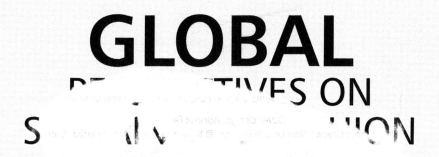

GLOBAL PERSPECTIVES ON SUSTAINABLE FASHION

Edited by

ALISON GWILT, ALICE PAYNE, AND EVELISE ANICET RÜTHSCHILLING

BLOOMSBURY VISUAL ARTS

LONDON · NEW YORK · OXFORD · NEW DELHI · SYDNEY

BLOOMSBURY VISUAL ARTS
Bloomsbury Publishing Plc
50 Bedford Square, London, WC1B 3DP, UK
1385 Broadway, New York, NY 10018, USA

BLOOMSBURY, BLOOMSBURY VISUAL ARTS and the Diana logo are trademarks of
Bloomsbury Publishing Plc

First published in Great Britain 2019
Reprinted 2019

A catalogue record for this book is available from the British Library.

Library of Congress Cataloging-in-Publication Data
Names: Gwilt, Alison, editor. | Rèuthschilling, Evelise Anciet, editor. | Payne, Alice, editor.
Title: Global perspectives on sustainable fashion / edited by Alison Gwilt, Evelise Anciet Rèuthschilling, and Alice Payne.
Description: London ; New York : Bloomsbury Visual Arts, 2019. | "Global Perspectives on Sustainable Fashion
showcases the global fashion industry's efforts to reduce the negative impacts associated with fashion production
and consumption. Illustrated throughout with infographics, photographs and diagrams of creative works, eighteen
essays focus on six regions, examining sustainable fashion in the context of local, cultural and environmental
concerns. Also included are 18 regional 'Spotlight' sections highlighting the differences and similarities across
regions by concentrating on examples of best practice, design innovation and impact on the community"—
Provided by publisher. | Includes bibliographical references and index.
Identifiers: LCCN 2018037997 (print) | LCCN 2018049769 (ebook) | ISBN 9781350058156 (epub) |
ISBN 9781350058163 (epdf) | ISBN 9781350058132 (pb : alk. paper) | ISBN 9781350058149 (hb : alk. paper)
Subjects: LCSH: Clothing trade—Environmental aspects. | Clothing trade—Moral and ethical aspects. |
Fashion—Environmental aspects.
Classification: LCC TT497 (ebook) | LCC TT497 .G55 2019 (print) | DDC 746.9/2—dc23
LC record available at https://lccn.loc.gov/2018037997

ISBN: HB: 978-1-3500-5814-9
        PB: 978-1-3500-5813-2
        ePDF: 978-1-3500-5816-3
        eBook: 978-1-3500-5815-6

Typeset by RefineCatch Limited, Bungay, Suffolk
Printed and bound in Great Britain

To find out more about our authors and books, visit www.bloomsbury.com
and sign up for our newsletters.

CONTENTS

LIST OF FIGURES, TABLES, AND ILLUSTRATIONS

FIGURES AND ILLUSTRATIONS

TABLES

PLATE SECTION

ACKNOWLEDGMENTS

We would first like to thank everyone who has contributed to this book; our authors and their institutes, and the organizations, companies, designers, and activists who kindly gave permission to include images of their work. We also wish to give thanks to Orsola de Castro (Fashion Revolution) for providing such a powerful and insightful Foreword.

While we thank all at Bloomsbury Publishing for their support, we are especially grateful to Georgia Kennedy for her enthusiasm for the proposal and support throughout the development of the manuscript. We also wish to thank our respective institutions: University of South Australia; Federal University of Rio Grande do Sul; and Queensland University of Technology.

Finally, we are grateful to our family (Ian and Dylan, Pedro, and Dan, Willa, and Theo), friends and colleagues for their love and support during the development of this book.

LIST OF CONTRIBUTING AUTHORS

Anne Anicet gained a PhD in Design (University of Aveiro, PT) and an MA in Clothing Design and Marketing (University of Minho, PT). She has completed specialization courses in Fashion Design (IED, Torino); Bachelor of Fine Arts (UFRGS, Brazil); and Technologist in Fashion and Style (UCS, Brazil). She has taught for ten years at the Uniritter Bachelor's Fashion Design Graduate and Postgraduate Program. She is currently a researcher at the UFRGS Sustainable Fashion Center, and Executive Director and designer at Contextura.

Duygu Atalay is a researcher and an international designer working for Italian, Turkish, and Austrian brands. Having worked as a research assistant for three years at Izmir University of Economics, and as a full-time lecturer at Istanbul Arel University, she is currently Assistant Professor at Beykent University. Her research interests include sustainable design, craft production, gender studies, and design education.

Taylor Brydges is an economic geographer from Toronto, Canada. Broadly, her research explores economic competitiveness, innovation, and entrepreneurship in the cultural and creative industries. A dominant theme in her research relates to exploring the contemporary nature of work in the creative economy, and the impact of digital technologies on patterns and spaces of

labor and entrepreneurship. Her research uses the fashion industry as a case study to explore these dynamics. Currently, she is conducting research on sustainability in the fashion industry drawing on case studies from Canada, Sweden, and Switzerland.

Ana Cristina Broega is a lecturer at Minho University, teaching in the course of Shoes and Garment Design, Fashion Design, Multifunctional Clothing Design and Comfort, and holds a degree in Textile Engineering, MSc in Design & Marketing and PhD in Textiles Physics. She is a researcher at the Textile Science and Technology Center at the University of Minho, in the area of Clothing and Footwear Comfort, Creativity, and Sustainable Fashion Design. Ana Cristina is also the Director of the MSc in Fashion Design and Communication, and is a member of various Scientific Committees of International Congress and Conferences on Design and Fashion, and President of CIMODE (International Conference of Fashion and Design).

Cariane Weydmann Camargo is a design academic, consultant, and researcher exploring sustainability and social innovation in the fashion area. Her PhD research focuses on the transition process from conventional to ethical fashion, framing how design activism can catalyze social and cultural changes. She has experience in the field of fashion design, with an emphasis on innovative project development through a strategic design approach. She teaches fashion design theory, products, and systems development, as well as sustainable design strategies at Unisinos University. She has coordinated, and been an activist, at the Fashion Revolution Week in Porto Alegre, Southern Brazil.

Huantian Cao is Director of Graduate Studies, Co-Director of Sustainable Apparel Initiative and Professor in the Department of Fashion and Apparel Studies, University of Delaware, United States.

Martha Carper is Assistant Professor in the Department of Fashion and Apparel Studies, University of Delaware, United States.

Jennifer Craik is Professor of Fashion at Queensland University of Technology, Brisbane, Australia. She is author of several books on fashion and arts and cultural policy. Current research projects include fashion in the Asia Pacific region especially focusing on contemporary Indigenous fashion design and the impact of contemporary Chinese fashion design on the restructuring of the fashion industry in Greater China.

Marilyn DeLong PhD and Associate Dean for Academic Affairs, is Professor of Apparel Studies in the College of Design at the University of Minnesota. Her scholarly research is focused upon design history, education, perception, and material culture. Current topics of research include apparel design, education across cultures, sustainable attitudes and practices of consumers. Published titles include *Color and Design* (co-editor), published by Berg in 2012; and *The Way We Look* (author), published by Fairchild in 1998. DeLong is author of numerous journal articles in such venues as *Fashion Theory, Clothing and Textiles Research Journal, Senses & Society, Textile,*

Qualitative Market Research, and *Journal of Fashion Marketing and Management.* DeLong has been co-editor of *Fashion Practice, The Journal of Design, Creative Process & the Fashion industry,* from its inception in 2009.

Marsha A. Dickson is Irma Ayers Professor in the Department of Fashion and Apparel Studies, and co-director of the Sustainable Apparel Initiative at the University of Delaware. She is internationally recognized for her research and teaching on social responsibility in the apparel industry, having published books on social responsibility and fair trade, and peer-reviewed journal articles on consumer and business practices that are based on field research carried out around the world. Dr. Dickson has received several awards for her academic and industry contributions in social responsibility, including—most recently—International Textile and Apparel Association Fellow in 2016.

Potlako L. P. Disele is a lecturer at the University of Botswana. She has been a lecturer since 1999 after serving in the Government of Botswana for twenty-three years as a Community Social Worker and a Trainer of Trainers. Her area of specialization ranges from social work and community development, social work and probation obtained from Botswana Agricultural College; she has a BSc Home Economics—majoring in textiles and clothing from University of Wales, MA in Fashion and Textile Studies from De Montfort University, and PhD in Clothing and Textile Technology, majoring in Dress and Culture obtained from Manchester Metropolitan University. She has published on dress and culture issues.

Tiziana Ferrero-Regis is Senior Lecturer in Fashion at Queensland University of Technology. Tiziana combines both professional and academic backgrounds in fashion having worked in Milan for more than a decade as editorial coordinator and writer for Italian *Vogue*. Her scholarly publications are in the field of fashion studies, and include industry approaches to cultural identity. Tiziana's research interest in global labor flows and sustainability stems from her visits to communities of women in India in 1989. Tiziana is a member of the Design Institute of Australia and was the recipient of the Women in Research Scholarship at QUT.

Angela Finn, PhD, is a Senior Lecturer and Learning & Teaching specialist within the School of Fashion & Textiles, RMIT University. Her research focuses on the design, production, and consumption of fashion and fashion education. She has published journal articles and book chapters on these topics and presented at international conferences. Her most recent research examines creative practice in the context of Fashion as an emerging discipline. As Deputy Head, Learning and Teaching (2015–17) she was able to work with the Fashion Department at RMIT Vietnam on the Fashion Colloquia held at the Ho Chi Minh campus in 2016.

Lily C. Fidzani, PhD, is an Interior Design lecturer at the Department of Family and Consumer Sciences, University of Botswana. Her research interests are in human behavior in different built (interior) environments. The focus is on the impact of housing and interior environments, on special population, personalization, and the impact of design on human development, children, and adolescents.

Miguel Angel Gardetti, PhD, holds two Master's Degrees: one in Business Administration from the IAE Business School (Universidad Austral, Argentina); and the other one in Environmental Studies and Sustainable Development from the

Universidad de Ciencias Empresariales y Sociales (Argentina). In the field of sustainable textiles and fashion, he founded the Sustainable Textile Centre. Moreover, he was a professor at different Latin American universities, and participated both as trainer and instructor in projects of the Inter-American Development Bank. Between 2012 and 2015, he was also a member of the Consulting Board of the "Future Fashion" Project run by MISTRA (a Swedish government foundation that conducts research into environmental topics).

Sumith Gopura is a lecturer specializing in fashion design and product development at the Department of Textile and Clothing Technology, University of Moratuwa, Sri Lanka. His research interest consists of creativity, fashion design, apparel value chain, and teaching and learning in higher education. Gopura formerly worked in the Sri Lankan export apparel manufacturing industry as a designer.

Alison Gwilt, PhD is a fashion design researcher, author and consultant. She explores and promotes a range of innovative design methods and approaches that enable the fashion and textiles community, from educators, to producers, and consumers, to adopt more sustainable and ethical practices. Her work focuses on the use of positive/sustainable design interventions that challenge the current production and consumption paradigm. Alison's books include *Shaping Sustainable Fashion* (2011), *A Practical Guide to Sustainable Fashion* (2014) and *Fashion Design for Living* (2015). Following her role as reader in fashion and sustainability at Sheffield Hallam University, UK, Alison relocated to Australia in 2017. She is currently associate professor in design at the University of New South Wales and adjunct senior research fellow at the University of South Australia.

Jennifer Hoover, PhD, has been playing with string as a hand-spinner, knitter, and weaver since about 2006. She earned a BA in Anthropology and MSc in Textiles, both from UC Davis. Her thesis research examined the material expression of place in wool fiber, from the perspective of a novice wool classer training with shearing crews in California. As a 2017–18 Fulbright-Nehru student researcher, she studied wool production in the Indian Himalayan state of Himachal Pradesh. Her research interests include exploring craft and place through post-humanist feminist theoretical lenses.

Kathleen Horton is Senior Lecturer in Fashion at Queensland University of Technology, Brisbane, Australia. Her teaching and research centers on the aesthetic, political, and social aspects of fashion design practice across both historical and contemporary contexts. In 2010, Kathleen founded the Stitchery Collective, a fashion design cooperative that explores innovative models for the production and consumption of fashion in the twenty-first century.

Eunsuk Hur is a lecturer and designer whose work is pushing the boundaries of fashion and textiles by exploring alternative solutions for a creative economy and future sustainability. She is particularly interested in "sustainability," "co-creation," and "social enterprise" in the area of fashion and textile, and creative business. She gained her PhD in sustainable fashion from the School of Design, University of Leeds and Master of Textile Future degree in Central Saint Martins in London. She is currently working as a Teaching Fellow in the School of Design at the University of Leeds.

Alana James Senior Lecturer in Fashion at Northumbria University, Newcastle. Specializing in fashion design and process, she teaches a wide range of students including undergraduate and postgraduate groups across fashion and textile disciplines. Alana's current research explores the relationship between fashion consumers and retailers in the ethical purchasing process. Wider research interests include supply chain transparency, social and environmental responsibility, and the increase of sustainability pedagogy to educate future generations of designers. She has presented research at various events in the UK, Asia, and North America, spanning both academic and industry forums.

Deb Johnson is the Founder and Executive Director of the Pratt Institute/Brooklyn Fashion + Design Accelerator, a hub for ethical fashion and responsible technology that promotes triple bottom line values that link financial success to an ethical and sustainable supply chain. Deb also founded the Center for Sustainable Design Strategies at Pratt Institute and has been leading the integration of sustainability into Pratt's art, design and architecture programs for over fifteen years. Johnson chaired Pratt's Industrial Design program from 1997 to 2005.

Maggie Jonk is a designer, Middle Eastern fashion and design researcher, and sustainable design disciple. As an active member of the design movement within the Middle East, Maggie has developed a multi-disciplinary design practice, which draws from her interests in culture, craft, and ethical and honest interactions. Her background and interests, including anthropology, language, yoga and meditation, sustainability, and travel, are a constant inspiration, and she finds opportunity in the challenges of participating in an emerging market through creative problem solving, patience and understanding. Maggie holds a Masters of Art in Fashion from Ryerson University, and currently is managing her studio and work as a design consultant in Dubai, United Arab Emirates.

Şölen Kipöz is an associate professor at the Department of Fashion and Textile Design at Izmir University of Economics, teaching a number of courses on design and theory at bachelor, masters and doctorate level. She produces publications and conceptual design works on ethical, social and sustainable fashion. Following her one-person exhibition "Ahimsa: The other life of clothes (2012)," her book on *Sustainable Fashion* (2015), which she edited and published in Turkish, has increased interest in the possibility of building a responsible design/consumption culture.

Faith Kane is a design researcher and educator working in the area of textiles and materials. Her research interests include design for sustainability, collaborative working in the design/science space, and the role and value of craft knowledge within these contexts. She is a senior lecturer and the Programme Leader for Textiles at the School of Design in the College of Creative Arts at Massey University in Wellington, New Zealand. She is also an editor of the *Journal of Textile Design Research and Practice*, published by Bloomsbury.

Susan B. Kaiser is Professor of Gender, Sexuality and Women's Studies; Design; and the Textile and Cultural Studies Graduate Groups at the University of California, Davis. Her research and teaching bridge the fields of fashion studies and feminist cultural studies. Recent and current interests include issues of space/place and time, and possibilities for critical fashion studies through popular and political cultural discourses. She is the author of *The Social Psychology of Clothing* (1997) and *Fashion and Cultural Studies* (2013), and more than 100 articles and book chapters in the fields of textile/fashion, gender, consumer and cultural studies, and sociology.

Mariangela Lavanga is Assistant Professor in Cultural Economics at Erasmus School of History, Culture and Communication, Erasmus University, Rotterdam. Prior to this, she worked as research fellow at the Department of Geography, Planning and International Development Studies at the University of Amsterdam. Her work brings together cultural economics and economic geography. She has researched and published on the relationships between the creative industries, the economy, and cities with special attention to sustainable development; her most recent research interests focus on independent fashion designers, their careers, entrepreneurial strategies, and locational behavior, slow fashion, temporary clusters, and fashion intermediaries.

Benny Ding Leong is the Assistant Professor, leaders of the Asian Lifestyle Design Lab and the MDes International Design & Business Management program at the School of Design, Hong Kong Polytechnic University. Leong has found and co-founded the Lifestyle Design Research Network of China and the Chinese Network on Design for Sustainability respectively in China. He is also an Advisory Committee Member of the Korean Future Design Research Institute, and a former advisor to the Innovation Design Center of the Huawei Device Co., Ltd.

Ana Livni, was born in Montevideo. She works in the fashion industry and is the owner of her own slow fashion brand, Ana Livni. She is a graduate of the School of Industrial Design Center (EUCD-Montevideo) and has a postgraduate in Fashion Management Mercosur and Industrial Design Center from POLIMODA in Florence, Italy.

Tasha L. Lewis is an associate professor in the Department of Fiber Science & Apparel Design at Cornell University where she teaches in the area of fashion design management. Her research interests include the disruptive impact of technology in the apparel industry, global and domestic apparel production issues, and the significance of social responsibility and sustainability throughout the apparel supply chain.

Suzanne Loker is a Professor Emerita in the Department of Fiber Science & Apparel Design at Cornell University, USA, having also held faculty and administrative positions at the University of Vermont, University of Idaho, and Kansas State University. Loker has published widely on topics about the apparel industry, international apparel production and marketing, with particular interest in emerging technologies and business practices, such as social and environmental responsibility/sustainability and mass customization technologies including body scanners used to improve apparel design and manufacturing. She co-authored the book, *Social Responsibility in the Global Apparel Industry*, with Drs Marsha Dickson and Molly Eckman.

Seoha Min is an assistant professor in the Department of Consumer, Apparel and Retail Studies at the University of North Carolina at Greensboro. She earned a PhD degree majoring in Apparel Design with a minor in Anthropology at the University of Minnesota (UMN). Her research interests are focused upon aesthetics and design, cultural aspects of design, and sustainable design practices—all within the framework of improving our understanding of design and its impact on humans and society.

Richie Moalosi is an associate professor of Industrial Design and Head of Department of Industrial Design and Technology at the University of Botswana. He holds a PhD in Industrial Design from Queensland University of Technology, Australia and MA in Design from the University of Wolverhampton. His research interests are in sustainable products and services, culture and design, and design education. He is also interested in cross-cultural collaborative research projects.

Laura Morgan is a design practitioner and researcher in the Textile Design Research Group at Loughborough University and the Textile Engineering and Materials Research Group at De Montfort University. Laura's research interests are concerned with addressing sustainability through process and material innovation for textiles. Through interdisciplinary research and practice, she works with multiple industry stakeholders, utilizing emerging digital technologies, specifically investigating laser-textile techniques to improve sustainability, circularity, and agility in material processing and textile surface design.

Sophia N. Njeru, PhD, is an educator, researcher, and consultant in the Department of Fashion Design and Marketing at Machakos University, Kenya. Njeru has several years' experience of university teaching and administration experience and is passionate about ethnic dress, sustainable fashion design, and textiles. She was an external examiner 2015–17 at the Department of Art and Industrial Design, Kyambogo University, Uganda. Njeru has facilitated postgraduate colloquiums, reviewed and edited conference papers, published extensively, and presented papers in international scientific conferences. Her membership of professional associations include International Federation for Home Economics, Network for Afrika Designers, and Learning Network on Sustainable Energy Systems (LeNSes).

Laura Novik is Professor of Sustainable Design at Universidad de San Andrés, Buenos Aires, Chief of Strategic Collection Management postgraduate program at Pontificia Universidad Católica de Chile, and founder and senior partner at Blink Design, a consultancy that works with companies and governments operating in the Latin American design and fashion markets. She has published academic and scientific articles on design and Latin American fashion (*Berg Encyclopedia of World Dress* and *Fashion: Latin America and the Caribbean*, Diseña and ARQ – PUC Ed. Chile, Estação das Letras y Cores Publishing). She is also the leader of Raíz Diseño (Design Root) platform that promotes Latin American sustainable design, focusing on development comunities and design as a force to change unequal social conditions.

Noël Palomo-Lovinski is an associate professor at Kent State University in Ohio. She received her BFA in Fashion Design from Parsons School of Design, MA in Visual Culture from New York University, and MFA in Textiles from Kent State University. Noël's research focus concerns design responsibility and sustainable practice, future needs of fashion design education, local manufacturing, and the relationship between culture and design.

Alice Payne, PhD is a senior lecturer in fashion at Queensland University of Technology, Brisbane, Australia. Her research centres on sustainability concerns throughout textile and apparel industry supply chains. Alice has examined perspectives on sustainability along the cotton value chain, the cultural and material flows of post-consumer textile waste, and design processes of mass-market product developers, independent fashion designers, and social entrepreneurs. Alice is also an award-winning designer, investigating design for sustainability in

fashion via practice-led research. In her recent design project *Shrinking Violets,* Alice explores the potential for design for disassembly in fashion. Her design work has been exhibited in galleries in Sydney, Canberra, Brisbane and London.

Anne Peirson-Smith, PhD, is Assistant Professor at City University of Hong Kong with an industry background in the creative industries. She teaches and researches fashion studies, fashion communication, popular culture, and the creative industries, and has published widely in these fields. She is co-author of *Public Relations in Asia Pacific: Communicating Effectively Across Cultures* (John Wiley, 2010). She is associate editor of the *Journal of Fashion, Style and Popular Culture* (Intellect Books) and co-editor of *Global Fashion Brands: Style, Luxury & History* (Intellect Books, 2014) and *Transglobal Fashion Narratives: Clothing Communication, Style Statements and Brand Storytelling* (Intellect Books, 2018).

Dolly Viviana Polo-Flórez is an industrial designer (Universidad Jorge Tadeo Lozano). She has a Master's in Education Human Development, and is currently an Education Doctoral Candidate. Experienced in research, education, especially learning methods for children and adults, she is also involved in the design, development, and diversification, at an industrial level, of clothing and garment accessories. Dolly is also Associate Professor of Apparel / Costume Design in the Faculty of Architecture, Art and Design at the Universidad de San Buenaventura Cali-Colombia.

Harsha Rani is Assistant Professor in the Department of Fashion Management Studies, National Institute of Fashion Technology Bhubaneswar. She holds an MBA in Marketing and International Business from Amity University, Noida, and BTech in Textile

Engineering. She is pursuing her PhD from Utkal University (Odisha) in the area of sustainable fashion and technology. She has more than eight years' experience in the industry (both domestic and international assignments), academic teaching and research. Her teaching and research interest lies in digital retail, fashion e-commerce, entrepreneurship, and consumer behavior.

Yaone Rapitsenyane is a lecturer in Sustainable Design at the University of Botswana. He has a BDes in Design and Technology and an MSc in Sustainable Product Design, with a PhD in developing Design and Sustainable Product Service Systems capabilities in SMEs, from Loughborough University. His research interests include imparting design capabilities in manufacturing SMEs, developing sustainable business models for SMEs, exploring Product Service Systems in dominant economic sectors, and developing sustainable PSS curricula for African universities. He contributes in multi-disciplinary and multi-stakeholder projects and hosts a global service jam at the University of Botswana.

Vibeke Riisberg holds a PhD in the evolution from analogue to digital processes of printed textiles. She is an experienced textile designer and educator currently employed as Associate Professor at Design School Kolding, Denmark. Her research interests include holistic approaches to sustainable fashion and textile design, handling of textiles in service systems, design and aesthetic experience in relation to institutional contexts such as office environments and hospitals and in the private sector the sharing of baby clothing. Riisberg has published internationally, served as PhD supervisor, appointed member of PhD committees and as reviewer for academic journals and conferences.

Darniya Roy is Assistant Professor in Fashion Design Department, National Institute of Fashion Technology, Bhubaneswar. She holds a Master's degree from NIFT. She has more than 8 years' experience in industry, teaching, and research. Two of her papers have been published in the last two IFFTI Conference Proceedings. Her research interest includes sustainable fashion, tribal art forms, tribal lifestyle, Indian handlooms, and handicraft.

Mercy Rugedhla is a lecturer of Clothing and Family Studies at Solusi University. She is studying for a PhD in Clothing and Textiles at the University of Botswana. She holds an MSc and BSc in Family and Consumer Sciences and a Diploma in Education. She also did Basic Counseling and Communication and HIV peer-education counseling. She has served as Acting Headmistress, Dean of Women, and Teachers' College Lecturer in Home Economics and Art and Design. Mercy is deeply committed to improving the community and often conducts community-based programs to empower people with family- and consumer-science-related skills.

Evelise Anicet Rüthschilling, PhD is a full professor at the Art Institute of the Federal University of Rio Grande do Sul, Brazil. She completed a postgraduate course in fashion design at The Art Institute of Chicago, USA (1994); Master of Fine Arts at UFRGS (1994); PhD in computer education at UFRGS (2002), and postdoctorate in surface design and sustainable fashion at the Center for Design and Sustainability, PG Design, UFPR (2012). She is a guiding teacher of masters and doctorate courses in design, PGDESIGN-UFRGS. Evelise also coordinates the Research Center for Surface Design UFRGS, where she is responsible for structuring this field of knowledge, and she is the author of the book *Design de Superfície*

(Surface Design) (2008; 2013). Evelise also coordinates the Research Center for Sustainable Fashion, both laboratories are part of the Laboratory for Imaging and Technology – LIT – UFRGS. Evelise is a founding member of ABEPEM, Brazilian Association of Studies and Research in Fashion, which completes in 2019, marking 15 years of the largest scientific congress of fashion in Brazil: *Colóquio de Moda* (Fashion Colloquium).

She develops applied research in surface design and sustainable fashion at the studio Contextura, which is a sustainable fashion laboratory.

Goutam Saha, PhD, is Associate Professor in Fashion Management Studies Department, National Institute of Fashion Technology, Bhubaneswar, India. Holding a PhD in marketing, he has more than seventeen years' experience in industry, teaching, research, and editing. His research paper was awarded First Prize at the IFFTI Annual Conference, Italy 2015 in the Senior Faculty category. He contributed an edited volume—*Entrepreneurship: Perspectives & Paradigms*, published by Macmillan—and other research papers in publications including the *Journal of Fashion Marketing & Management* (Emerald) and the *South Asian Journal of Management*. His teaching and research interest lie in Sustainability and Fashion, Fashion Business Analytics, Entrepreneurship, and Social Entrepreneurship.

Elena Salcedo-Allende has more than seventeen years' experience in the fashion industry, and six years working as a sustainability advisor focusing on Sustainability Culture and Change Management. Currently Elena coordinates the Professional Summer Course in Sustainable Fashion at Istituto Europeo di Design (IED) in Barcelona and lectures at ESADE and IED Barcelona. Her books include *Moda ética para un futuro sostenible* (Ed. Gustavo Gili, 2014) and *Moda y Empresa* (Ed. Granica, 2004). Elena holds a BA and MBA from ESADE Business School and CEMS Master in International Management from Vienna University of Economics and Business.

Ayesha Siddequa is a CSR professional, consultant, and design activist who wants to make a difference in an industry that she is passionate about. In her view: "The philosophy of our success lies in our belief that every modern fashion brand should give back to the community and be at one with the environment." Ayesha is the Founder and Creative Director of *Future Fashion*, a "pioneering Ethical Fashion platform" in the Middle East. She is also the UAE Country Coordinator for Fashion Revolution Day, a member of the International Executive Board at The Global Sustainable Fashion Week organized by National Fashion League Association (NFLH), Hungary, and a proud Guinness World Record holder.

Jinsong Shen is Professor of Textile Chemistry and Biotechnology at the School of Design, De Montfort University in UK. He holds a BSc and MSc in textile chemistry from Donghua University and a PhD in protein chemistry from the University of Leeds. Prof. Shen is extensively involved in the research of protein materials, the development of biotechnology for the textile wet processes, and the functional finishing to enhance fiber properties and fabric performance. His current interests lie in the areas of textile biotechnology, sol-gel technology, nanotechnology and flame-retardant technology, and their applications leading to the development of protective garments and multi-functional materials.

Desiree Smal is a lecturer in fashion design on undergraduate level and supervision of postgraduate students. Her area of research specialization is in environmental sustainability in fashion design praxis. Desiree's current research interest is primarily based in the discipline of fashion design and focused particularly on sustainable design within the fashion industry on a global and national level, as well as on indigenous knowledge systems in relation to environmental sustainability. In addition, Desiree is passionate in developing the discourse in the discipline of fashion design and design education in South Africa.

Lauren Solomon is a Doctoral Candidate, Practitioner, and Associate Lecturer in Fashion at the Queensland University of Technology. Lauren's current research explores how fashion activism can be used to intervene in global fashion production networks. Using practice-led research, she recently collaborated with a local trade union in Cambodia to run a capacity-building training program for garment workers. Lauren aims to increase worker agency, contest existing power relationships in the fashion industry, and educate the next generation of practitioners about ethical industry practices.

Doris Treptow-Novacs has been teaching at the Savannah College of Art and Design since 2005. Courses she leads include Sustainable Practices for Fashion, Computer Aided Fashion Design, Trend Forecasting, and Introduction to Textiles. Brazilian-born, Doris has an MFA in Fashion from SCAD (USA), an MA in Fashion Design and Production from UDESC (Brazil), and is the author of *Inventando Moda: Planejamento de Coleção*.

John Tyrer was educated at Cranfield and Loughborough Universities in Mechanical Engineering. Prof. Tyrer joined Loughborough University as a lecturer in Engineering Design in 1983. He became a Senior Lecturer in 1988 and Professor of Optical Instrumentation in 2007. He has four primary research interests: Optical Measurement/Detection; Holography; High-Power Laser Processing; and Laser Safety. He lectures in high-power laser material processing, ballistics and rocketry, design of machine elements, optical metrology, and experimental bio-mechanics. The use of high power lasers for advanced textile manufacturing, and the development of novel textile performance, have been areas of interest for twenty-five years.

Jennifer Whitty is a sustainable design educator, researcher, designer, and activist. Originally from Ireland, she teaches and practices at Massey University's School of Design in New Zealand. She is focused on developing new systems for alternative ecologies of fashion practice, which are connected to and have an impact on society. She strongly believes in the positive aspects that fashion can impart to both the individual and to our culture. She is involved in taking action to catalyze change by developing alternative roles for the fashion designer through activism, social innovation, and transition design.

Gloria Wong joined The Hong Kong Polytechnic University in 1988, was Fashion Course Leader in the School of Design, and is currently Senior Teaching Fellow at Institute of Textiles & Clothing. She is significantly involved in international events collaborating with overseas designers, activists, and academics. Meanwhile Gloria has been actively exhibiting internationally fiber art and fashion costumes that combine the use of traditional crafts and innovative technologies, aiming to unravel new meanings behind culture, gender, sustainability, and fashion in her works.

FOREWORD

The world of fashion is changing.

As all industries take stock of human impact on the planet and its inhabitants, the fashion industry is looking at reinventing itself to secure both its relevance and its survival in the anthropocene era.

The fashion industry is populous—it employs directly over 75 million people, many of whom are young women—and encompasses many other industries such as agriculture, transport, education, and communication. Fashion is also one of the most polluting and socially exploitative industries in the world; we are producing over 100 billion garments per year, according to Greenpeace, and clothing production has more than doubled since 2000, yet 40 percent of what we buy is left unworn. The weight of this mass production is unsustainable, socially and environmentally, both during the production phase, and later on, at the end of clothing's useful life. And, crucially, it affects 100 percent of the population: you may well not be interested in fashion, but you still have to wear clothes.

We cannot keep glossing over these disturbing facts, especially when we can be part of the solution. Imagine your wardrobe as being part of the fashion value chain—somewhere inbetween the cotton seed being sown and the final disposal of a garment—and imagine that every day, when you chose what to wear, you are making a statement: does this dress fit my ethos? Who made it? And in what conditions? Do my ethic and aesthetic match? This is why we need to arm ourselves with knowledge, and stake our claim for a fairer future, because knowledge is the key to making changes.

At Fashion Revolution,[1] we encourage our audience to be curious, find out, and do something, because we know that sustainability is complex and understanding its multiple subjects requires dedication and assiduousness, but we also know that this journey is incrementally a part of everyone's roadmap.

The vision of an exemplary fashion industry is clear to me: mass production designed to provide safe jobs and living wages to millions of people, products made with biodegradable and recyclable materials and innovative production systems that look at the full life-cycle and closed-loop technology; alternative models to consume clothes, such as leasing, swapping, and mending; a luxury industry that focuses on quality over quantity, and space for thousands of small, independent entities that champion local manufacturing, heritage, and design. *Global Perspectives on Sustainable Fashion* demonstrates how designers and producers around the world are working to make that vision a reality.

Orsola de Castro,
Founder and Creative Director,
Fashion Revolution

NOTES

1. Fashion Revolution was born as a result of the Rana Plaza factory collapse disaster in Bangladesh in 2013, when a building collapsed killing 1,134 garment workers and injuring many others. Since then we have become a powerful global movement for positive change, respect, and honesty, highlighting and encouraging the importance of a fashion industry that is firmly focused on transparency and environmental sustainability.

   Our aim is to create connections throughout the fashion supply chain, to tell stories and ask questions, activating designers, brands, students, garment workers, citizens, media, parliamentarians, cotton farmers, celebrities . . . in short, to bring together the people who wear clothes with the people who make the clothes we wear.

INTRODUCTION

Fashion plays an important role in many lives, but in the twenty-first century, the environmental and ethical challenges inherent in the global fashion system have reached a critical point. At the risk of hyperbole, the concerns of sustainable fashion affect nothing short of the entire world: the practices of all humans who wear clothes, the well-being of the world's 60 million garment workers and 250 million cotton growers, the farms and forests that provide cotton and viscose, the oil fields providing petrochemicals for synthetic fiber, the animals providing fiber and hides, the growing mountains of waste, and the economic paradigms that require fashion's systems of production and consumption to grow *ad infinitum.* As the fashion and sustainability discourse gathers momentum internationally, it is imperative that companies and individuals alike collectively work to reduce the impacts from producing and consuming fashion garments.

Ever present in our mind is that fashion's issues are symptomatic of increased levels of consumption. While the over-consumption of fashion clothing in the developed North has been problematic for many years, the levels of consumption are increasing everywhere. The challenge, as we see it, is to find approaches that support behavioral change—that includes encouraging consumers to buy less and do more

to help keep materials in circulation for longer. This may appear idealistic, but in reality industry's fashion visionaries—from designers of luxury fashion brands to editors of high-profile fashion magazines—are beginning to influence the way that consumers perceive sustainable fashion. At the same time there is a proliferation of non-governmental organizations (NGOs), industry networks, and government-backed initiatives that provide advice, resources, and tools to support fashion brands, labels, and companies to show their "commitment to change" (Copenhagen Fashion Summit, May 2018). But we ask, where is this change happening globally, and how?

Global Perspectives on Sustainable Fashion brings together, for the first time, voices from different communities, countries, and continents. The contributions in this book chart the many varied environmental, ethical, social, and economic aspects that are shaping the evolution of sustainable fashion in different nations. We began the project with questions: how is the movement toward sustainable fashion evolving around the world? Are there similarities and differences to be found in approaches to sustainability and circularity across the regions? And how do we see fashion in a global system developing in the future? We chose not to "define" sustainability for our authors; rather, we have let our authors explore the field from their own perspective. The contributions represent a wide range of current and ongoing research projects and activities that are occurring in countries around the world—and they demonstrate, collectively, that regardless of the scale of the project or work being conducted, change *is* taking place.

We have organized this book into six "continents." The regional essays explore and debate the development of sustainable fashion in the context of specific domestic economic, cultural, environmental, and ethical goals and concerns. Regional "Spotlight" sections serve to highlight differences and similarities across regions by concentrating on examples of best practice, design innovation, and impact in the community. They introduce and explore cross-national initiatives, the work of NGOs and activist groups, and fashion brands and companies working in established and emerging markets.

Our journey starts with Latin America. In 1992 (and again in 2012) Brazil hosted the United Nations Conference on Environment and Development, commonly known as the "Earth Summit," in Rio de Janeiro. Among the achievements from the 1992 conference the Climate Change Convention was agreed, the environmental action plan "Agenda 21" was announced, and the three pillars of sustainable development were recognized for the first time (UNEP n.d). Many of our authors refer to the original economic, environmental, and social pillars of sustainability, as well as the newer fourth dimension—cultural. And so we return to Brazil, where Evelise Anicet Rüthschilling reflects on how sustainability is currently applied within the Brazilian fashion system, and explores why the circular economy may support a fashion ecosystem that benefits society in Brazil. Anne Anicet and Cariane Camargo go on to explain the significance of Fashion Revolution in the state of Rio Grande do Sul that has led to a growth in collaborative

partnerships between the academic, industrial, and retail sectors, which are supporting local traditions that socially and economically benefit the community. Laura Novik traces the steps of the *Raíz Diseño,* a project established to form a transnational network for Latin American designers, and reveals how some of the fashion designers are demonstrating "… the silent forms of resistance from within the field of design," Ana Livni examines the resurgence in interest in Uruguay for locally produced wool fiber. Defined by Livni as a naturally "slow" country, Uruguay's producers eagerly embrace wool as a key fiber in the development of sustainable textile materials and fashion products. In Argentina, Miguel Angel Gardetti examines the sustainability practices of eighteen local independent fashion design brands to see whether there is a need to improve the ways in which brands communicate (and not selectively disclose) their actual sustainability credentials in the marketplace. Finally in this first section, Dolly Viviana Polo Flórez takes us to Colombia, where she reflects on the three main approaches to sustainable production adopted within the Colombian fashion industry: producers working with local communities; producers engaging with traditional techniques; and closed-loop approaches to production.

Producers and retailers in North America and Europe are seen as the major instigators of fast fashion. Well-known global brands from these regions distribute and sell large volumes of fashion clothing all around the world, but they frequently rely on manufacturers based in other nations to produce their inexpensive goods. In response, government agencies, researchers, activists, and NGOs based in North America and Europe have been actively encouraging change in the fashion industry and we present some of the current debates in Parts 2 and 3. Across North America, in Part 2, our authors highlight a number of initiatives, brands, and small fashion start-ups that support localism and involve industry and consumers working to reduce the impacts of fashion clothing. Tasha Lewis and Suzanne Loker discuss the ways in which US brands are encouraging user consumers to take action and see fashion through a new paradigm, the circular economy. Meanwhile, Noël Palomo-Lovinski considers the impact of a declining clothing manufacturing industry in Cleveland, in the Midwest, and discusses how local pattern- and garment-makers are working as a connected network to form a new garment district. The "... inextricable entanglement of local environmental settings and global economic systems" is explored by Jennifer Hoover and Susan Kaiser, who trace the complex journey of processes through which wool fiber travels. Doris Treptow-Kovacs presents the local / global story of Preloved, the Canadian brand founded by Julia Grieves, which remanufactures discarded clothing on-site in Toronto and distributes in domestic and international retail markets. Subsequently Taylor Brydges explores how and why independent fashion labels in Canada are enthusiastically supporting the "Made in Canada" strategy, at a time when the industry appears to be lacking government support and funding. Finally in Part 2, while automation in manufacturing may be seen as a contributor in the demise of local garment districts, Deb Johnson presents the case for technology as an opportunity for innovation that supports the design of "... really 'smart' garments and functional textiles from the outset." In bringing technology and sustainability together, Johnson argues that systems-based innovation may emerge.

In Part 3 we present perspectives from Europe. In the first essay, Alison Gwilt and Alana James explore the notion of garment longevity, and discuss how the UK High Street could re-evaluate its existing practices and look to circular approaches that aim to reduce textile waste. At the same time, Mariangela Lavanga reflects on the progress made by producers, organizations, and consultancies in leading sustainable development and the circular economy in the Netherlands. Ana Cristina Broega describes the moves being made in the Portuguese fashion industry, particularly by small businesses, to develop ethically made and locally produced products, but suggests that Portuguese brands need to communicate these efforts more effectively to consumers. Meanwhile, Vibeke Riisberg discusses a product-service system model provided by VIGGA, a Danish company that specializes in offering a subscription service for leasing baby clothes. Elena Salcedo-Allende examines how sustainability in the luxury sector is helping redefine its consumer market, and provides a specific focus on the Spanish brand, Teixidors. To conclude this section, Laura Morgan, Faith Kane, John Tyrer, and Jonsong Shen describe a new advancement in surface color and patterning in sportswear, which uses laser processing to reduce resource consumption, improve material cyclability, and enable production-on-demand.

Asia is the world's most populous region and includes many countries that are important sourcing destinations for globalized fashion production. However, alongside the economic benefits of large scale manufacturing are attendant environmental and social challenges. In Parts 4 and 5, contributors examine the different forms and scales that fashion production takes across Asian regions. In Part 4, Gloria Wong and Benny Leong explore China as the "world's factory," and Hong Kong and China's rapid development in greening the apparel industry. Anne Peirson-Smith's Spotlight on Hong Kong-based NGO Redress highlights the grassroots activities occurring to shift consumption norms through innovative marketing and communication. Eunsuk Hur also explores changing approaches to purchasing practices through highlighting collaborative consumption models in South Korea. Turning to India, Goutam Saha, Darniya Roy and Harsha Rani explore the work of women workers in the informal economy, in which workers, activists and unions have come together to empower female craft workers through SEWA, a union now found throughout South Asia. Sumith Gopura's Sri Lankan spotlight showcases the connections between the Sri Lankan export apparel industry and local fashion entrepreneurs redirecting pre-consumer textile waste. In Turkey, a country with a powerful manufacturing industry and deep-rooted craft traditions, Şölen Kipöz and Duygu Atalay explore the slow and sustainable approaches in which Turkish designers reflect on their Anatolian heritage.

Part 5 focuses on South East Asia and Oceania, with contributors exploring the tensions between local and global manufacturing, as well as the cultural traditions and craft practices that may support ethical making and wearing. Seoha Min and Marilyn DeLong's exploration of the practices of renting wedding dresses in Asian countries such as Thailand reframes traditional practices as a marker of ethical consumption. Issues of cultural sustainability are explored through Jennifer Craik and Kathleen Horton's spotlight on Australian Indigenous fashion designers and their work to create fashion objects and experiences that articulate cultural identity. Angela Finn, writing on Vietnam, explores the local Vietnamese designers who develop environmentally aware, ethically manufactured fashion that draws on local heritage, proposing that an ethical "design economy" and a "making economy" are each futures for fashion in the region. Lauren Solomon shares insights from Cambodian garment workers, unions, and NGO

representatives as they work to shape a more equitable industry for Cambodia's primarily female workforce. In the Australian essay, Alice Payne and Tiziana Ferrero-Regis discuss the pragmatic challenge of restoring local manufacturing, even as a desire for local fashion stories emerges. Jennifer Whitty's Spotlight case study from New Zealand highlights the role of fashion educators in promoting social enterprise to tackle post-consumer waste.

In the final section we explore Africa and the Middle East. Desiree Smal begins by exploring some of the key findings from her recent study on the principles that drive a designer in business in South Africa to consider environmental sustainability, and how they inform their design and manufacturing practices. Next, Marsha A. Dickson, Huantian Cao, and Martha Carper examine the South Africa Sustainable Cotton Cluster, and discuss several recommendations that arose from their study of the initiative, which may be useful for other sustainability-focused country-level initiatives. Yaone Rapitsenyane, Sophia Njeru, and Richie Moalosi reflect on the interventions that are needed to assist and support the Botswanan and Kenyan fashion industries to adopt sustainable product-service system business models. Meanwhile, Mercy Rugedhla, Potlako Peoesele Disele, Richie Moalosi, and Lily Clara Fidzani explore the significance of indigenous knowledge in the design and production of eco textiles for traditional dress worn by Zimbabwean women. In this section we then move to the Middle East, where Ayesha Siddequa explores the sustainability themes set within the UAE Vision 2021 framework, and the positive impact that these may have on Dubai's fashion industry. Finally, Maggie Jonk discusses the preservation of traditional, cultural textiles practice in Egypt through the work of researcher, collector and designer, Shahira Mehrez.

In closing, this book aims to contribute to, and expand on, the discourse concerning the international movements toward a sustainable and circular global fashion system. The cases presented throughout this book demonstrate the committed, passionate work going on around the world to foster more equitable and responsible industries, extending from agriculture through to retail. But beyond fashion's challenges, the local stories speak to the cultural significance of fashion—in both its making and its wearing—as a source of inspiration and a marker of identity. Our hope is every reader will discover something fresh about the world that we inhabit and fashion's place within it.

Alison Gwilt, Alice Payne, and
Evelise Anicet Rüthschilling

REFERENCE

Copenhagen Fashion Summit (2018), *Archive: 2018*
    https://www.copenhagenfashionsummit.com/archive
    Accessed 22 May 2018.
United Nations Environment Program (n.d), *A brief
    history of sustainable development* [Online].
    Available at: http://web.unep.org/post2015/history.
    php Accessed 5th March 2018.

LATIN AMERICA

PART 1

CHAPTER 1.1

SUNSHINE ON A CLOUDY DAY
Sustainable Fashion in Brazil

Evelise Anicet Rüthschilling, Federal University of Rio Grande do Sul, Brazil

INTRODUCTION

Brazil occupies 47 percent of the territory of South America. Its population of 207 million inhabitants is composed of different ethnic groups from many parts of the world, resulting in a multi-cultural nation that loves Nature. This essay focuses on sustainable fashion design in the context of contemporary Brazilian society. The text drawn on information strands from three key sectors: the environment, people, and the economy.

The objective of this essay is to present a mapping of the current scenario in sustainable fashion, identifying the production, consumption, and disposal guidelines that are being followed, the Brazilian way of doing things, success stories, fragilities, and the vision of the future.

The study[1] covers the traditional large-scale production system, and the corresponding system of retail and consumption, in relation to different types of businesses emerging from slow fashion, such as rural and digital associativism, phenomena of social innovation, and solidarity economy projects. It identifies the available raw materials and fashion brands with sustainable intent that are making contributions to a change in the system of production.

The discussion of the results presents the circular economy as a link between the two trends observed, identifying the capacity to promote the transition to a fashion production ecosystem while having a positive impact on society. The relationships in this field are networks that are simple in their purpose but complex in their transactions, constituting a multi-dimensional fabric of relationships that function in movements reminiscent of a spiral.

FAST FASHION

The Brazilian textile and clothing industry (traditional and fast fashion) currently has a contingent of 29,000 legally operating companies, providing 1.5 million direct jobs and 8 million indirect jobs, of which 75 percent are held by women (ABIT 2017). The industrial apparel chain in Brazil is one of few complete chains in the West (comprising fiber production, spinning, weaving, processing, manufacturing, and strong retail), and is the fourth largest industrial garment manufacturer in the world in terms of volume of production. Self-sufficient in the production of cotton and fast advancing in the productivity of petrochemical fibers (extracted from the Petroleum Pre-salt basin), soon the country will be in a position to stop importing synthetic fibers. Brazil is a world leader in the beachwear, jeanswear, fitness, and lingerie segments, and Brazilian Fashion Week is among the five biggest fashion weeks in the world (ABIT 2017). Financial reports at the end of 2017 (ABIT 2017) indicate the beginning of economic recovery, with an increase in production, retail sales, and jobs, as well as a general repositioning of fashion chains to pay more attention to sustainable issues in order to align with external markets and foster exports as a solution to correct the trade balance.

Analysis of corporate policies for the sustainability of Brazil's largest clothing and fashion brands take into account codes of conduct, sustainability reports, and certifications. Results show the presence of controls in the following aspects: social standards (working conditions, legal employment rules, health, safety, discrimination, human traffic, relationships); environmental standards (management of water, waste, greenhouse gas emissions (GHG), effluents, energy and substances dangerous to people and habitat); product safety (chemicals) and ethical integrity (ABIT 2017). Entrepreneurs are aware that these controls will ensure the competitiveness of Brazilian companies in the domestic and international markets, with a focus on the United States, Japan, and the European Union. On the other hand, they are also aware that most Brazilians cannot afford the higher costs generated by cleaner and more sustainable production.

The vision of the future of the Brazilian textile and clothing industry is based on two main pillars: investment in certifications and compliance of products with sustainability standards; and Advanced Manufacturing, also called "Industry 4.0," which comprises several integrated automated systems (Bruno 2016). In retail, chain stores offer products for the whole family within the security of air-conditioned malls, and these stores are responsible for the largest volume of clothing purchases in Brazil. According to ABVTEX (2017), the increase in consumer-awareness campaigns for ethical and socio-environmental causes, and the adverse scenario of the economic recession, which affected mainly the middle class and poorer sections of the Brazilian population, forced the executives of these companies to create monitoring systems for suppliers and subcontractors, called the Sustainable Supply Chain (SSC). They also signed the National Pact for the Eradication of Slave Labor in Brazil (Federal Senate 2017). Together, these initiatives send auditors on unannounced visits, and are monitored by various institutions (ABVTEX 2017). International suppliers are governed by protocols such as the Business Social Compliance Initiative (BSCI), WCA (Workplace Conditions Assessment), and SMETA (Sedex Members Ethical Trade Audits).

The future focus is on the more conscious consumer, who buys fewer products, but of higher quality, aiming at greater durability. This consumer is concerned with the ethical values of the companies—for example, responsibility and transparency, considered essential in relations with employees, suppliers, customers and the community as a whole.

SLOW FASHION

"Slow" ideology has recently been gaining favor, proposing a rethinking of the actions and processes underlying the relationship between clothing and user—the latter no longer referred to as a "consumer." The user may temporarily use the piece through a rental service, buy it at a second hand market, or purchase an individual piece that will last a long time, without going out of fashion, and which has a proper disposal system in place, usually by returning it to its manufacturer, in a circular system.

Unhurried fashion operates though a low-scale production system and creates trend-free fashion, seeking innovation, timeless design, clean processes, and raw materials that are less polluting. It preserves natural resources, encourages manual labor, and values quality over quantity by manufacturing meaningful clothing. The following are the main natural raw materials found in Brazil and considered alternatives for use in slow fashion. Next, we present the main Brazilian brands that focus on sustainability.

Natural Raw Materials

Brazil has a rich green chain of biological-fiber production, which appeals to manufacturers and consumers due to its renewable, carbon-free, and biodegradable credentials. Thus, older and more traditional fibers are now those of the future, but in a form enhanced by contemporary scientific and technological development. Extractive activities based on family agriculture produce rubber, vegetable fibers (cotton, bamboo, coconut, jute, sisal, flax, and hemp), and animal fibers (silk, wool) and fish and bovine leather with ecological tanning (Sarmento 2014).

The *Algodão Brasileiro Responsável* (ABR) program (Responsible Brazilian Cotton Program) (EMBRAPA 2018) incorporates the criteria for granting a marketing licence and is certified by the Better Cotton Initiative[2] (BCI), the largest Brazilian differential in the international organic cotton market being the production of naturally colored—that is, undyed—organic cotton. Since 1984, the Empresa Brasileira de Pesquisa's program called Embrapa Cotton has regenerated and revived the colored primitive species of the cotton plant, which became almost extinct during the Industrial Revolution because its fibers were not long enough to support industrial spinner rotor speeds.

Researchers improved the Brazilian northeast's cotton fibers through natural selection. They obtained colored organic cottons in twenty-two shades, ranging from off-white, beige, green, and brown to reddish, and new tones are in development currently. These fibers today generate strong yarns that offer high productivity, colorfastness, dimensional stability, resistance to pilling, and other quality criteria as greater plant diseases resistance, and can be processed by automated textile factories while saving 70 percent of water in comparison to other yarns.

Brazil has the best-quality colored cotton fiber in the world, which, as well as being ecologically friendly, has the advantage of dispensing the chemically polluting processes of bleaching and dyeing. This is an advantage in the manufacture of clothing, especially products designed for children and people allergic to dyes or synthetic fibers.

In the use of colored organic cotton, the Natural Cotton Color brand[3] stands out. It operates in the clothing, footwear, and accessories sectors, while maintaining ecological and socially just practices. It is a fashion company fully supported by Embrapa Cotton (EMBRAPA 2018) that also sells fabrics made with organic colored cotton at Première Vision, Paris, and Biofach, Germany. It represents Brazil in the main international sustainable fashion fairs such as Pure London and Ethical Fashion Show in Berlin,[4] and exports to more than ten countries, including Japan, Canada, the United States, Germany, France, and Saudi Arabia.

Regarding silk, O Casulo Feliz (The Happy Cocoon)[5] is a sustainable business that started out thirty years ago. Located in the south of Brazil, it developed a manual way to produce silk yarns, taking advantage of the cocoons unsuitable for industrial processing, and using them in new products for fashion and home decor with handmade appeal. The various types of yarns and fabrics result from blends with cotton, linen, and PET in light dyeing tones using natural plants, promoting the circularity of production processes, focusing on zero waste, and guaranteeing extra remuneration for small farmers and local entrepreneurs. The main Brazilian brands that use this certified organic silk in their collections are Osklen, Animale, Grama, Erika Ikezili, and Mário Queiroz (The Happy Cocoon 2017).

The state of Rio Grande do Sul has a long economic tradition based on farming systems, cooperativism and rural associativism. Wool production there suffered a decline in sales due to increased competition from synthetic fibers, which are more easily maintained, but recently the scenario has begun to change. The market is improving due to renewed appreciation of the advantages of wool, a fiber with unique properties and morphology, such as the ability to maintain moisture and regulate body temperature, its antibacterial and UV protection properties, and its non-flammable and biodegradable nature. It also offers the possibility of extracting by-products such as lanolin, and is a renewable source that may be harvested without the slaughter or mistreatment of animals. Like cotton, it also naturally comes in a range of colors, from natural whites and browns to black (Gestão no Campo 2017) (Field Management).

Another advantage of wool is the possibility of reducing the number of production stages by exploiting its properties of plasticity, as it can pass from the fiber stage directly to the final product stage by means of the felting process, which has a low pollution impact, and therefore offers reductions in environmental and financial costs. These are millennial techniques that contemporary designers are once again seeking to use, and to combine with expressiveness, well-being, and sustainable practices.

One key Brazilian market advantage is its natural rubber, originating in the Amazon region (Sarmento 2014), which spread its elastic, non-slip, impermeable and electrical insulation properties all over the world. It is an important natural raw material and a renewable source that helps the restoration of the forest and protects these public areas against the illegal exploitation of the wood, as well as generating income for families that inhabit the Brazilian northwest. The extraction of rubber native to the Amazon is assisted by various internationally protected and regulatory bodies, such as the World Wide Fund for Nature (WWF),[6] as well as special projects by universities and designers. The collection of latex from the trees is traditional and perennial, as each tree continues to give rubber and financial support to many generations of rubber tappers. There is a renewal of interest observing the environmental impact in the use of natural rubber in footwear and accessories, such as necklaces and handbags—for example, in the work of designer Flávia Amadeu.[7]

There are many more possibilities for the exploitation of other natural raw materials, such as banana and pineapple fibers, but it is not possible to discuss them all in this chapter. What remains is the certainty that we must constantly re-evaluate the use of natural materials and traditional processes from the perspective of sustainable development.

SUSTAINABLE FASHION BRANDS

The wealth of natural resources in Brazil is inspiring, fostering the emergence of fashion brands committed to sustainable principles. The following are some of the names involved that have slow fashion characteristics in a consolidated market and within contemporary systems of thinking that contribute to a sustainable fashion chain in Brazil.

Flávia Aranha[8] is a São Paulo brand that believes consuming is a political act and that it is possible to redesign the market through consumer choices. The designer makes clothes, accessories, shoes and decorative objects that put the customer in contact with biodiversity and traditional knowledge through the use of biodegradable materials, based on organic family farming. Through affective design principles, she carefully selects her suppliers of certified raw materials and the artisan processes of natural dyeing and botanical printing on silk, controlling the conditions in which her products are made and reducing the negative impacts of waste generated by the production. The result is fashionable products with timeless design, technical durability, and comfort. In her shop, artefacts from groups and places that participate in the production are displayed. The brand also offers product maintenance services and represents Brazil in international sustainable fashion fairs, such as the Ethical Fashion Show in Berlin.

Agustina Comas[9] has experience in the production of luxury clothes, which gave her a sense of the scale of waste in luxury fabrics production. Her brand's flagship initiative is the upcycling of scraps and pieces of clothing that have been subject to production errors or have not passed quality control. In a very creative way, she has generated single-piece production line methods, selling them online and at sustainable fashion events. As Binotto and Payne (2017) say in regard to the reuse of waste textiles: "[W]aste is connected to notions of value, which are ever

Figure 1.1.1 Flávia Aranha design, hand-woven blouse made with genetically colored organic cotton
Image reproduced courtesy of Flávia Aranha. *Copyright © Flávia Aranha. Photographer: Caio Ramalho*

shifting. It is a state that things can move in and out of. Items, goods and leftovers formerly considered waste can be re-categorized and reclaimed with fresh value ascribed to them." (Binotto & Payne 2017: 7). Agustina also creates fabrics from scraps and selvedge: one example is Oricla, which is rich in tactile textures and used in joint collections with another designer, Fernanda Yamamoto.[10]

Insecta Shoes,[11] a brand of vegan footwear, was established in 2014 and collects clothing from secondhand stores to make shoes. Today it

Figure 1.1.2 Happi Sutorito Oricla made in partnership with Japonique
Photographer: Mariana Cobra. Model: Elisa Montouto

is known for its printed fabric shoes (floral, animal world, and vintage universe), classic models, flats, genderless footware (such as Oxfords), as well as boots and sandals with recycled rubber soles. These classic shoes are revived as green and fun fashion products, combining comfort, cheerful style, and ecological awareness. The winner of the Ecoera Brasil 2015 Award, the company is B+ certified. In addition to an online operation, it has physical stores in Brazil and points of sale in the United States, Canada, Germany, and Spain.

Contextura[12] emerged in 2010 as a company conducting scientific and artistic research with the objective of testing in the real world the sustainable strategies studied in an academic environment. The brand mixes artisanal techniques (surface treatments) and digital technologies, which are its differential in the market. Creation follows slow design principles (timeless, versatile clothes with durability and ease of maintenance), and upcycling and zero-waste policies (Rüthschilling & Anicet 2018), using natural fabrics, recycled PET, and biodegradable synthetic fibers. The sales system combines e-commerce, physical points of sale, and personalized service in the showroom. The business model aggregates local raw materials, networks of services providers, social inclusion, and partner companies, with a view to circularity. The brand is a signatory of the 2020 Circular Fashion System Commitment—Global Fashion Agenda—Copenhagen Fashion Summit[13] and winner of the 2018 Ecoera Award—category people.[14] (See Figure 1 in the plate section.)

Márcia Ganem[15] is an internationally recognized Bahian creator. She makes a contribution to the national culture, updating traditional knowledge of handmade lace techniques and using it in contemporary clothing design generated with polyamide fibers recovered from industrial surplus, creating new tactile textures of singular beauty. Her academic research developed the Dialogical Design methodology in the Handicrafts Traditions (Ganem 2016), which feeds into the sustainability and permanence of the work and to ensuring the survival of lace communities through the production of haute couture pieces.

Undoubtedly, Brazil has a large number of brands with a slow fashion profile with a sustainable intention, but it was decided to present here brands using different market approaches, both of which were studied in this academic research.

SPECIAL PROJECTS

The survey gathered results of projects and initiatives for sustainable fashion, and these are listed below.

Ahlma[16] functions as an axis of collective co-creation of shared fashion ranges, services, stories, and experiences in a community of partners, producers, suppliers, and consumers. It looks for fertile solutions to make fashion serve people's lives, bearing in mind that there are already too many clothes in the world, and too much waste from the clothing industry. It is a *carioca* (meaning native to Rio de Janeiro) movement coordinated by André Carvalhal, who designs new forms of conscious consumption focused on the Millennial generation, creating new types of relationships between time, space, people, education, work, and consumption. He exerts a powerful positive influence on the young in Brazil.

The project called Ateliê Vivo ("Living Atelier") in São Paulo is a public library of modeling patterns donated by prominent Brazilian stylists, where people from the community can register, having made a financial donation of their choice, to produce their own clothes under the guidance of volunteer instructors. The goal is to encourage the culture *maker* and a DIY approach, thereby, reducing consumption.[17]

The Instituto-E (E-Institute) is an OSCIP— civil society organization of public interest— promoted by the fashion brand Osklen that emerged from the e-brigade, an environmental activism movement that transforms concepts into attitudes. It acts as an interface between the various initiatives of sustainable development and agents of society, and its mission is to share information, in order to improve education and safeguard Brazil's natural and cultural heritage.[18]

The EcoEra Award, coordinated by the fashion model Chiara Gadaleta, with the support of *Vogue* magazine and System B,[19] sets out to identify companies in Brazil that employ conscious practices throughout their production chain. Since it was established in 2015, the Award created a "big picture" of the fashion, beauty, and design markets with social, economic and cultural environmental sustainability indicators (see note 13).

NEW BUSINESS MODELS IN NETWORKS

The extraction of natural raw materials and the recycling of chemical fibers are usually linked to networks of socio-economic projects and actions of associativism, solidarity economy, and Fairtrade. Characteristic of Brazil, these are run by organized groups of individuals who are on the margins of the labor market, due to the isolation of their home location and/or due to lack of professional qualifications and job opportunities. The goal is to overcome difficulties and generate social benefits and economic survival (Bossle 2011). The notion of associativism (FIEP 2017) lies in the belief that, together, it is possible to find solutions, share burdens, and face the challenges that life presents; this collaboration can occur among workers, professionals, and companies.

In the current scenario of economic challenges in Brazil, which strongly affect the companies in the textile and clothing production chain, and the general low level of education, employment opportunities are scarce, generating a large contingent of unemployed, but not unoccupied, people. This situation explains the emergence of solidarity economy ventures, an economic model on the rise in the country.

Note the existence of several associations established by individuals (mostly women) based initially on family agriculture, which in turn create cooperative networks with alternative forms of business, and whose products are distributed across several Brazilian states. In this way they manage all links in the ecological textile chain: planting, spinning, weaving, confectionery, handicrafts, collection and recycling of fabrics, management, trade, and finance.

As we can see, these sociodiversity-based ventures establish strong ties between those who produce, finance, market, and use products, showing a promising path to change within the fashion chain.

CO-WORKING

Currently, Brazil offers approximately 224 educational courses in Fashion Design, including those covering technological aspects, those at baccalaureate level, and some covering related areas (Neira 2017). This social phenomenon brings to the labor market a large contingent of young professionals every year. They are part of the Millennial generation, born in the digital era. A few take up industrial posts, many establish their own brand, and others provide services in the fashion system. Most of them inhabit the virtual dimension of social networks and organize themselves into co-working groups, participating in online and offline communities, inventing new ways of working for both professional achievement and economic survival. If there are no jobs, they invent alternative forms of business.

In this context, cooperation networks are extremely popular and span the entire industry and workforce, from the rural employee to the young professional graduate or large companies. All parties make use of information and communication technologies (ICTs) to organize and be effective in their work. The broad array of technology resources available today on the internet provide new forms of communication, data access and process management, reducing costs and accelerating production and distribution.

CIRCULAR ECONOMY

Cooperation networks rely on electronic technology. Digital environments are emerging that are also open, inclusive, transparent, profit-oriented organizations or not; they bring together people who undertake, invest in, and work on fashion projects, interacting in physical and virtual spaces. Industrial society thus transmutes itself into a networked society, generating new patterns of interactions between actors with economic, political, managerial, and social implications. In this new system, the individual is a node of the network and exerts systemic responsibility, contributing to the best of his or her abilities for the improvement of all.

There are also decentralized networks of alternative peer-to-peer (P2P) economic systems, i.e., platforms without third-party mediation in commercial transactions, where confidence is expected in the construction of an alternative financial system, reducing costs and boosting stakeholders. These technologies are used to support and control services, products, and payments systems. The close relationship between technology and green products—even traditionally made or handcrafted products—can now be managed and marketed through electronic technology, creating an environment conducive to managing the circular economy.

According to Webster, "Information and communications technology (ICT) and the circular economy have a very deep relationship between this big picture/different system orientation. The very means through which we can imagine prosperity in a circular economy is through a digital-meets-systems perspective" (2015: 2461). We are living a new revolution by expanding the role of digital technologies through enhancing online systems such as tracking and applications for mobiles, among many other features that build feedback-rich systems perspectives.

The paradigm shift from linear to circular industrial production is emerging today in the world as a resource for the survival of the population and the planet. In a circular economy focused on the fashion production chain, design and manufacturing systems are intentionally designed to produce products that, at the end of their life cycle, can be reused, regenerated, or recycled, advancing immediately as input into a new cycle, which in turn generates new products. Thus, it aims to increase resource efficiency (energy, water, material extraction) and clean technologies in product manufacturing, reducing environmental, social and economic impacts (Ellen MacArthur Foundation 2017).[20]

In this context, it is evident that the cycles start in one or more companies, or local productive arrangements, and develop in the form of spirals, that is, they are 3D spatial cycles, in continuous movements of expansion, enlarging the networks of stakeholders' cooperation. Thus, the mental and graphic representation proposed here illustrates the continuous flow of regeneration of technical and biological inputs (McDonough & Braungart, 2013) from a growing contingent of producers and service providers.

The spiral form represents the genesis of life, nature as a measure and model in its convolutions, wind, clouds, planets, seed germination, life from its micro dimension to the macrocosm. Meaningful for many cultures and in many time periods, the spiral captures very well the energy that comes from the movement of people and textile materials passing around them, close to each other, creating new possibilities.

The spiral illustration shown here is inspired by the book *The Espirals of Fashion* by the French author Vincent-Ricard (1989), who associates the creative evolution of fashion with spirals, as imagined by Vladimir Nabokov:

> The spiral is a spiritualized circle. In the spiral form, the circle, uncoiled, unwound, has ceased to be vicious; it has been set free … Twirl follows twirl, and every synthesis is the thesis of the next series.
>
> [1989] 2018: 265

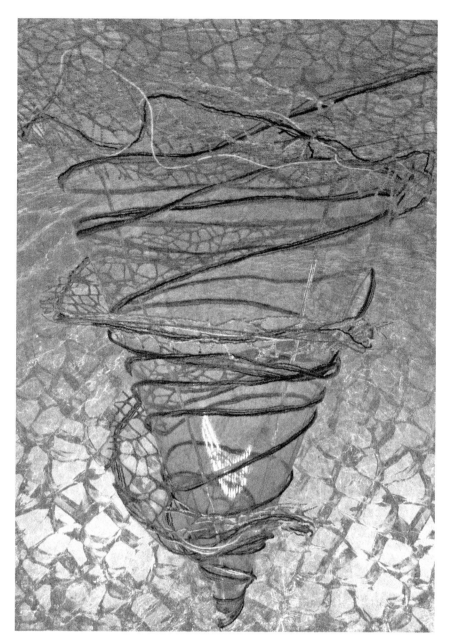

Figure 1.1.3
The sustainable
fashion spiral
Image reproduced
courtesy of Evelise
Rüthschilling and Paula
Godecke

CONCLUSION

These research results show that the predisposition of Brazilian producers to work in cooperative networks, their love of Nature, domain of technological expertise, and the social maturity reached in labor through actions in favor of social capital, constitute a favorable scenario to the new textile economy. That said, the process of evolution and transition from the old values to a more just and efficient society is complex and can be slow.

Brazil is a country of continental size; it displays great contrasts—poverty and wealth, low and high technology—and great possibilities that, if properly harnessed, can promote the transition from the textile industrial line chain to a circular system, constantly advancing in order to create better conditions for life, work, and income.

NOTES

1. This essay shares the data collected and systematized through the research projects Mapping Sustainable Fashion in Brazil conducted by the Research Center on Sustainable Fashion, UFRGS, RS, Brazil – NMS-UFRGS, from 2015 to 2018.
2. https://bettercotton.org/
3. www.nccecobrands.com
4. http://ethicalfashionshowberlin.com/
5. www.ocasulofeliz.com.br
6. www.wwf.org.br/
7. www.flaviaamadeu.com/
8. http://flaviaaranha.com/
9. https://comas.com.br/
10. www.fernandayamamoto.com.br/
11. www.insectashoes.com/
12. www.contextura.art.br
13. www.globalfashionagenda.com/commitment/
14. https://vogue.globo.com/EcoEra-Chiara-Gadaleta/noticia/2018/03/os-vencedores-da-3-edicao-do-premio-ecoera.html and https://www.consumoconsciente.com.br/
15. www.marciaganem.com/
16. https://ahlma.cc/
17. www.atelievivo.com.br/
18. http://institutoe.org.br/
19. www.bcorporation.net/
20. www.ellenmacarthurfoundation.org/

REFERENCES

ABIT (Associação Brasileira da Indústria Têxtil) (2017), Available online: www.abit.org.br/cont/perfil-do-setor (accessed December 10, 2017).

ABVTEX (Associação Brasileira do Varejo Têxtil) (2017), Available online: www.abvtex.org.br (accessed May 28, 2017).

Algodão Colorido (Colored Cotton), Available online at: https://www.embrapa.br/en/busca-de-publicacoes/-/publicacao/896908/o-algodao-colorido-da-embrapa (Accessed July 8, 2018).

Binotto, C. and A. Payne (2017), "The Poetics of Waste: Contemporary Fashion Practice in the Context of Wastefulness," *Fashion Practice*, 9 (1): 5–29. Available online: https://doi.org/10.1080/17569370.2016.1226604 (accessed September 29, 2017).

Bossle, M. (2011), *Comércio justo no Brasil e a comercialização de produtos do algodão orgânico.* Dissertação de Mestrado Universidade Federal do Rio Grande do Sul, Brasil. Available online: www.lume.ufrgs.br/handle/10183/30370 (accessed July 28, 2017).

Bruno, F.S. (2016), *A quarta revolução industrial do setor têxtil e de confecção: a visão de futuro para 2030.* São Paulo: Estação das Letras e Cores. Available online at: http://arquivos.portaldaindustria.com.br/app/conteudo_18/2016/06/21/11146/Aquartarevoluoindustrialdosetortxtiledeconfeco.pdf?r=0.708670839781 (accessed November 4, 2017).

EMBRAPA (*Empresa Brasileira de Pesquisa Agropecuária*) (2018), Available at: www.embrapa.br/en/web/portal/library/ (accessed May 20, 2018).

FIEP (Federação das Indústrias do Estado do Paraná, Brasil) (2017), "Conceito de Associativismo." Available onlineat: http://www.fiepr.org.br/para-sindicatos/pda/o-que-e-associativismo-1-20743-320690.shtml (accessed October 16, 2017).

Ganem, M. (2016), *Design dialógico: uma estratégia para gestão criativa de tradições.* São Paulo: Estação das Letras e Cores.

Gestão no Campo (2017), (Field Management) [online]. "A cadeia de produção de ovinos." Available online at: http://www.gestaonocampo.com.br/biblioteca/a-cadeia-de-producao-de-ovinos/ (accessed June 12, 2017).

McDonough, W., and M. Braungart, M. (2013), *The Upcycle: Beyond Sustainability, Designing for Abundance*. New York: North Point Press.

Nabokov, V. ([1989] 2018). *Speak, Memory: An Autobiography Revised*. New York: Vintage Books International.

Neira, L. (2017), "Precisamos falar sobre educação em moda. dObra[s] – Revista da Associação Brasileira de Estudos de Pesquisas em Moda, São Paulo. v. 10, n. 21 (2017), pp. 1–7. Available online at: https://dobras.emnuvens.com.br/dobras/article/viewFile/560/455 (accessed December 22, 2017).

Rüthschilling, E. and A. Anicet (2018), "Slow Surface Design and Contemporary Technology Applied in Fashion," *Revista Moda Palavra* online journal. UDESC/CEART. v.11,n. 21, Jan/June 2018. Available online: www.revistas.udesc.br/index.php/modapalavra (accessed January 6, 2018).

Sarmento, F. (2014), "Design for sociobiodiversity: Prospects for sustainable use of rubber in the Tapajos National Forest," PhD thesis, Faculdade de Arquitetura e Urbanismo. São Paulo, USP, Brazil. Available online: http://www.teses.usp.br/teses/disponiveis/16/16134/tde-28072014-111246/pt-br.php (accessed June 13, 2017).

Senado Federal Brasileiro (2017), *Pacto Nacional pela Erradicação do Trabalho Escravo*. Available online: https://www.senado.gov.br/noticias/Jornal/emdiscussao/trabalho-escravo/ongs-contra-o-trabalho-escravo/pacto-nacional-pela-erradicacao-do-trabalho-escravo.aspx (accessed September 21, 2017).

Vincent-Ricard, F. (1989), *As espirais da moda*. Rio de Janeiro: Paz e Terra.

Webster, K. (2015), The Circular Economy: A Wealth of Flows. 2nd ed. (English edition; eBook published 2016) Cowes: Ellen MacArthur Foundation. Available online at: https://www.ellenmacarthurfoundation.org/publications/the-circular-economy-a-wealth-of-flows-2nd-edition (accessed December, 2017).

CHAPTER 1.2

A SPOTLIGHT ON: FASHION ACTIVISM
The Impact of the Fashion Revolution Movement in Brazil

Anne Anicet, Research Center on Sustainable Fashion, UFRGS, RS, Brazil
Cariane Weydman Camargo, Universidade do Vale do Rio dos Sinos, UNISINOS, RS, Brazil

Fashion linked to ephemerality, consumerism, and planned obsolescence has imposed a high cost on both society and the environment. Even today, most methods of production of fibers, materials, and products prioritize profits rather than ethical values, by taking into consideration neither the limits of our planet's resilience nor consumers' and workers' safety and health.

This model of development has caused a number of social-environmental disasters, such as the collapse of the Rana Plaza complex on April 24, 2013, in Bangladesh, where more than 1,000 people died and 2,000 were injured. In response to this tragedy, the Fashion Revolution Movement was established by Orsola de Castro and Carry Somers in London with the aim of increasing consumer awareness of the true cost of fashion at all stages of the production, consumption, and disposal processes.

By posing the simple question *#whomademyclothes*, Fashion Revolution has been able to provoke reflection on the transparency of the fashion supply chain and to inspire people from more than ninety countries to think differently about what they wear. Held every year, in the week of April 24, the movement has spread all over the world; for instance, from 2015 to 2016, there was a 448 percent increase in the number of people involved in the movement through participation in numerous online and physical actions, such as activities proposed by universities, sustainable brands, non-governmental organizations, and labor unions, among others.

In Brazil, the movement started in 2014 during ECOERA in Sao Paulo, and very quickly spread to the major Brazilian capitals. In 2015, fifteen events were held in twelve different cities. In 2016, the promotion of ethics in fashion was seen in fifty-four events in twenty-nine cities, and thirty-one universities participated in an action specifically directed at the academic setting

through the production of flags made out of fabric scraps. This involvement with the ethical movement in Brazil keeps growing even outside of Fashion Revolution Week, as increased ongoing participation in social networks shows. In January 2017, the @fash_rev_brasil Instagram account had more than 8,000 followers, and *#whomademyclothes* hashtag had been used more than 4,000 times[1]; on Facebook, the Fashion Revolution Brasil page had more than 19,000 likes[2], and posts have been frequently commented on and shared. By April 2018, fashionrevolution.brasil had 34,337 Facebook followers and roughly the same number of likes, while @fash_rev_brasil 39,000 followers.

In the city of Porto Alegre, in the south of Brazil, Cariane Camargo coordinated the events of the Fashion Revolution Week in 2016 and 2017, with the support of Research Center on Sustainable Fashion at the Federal University of Rio Grande do Sul—UFRGS[3]. The activities intended for a wide audience had significant

Figure 1.2.1 Fashion Revolution Day, Universidade Federal do Rio Grande do Sul
Image reproduced courtesy of the Research Center on Sustainable Fashion, UFRGS, RS, Brazil

impacts on society. Exhibitions, lectures, documentaries, performances, informal meetings in fairs, brand stands, and studios, as well as round tables with representatives of the textile chain and footwear and accessories industries, were held, alongside intensive activities that took place on social networks and were supported by traditional media. The end result was a change of mindset in the state of Rio Grande do Sul in terms of the transparency of the fashion production chain in Brazil.

Parallel to this, several schools and eleven fashion, design, and art colleges developed the Project Fabric Scrap Flag to address the values of the Fashion Revolution Movement with students. The topic was introduced through the film *The True Cost*, which introduced some of the movement's history. A comprehensive debate raised students' awareness of the poor working conditions in the fast fashion chain. Later, students from different disciplines and extension projects gathered to design flags made out of fabric scraps disposed of by the clothing industry. The phrases *Who made my clothes?* and *Fashion Revolution* could be seen on the big, colorful flags. The flags were exhibited in schools and also in public, encouraging students and the community as a whole to think about the true cost of fashion. Such activities in educational institutions foster students' awareness, thus preparing them, as professional designers of the future, to act in accordance with the mission of changing society.

Adherence to the sustainable cause has been beneficial to the state of Rio Grande do Sul, as it has fostered a union of the academic, industrial, and retailing sectors, and wider society. This has yielded positive results, including the instigation of collaborative actions that have improved the local economy by reviving the traditional value placed on its farming activities, such as wool production. In the fashion production chain, Rio Grande do Sul, which is characterized as a "slow" state, has always been adversely affected by competitors from other, more highly industrialized Brazilian states. This is the time for Rio Grande do Sul to be both nationally and internationally acknowledged as a state that produces sustainable fashion by generating revenue through supporting its local traditions.

Figure 1.2.2 Fashion Revolution Week in Porto Alegre, RS, Brazil
Image reproduced courtesy of the Research Center on Sustainable Fashion, UFRGS, RS, Brazil

NOTES

1. www.instagram.com/fash_rev_brasil/. Accessed January 16, 2017.
2. https://www.facebook.com/fashionrevolution.brasil/. Accessed January 16, 2017.
3. www.ufrgs.br/mmt/acervo/5/Fashion-Revolution-PortoAlegre/. Accessed July 8, 2018.

CHAPTER 1.3
RAÍZ DISEÑO
The Journey of a Silent Resistance

Laura Novik, Universidad de San Andrés, Buenos Aires, Argentina

THE JOURNEY

Latin America always existed under the sign of utopia. I am also convinced that utopia has a time and a place. It is here.

The echo of Latin America resonates in Thomas More's *Utopia* as an influence that takes on new meaning 500 years after its publication. Both a political treaty and travelogue (Jameson 2007), inspired by Americo Vespucci's last journeys (Borges Morán 1995), its text transports us to the "end of the world," a metaphor for humankind's eternal search for perfection (Marin 1973). This essay presents an exploration of reflections on ethical fashion across Latin America, the same geography that inspired the Morean *Utopia*—and from where we can uncover subtle forms of resistance.

This research arose in the context of the travels organized by Raíz Diseño (in English, "Design Root"), an independent platform created in 2007 as a transnational network of Latin American designers. Most of them had already been working for two decades within the Mercosur market to integrate local forms of

knowledge and ethical business practices into the design and manufacturing processes. In the current context of emerging economies, the fast fashion problem and the evolution of the world financial crisis that has affected the so-called central countries, peripheral fashion design has begun to add its polyphony of voices and experiences to tackle the many problems of the global agenda on the environmental, social and cultural fronts.

The Raíz Diseño project arose in this context as a platform for meetings and inspiration, and has become a central actor in consolidating sustainable design in Chile and Latin America. With this focus, Raíz Diseño began contacting leaders of standout projects, businesses, and institutions whose work shows that the future of markets does not only involve buying and selling. In the future, as well as in the emerging present, economic exchange will be tied to land, the environment, and the well-being of humankind, in addition to ethics and profitability. Also, far from being, as some may expect, frivolous, poor, or unattractive, the new creative scene is seeing successful cases of alternative approaches that have become sustainable businesses, precisely because they connect with people's sensibilities.

These are silent forms of resistance from within the field of design.

DESIGN IS RESISTANCE

In a world that hastily absorbs, creates, digests, and eliminates wealth, new forms of resistance emerged and became consolidated in the Latin American region as recently as the end of the last century. Public conscience shifted toward the search for an ecological balance regarding communities and their territories. Since the dawn of the new millennium, Latin American designers, businesspeople, artists, and inventors have set out to creatively reduce the ecological impact of contemporary lifestyles through the dematerialization of consumer society.

A tool that the *gauchos* employed to make better use of raw leather was the point of departure of a unique tool that draws between fifteen and thirty meters of plastic ribbon from a PET bottle. Designed by the Argentine Alejandro Sarmiento, these ribbons can be used in different artisanal and domestic processes, such as basketry, woven fabric, crochet, and knitwear, or by using a thermal-shaping process that simply uses hot water. Named *Contenido Neto* (or "Net Content") (www.contenido-neto.com), the system starts out by turning PET bottles into strands, which are then turned into tools for the design of all kinds of objects, from cleaning implements to lamps and fashion accessories. In Raíz Diseño's 2007 Observatorio de Tendencias Emergentes (or "Emerging Trends Observatory"), Sarmiento explained that the idea originated on a trip during the mid-nineties to New York where he witnessed the disposal by North American consumer culture of objects that were still in good condition. Upon his return, Sarmiento began experimenting with industrial design elements taken out of context and using recycling strategies. This hybrid approach, born from everyday technology and rethought for the purpose of recycling urban waste, is one of the most acclaimed innovations from this designer (Muzi 2007), who is a pioneer of the field in Latin America, and who has won many national and international awards.

The Argentinian economic debacle of 2000 and 2001 pushed designers to shift their focus away from the object; instead, they began to concentrate on open-source systems capable of changing their environment and their society. *Contenido Neto* is an example of this "community-oriented design" shift with an egalitarian focus (Julier 2017). A simple, low-tech instrument, it functioned as a solid waste management system and provided a source of employment for the *cartoneros* (unemployed people, who became urban recyclers) and youth during Argentina's financial crisis (Picchi and Cambariere 2006). Alejandro Sarmiento's approach became an inspiration for a generation of Argentine designers who understood social and environmental imbalances as two sides of an economic model that was undergoing a crisis.

A few years later, on the other side of the Andes, recycling emerged as an activity for students who used their university's waste to make jewelry for a teen clothing brand. This is how Modulab appeared, a brand led by the Chilean industrial design couple Pamela Troncoso and Felipe Ferrer, also present at Raíz Diseño's 2007 Observatorio de Tendencias Emergentes. This is an example of how recycling in the context of a market economy, as in Chile, can become a waste management service for the corporate world. Modulab was a pioneer in Chile, and over time, Troncoso and Ferrer discovered that their growth and value was tied to "tackling sustainability by linking up with businesses (corporations), to which we lend our services. Modulab is a bridge between design and waste management that takes a hybrid leap from crafts to industry." They specialize in producing containers and handbags, and, as a laboratory exercise, they search the city for industrial waste materials that they can later turn into fashion accessories. The brand establishes long-term rapport with its clients, some of which share its sustainability efforts, like cosmetics company Natura, outdoor clothing company Patagonia (Guerrero 2016), and government (e.g., Plataforma Urbana 2012). Some of these are also part of its CSR program, such as the Coca Cola Company and Tiendas París (Tiendas Paris 2013). During this time, Troncoso and Ferrer participated in Raíz Diseño's festivals, runway shows and exhibitions, which they described as "a space of inspiration, gathering, and motivation. We were the first, the only business of our kind. Therefore, finding Raíz Diseño, and being part of a collective, connected us to other designers who spoke the same language. They created networks that continue today."

In 2010, Pasarela Raíz Diseño's catwalk devoted to ethical fashion presented two emerging brands that made binary use of art and textile recycling: Híbrida, from Chile, and Cosecha Vintage, from Argentina. Híbrida (www.hibrida.cl) was created in 2008 by artist Angélica Delgado and sociologist Eduardo Sepúlveda. The couple discovered the potential of using waste from the fashion industry to produce jewelry to materialize their ethical and aesthetic visions. Through variations of the *embarrilado* (a traditional indigenous technique), they make pendants, chokers, bracelets and bangles in organic volumes. Sometimes, they broaden their scale so the objects become true chrysalises with strong aesthetic power, which they use to raise awareness on the value of reusing, recycling, and reducing the footprint of consumption. The artists share their commitment to the environment with Cosecha Vintage (www.cosechavintage.com.ar), a company created in 2009 by artist Ale Gougy. In a workshop at Centro Metropolitano de Diseño de Buenos Aires (Buenos Aires Metropolitan Design Center), Gougy became aware of the fact that nylon socks could take up to 2,000 years to biodegrade. After that, she decided to make nylon socks a central "raw material" in her collection. In her workshop, she turns these socks into threads, mixes them with natural fibers, and weaves delicate and romantic crafted clothing with this material. An award-winner at the Bienal Iberoamericana de Diseño (BID) awards in 2011, she represents her country at major fashion events throughout the world and in national runway shows. Her collections evoke the aesthetics of a pre-industrial past, in which Gougy recalls her own family history and tells us about the new harvest (*cosecha*) that arrives with sustainability.

Figure 1.3.1 Collar Troncocônico
2011 for Raíz Diseño exhibition to Fair Ropero Paula. Photo & post: Pilar Castro/Hair & Make up: Margarita Nilo/Model: Sade H.

RESISTING THROUGH WHAT IS LEFT

12na's (12na.com.ar) founders, Mariano Breccia and Mechi Martínez, moved to Chile searching for used clothing from the First World that were sold in bulk, by the kilo or by the dozen. The latter number inspired the brand's name, that was later transformed into a verb—*doceñar* (a hybrid of "dozen" and "designing"). *Doceñar* is an action that means much more than recycling, reusing, and re-signifying clothes. It means creating value from precariousness, and turning the logic of fashion upside down. They began with collections of unique items that were exported to the United States, Japan, and Germany, in an ironic reversal of the tide of discards from the global fashion industry.

From 2008 onwards, 12na has showcased its creative progress at Pasarela Raíz Diseño, where it won the award for best collection in 2012. Their endeavors went far beyond apparel to include urban installations and collective workshops in festivals like Lollapalooza, and in sustainability gatherings, such as the Malmö Festival (www.malmofestivalen. se) in Sweden. Its distinctive features were precise textile recycling, an appreciation for local marginal cultures, a critical stance toward contemporary consumerism, a strong commitment to sustainable practice, and collective creation (Docena 2017). For Raíz Diseño, 12na was always more than a clothing brand, and for 12na: "Raíz Diseño was a platform that contextualized our ideas. Its contents sparked a need to deepen our approach and to think of ourselves beyond a brand of recycled clothes, which is what we were when we participated in the first catwalk. With this in mind, we began experimenting in other areas that allowed us to become the textile recycling platform that we are today."

Another project that finds in precariousness a way of reflecting on the political dimensions of hyper-consumption is Telas del Futuro (or "Fabrics of the Future"), by fashion designer Juana Díaz. A daughter of exiles, she returned to Chile in the 1980s after living in Barcelona and London with her parents. During her time abroad, she encountered punk culture, which Juana says inspired many of her aesthetic interests, and even her combative attitudes, as a step toward the discovery of the potential of used clothing.

Scarcity of materials has been a constant throughout her career, a situation that led her to use discarded clothes and fabrics as the raw material for her first sculptural work. Thanks to this formula, she won the FONDART award (Fondo Nacional de las Artes, or National Fund for the Arts) in 2000. Later, she put forward a new reflection on sustainability through reused surfaces, textile art, political attitudes and poetry. This is how, in 2010, Telas del Futuro was born and presented in Pasarela Raíz Diseño, a space that, Juana declares, allowed her to "discover the ethical dimension of production, to build a coherent storytelling, alongside a way of life." Telas del Futuro was selected for the Bienal de Diseño Iberoamericano (BID) 2011. Since then, Díaz has been leading ethical fashion movements, and taking steps to place her brand in the international market, together with other brands that share her philosophy (such as 12na), and is established as one of the leading voices in fashion in her country. For Juana Díaz, "fashion is a means to reflect on how we are and to create better living conditions for people," in what she calls "ModaconSentido" (or "FashionwithaPurpose").

RESISTING WITH THE VOICE

At a time of revolutionary trends, with viral advertising campaigns and curated images that demand change in the system of fast fashion,

Figure 1.3.2 Telas del Futuro designer, Juana Díaz Allende *Photographer: Juana Diaz Alliende*

ingredients and, above all, on celebrating the act and the time of eating. These were some of the points that these designers began to consider in fashion, in an intuitive way. Soon after, "without rush, but without pause," as their slogan says, they started promoting local products, establishing ties between traditional and technological elements that, in addition to their artistic focus and their connection to the industry, led them into the field of slow fashion around 2005. In 2007, when the term "slow fashion" started gaining ground in the international press, they were invited to the first Pasarela Raíz Diseño in Chile, which presented the concept to local society. At that time, the brand Ana Livni was already expert at choosing locally sourced materials, using ethical work practices and setting fair prices. Their collections were conceived as an evolution, with only one annual launch, with no seasons, and without sales and other commercial formulas. When people walk into their store to see what is new, Ana and Fernando take the opportunity to spread the word on the benefits of conscious consumption. As they explain in their manifesto, "There is no beauty if it is not good"—a summary of their ethical and aesthetic position.

Another leading figure that adopts a critical stance is Brazilian designer Ronaldo Fraga (www. ronaldofraga.com.br), who has been a sort of a guide for Raíz Diseño. One of his most valuable contributions in the realm of ethical fashion is addressing issues on the global agenda related to the environment and society and tackling them with honesty, a critical viewpoint, and a political standpoint. He is called "the poet of fashion" because his collections tell stories, and because his runway shows can be understood as small performance pieces that point out uncomfortable or forgotten realities. During times of fast production and consumption, Fraga uses fashion to transform minds. He reaches global audiences

other forms of resistance have arisen in South America, waving fashion as a political flag. Fashion continues to raise its voice to influence its audience among today's severe humanitarian and environmental problems. Ana Livni in Uruguay was one of the first brands to embrace sustainability. The creative couple behind this brand, Ana Livni and Fernando Escuder, were inspired by the slow food movement. During a trip to Italy in 2001, as members of the Mercosur Design graduate program, they discovered ways of protesting against the fast food industry based on conscious consumption, choosing locally sourced products, using natural, good-quality through topics that stir society: his clothes speak about love, about pollution of the San Francisco River, about production in China, or about refugees. His runway shows in the Sao Paulo Fashion Week always go viral, and he himself is an avid user of social networks, with active Instagram, Facebook, and Twitter accounts. His message is disseminated through other media as well, such as TV, books, and conferences in Brazil, Latin America, and the rest of the world. Ronaldo Fraga's fashion is a message, a different way of resisting creatively.

RESISTING THROUGH YOUR VIEW

Form does not follow function, but emotion. It communicates a worldview. Therefore, I believe this is a great opportunity for Latin America. The market needs to reveal other voices. And our mission is to make them heard. The transformative potential of visibility is self-esteem.

Adélia Borges, Raíz Diseño Symposium, Temuco, Chile (Cambariere and Luján 2007)

"Wash one's eyes to see more clearly … Or close them to look again, recognize the other and his place," explained Heloissa Crocco to the audience in the Symposium Raíz Diseño ("Design for emerging communities"), which was held in Temuco, the heart of the *comunidad mapuche*. Crocco, a Brazilian industrial designer who began her work in 1980 as a crafts designer, cofounded the Laboratorio Piracema de Design along with historian José Nemer. This center for interdisciplinary research on Brazilian culture's formal expressions pioneered the links of designers with the craft-making world, and facilitated the development of new products.

Inspired by the reflections of Aloísio Magalães—another pioneer of Brazilian design in the 1970s—and with the sponsorship of groups such as Sebrae (Serviço Brasileiro de Apoio às Micro e Pequenas Empresas, or the Brazilian Service for the Development of Small and Medium Businesses) and Artesol (Artesanato Solidário, or Solidary Handicraft), the group fostered a design methodology with a strong anthropological influence that eschewed shallow viewpoints that might otherwise have jeopardized the cultural identity of their work.

Piracema is an indigenous word: in the Tupy language, it describes the natural migration of fish that swim upstream in the rivers to spawn. This image of diving into the origins and establishing vanguard practices from there is the source of inspiration for their "experiences" (*vivencias*), as they called their visits to indigenous communities. The photographer's camera captures exotic treasures to visitors' eyes that go unnoticed by locals, zooming in on people and their immediate environment and zooming out onto the landscape. Respect is the essential tool in this method, and the notion of "intervention" is absent when developing a product inspired by these treasures. In this model, design comes in to a place to establish branding strategies, and to assemble collections aimed at making those local communities visible to the market.

Honoring the value of travelling, these experiences join a tradition that started in the 1970s and 1980s in Colombia, where Artesanías de Colombia's "Design Laboratories" (Ramírez Cendar 2012) and the Arts and Textiles Program at Universidad de Los Andes (Guerrero 1994) took its first steps toward bringing the field of design closer to that of craftwork. Heloisa Crocco visited this school in the late 1970s, and remembers this episode as a transformative trip (Raíz Diseño 2007). This was one of the most important academic research centers on Andean craftwork, and established a model of design that was focused on the innovation of the artisan sector. The methodology involved students and professors travelling to indigenous territory, where they experienced transformative exercises and the awakening of new ways of seeing.

Raíz Diseño aimed to take the experiences of Colombia, Brazil, and the Travels of Amereida (Universidad Católica de Valparaíso) to the next level: establishing relationships between creative people based on equality, as a laboratory for inspiration and co-creation that entrepreneurs, designers, artisans, and institutions could use for their common and mutual benefit. Two examples of this are Fundación Ona and the Chilean artist and jeweler Pamela Cavieres.

"Alma" is the jewelry collection based on textile recycling that Cavieres created during one of the Travesías to Atacama. Before joining the trip, Raíz Diseño invited the group to think of the desert as a space of open questions about the universe and the human condition. With this input, the artist prepared her work material for the journey where she took new perspectives from Dava Newman, an engineer at MIT who presented NASA's Biosuit, one of their new spacesuits, and the research team from the Design School of the Universidad Católica de Chile, who showed their research on Andean colors. Cavieres continued her project after returning to Santiago, where she printed the photographs of a nocturnal desert journey on reused textiles. She began to fold this star-like surface to create a relief that was like the stones of the desert road, fragments of the "Alma" ("Soul"), per Pamela Cavieres.

These journeys inspire designers, but also artisans, who draw on that inspiration to deepen their own work. In turn, this has aroused the interest of public institutions such as INDAP (Chilean National Institute for Agricultural Development), and private foundations such as Fundación Ona (www.fundacionona.org), whose work is devoted to fostering the crafts sector. For some years, Fundación Ona, along with the CSR program of the Chilean retail company Almacenes París, have promoted Volver a Tejer ("Knitting Again"), a collection of items made by Chilean artisans that are for sale to the public (Andulce 2017). This Fairtrade program selects innovative pieces created by the artisans who participated in Raíz Diseño's Travesías. The artisan Egon Muñoz Quezada, winner of the Sello de Excelencia a la Artesanía (Seal of Excellence in Craftsmanship), told his colleagues about his experience in the Travesía Raíz Diseño Chiloé 2014: "It is very inspiring. You share three days of work with designers, experts from different countries, and other artisans from Chile. New ideas are plentiful ... but what was funny was that at first I thought the designers did not know anything, because they suggested very strange and crazy ideas. But at the end of the day, I realized that my mind had opened up like never [before] with those propositions."

Travesía Raíz Diseño is a gathering of different worlds that works through ceremonies and choreographies by creative professionals of different origins, but also through many other means: the exchange between equals of knowledge in inter-learning workshops with no creative director (where one learns from others, be they artisans or designers); on walks where each traveller is alone, while also in company of colleagues with whom they share offerings—sometimes objects, sometimes installations or performances; through the land, which is part of the process, and receives a ceremony of gratitude led by a shaman at the end of the trip; through continual coexistence of artisans, designers, and artists, who are all lodged in the same place and share culinary wisdom during collective dinners;

and also through meetings with the local host community, in which all share their knowledge in conferences that are open to the public (Pérez 2013). Each movement in this choreography enlivens the spirit of resistance of the participants, while also making them aware of their place in a collective with diverse viewpoints and shared goals that contribute to the evolution of ethical fashion in the region.

REFERENCES

Andulce, P. (2017), "Herencia textil nortina. El Tesoro de los Andes," Revista Full Diseño. *La Tercera*. Available online at: http://www.masdeco.cl/herencia-textil-nortina-el-tesoro-de-los-andes/ (accessed May 12, 2017).

Borges, Morán, P. (1995), "La inspiración americana de la Utopía de Tomás Moro," *Mar Oceana: Revista del humanismo español e iberoamericano*, 2: 91–111.

Cambariere, L. (2007), *Cuando la forma sigue a la emoción*. Página 12, p.8. Available online at: http://www.pagina12.com.ar/diario/suplementos/m2/10-1341-2008-01-02.html (accessed March 12, 2017).

Crocco, H., and J. Nemer (2007), *Heloisa Crocco: Topomorfose*. Porto Alegre: Leitura XXI.

Docena (2017), "Doceña water." Available online at: https://vimeo.com/214917592 (accessed March 12, 2017).

Eynaudi, P. (2006), "Jóvenes empresarios apuestan por el reciclaje en el diseño," Suplemento Economía y Negocios, *El Mercurio*. Available online at: http://www.economiaynegocios.cl/noticias/noticias.asp?id=15068 (accessed February 21, 2017).

Guerrero, A. (2016), "Repararán gratuitamente ropa 'outdoor' para cuidar el medioambiente," *America Retail*. Available online at: http://www.america-retail.com/industria-y-mercado/repararan-gratuitamente-ropa-outdoor-para-cuidar-el-medioambiente/ (accessed March 12, 017).

Guerrero, M. T. (1994), "Origen del arte textil colombiano contemporáneo," *Revista Historia Crítica*, 9 (Jan–June). Departamento de Historia de la Facultad de Humanidades y ciencias Sociales de la Universidad de los Andes, Bogotá.

Jameson, F. (2007), *Archaeologies of the Future: The Desire Called Utopia and Other Science Fictions*. London/New York: Verso Books.

Julier, G. (2017), *Economies of Design*. London: SAGE Publications.

Marin, L. (1973), *Utopiques: jeux d'espaces—Collection Critique*. Paris: Editions de Minuit.

Moro, T. (1984), *Utopía*. Intro., trans. and notes by Joaquim Mallafrè Gavaldà. Barcelona: Editorial Planeta.

Muzi, C. (2007), *Genealogías de Sur: Conductas de Diseño*. Buenos Aires: MALBA.

Paul, M. G. (2011), "Diseñando la experiencia," Revista Masdeco, *La Tercera*. Available online at: http://www.masdeco.cl/encuentro-disenando-experiencia/ (accessed March 12, 2017).

Pérez, R. (2013), "Conferencias del Desierto y Laboratorio de Innovación. Travesía Raíz Diseño," Departamento Audiovisual Universidad de Antofagasta. Available online at: https://www.youtube.com/watch?v=DJlRVZv05hs (accessed February 2, 2017).

Picchi, F., L. Cambariere, and C. Muzzi (2006), *Woven from Waste: Alejandro Sarmiento*. Milan: Editoriale Domus Spa.

Quinta Bienal de Diseño (2014), *Pensamiento Global, Creatividad Local*. Santiago de Chile: Ed. Pontificia Universidad Católica/Universidad del Desarrollo.

Raíz Diseño (2007), Comments by Heloisa Crocco at the Design Symposium for Emerging Communities, Temuco, Chile.

Ramírez Cendar, D. (2012), "Notas sobre la historia de Artesanías de Colombia S.A. y la artesanía colombiana," Ponencia presentada en el Seminario "Políticas públicas para el sector artesano de América Latina" (October 15–19, 2012). Available online at: http://repositorio.artesaniasdecolombia.com.co/bitstream/001/2595/1/INST-D%202012.%20110.pdf (accessed February 2, 2017).

Ribeiro, D. (1982), "La nación latinoamericana," *Nueva sociedad*, 62: 5–23.

Tiendas Paris (2013), Modulab en París 03/12/2013. Available online at: https://www.youtube.com/watch?v=kAmtBYr0gLM (accessed January 15, 2017).

Tiendas Paris (2014), "Proyecto Modulab," París sostenible. Available online at: https://www.paris.cl/guias/rse/2014-modulab.html (accessed January 15, 2017).

CHAPTER 1.4

A SPOTLIGHT ON: THE PRODUCTION OF WOOL FIBER IN URUGUAY

Ana Livni, brand owner/designer, Uruguay

The inhabitants of this small country in south-eastern South America number just over 3 million, in an area of 176 215 km². However, despite its small population and geographic limitations, Uruguay is privileged in terms of textile resources, and in particular, one of the most sustainable fibers: wool. At the end of the 1980s, sheep numbers peaked at 24 million head of sheep, but currently are around 6.5 million animals.

In the 2014–15 harvest alone, 39.3 million kilograms of wool were exported from Uruguay to forty markets worldwide, demonstrating that, despite the decline in the sheep numbers, the wool business is still extremely important to the country. In turn, interest in working with this natural and sustainable fiber is growing among local textile producers. Today, there are more than twenty national companies that work exclusively with natural wool.

From the shearer to the designer responsible for thinking about the clothes that will be manufactured in this fiber, many people are involved in the wool production chain, in which respect for the animal and dedication to it are a source of national pride. Characterized by

working in an artisanal way, focusing on quality and not on quantity, wool producers, companies that make textile yarn, weavers, seamstresses, and clothing designers form a team that constructs a truly national textile.

Due to its natural characteristics, Uruguay is a "slow" country, where sustainable design is important for both its people and the textile industry. There is respect for rural culture and a favorable climate for the production of top-quality raw materials, all of which increase craftsmanship and industrial activity. With the incorporation of design into the industry in the 1990s, Uruguay's brands have begun to transcend its national borders, and some of these have a long and proud history, such as the Manos del Uruguay Cooperative, Ana Livni, a pioneer of the Latin American slow movement in fashion, the Montelan textile company with its current Don Baez clothing range, or others such as Quiroga-Quiroga or Textural. These and many others have creatively introduced different methods for sustainable textile design.

Wool always has been the main fiber used in Uruguay's sustainable fashion sector. Its growth

Figure 1.4.1 Ana Livni design
Model: Stefania Tortorella. Photographer: Rafael Lejtreger. Make-up: Inés Silvera. Hair: Roberto Tajes; Direction and design: atelier Livni-Escuder

continues, both in national projects and in events at which it is the star of the show, such as Expo Lana, the "Day of weaving in public," or meetings that are held to weave in support of disadvantaged organizations, which are already part of the national identity.

Uruguay has a promising sustainable future ahead of it if it continues to use wool from local brands, brands which are now seeking to innovate by incorporating new sustainable materials too, such as ceramics, hemp, flax, silk, organic cotton, and even reused tyres. For example, a new material composed of wool and hemp is being developed as part of a joint project between the Cañamama, Miem, and CTPS brands to aid the industrialization of the commercial hemp industry in Uruguay.

Similarly, the range of available products is expanding. Previously, the focus was on women's clothing, but today new sustainable brands have appeared that focus on other areas, such as menswear, childrenswear, underwear, and accessories. Such labels include Rufinna, Let Flow,

Terra, Canica, Ruta10, Bamba, Maria Lasarga, Rania, Savia, Agnes L., and Fuerza Natural e Estudio Null, to name just a few.

Design has been transformed into a productive matrix, in which artisans and creators investigate new paths. Advances toward sustainable fashion extend beyond the clothing projects themselves; in April 2016, for example, the first blog on sustainable fashion appeared. Called *SlowfashionUY*, and written by the student Macarena Algorta of the Design Centre of the University School, it maps the number of enterprises and informs the public about events, opportunities for students, and emerging national and international projects.

In June 2017, the first MOLA (Moda Latinoamericana) event took place with the participation of several Latin American countries, making Montevideo the sustainable fashion capital of the region for the three days of the event, which consisted of talks, conferences, exhibitions, workshops, and parades. At the same time, the international festival on artistic recycling, DrapArt, originally founded in Spain, was held for the second consecutive year, during which several designers revealed recycled clothing alternatives using industrial waste.

Uruguay, with its quiet people, with its disregard for the hectic pace of modern life, and its appreciation for textiles and handcrafted work, holds in its DNA the basis for a sustainable fashion industry, which is now developing, aligning the country with the rest of the world. This process will be taken forward by young people or students who choose to approach the subject in national competitions like Lúmina, who participate in projects such as the Rediseña Montevideo shopping complex and Integra Escuela Pablo Giménez, or who present their final projects in their fashion design courses. It can be said, then, that sustainability is growing and will play an increasingly role in this small country with such a bright future.

REFERENCES

http://www.ine.gub.uy/documents/10181/39317/Uruguay_en_cifras_2014.pdf/aac28208-4670-4e96-b8c1-b2abb93b5b13

https://www.welcomeuruguay.com/datosutiles/algomas.html

http://www.elobservador.com.uy/la-poblacion-ovinos-alcanzo-el-nivel-mas-la-historia-n984160

http://www.elobservador.com.uy/un-uruguay-mas-vacas-y-menos-ovejas-n1014320

http://presidencia.gub.uy/comunicacion/comunicacionnoticias/datos-exportacion-lana-2014-2015

cañamama

http://www.molaevento.com/

https://www.draparturuguay.org/

http://www.analivni.com/MODAlenta-SLOWfashion/ANA_LIVNI.html

INDEPENDENT FASHION DESIGN IN ARGENTINA
Is "Sustainablewashing" a Concern?

Miguel Angel Gardetti, Center for Studies on Sustainable Luxury, Argentina

INTRODUCTION

Many entrepreneurs—or, in the author's (2016) phrase, "transformational leaders"—as well as manufacturing sustainable products, are revolutionizing the entire supply chain. They have created a business model that integrates profits with the best interests of society. Becoming a sustainable brand takes significant time and resources, and involves risks. However, these difficulties did not discourage many designers and brands from their attempt to reap the benefits of making the "outside" "sustainable" without making the necessary investments on the "inside" (Berrone 2016). This seems to be the case for the "Independent Fashion Design" sector in Argentina, since in a very short period, many of these designers define themselves as "sustainable" when they communicate to their customers, and sell their products.

This essay—which begins with a detailed explanation of the meaning of being sustainable in the textile and fashion sector, and advances the concept of "sustainablewashing"—features research and analysis of eighteen brands that can be considered independent fashion design brands. The essay ends with an analysis of this topic, and some recommendations for future research.

METHODOLOGY

To develop this research, the author collected publicly disclosed background information about the companies (through websites, social networks, and specialized magazines in design and fashion). Eighteen brands, in this study named as M1, M2, etc., were included in the research, of which sixteen are based in Buenos Aires City, one in Rosario City (Province of Santa Fe) and one in San Miguel de Tucumán City (Province of Tucumán).

SUSTAINABILITY IN FASHION, "SUSTAINABLEWASHING," AND INDEPENDENT FASHION DESIGN

What Are "Sustainable" Textiles and Fashion?[1]

"Sustainability" implies a model encompassing economic, environmental, and social aspects, which are dynamic and interact with one another, each factor being influenced by the other two. It also implies integrating the short term into the long term with a multi-disciplinary approach. This understanding illustrates the systemic aspect of sustainability. In other words, in order to understand sustainability, it is essential to begin to understand the "big picture." This implies acknowledging that sustainability is about well-being and the long term, and it is also about developing an "actual" awareness of its implications. Rather than going from the particular to the general, we should better start from the general and then turn to the particular, i.e., we should be able to think in the long term, considering its implications, and why it is important to practice sustainability. This "big picture" approach will enable us to spot the aspects involved in being sustainable in textiles and fashion. For the sake of clarity, the conception of this "big picture" will not include economic sustainability, which may be defined as the assurance of ongoing and sufficient cash flow to ensure readily available funds while making positive returns for the company (or the brand). Figure 1.5.1 depicts those aspects involved in being sustainable: environmental aspects, consumer's issues, design, and innovation. It also includes technological aspects, social aspects, business models, marketing and communication, and raw material aspects.

Environmental issues encompass the efficient or inefficient use of water, energy and soil, and carbon dioxide (CO_2) emissions into the atmosphere. They also include the use, handling, and transport of both hazardous and non-hazardous materials and substances, and waste management in its broadest sense.

As regards the **consumer**, the issues include information access and consumer's responsibility in their purchase decisions, which is relevant to a discussion of taking care of clothes purchased.

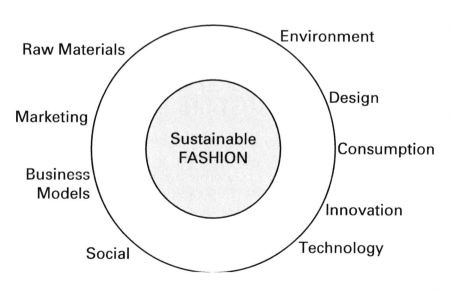

Figure 1.5.1 Aspects involved in sustainable fashion and textiles
Source: Gardetti (2017). Published with the permission of Editorial LID, Buenos Aires

In connection with **designers**, these aspects include their leadership or roles that, according to Williams (2015) are: designer as determiner (creator of boundary objects); designer as condition creator (creator of learning objects); and designer as co-creator (facilitator). Here, we could add the core concept from Papanek (1971): that designers should design items that people need and not those that people want. Reappraisal of native culture and consideration of other cultures (Eastern culture, for example) are also related to design.

Innovation is a complex topic since "incremental continuous improvement" has been over-promoted in the last few decades, backed up by our current mindset. We should be asking ourselves what type of innovation we need in order to achieve sustainability, and the answer will lead us to "disruptive innovation," supported by a "fracture" or "discontinuance" with respect to our current mindset. We should "think differently," underscoring that the disruption is to "think *very* differently." Most brands assume very defensive stances that protect and nurture that which has served them well in the past, even in the face of change (Teece et. al. 1997; Christensen 1997). That is to say, brands react by increasing their commitment to the "existing" products, processes, and markets.

Technological aspects include process- and product-related issues while **social aspects** encompass labor rights, human rights, social inclusion, human trafficking, modeling, anti-corruption, and knowing and understanding the fast fashion issue.

With regard to **business models**, the main issue is to develop a new type of model promoting sustainable fashion.

In connection with **marketing**—considered here as a communication instrument—the issues include responsibility and customer- and consumer-relations management tools.

Finally, we have **raw materials** in the broadest sense, and also issues related to the use of water, energy, and soil. This also includes animal and recycling issues. Thanks to techniques such as redesigning, cutting, and making from scratch an entire new garment or parts of one from old pieces of fabrics (which may be vintage) and accessories, it is possible to create unique pieces. These creations are challenging the widespread idea of the reduced value of used materials, and prove that *upcycling* adds value to an object through its recovery. This is in contrast to *downcycling*, which is older than upcycling, in which the recycled material's value is lower than that of the original item. Figure 1.5.2 depicts the aspects mentioned above to achieve sustainability, or what the "big picture" is.

Given the systemic character of sustainability, all of the aforementioned aspects are inter-connected. Finally, we have *transparency*, which is an aspect related to the brand/start-up/company's *supply chain* (Figure 1.5.3). Tracking and monitoring the supply chain *per se* is essential for the sustainable management of the groups of interest. From sourcing the raw material to the retail business, the supply chain has different impacts on the groups of interest, and the end product affects the environment as well as society.

GREENWASHING OR SUSTAINABLEWASHING?

Jay Westerveld, an environmental activist, has noted that the word "green" has been indiscriminately used by hotel companies in an attempt to build an environmentally committed reputation while their actual purpose was to make profit (Ottman 2011: 132). In 1986, Westerveld defined "greenwashing" as a "marketing or Public Relations attempt to

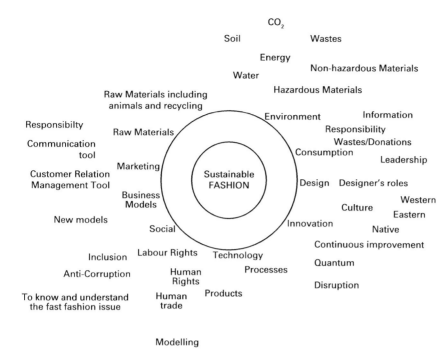

Figure 1.5.2 Every aspect related to the concepts of sustainable textiles and fashion: the "big picture"
Source: Gardetti. Published with the permission of Editorial LID, Buenos Aires

mislead consumers by making them believe that a company develops environmentally-friendly policies and procedures" (Berrone 2016: 106). Berrone (2016: 106) defined it as "the act of making false or misleading statements about products, services or environmentally friendly practices to obtain a series of benefits"; that is to say, it is a concept that considers the extent of advertising or communication on the one hand, and on the other, the extent to which commitments are fulfilled.

Additionally Berrone (2016: 119) says that communication strategies may fall into two categories when greenwashing: "product level" (where the environmental benefits of a product or service are communicated) and "corporate level" (where a company's environmental practices are communicated). Most of the environmentally friendly statements made by companies and/or brands tend to be made about a specific product or service (i.e., at a product level).

In turn, Lyon and Maxwell (2011) define greenwashing as a selective disclosure of positive information about a company's environmental or social performance, while withholding negative information on these dimensions, while Marquis and Toffel (2012), along the same lines, state that it is a type of selective disclosure, whereby companies disclose positive environmental actions while concealing negative ones to create a misleadingly positive impression of overall environmental performance. Finally, TerraChoice (2007) refers to greenwashing as a marketing claim that misleads consumers about the environmental benefits of a product or service.

Based on the aforementioned definitions of the concept of greenwashing, the following definition has been prepared for this chapter: a marketing claim to mislead consumers by the selective disclosure of positive information about a company's environmental or social performance to distract attention from negative aspects. We

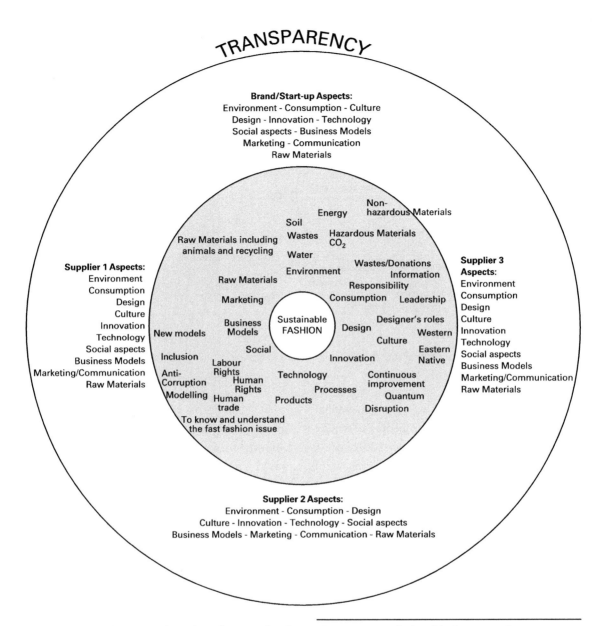

will call this "sustainablewashing," instead of greenwashing.

Figure 1.5.3 Relationship between the aspects involved in sustainable fashion and transparency
Image prepared by the author

ANALYSIS

The brands discussed in this chapter were analyzed based on the aspects presented above. Table 1.5.1 shows the raw materials used by each brand and their end products.

As shown in the table, the most widely used raw materials are: cotton (e.g., M1, M3, M4, M14, M16, M18), organic cotton (M6, M7), sheep wool, including wool from merino sheep (M3, M9, M14, M17), secondhand clothes (M1, M17),

TABLE 1.5.1

BRANDS, RAW MATERIALS USED, AND PRODUCTS OFFERED

Brand names for the paper	Products offered	Raw materials used
M1	Women's clothing, swimwear, accessories and footwear	Denim, jersey, eco-leather, satin, cotton, Lycra, felt, neoprene, linen
M2	Women's clothing	appliques (sequins, beads, etc.), velveteen, wool from Merino sheep, acrylic, viscose, elastane, nylon, wool, alpaca, cotton, polyester, denim, rayon, spandex
M3	Women's clothing	hand- and loom-knitted fabrics (*aguayano*, *boyaca*, *picote*, *randa*). Cotton, llama and sheep wool
M4	Unisex clothing and accessories	polyester, cotton, knitted fabrics, viscose, gauze, silk, denim . . .
M5	Women's clothing and accessories	Morley, cotton, water-based and natural dyes (maté leaves, onion peel, tea, poplar leaves, etc.). Viscose, modal, organic 40/1 jersey
M6	Women's clothing, swimwear	viscose, polyester, cotton, Peruvian Pima cotton, linen, silk, Italian wool, felt, organic cotton, mercerised cotton, Tence, rayon, spandex, Lycra
M7	Women and men's clothing	Cotton and second hand clothes. Zipper, clasps, appliques, and non-commercial materials. Main recycled shirts
M8	T-shirts	Organic 40/1 jersey. Low environmental impact dyes
M9	Women and men's clothing	100% natural felt, wool from Merino sheep, natural dyes
M10	Accessories (totes, bags, clutches, wallets)	Plastic bags, packaging films, (polyethylene) packaging

Brand names for the paper	Products offered	Raw materials used
M11	Women and men's clothing. Pyjamas. Redesign and remake of second-hand clothes	Second hand clothes, mainly shirts
M12	Women's clothing	Natural dyes (e.g., maté leaves), felt, cotton, natural linen, jute yarn
M13	Women's footwear, clothing and accessories	Morley, denim, velvet, microfiber, brocade, synthetic patent leather, Pima cotton, satin
M14	Women's clothing, swimwear. Accessories Home accessories (cushions and throws)	viscose, cotton, elastane, wool from Merino sheep, Dralon, mohair, polyamide, rabbit fur
M15	Women's footwear, clothing and accessories.	Jute, raffia, wood, patent leather, synthetic leather, suede
M16	Women and men's clothing Rucksacks.	Leather, cotton, felt, wool, linen
M17	Women clothing and jewels	Bronze, cotton, wool
M18	Women's clothing	Cotton

Source: prepared by the author

viscose (M4, M5 M14), and linen (M1, M12, M16). As for end products, women's clothing (e.g., M1, M2, M5, M7, M11, M14, M16, M18), men's clothing (M7, M9, M11, M16), and accessories (e.g., M1, M5, M10, M14, M15 and M16) prevail.

The analysis was divided into the following points:

a. **"Generic-style communication":** used when brands communicate ideas, concepts, practices, and strategies generally to show that they are sustainable. Some examples are:

M1 Sustainable design with decent workshops.

M8 Our purpose is to promote and develop sustainable practices while actively collaborating with social inclusion practices, environmental care, Fairtrade, corporate social responsibility and sustainability.

M12 We promote a different fashion concept, one based on [a] non-automated process that offers less quantity but more quality. A fashion that helps raise awareness of the pressing need to protect the environment, revalues small producers, and implements Fairtrade practices.

b. **"Misleading" information:** when brands fail to explain whether "sustainable" refers to the brand itself or to a product line only. This is the case with M2 when referring to its X1 line.

c. **"Overstatements":** when brands use ostentatious language to convey their ideas. For example, brand M6 says that "it drifts away from fashion '*fierceness*' and frenzy."

d. **Partial information:** when the brand offers partial information about its raw materials or processes. For example, M5 explains the beauty of organic cotton, but fails to mention the water footprint—i.e., the negative environmental impact—of this fiber.

e. **Promotion of local production:** when brands refer to, and claim to promote and defend, local production, but reality shows something either totally or partially different. For example, M5 imports its materials but claims the product is "100% made by Argentinians to revalue local labor." Another aspect of this point is when brands claim to promote "Argentine" design, but part of the information is in a foreign language, such as English. This is the case with brand M10.

f. **No environmental impacts:** when brands claim that their production processes or "sustainability" strategies eliminate negative environmental impacts. This is the case with M10 when it asks consumers to "help it clean the planet."

g. **Transparency:** brands often mention transparency (e.g., M11), followed by vague or generic consumer information about processes. In connection with production processes, there are references to "decent workshops" (M10), "regulated free of forced labor workshops" (M5), "social workshops" (M8), or "workshops compliant with fair trade rules" (M11), but none of these brands specify what these rules are.

h. **Cruelty-free:** M13 claims that it is a "cruelty-free" brand that makes designs using synthetic fabrics to avoid animal cruelty, and M15 claims that among "our materials we use the best synthetic leather." However, it does not explain the impact of these synthetic fabrics. None of the above cases mentions the environmental impact of the used synthetic material.

i. **Luxury design and sustainable luxury:** Some brands use the "sustainable luxury" concept to define themselves. However, the attributes of sustainable luxury, such as exclusiveness, excellent quality, high-level innovation, creativity, and offering luxury consumer experiences at points of sale, are not always mentioned by the designers. For example:

M3 Refers to "sustainable luxury" based on their garments' "durability."

M4 Express gratitude for being characterized as a "sustainable luxury" brand on social media.

j. **Certification "scope":** in some cases, a brand that uses a certified raw material "extends" such certification to its entire production process. One example is M5, when it claims that "the entire process is certified by OCS (Organic Content Standard)."

k. **Websites:** some brands promote their websites on their Facebook pages but, when you click on the links, the sites seem not to exist. This is the case of M9, which displays the message "This site can't be reached" (attempts from January to April, 2017).

l. **Contradictions:** for example, brand M18 promotes "local identity" using cotton. It is up for debate whether or not cotton is part of the Argentine "identity," and the brand does not refer to the negative environmental impact of this material.

m. **A "reductionist" view of sustainability:** we have examined the meaning of sustainability in the textile and fashion sector when a brand defines itself as sustainable. However, these types of definitions miss several important aspects, such as water use, power use, and carbon footprint, among others. At least some of these aspects are missing in the cases of all the brands. (See Table 1.5.2 in Conclusions.)

CONCLUSIONS

Based on the aspects described in the above section, Table 1.5.2 illustrates each of the eighteen brands and the aspects inherent to sustainability in textiles and fashion (refer to the section "What does sustainable textiles and fashion mean?" in this chapter).

Some of the results worth mentioning are:

- Only M7 refers to the water footprint or power use.
- Only M8 refers to soil issues.
- None of the brands refers to CO_2 emissions.
- The only brands to refer to the waste issue are M7, M11, and M18.
- The brands make almost no reference to any of the three classes of innovation, despite their being closely connected to creativity, an essential design factor.
- No brand refers to human "trafficking" (deeply rooted in the industry), or to corruption (the latter being a factor related to the former).

- Only occasional reference is made to human rights and labor rights.

Taking into account the above results, we should ask ourselves an important question: what is the current focus of Argentine sustainable fashion, based on these eighteen brands? The answer appears to be only material issues (i.e., raw materials) and some aspects related to the social and the environmental dimensions, as shown in Figure 1.5.1. While it may be redundant, please note that the shaded areas in the figure take up only part of the main aspect.

The definition of "sustainablewashing" used for this chapter states that it is a marketing claim used to mislead consumers by the selective disclosure of positive information about a company's environmental or social performance in order to distract attention from negative aspects. While it can be interpreted that some brands have ethical problems, simply omitting information to obtain an economic or image profitability also goes against the principles of sustainability. Moreover, some brands, such as M1, M3, M4, M5, M6, M7, M8, M11, and M12 are related to initiatives like the Fashion Revolution Day and Clean Clothes Argentina—in some cases, closely. Additionally, some designers were educated and trained in the Programme on Training Leaders for the Change in the Textile and Fashion Sectors, held by the *Centro Textil Sustentable* (Sustainable Textile Center) and the United Nations Global Compact Argentine Network, or in fashion sustainability programmes at the *Centro Metropolitano de Diseño* (Metropolitan Design Center). Against this framework, we may conclude that there is a reductionist view of the concept of sustainability and that these brands, to a large extent, implement "sustainablewashing."

TABLE 1.5.2

BRANDS AND THEIR RELATIONSHIP WITH ALL THE ASPECTS INHERENT TO SUSTAINABILITY
NOTE: THE CHECK-MARKED ASPECT IS NOT MENTIONED BY THE BRAND

Brand	Environment							Consumption		
	Water	Energy	Soil	CO_2	Wastes	Hazardous Materials	Non-hazardous Materials	Information	Responsibility	Wastes/ Donation
M1	×	×	×	×	×	×	×	×	×	×
M2	×	×	×	×	×	×	×	×	×	×
M3	×	×	×	×	×	×	×		×	×
M4	×	×	×	×	×	×	×			
M5	×	×	×	×	×	×	×		×	×
M6	×	×	×	×	×	×	×	×	×	×
M7			×	×		×	×			
M8	×	×		×	×		×			×
M9	×	×	×	×	×	×	×	×	×	×
M10	×	×	×	×	×	×	×			×
M11	×	×	×	×		×	×			
M12	×	×	×	×	×	×	×	×	×	×
M13	×	×	×	×	×	×	×	×	×	×
M14	×	×	×	×	×	×	×			
M15	×	×	×	×	×	×	×	×	×	×
M16	×	×	×	×	×	×	×	×	×	×
M17	×	×	×	×	×	×	×	×	×	×
M18	×	×	×	×		×	×			×

Source: prepared by the author

Brand	Design					Innovation			Technology
	Leadership	Roles	Cultures			Continuous Improvement	Quantum	Disruption	Processes
			Western	Eastern	Native				
M1		×		×	×	×	×	×	×
M2		×		×	×	×	×	×	×
M3	×		×	×		×		×	
M4	×			×	×	×		×	
M5	×			×	×	×	×	×	×
M6	×	×		×	×	×	×	×	×
M7	×			×	×	×	×	×	
M8	×			×	×	×	×	×	×
M9	×		×	×		×	×	×	
M10	×			×	×	×	×		×
M11	×			×	×	×	×	×	
M12	×	×		×	×	×	×	×	×
M13	×	×		×	×	×	×	×	×
M14	×	×		×	×	×	×	×	×
M15	×	×		×	×	×	×	×	×
M16	×	×		×	×	×	×	×	×
M17	×	×		×		×	×	×	×
M18	×			×		×	×	×	×

Source: prepared by the author

Brand	Social Aspects						Business Models			Marketing		Raw Materials		
	Human Rights	Labor Rights	Human Trade	Modelling	Inclusion	Anti-corruption	Fast Fashion?	Business Model	Respon-sibility	Commu-nication	Customer Relation	Raw Materials	Animals	Recycling
M1	×	×	×	×	×	×	×	×			×			×
M2	×	×	×	×	×	×	×	×	×	×	×	×		×
M3	×	×	×			×		×	×	×	×			
M4	×	×	×	×	×	×		×				×	×	
M5			×			×	×	×	×					×
M6	×	×	×	×	×	×	×	×	×	×	×			×
M7			×			×								
M8	×		×	×	×	×		×						×
M9	×	×	×	×	×	×	×	×					×	×
M10	×	×	×	×	×	×		×					×	
M11				×	×		×							×
M12	×	×	×		×	×	×	×	×				×	×
M13	×	×	×	×	×	×	×	×	×	×	×			×
M14	×	×	×	×		×		×	×					×
M15	×	×	×	×	×	×	×	×	×					×
M16	×	×	×	×	×	×		×	×	×	×			×
M17	×	×	×	×	×	×	×	×	×	×		×	×	×
M18			×		×	×		×				×	×	×

Source: prepared by the author

RECOMMENDATIONS

This fieldwork could be supplemented by interviews with designers (entrepreneurs) in order to learn and to analyze the reasons why they prepare these types of misleading communications.

LIMITATIONS

As noted earlier, eighteen brands were researched, based in Buenos Aires City, in Rosario City (Province of Santa Fe), and in San Miguel de Tucumán City (Province of Tucumán) respectively. This may not be representative of Argentina as a whole.

ACKNOWLEDGEMENTS

This essay was prepared in collaboration with Lic. Stefanía Ferre.

NOTES

1. This section is adapted from Chapter 5 of the author's book *Textiles y Moda: qué es ser sustentable*, Buenos Aires: Editorial LID, 2017.

REFERENCES

Berrone, P. (2016), *Green Lies: How Greenwashing Can Destroy a Company and How to Go Green without the Wash*. Lexington: Fundación BBVA.

Christensen, C. M. (1997), *The Innovator's Dilemma: When New Technologies Cause Great Firms to Fail*. Boston: Harvard Business School Press.

Gardetti, M. A. (2017), *Textiles y Moda: ¿qué es ser sustentable?* Buenos Aires: Editorial LID.

Gardetti, M. A., and M. E. Girón (2016), *Sustainable Luxury and Social Entrepreneurship: More Stories from the Pioneers*. Sheffield: Greenleaf Publishing.

Gjerdrum Pedersen, E. R., and K. Reitan Andersen (2013), *The SocioLog.dx Experience: A Global Expert Study on Sustainable Fashion*. Copenhagen: Copenhagen Business School and Mistra Future Fashion.

Lyon, T. P., and J. M. Maxwell (2011), *Greenwash: Corporate Environmental Disclosure Under Threat of Audit, Journal of Economics & Management Strategy*, 20(1): 3–41.

Marquis, C., and M. W. Toffel (2012), *Scrutiny, Norms, and Selective Disclosure: A Global Study of Greenwashing*. Boston: Harvard Business School working paper, 11–115

Ottman, Jacqueline A. (2011), *The New Rules of Green Marketing: Strategies, Tools, and Inspiration for Sustainable Branding*. Sheffield: Greenleaf Publishing.

Papanek, Victor (1971), *Design for the Real World: Human, Ecology and Social Change*. 2nd ed. Chicago: Chicago Review Press.

Teece, D. J., G. Pisano, and A. Shuen (1997), "Dynamic Capabilities and Strategic Management," *Strategic Management Journal*, 18(7): 509–33.

TerraChoice (2007), *The Six Sins of Greenwashing*. Ottawa: TerraChoice Environmental Marketing Inc.

Williams, D. (2015), "Fashion Design and Sustainability," in R. S. Blackburn (ed.), *Sustainable Apparel: Production, Processing and Recycling*, 163–85. Cambridge: The Textile Institute and Woodhead Publishing.

CHAPTER 1.6

A SPOTLIGHT ON: SUSTAINABLE FASHION IN COLOMBIA
Perspectives and Scope

Dolly Viviana Polo Flórez, Associate Professor of Apparel Design Program, Universidad de San Buenaventura. Cali-Colombia.

Colombia has one of the highest growth rates in the fashion sector in Latin America. In this process, foreign investment has been consistent, and the country is recognized for its services of outsourcing and *maquil*—the manufacture of a specific process—for companies known as *marquistas* (which provide manufacturing for foreign brands in line with their quality standards). In both cases, technological capacity is low to medium.

Mainly family-owned, most of these businesses grow to be medium-sized, and tend toward progressive improvement of efficiency in their means of production, focusing on the market for casualwear, footwear, and jewelry for men, women, and children. The mix of techniques and technologies employed allows the companies to advance in technical terms, and allow them to work on short-term projects.

Environmental awareness and ethical work practices have also been phased in, allowing for the incorporation of the sensibilities of the user/client and their eco-friendly lifestyles as an essential component of sustainable fashion and clothing. Companies operating in the fashion industry follow technical regulations, but developments regarding the generation of technology are still in process. Slow fashion and eco-fashion models in small- and medium-scale industries are making sustainable clothing more visible in Colombia. Both models are presented as common ground for development and the promotion of human welfare, prioritizing community and external commitment to ethical practices. The tendency toward ethical and socially aware fashion has been promoted by the Colombian government through policies of social innovation, and also by companies' approach toward the incorporation of social and sustainable policies. By these means, the projects of social innovation of fashion demonstrates a clear path in terms of sustainability, ethics, and social fashion, and generates a platform for production (Watson et al. 2017: 7).

Non-governmental organizations (NGOs) also outsource processes, prioritizing the economic development of vulnerable groups by allowing them to work in multiple flexible ways. Large industries are focused on manufacturing garments and clothing and on the associated processes, with a proportion of about 49 percent using textile imports (ProColombia 2014: 2), meaning that the national textile industry has reduced production; a direct consequence of this (in a cause-consequence loop) is the high number of FTAs (Free Trade Agreements) signed with different agencies and countries.

....

Three characteristic fields of sustainable fashion in Colombia are:

1. *Direct work with communities,* incorporating practices of fabrication and hybridization with parts and materials generated industrially. For example, Artesanías de Colombia has, since 1964, developed a series of projects that help consolidate the identity of indigenous and rural cultures. The production processes, linked to ancestral techniques and materials, are regulated by governmental entities that moderate such work with communities to prevent their exploitation, and to promote their preservation as part of the national heritage. In this product category, price differentiation is a key factor, as there is a captive market that is willing to pay more for an exclusive and highly identifiable product. These projects are directly correlated with their regions. One example is that of Wayuu products, as well as the typical customs that are part of their local festivities, such as carnivals and fairs (Figure 1.6.1). Another example is the textile work of the Nasa Community that is now regarded as a valued input into the industry (Figure 1.6.2).

Figure 1.6.1 Kametsa waistcoat Moda Viva— Artesanías de Colombia
Image reproduced courtesy of Artesanias De Colombia/ Monica Barreneche

2. *Companies working with ancestral techniques connected with industrial processes.* An example in this field is Adriana Santacruz, with the Precolombino Indigenous Loom. In this model, families of artisans work together with their company, fusing craft techniques with clear design concepts. It links social programs with labor and is located in the region of Los Pastos, to the southwest of Nariño, Colombia.

3. *Circular systems.* Finally, there is the model of *neoartesania,* which is a circular system using the closed-loop concept to avoid creating waste and to conserve waste products that

Figure 1.6.2 Advertising image, Adriana Santacruz
Image reproduced courtesy of Juan Santacruz

would otherwise go to landfill. It considers waste and discarded materials as resources that begin the life cycle of a new product (Sinha et al. 2016: 12). The organization of the mode of production is performed in a controlled way. An example of this model is the company Croquis, from the city of Cali, that makes hand-painted clothing (see Figure 5, plate section).

The Report of the Copenhagen Fashion Summit (Global Fashion Agenda & The Boston Consulting Group 2017: 22) found great variety in different contexts in the use and consumption of water, energy, chemicals, and waste, as well as in labor practices, health and safety, community and external engagement, and ethical practices, resources that assume about 80 percent of consumption in the production cycle. In Colombia, the focus on sustainability comes from small- and medium-sized enterprises, since they can have greater control over the processes.

ACKNOWLEDGEMENT

Thanks to Artesanías de Colombia, Adriana Santacruz, and Croquis.

REFERENCES

Global Fashion Agenda, & The Boston Consulting Group (2017), *Pulse of the Fashion Industry 2017*. Copenhagen: Global Fashion Agenda & The Boston Consulting Group.

ProColombia (2014), *Colombia: Crecimiento, confianza y oportunidades para invertir. Sistema Moda*. Bogotá: ProColombia-Gobierno de Colombia.

Salcedo, E. (2014), *Moda ética para un futuro sostenible*. Barcelona: Gustavo Gilli.

Sinha, P., S. Senthilkannan Muthu, and G. Dissanayake, G. (2016), *Remanufactured Fashion: Environmental Footprints and Eco-design of Products and Processes*. Singapore: Springer Science+Business Media Singapore.

Watson, D., J. Eder-Hansen, Global Fashion Agenda, S. Tärneberg, and PlanMiljø (2017), *A Call to Action for a Circular Fashion System*. Copenhagen: Global Fashion Agenda 2017.

NORTH AMERICA

PART 2

INDUSTRY LEADERSHIP TOWARD SUSTAINABLE FASHION THROUGH USER CONSUMER ENGAGEMENT
North America

Tasha L. Lewis, Cornell University, USA
Suzanne Loker, Cornell University, USA

INTRODUCTION

Sustainable fashion in North America represents a diverse mix of large and small companies, as well as designers and entrepreneurs, who are defining sustainability for the twenty-first-century apparel industry. Their activities are re-shaping the landscape for sustainable fashion by challenging consumer acceptance of *new* and *used, re-fashioned, slow* and *fast* fashion. The ultimate goal is a sustainable, cradle-to-cradle life cycle for its products where even the end-of-life phase of clothing does limited damage to, or even feeds, the earth and its people through innovative reuse and disposal reduction and management. Yet, success is dependent upon engaging the *user consumers*—people who wear and maintain, enjoy and become attached to, repurpose, or give away or discard their clothing. The human factor, engaging and involving user consumers in actions toward sustainable apparel, is conscientiously being addressed by the apparel industry.

LIFE-CYCLE ANALYSIS OF APPAREL AND THE CIRCULAR ECONOMY: CONSUMER CONCEPT

Life-cycle analysis and the circular economy are often presented as a continuous circle following the cradle-to-cradle concept that waste = food (McDonough & Braungart 2002). Representing each step of the product supply chain from fiber to end user, the garment life-cycle analysis evaluates each process for waste, ways to reduce and eliminate waste, and ways to turn waste into new biological (e.g., cotton and linen) and technological (e.g., polyester and nylon) materials as good or better than the initial materials. The circular economy framework (Ellen MacArthur Foundation 2016) has emerged as a reaction to the linear economy characteristic of a "take-make-dispose" society where consumption is focused on limited use and disposal, usually to landfills or as other contaminants (Sauvé, Bernard & Sloan 2016). In the circular economy, the goal is to think systemically and make plans for waste use at every stage of the life cycle—fiber growth and manufacture, product development, remanufacturing, and remaking. In other words, the product's end-of-life is considered for its impacts on the environment and society at all times. Since the consumer is a major actor at the end-of-life stage, it is vital to educate and engage them in the circular economy.

Winakor (1969), with her inclusion of care, storage, and disposal actions along with acquisition in the use phase of a clothing garment, provides an early understanding and elaboration of user consumers' roles even before environmental sustainability was considered a factor. Others embrace the use phase in a do-it-yourself (DIY) sort of way, such as the Loveyourclothes.com website, featuring four consumer actions for sustainability: buying new clothes; care and repair; refurbishing; and upcycling.[1] Fletcher (2008) describes the importance of participatory design in building a more sustainable fashion paradigm. In her 5 ways and Local Wisdom Projects (Fletcher n.d.) she describes how user-makers can be part of the solution with their ideas and active engagement in the redesign process. Going beyond DIY actions and making the connection between user consumers and industry programs, Lewis (2015) categorizes the reuse and discard options of the clothing-use phase, often involving

the consumer: thrift and shop; technology-enabled reuse; upcycling; and downcycling.

Expanding the current focus of the use phase on purchase/acquisition and treating the consumer as a user, in this essay we will add consumer involvement to the discussion of end-of-life and re-conceptualize the consumer's role as *user consumer*. That is, the user consumer buys or makes/remakes the apparel product, maintains and modifies it, adds emotional and social ownership value to it through wear, and stores it until finding a proper end-of-use method or its next owner. Incorporating the owner's actions and connections to the garment in life-cycle analysis and within a circular economy enriches the options for garments' second lives.

ISSUES SURROUNDING USER CONSUMER SUSTAINABILITY ENGAGEMENT/ACTIONS

Information, Accessibility, and Motivation

Probably the most important deterrent to user engagement is lack of information. Although academics and industry have been discussing sustainability for over two decades, consumers are just realizing that textile product waste is a problem. Indeed, it is estimated that over 20 billion pounds of textiles are deposited into US landfills each year (Clancy 2014) representing over 80 percent of the annual generation of textile waste according to the US Environmental Protection Administration (EPA n.d.). This waste is attributed to both consumers and sellers of apparel in the United States and elsewhere in North America, so tackling the waste problem must address both consumer behavior and company practices. To change behaviors, information is crucial; user consumers need to know about the detrimental effects of clothing disposal to landfills, incineration, and secondhand markets as well as the innovative industry progress in recycling fiber, upcycling clothing/textile waste by redesign, repurposing, and technology-assisted alternatives such as renting and swapping.

Accessibility is another requirement. Some apparel firms offer take-back programs where consumers can send worn garments back to producers, such as Patagonia's "Worn Wear"[2] and Eileen Fisher's "Green Eileen," either mailing or bringing them to a small number of locations. Until the accessibility of such programs increases, however, user consumer involvement will be limited. Even the strategies of philanthropic organizations are not well known to all user consumers. While many North American consumers recognize that Goodwill, Planet Aid, and others collect used clothing, they may not fully understand that most of the clothing collected through these channels is diverted to third-world markets or downcycled (Secondary Materials and Recycled Textiles n.d.). Engaging consumers to be part of alternative end-of-use strategies will result in more textile product waste returned to a fiber state, recut and redesigned, or upcycled into higher-valued products.

Motivating user consumers to action is a third necessity. Sustainability is a concept accepted by many to be helpful to the planet, but how can it be applied to clothing? The food industry provides a model for user consumer engagement and involvement by its success in motivating local food purchases by increasing user consumer knowledge about growing and harvesting conditions to the nutritional quality and environmental effects of long-range distribution channels. User consumers feel good about buying from farmers' markets and knowing where their food comes from. Local recycling programs for bottles, plastics, and even food waste provide another model that reduces landfill disposal. While locally sourced will be an unlikely option for most North American apparel and textile user consumers, they can be motivated by additional knowledge and accessibility to alternatives that make them feel good about how they use, reuse, recycle, and dispose of their textile products. The following sections highlight a spectrum of innovative practices focusing on consumer education, industry transformation and collective action—all of which can resonate with the user consumer.

INDUSTRY LEADERSHIP IN USER CONSUMER ENGAGEMENT

Industry is leading the way toward a circular economy that engages user consumers through awareness education, zero-waste community actions, take-back programs, and closed-loop systems. These efforts are still somewhat small in scope and effect and known primarily by self-selected user consumers. Still, these strategies provide innovative models that can be expanded and adopted.

Education and Collaborative Actions

Patagonia

The outdoor clothing company Patagonia is a long-time advocate for sustainability through education, environmental stewardship, innovative sustainable production and life-cycle business strategies, and leadership in industry collaborations toward a more sustainable apparel industry. The business embraces life-cycle analysis, evaluating every step in its supply chain; modifies strategies of procurement and manufacturing processes to lessen the impact on the environment; and communicates their approach to other brands and retailers as well as consumers to help others adopt more sustainable practices. Patagonia acts sustainably and passes that message on to user consumers and its industry competitors. As noted earlier, its "Worn Wear" take-back program was one of the first such initiatives, and encourages user consumers to buy for quality and long wear and then to return garments to Patagonia stores for reuse and remaking.

Patagonia uses its website (Patagonia.com) in a variety of ways to communicate with and engage its customers. The Footprint Chronicles of the Common Threads Project[3] tracks the journey of one garment on a world map, annotating each stop with specific amounts of energy and carbon footprint spent on the product through design choices, manufacture, and transport. All products are now analyzed online on Patagonia.com so that consumers are provided with this sustainability information along with style, fiber content, and size information. In addition to product details, Patagonia catalogs provide factual information about the environmental effects on our planet caused by humans and ways to think about it in terms of our purchase, use, and disposal of clothing. Patagonia's Black Friday *New York Times* ad on November 25, 2011, is an example of its activist communication strategies aimed at engaging consumers (and industry) in the fight for saving the environment by lowering consumption through longer wear, reduction, repair, reuse, and recycling (see Figure 2.1.1). Patagonia writes critically of their actions, taking the stance that any production negatively affects the environment, sustainability is a journey, and we can always do better. For example, Hepburn

(2015) argued that in fact the Black Friday advertising campaign actually *increased* sales, and thus consumption. Patagonia's stance encourages both the industry and consumers to understand that we need to continue finding ways to be more sustainable yet we will never be totally sustainable.

Patagonia has engaged industry in collaborative actions aimed at saving the planet through intentional acts in the design, production, distribution, and use phases of a garment's life cycle. 1% for the Planet[4] was first initiated by Patagonia founder Yvon Chouinard and Blue Ribbon Flies founder Craig Mathews in 2002 to increase business involvement in environmental sustainability. It now has more than 1,400 international member businesses listed on its website that pledge to contribute 1 percent of their sales to the organization. 1% for the Planet has spent tens of millions of dollars from membership donations since 2002 to support non-profit organizations dedicated to high impact environmental projects.

Patagonia was instrumental in the Sustainable Apparel Coalition that grew out of its work with the Outdoor Industry Association (OIA) to develop a tool that would evaluate a business's efforts in sustainability. Partnering with WalMart, also working on a sustainability tool or scorecard, about ten apparel and footwear CEOs were invited to a 2009 meeting to discuss working together toward sustainability. The Sustainable Apparel Coalition was initiated with its core project to combine and scale the OIA and WalMart tools into a single, industry-wide sustainability assessment tool. The result is the Higg index with modules to assess environmental impacts for Facilities, Brands, Retailers, Rapid Design, and Design and Development. These are accessible online to both members and non-members—another sharing tactic led by Patagonia to help other businesses and the

DON'T BUY THIS JACKET

Figure 2.1.1 Patagonia Black Friday advertisement

Image reproduced courtesy of Patagonia

It's Black Friday, the day in the year retail turns from red to black and starts to make real money. But Black Friday, and the culture of consumption it reflects, puts the economy of natural systems that support all life firmly in the red. We're now using the resources of one-and-a-half planets on our one and only planet.

Because Patagonia wants to be in business for a good long time – and leave a world inhabitable for our kids – we want to do the opposite of every other business today. We ask you to buy less and to reflect before you spend a dime on this jacket or anything else.

Environmental bankruptcy, as with corporate bankruptcy, can happen very slowly, then all of a sudden. This is what we face unless we slow down, then reverse the damage. We're running short on fresh water, topsoil, fisheries, wetlands – all our planet's natural systems and resources that support business, and life, including our own.

The environmental cost of everything we make is astonishing. Consider the R2® Jacket shown, one of our best sellers. To make it required 135 liters of

COMMON THREADS INITIATIVE

REDUCE
WE make useful gear that lasts a long time
YOU don't buy what you don't need

REPAIR
WE help you repair your Patagonia gear
YOU pledge to fix what's broken

REUSE
WE help find a home for Patagonia gear you no longer need
YOU sell or pass it on*

RECYCLE
WE will take back your Patagonia gear that is worn out
YOU pledge to keep your stuff out of the landfill and incinerator

REIMAGINE
TOGETHER we reimagine a world where we take only what nature can replace

water, enough to meet the daily needs (three glasses a day) of 45 people. Its journey from its origin as 60% recycled polyester to our Reno warehouse generated nearly 20 pounds of carbon dioxide, 24 times the weight of the finished product. This jacket left behind, on its way to Reno, two-thirds its weight in waste.

And this is a 60% recycled polyester jacket, knit and sewn to a high standard; it is exceptionally durable, so you won't have to replace it as often. And when it comes to the end of its useful life we'll take it back to recycle into a product of equal value. But, as is true of all the things we can make and you can buy, this jacket comes with an environmental cost higher than its price.

There is much to be done and plenty for us all to do. Don't buy what you don't need. Think twice before you buy anything. Go to patagonia.com/CommonThreads or scan the QR code below. Take the Common Threads Initiative pledge, and join us in the fifth "R," to reimagine a world where we take only what nature can replace.

patagonia®
patagonia.com

TAKE THE PLEDGE

*If you sell your used Patagonia product on eBay® and take the Common Threads Initiative pledge, we will co-list your product on patagonia.com for no additional charge.
© 20_ Patagonia, Inc.

industry as a whole to engage in the issue of social and environmental sustainability.[5]

Product Stewardship: Takeback Programs

Eileen Fisher, Renew, Irvington, New York, USA

One of the premier retailer takeback programs in the US is operated by apparel brand Eileen Fisher. The company began its customer takeback program in 2009 under the name "Green Eileen" as part of the Eileen Fisher Foundation to support its charitable efforts aimed at helping women and girls. Green Eileen organizationally moved into Eileen Fisher, Inc. in 2013, but the donations to women and girls through community efforts and non-profits continue. The company takes back only its own branded products from customers and provides a $5 coupon incentive in exchange for each item that is returned to any of their retail locations. When the program began, there was a huge response from Eileen Fisher's customers. Many had retained the brand's timeless items in their wardrobes for several years and the return of these used items to the company provided a robust inventory as the initiative was rolled out (Lewis 2015).

Today, the Green Eileen program has been renamed "Renew"[6] and incorporates processes for renewing and remaking the garments that are too damaged to be re-worn. Renew brings in almost $3 million annually with two processing centers/warehouses in the US—one in Seattle, Washington, and the other in Irvington, New York. In addition, at its Irvington location, a fully operational reuse facility where a staff of innovative "Remade" designers is charged with determining the creative destiny of the various used garments returned in damaged condition

to the company, according to a conversation with C. Gama, March 9, 2017. The new facility incorporates the existing processing center and links it to a new Renew retail store as well as a new Remade design studio, showroom and manufacturing facility. This vertically integrated space is both design lab and factory with the capacity to inspire consumers and serve as a model for other apparel industry brands. According to the Eileen Fisher web site (n.d.), by 2020 the company expects to have taken back over 1 million garments and it is physically preparing for the ever-increasing volume. Eileen Fisher also operates a separate Lab store in Irvington, which serves as multi-purpose retail and maker space; it showcases local artisans and hosts workshops in support of creative upcycling using items collected from the takeback program that are too damaged to be re-worn. In addition, the company will be opening a new store outside of Irvington called "Fisher Brooklyn" to further engage consumers with workshops that enable re-worn and reuse behavior. These community-facing spaces allow for a deeper engagement with sustainability for both the brand and its customers.

Eileen Fisher continues to grow and re-shape the Renew program as part of its Vision 2020 initiative to make its supply chain 100 percent sustainable and transparent (McGregor 2015a). The company's extended product stewardship considers the impact of new garment development and the ability to reuse or recycle the garment when it comes back through the takeback program. The company has already begun to scale its ability to takeback more of its garments for recycling, reselling and repurposing.

Both Patagonia and Eileen Fisher have cultivated sophisticated takeback programs that raise consumer awareness while simultaneously incentivizing the user consumer to take

Figure 2.1.2 Eileen Fisher's Renew sorting and storage space for takeback program, Irvington, NY
Photo by Helen Trejo

actionable steps to make an impact (i.e., returning and buying used clothing). New shopping channels for the purchase of high quality used clothing is a growing sector in North America with the emergence of popular secondhand clothing "re-commerce" sites like ThredUP[7] and remanufacturing businesses like the Renewal Workshop in Oregon.[8] Engaging the consumer in extended use behavior is a key contributor to a closed-loop, circular economy for apparel.

Closed-Loop Systems

Fibershed, San Geronimo, California, USA

California-based, Fibershed (n.d), emphasizes the use of local fiber, dye, and labor in its effort to build "a bridge between individuals and the biologic context of the raw materials that clothe them."[9] Founded in 2010 by Rebecca Burgess, the non-profit began as her personal journey to create a 100 percent regionally sourced wardrobe. In 2014, the organization conducted a feasibility study for the establishment of a closed-loop, vertically-integrated textile production facility using local wool. Today, Fibershed leads several initiatives that explore the intersection of local and sustainable fashion. The organization focuses on three key areas: education; textile economics; and fiber systems research.

In their home base of northern California, they have recently launched the Community Supported Cloth Project. Modeled on the Slow Food movement's Community Supported Agriculture Project, their project seeks to provide transparency and support sustainable textile production through economies of scale. Climate Beneficial Wool, a collaborative project between Fibershed and a local ranch to create a Carbon Farm Plan in partnership with the Carbon Cycle Institute, also exemplifies Fibershed's focus areas. The overarching goal of the project is to offset the greenhouse gas emissions associated with wool production. Another project, Soil-to-Soil, represents Fibershed's regenerative fiber system research. The Soil-to-Soil framework is a method

Figure 2.1.3 Fibershed certified fiber
Photo by Helen Trejo

to develop fabrics and dyes that allow garments at the end of their life to become compost (Scarano 2016b) making them "food" for the creation of new plant- or animal-based fibers, a closed-loop system (McGregor 2015b). Outdoor brand, The North Face, partnered with both Fibershed and the Sustainable Cotton Project in 2014 to launch the "Backyard Hoodie" garment, which emphasized the use of raw materials and production within 150 miles of The North Face's San Francisco headquarters (Lamicella 2014). The project was immensely successful in terms of consumer demand and the company expanded the project in 2016 with the Backyard Project Collection (Friedman 2016).

Recycled and Reused Fiber

Martex Fiber, Spartanburg, South Carolina, USA

Martex has been in the recycling business for over forty years with expertise in the processing of post-industrial textile waste. In 2016, the company launched its own Zero Landfill and No Fiber Left Behind initiatives pledging to convert all of its collected textile waste into sustainable products (McGregor 2015d). A recycled denim collection, R3 Denim, was developed in 2016 in partnership with Denim North America (DNA). The chemical-free textile used for the denim is made of recycled cotton knit fabric waste (Scarano 2016a).

Evrnu, Seattle, Washington, USA

Similarly, Seattle-based start-up, Evrnu, collaborated with Levi Strauss to create jeans made from post-consumer textile waste. Using five cotton T-shirts, they were able to make a pair of 511 jeans using 98 percent less water than that required for a pair made from virgin materials

(Zaczkiewicz 2016). Evrnu's specialty is processing used cotton garments into new fiber that is stronger and more durable than virgin cotton. Co-founder Stacy Flynn started the company in response to the growing and environmentally unsustainable consumption and disposal rates of clothing. Evrnu's process is intended to replace the use of harmful textile processes used to create new materials, like polyester (McGregor 2015c).

Entrepreneurial Models: Recycled and Reused Textiles

Mimi Prober, New York, NY, USA

Mimi Prober is an artist, designer, and entrepreneur. Her work can be best described as sustainable luxury, and her design philosophy is to create modern heirlooms handcrafted from antique materials.[10] She merges new and old to build her collections and approaches fashion as art in order to create timeless pieces. She is passionate about preservation, fine and decorative arts, and also has museum experience working with historic costume and textile collections. Antique textiles, primarily from the eighteenth to early twentieth centuries, are the foundation of all of Mimi's pieces and she meticulously sources reclaimed handmade lace and other materials crafted from natural fibers (silk, cotton, or linen). Her collection consists of luxury, ready-to-wear designs as well as an exclusive line of custom atelier pieces, which are all zero-waste and made of 100 percent reclaimed materials, many of which make use of recovered fragments of antique materials. The luxury collection also includes natural and locally produced luxury fibers blended with the antique fragments to form a unique custom textile. Additional sustainable techniques include the use of natural dyeing, old hand-woven linen, and a signature lace felted textile (see Figure 2.1.4). Mimi's signature natural dye process uses botanical bundle-dye techniques to achieve natural colors from local flora and is applied to reclaimed lace to create her unique "watercolor lace." Local resources are integral to Mimi's designs and she actively engages with local New York farmers for dyes and materials used in her collections. The signature lace felted textile is a design element Mimi developed with local Hudson Valley fiber

Figure 2.1.4 Mimi Prober black cape coat with signature lace felted textile from the 2017 collection
Photo by Randy Brooke

farmer, Sara Healy, according to a conversation with Mimi Prober on March 9, 2017. Mimi works directly with Sara at her farm and fiber mill to create and produce the custom textile with the luxurious Cormo and mohair wool from sheep raised on the farm. Mimi has already expanded her material sourcing to the Paco Vicuña, a US breed of the South American fiber animal. Mimi was the first designer to bring this rare luxury fiber to the New York Fashion Week runway, having worked with a family-owned farm in Missouri (Victory Farm) to source the rare fiber. Mimi is also beginning to explore opportunities for using locally sourced linen from Maple Shade farm in Somer, NY. Mimi's creativity and focus on local production, meaningful quantities, and high value-added materials and processes represents the dedication necessary to ensure a sustainable profile for every garment.

Local Buttons, Toronto, ON Canada & INDEPCO, Port-au-Prince, Haiti

Sourcing used textiles for incorporation into new garments was the business model for Canada-based Local Buttons. Founded in 2010 by Anne Pringle and Consuelo McAlister, two recent college grads with international development backgrounds, Local Buttons sought to leverage the abundant supply of used clothing in Haiti's *pepe* (secondhand clothing) market in order to develop a business that would help Haitian earthquake recovery efforts, create jobs, and reduce the impact of used clothing imports on the local economy (Lewis & Pringle 2015). The export of used clothing has long been a method of post-consumer textile waste management. The flow of used clothing is usually from developed to less-developed countries where wages are lower and acquiring new clothing can be costly and difficult to access. Yet, importing used clothing into a developing country can also negatively impact domestic textile and apparel industries that are forced to compete with the cheaper imports and it was this issue that Local Buttons addressed.

A connection with Hans Garoute, the president of Haiti's National Institute for the Development and Promotion of the Sewing Sector (or INDEPCO), allowed Pringle and McAlister to develop their first upcycled fashion collection in 2012. INDEPCO was a non-profit organization with the mission of promoting the Haitian garment industry by serving as both an apparel manufacturing facility and a training center. Many of the workers at INDEPCO were experienced in tailoring techniques due to Haiti's apparel manufacturing history (it had been a major exporter in the 1980s for many US brands) and the widespread need to modify imported secondhand garments for the local population. INDEPCO created and altered production patterns, deconstructed the used clothing and

assembled new garments for export to Canada. Local Buttons wanted to promote the process of refurbishing secondhand clothing in Haiti as a viable business model for sustainable fashion and prominently featured images of Haiti in their photo shoots in order to share the narrative of where and how their garments were made with their customers (Lewis & Pringle 2015). Although the Local Buttons' project is over, it provides a model of utilizing local labor and used materials as a textile waste management strategy—one that requires engagement of new sets of communities including consumers, apparel brands, and even governments.

CONCLUSION

While emphasizing the perspective that sustainability will never be reached, we are encouraged that user consumers are becoming engaged through industry educational campaigns, more accessible alternative actions,

Figure 2.1.5 At INDEPCO, Anne Pringle and Consuelo McAlister sort through secondhand clothing to use in their upcycled collection, Port-au-Prince, Haiti
Photo by Danilo Ursini, reproduced courtesy of author

and motivating models. Industry recognizes that user consumers are important actors in the journey toward a circular economy in textile and clothing products. User consumers are ready and willing if given the information, options, and incentive to alter behaviors around apparel disposal and reuse. A well-developed infrastructure to support a circular flow of textiles and apparel is paramount to the ongoing engagement of the user consumer in order to avoid frustration and/or boredom associated with initiatives to divert textile waste from landfills. An apparel supply chain that effectively includes the remanufacture or refurbishment of used clothing can provide purchase alternatives to new clothing for consumers that avoid the resource consumption associated with use of virgin materials. When new materials are required as inputs along with refurbished or reclaimed products, a focus on local resources can bolster local economies, create new business models and encourage user consumers through community connections.

This essay is a glimpse at the changes driving a new paradigm for consumption, use and disposal of apparel inclusive of farmers, designers, entrepreneurs, retailers, and user consumers. All are stakeholders and drivers of a new circular economy for fashion in North America.

NOTES

1. www.loveyourclothes.com
2. www.patagonia.com/the-activist-company
3. www.patagonia.com/footprint
4. www.onepercentfortheplanet.org
5. www.apparelcoalition.org
6. www.fisherfound.com
7. www.thredup.com
8. www.renewalworkshop.com
9. www.fibershed.com
10. www.mimiprober.com

REFERENCES

Clancy, H. (2014), "Why American Eagle, H&M, Nike and Puma want your hand-me-Downs," *GreenBiz*. Available online at: https://www.greenbiz.com/blog/2014/07/30/american-eagle-hm-nike-puma-want-old-clothes (accessed September 25, 2017).

Eileen Fisher (n.d.), *Vision 2020*. Available online at: www.eileenfisher.com/vision-2020 (accessed September 25, 2017).

Ellen MacArthur Foundation (2016), *Towards the Circular Economy: Economic and business rationale for an accelerated transition*. Available online at: https://www.ellenmacarthurfoundation.org/assets/downloads/publications/Ellen-MacArthur-Foundation-Towards-the-Circular-Economy-vol.1.pdf (accessed March 30, 2017).

EPA (n.d.), *Advancing sustainable materials management facts and figures report*. Available online at: www.epa.gov/smm/advancing-sustainable-materials-management-facts-and-figures-report (viewed September 25, 2017).

Fibershed (n.d.), Available online at: www.fibershed.com (accessed March 28, 2017).

Fletcher, K. (2008), *Sustainable fashion & textiles: Design journeys*. London: Earthscan.

Fletcher, K. (n.d.), "Local Wisdom." Available online at: Kateflectcher.com/projects/local-wisdom (accessed April 16, 2017).

Friedman, A. (2016), "North Face expands made in U.S. backyard project collection," *WWD*. Available online at: http://wwd.com/fashion-news/sportswear/north-face-expands-made-usa-backyard-project-collection-10375245 (accessed March 30, 2017).

Hepburn, S. J. (2015), "In Patagonia (Clothing): A Complicated Greenness," *Fashion Theory*, 17(5): 623–45, from, DOI: 10.2752/175174113X13718320331035.

Lamicella, L. (2014), "The North Face unveils locally sourced, produced 'backyard' hoodie," *Sourcing Journal*. Available online at: https://sourcingjournalonline.com/north-face-unveils-locally-sourced-apparel-collection-ll (accessed March 30, 2017).

Lewis, T. (2015), "Apparel disposal and reuse," in R.S. Blackburn (ed.), *Sustainable Apparel: Production, Processing and Recycling*, 233–50. Cambridge, UK: The Textile Insitute and Woodhead Publishing.

Lewis, T., and A. Pringle (2015), "Local Buttons: Sustainable Fashion and Social Entrepreneurship in

Haiti," *NKA Journal of Contemporary African Art*, 37: 114–25.

McDonough, W., and M. Braungart (2002), *Cradle to Cradle: Remaking the Way We Make Things*. New York: North Point Press.

McGregor, L. (2015a), "'Eileen Fisher pledges to reach 100% sustainability by 2020," *Sourcing Journal*. Available online at: https://sourcingjournalonline. com/eileen-fishers-green-colored-glasses-lm (accessed March 30, 2017).

McGregor, L. (2015b), "Are closed loop textiles the future of fashion?," *Sourcing Journal*. Available online at: https:// sourcingjournalonline.com/are-closed-loop-textiles-the-future-of-fashion (accessed March 30, 2017),

McGregor, L. (2015c), "Evrnu wants to turn old clothes into new fiber," *Sourcing Journal*. Available online at: https:// sourcingjournalonline.com/evrnu-wants-to-turn-old-clothes-into-new-fiber (accessed March 30, 2017).

McGregor, L. (2015d), "Martex adds new fiber reclamation line," *Sourcing Journal*. Available online at: https://sourcingjournalonline.com/martex-adds-new-fiber-reclamation-line (viewed March 30, 2017).

Sauvé, S., S. Bernard, and P. Sloan (2016), "Environmental Sciences, Sustainable Development and Circular Economy: Alternative Concepts for Trans-disciplinary Research," *Environmental Development*, 17 48–56.

Scarano, G. (2016a), "Martex debuts R3 denim collection," *Sourcing Journal*. Available online at: https://sourcingjournalonline.com/martex-debuts-r3-denim-collection (accessed March 30, 2017).

Scarano, G. (2016b), "Fibershed leads the movement in sustainable textile systems," *Sourcing Journal*. Available online at: https://sourcingjournalonline. com/fibershed-sustainable-textile-systems (accessed March 30, 2017).

Secondary Materials and Recycled Textiles, (n.d.), "The lifecycle of rags." Available online at: https://www. smartasn.org/SMARTASN/assets/File/resources/ lifecycleofrags.pdf (viewed October 7, 2017).

Winakor, G. (1969), "The Process of Clothing Consumption," *Journal of Home Economics*, 6(18): 629–634.

Zaczkiewicz, A. (2016), "Evrnu partner to launch jeans made from waste," *WWD*. Available online at: http://wwd.com/fashion-news/denim/levi-strauss-evrnu-cotton-waste-made-jeans-10428397 (accessed March 28, 2017).

CHAPTER 2.2

A SPOTLIGHT ON: PATTERN MAKERS AND GARMENT MAKERS
Midwest, Ohio, Cleveland

Noël Palomo-Lovinski, Kent State University, USA

Pattern Makers, and its new sister company Garment Makers, is located in Cleveland, Ohio, a town at the heart of the United States' Midwest industrial Rust Belt. Run by partners Sean Bilovecky and Gwyn Strang, the businesses occupy a former manufacturing facility on Superior Avenue, hearkening back to the bygone days of the area's garment district.

Cleveland's garment district began blossoming as early as the 1860s as predominantly German Jews immigrated out of New York to expand their business opportunities (Dillon & Godley 2012: 41). Reaching its zenith in the 1920s, the Great Depression wiped out a significant number of businesses (Garfinkel 2015). Throughout the twentieth century, most of what Americans wore was made in the United States yet by the late 1990s, most garment manufacturing had completely left the Midwest (Garfinkel 2015; Novellino 2015).

Having attended the Fashion School at Kent State University, been in a rock band, and then becoming a father, Sean Bilovecky decided to try his hand at what he knew best: pattern making. In 2006, Sean created a profile on Makers Row, a manufacturing network that highlights the garment industry in the United States. Sean quickly achieved a top profile on the website due to his ability to create highly skilled and diverse set of pattern work. Pattern Makers provides a wide spectrum of production room services, working with established brands to start-ups. As a designer himself, Sean and his small group of employees can assist in the entire spectrum of small batch to large scale production attracting some very large-scale clients. Traditionally, Sean would then connect the designers for whom he had created production packets with the few remaining sewing manufacturers across the country, including New York City.

In 2016, Sean formed Garment Makers with partner Gwyn Strang, also a former designer and owner of the store House of Ill Repute. Housed in the same facility, Garment Makers seeks to pick up where Pattern Makers drops off, thereby offering the full gamut of the manufacturing

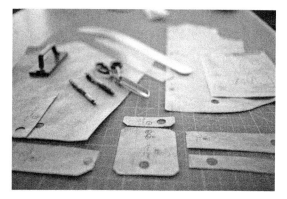

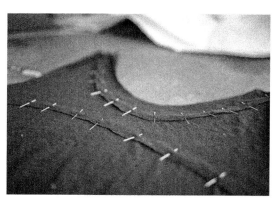

Figure 2.2.1 Images from the studios of Pattern Makers and Garment Makers, Cleveland, Ohio
Images reproduced courtesy of Sean Bilovecki

process, from conception to completion. Still in the formative stages, Garment Makers is focused on what they do best—cutting and sewing knits and athletic wear. The two partners are committed to developing and maintaining the highest quality product at consistent levels, thereby building a solid foundation of trust among potential clients.

A key advantage of being in a type of Renaissance of the American fashion industry is that manufacturers are a close-knit community. Some of the advantages of working with manufacturers outside of New York and Los Angeles that Sean cites include being able to provide quicker response times, greater involvement, and higher levels of collaboration between factories. If Pattern Makers receive work that they know another company in the United States can do better, they send the work to that business. Conversely, when other manufacturers receive knit cut and sew work, they send it to Garment Makers. Another plus to working with manufacturers in the United States for the American fashion industry is the level of transparency and accountability that is inherent not only in proximity but in a new ethos of wanting to do business the "right way." As the apparel manufacturing industry in the United States strives for resurgence, there is a palpable sense of wanting to do things differently, from instituting fair and equitable labor practices to ensuring better environmental and sustainability protection, and the highest level of resource efficiency.

The greatest benefit of working specifically in Cleveland is the low cost of real estate in comparison to other cities, which means that Sean and Gwyn can stream more revenue into paying all their employees above minimum wage, offering incentives for quality work. The primary disadvantage is that there are not enough skilled sewing operators to work at the level and speed that is required of industry-level work. Sean and Gwyn do a great deal of mentoring and instruction to help create a healthy workforce. The lack of skilled labor is seen as the primary hurdle across the United States to a more localized garment industry. Future success for the American garment industry will depend on vocational education resources that provide sewing skills or technical oversight in automated sewing, which is currently in the early stages of development. In either case, companies such as Garment Makers and Pattern Makers are at the forefront of an exciting set of new possibilities for the garment industry in the Midwest.

REFERENCES

Dillon, P., and Godley, A. (2012), "The Evolution of the Jewish Garment Industry, 1840–1940," in R. Kobin (ed.) *Chosen Capital: The Jewish Encounter with American Capitalism*, 37–61. New Brunswick, NJ: Rutgers University Press.

Garfinkel, S. (2015), "Garment Industry: Encyclopedia of Cleveland History," Case Western Reserve University. Available online at: https://case.edu/ech/articles/g/garment-industry/ (accessed December 19, 2015).

Novellino, T. (2015), "Made in the USA clothing: Rare but worth it," *New York Business Journal*, July 2. Available online at: www.bizjournals.com/newyork/.../made-in-the-usa-clothing-rare-but-worth-it.html (accessed July 21, 2015).

CHAPTER 2.3

CLASSING CALIFORNIA'S WOOL
From Local to Global Networks

Jennifer Hoover, University California, Davis, USA
Susan B Kaiser, University California, Davis, USA

INTRODUCTION

In fashion, as in food, "local" is the new "green." At Fibershed's 2015 Wool & Fine Fiber Symposium in Point Reyes, California, founder Rebecca Burgess presented a newly published handbook of regional fiber production. Intended to be examined by hand, it features samples of wool (as well as fiber from goats, rabbits, and alpacas) at every stage of processing, from cleaned but otherwise unprocessed locks to finished swatches. At the lunch break between lectures on pollinator-friendly pastures and the revival of rare sheep breeds, symposium participants perused the book, sampled locally produced cheeses, and tried their hands at the spinning wheel. Through these activities, Fibershed presents an alluring world in which one can feel good, ethically and sensually, by buying local.

Small- to mid-size businesses, individual textile artisans, and non-profit organizations such as Fibershed are pushing back against the trend of "fast fashion," positioning their work as "slow" and "local." Local fiber projects rest on the assumption of intrinsic connections between fiber and the places where it is grown, palpable in the textures of clothing fashioned from those fibers. At the same time, if they are to be profitable, fiber growers have to be sufficiently competitive to sell their wool in the global, as well as the local, marketplace.

This study explores intertwining material and social expressions of place in fiber through the first author's training as a wool classer: a worker on a shearing crew who performs a sensory evaluation of each fleece as it comes off the sheep. We find that a focus on wool collapses the binary opposition of *local* versus *global*, revealing the inextricable entanglement of local environmental settings and global economic systems. Close attention to the processes by which wool is transformed from an extrusion of the sheep's skin to a "second skin" for a human consumer reveals that such binaries are in constant flux.

WHY WOOL?
WHY CLASSING?

For both producers and researchers of textiles, wool provides a rich medium for the exploration of locality. Wool is inherently somewhat resistant to fast fashion, with necessarily long lead times due to an extensive chain of processing from fiber to finished product. The scenic qualities of the landscapes of wool production provide ample photographic material for retail websites and clothing tags—rugged mountains, idyllic farmsteads, and fluffy sheep (Pawson & Perkins 2013).

Early stages of this research included participant observation in a wide range of fiber-related activities: attending annual Fibershed symposia, other fiber festivals, and meetings of textile craft guilds; volunteering at small ranches that produce high-quality fleeces for hand-spinners; touring a wool mill under construction; and enrolling in shearing school at the University of California Hopland Research & Extension Center. The project then became more narrowly focused on the practice of wool classing, with the first author pursuing certification through the American Sheep Industry Association (ASI). Fieldwork was conducted with two industry professionals who have worked in the global wool industry for several decades: Ron Cole (who oversees ASI training of wool classers) and Ian MacKenzie (who works as a field agent for a wool broker in the US, and classes wool in New Zealand). In spring of 2016, Jen Hoover accompanied Ron and Ian on visits to multiple shearing sites in Kern County and spent three days in Solano County classing one ranch's clip of approximately 1,200 fleeces under Ian's direction.

Classing is required if a grower is to compete with longer, finer, premium wool in the global marketplace. This is in contrast to most wool in

California, which is sold as "Bellies Out": the dirtiest belly wool is separated from the remainder of the fleece, but no further sorting takes place. Yet classing plays a crucial role in projects strengthening national and regional wool production systems. ASI's efforts to improve the quality of wool produced in the United States include promoting the practice of classing in order to better compete with Australian wool. Within California, efforts to create and strengthen local wool supply chains currently focus on building mid-scale industrial infrastructure for processing of fine fiber into lightweight garments suitable for the state's relatively warm climate (Bieg et al. 2014). Critical to the endeavor is the selection of raw wool with characteristics that allow it to be processed into fine-gauge yarns smooth enough to travel through an industrial knitting platform without snagging, and soft enough for next-to-skin wear.

Wool classing offers a fruitful site of inquiry into entanglements between local and global. The wool classer stands at a node of interchange between the local rangeland ecology and the global textile economy. As we will show, this is not a simple one-way exchange, but a complex knot of feedback loops winding far afield from the point at which we pick up the threads.

LOCAL AND GLOBAL

Recent work in critical fashion studies (e.g., Kaiser 2013) follows geographer Doreen Massey in urging attention to routes and movement in discussions of place. Massey (1991) argues against discourses that pit globalization as a homogenizing and fragmenting force against romanticized notions of unique yet internally homogeneous local places. On the surface, discourses around local fiber appear to operate within a rather static, bounded understanding of place. Fibershed certification indicates that fibers, botanic dyes, and labor are sourced in "the backyard of the Bay Area" within a 150-mile radius of the organization's headquarters,[1] with exceptions for processes and products unavailable within that area (including fine-gauge wool milling). Other Fibershed-inspired projects identify fiber production regions outlined by state borders (Trejo 2014) or circles centered elsewhere (such as the Upper Canada Fibershed, which crosses national borders).[2]

In practice, however, "local" serves as shorthand for commitments that cannot be captured in a circle superimposed on a map. A wide range of consumer concerns—including animal welfare, environmental sustainability, and domestic manufacture (Bieg et al. 2014; Hebrok et al. 2012; Peterson et al. 2012)—become compressed into the idea of "knowing where" the wool came from. For many fiber enthusiasts, working with local wool is a way of supporting small family businesses, of ensuring that animals are treated humanely and that farmers practice environmentally sustainable techniques, and of cultivating personal relationships within a community of "fiber folk."

Local fiber enthusiasts, then, enact place, as Massey (1991) would put it, through "articulated moments in networks of social relations and understandings" (28). These networks extend far beyond whatever boundaries might be set to define a place, whether a town, nation, bioregion, or single ranch. Massey does not offer a metaphorical model for this type of interchange

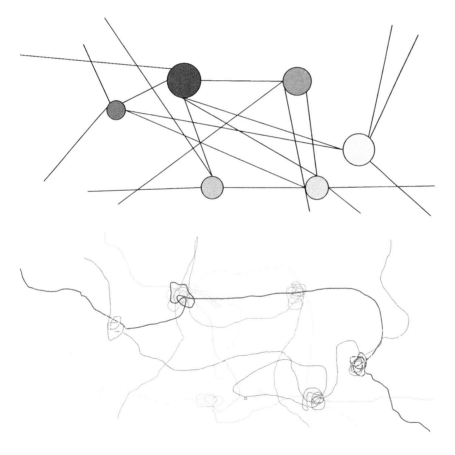

Figure 2.3.1 Nodes and knots
© *Jennifer Hoover*

between the local and the global, but other theorists do: knots. According to philosopher Michel Serres (2008), "(t)hrough their topological design...knots weld the local to the global and conversely" (303). Anthropologist Tim Ingold (2007) likewise envisions places as nets or "meshworks" of entangled strands traced by inhabitants as they move through life. Re-envisioning places as knots within a global meshwork counters discourses that treat "the local" as static, bounded, and internally homogeneous. Within each knot, multiple strands interlace such that a change to any one strand impacts several other knots and the entire structure. Each knot is unique and cohesive, yet internally diverse, unbounded, and continuously changing.

KNOTWORKS AND NETWORKS

Ingold adopts the term "meshwork" to highlight issues of flow and growth, revising Bruno Latour's use of "network" in naming Actor-Network Theory (Ingold 2010). Actor-Network Theory (ANT) is one branch of science and technology studies (STS), within which scholars seek to investigate entanglements of materiality and sociality. ANT and STS studies intermesh in ways that are familiar to fashion scholars, who understand how and why the material and social aspects of textiles cannot be considered in isolation from each other. The two fields resonate in their approaches to material/social entanglements and capacities to encompass ambiguity and contradictions.

Latour (2005) presents a series of "moves" by which ANT researchers may "reassemble the social" to include the material: localizing the global, redistributing the local, and connecting sites. Through these moves, Latour collapses the

hierarchical binary of local/global into a "flat" network of connections. To do so, he advocates forsaking the panopticon—the position of a comprehensive, commanding view—for the oligopticon—a position from which it is possible to see only a little, but to see it well. From the vantage point of the oligopticon, the researcher can follow the diverse trails that intersect at that point. Although Latour does not explicitly liken the oligopticon to a knot, his model resonates with that imagery and we engage with it as such.

LANDSCAPES OF WOOL PRODUCTION

From the oligopticon of the wool classer's table, one trail leads back to the pastoral landscapes across which sheep roam, and in which ethnographers have explored how humans and animals engage as active co-creators of place. Sheep quite literally shape the landscape through their grazing (Law & Mol 2008). The grazing patterns of sheep are in turn shaped by the social structures and practices of the shepherds and ranchers who tend them. And shepherds come to understand the land in specific ways through their care of sheep, walking and motor biking along routes traced by ovine and human feet over many generations (Gray 1999; Dominy 2000; Rebanks 2015).

The experiences of shepherds, as recounted in their own words and analyzed by researchers, exemplify the concept of "taskscape" developed by Tim Ingold. Ingold regards the landscape as an embodiment of a series of interlocking cycles and as "an enduring record of—and testimony to—the lives and works of past generations who have dwelt within it" (Ingold 2000: 189). His "taskscape" conveys an active, temporal sense of place; the seemingly static landscape is merely a "congealed" form of the taskscape.[3] In an ethnography of high-country sheep stations in New Zealand, Michèle Dominy (2000) posits a similar relationship between wool and the cyclical work that produces it. Her account of the seasonal round of wool growing culminates in the shearing shed: "the conceptual site for distilling the landscape and pastoral activities of the year into fleece" (Dominy 2000: 189). Dominy concludes that "the fleece signifies the landscape" (190).

As wool grows, it becomes a timeline of the conditions experienced by the sheep over the course of a year. The major characteristics of fiber quality—fiber diameter, length, and strength—are all impacted by a combination of environmental conditions including temperature, day length, and quantity and quality of feed and water (Khan et al. 2012). These variables fluctuate seasonally and as sheep move from one grazing ground to another, either cycling through pastures on a ranch or ranging more widely across public lands. Long-term stresses, such as the multi-year drought in California, result in weakness throughout the staple length known as "tender" wool. A short-term stress (caused by

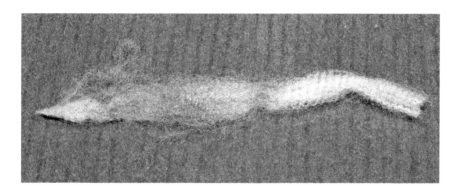

Figure 2.3.2 Wool break
© *Jennifer Hoover*

Figure 2.3.3 Paint-branded sheep
© *Jennifer Hoover*

lambing, predation, or illness) can cause a sharply delineated break across the lock. Environmental factors (e.g., vegetable matter, bits of propylene twine, dirt) and shepherding practices (e.g., paint applied to the sheep to aid in flock management), as well as natural conditions (e.g., kemp [stiff, medullated fibers] and pigmented wool[4]) can also contribute to the "contamination" of fleece.

Growers aim to minimize "contamination" of fleece, and maximize growth of high-quality wool, through a combination of breeding programs and management of interlocking seasonal and geographic cycles. The skill required to do so develops in an iterative process of observing the results of one year's shepherding work, and adjusting practices accordingly. The knowledge gained in this way is deeply embedded in the environment in which it develops.

ENSKILLED SENSES

Like wool growing, classing requires development of skill within a specific environment. The structure of the ASI wool classer certification explicitly acknowledges the embodied and emplaced nature of the practice. Prospective wool classers take a three-day course in which general information is presented in lectures and written materials, then engage in extensive practice under the guidance of a higher-ranked classer before working independently. Classers first work within local flocks, and can progress toward national certification through experience with an increasing variety of sheep breeds and geographic regions.

Classers conduct their evaluations through rapid visual and tactile inspections. The first clues to fleece quality come as the classer throws a fleece onto the sorting table. The heft of the fleece and its visual density suggest whether the fiber is long enough to warrant closer examination. Classers confirm this evaluation by tugging out a lock to compare against a measure on their own bodies, such as a finger known to be three inches long (the desired fiber length). Once adequate length is established, a quick tug on either end indicates the fiber strength. "Short and tender" fleeces are set aside without further evaluation. Classers evaluate fineness of fiber diameter by feel, either on their hands as they perform the other evaluations or against a more sensitive area of skin such as the inner forearm or under the nose. They may pull a lock apart laterally to see how the fibers interact with each other, a visual clue to fineness. Classers also look for contaminants, and may remove heavily contaminated sections of wool, usually found at the edges of the shorn fleece.

Fleeces are sorted into "lines"; the number and designations vary, because there are no fixed grades of wool. Each flock is classed relative to itself, with the majority of fleeces feeding into the "A line." Classers create other lines for fleeces significantly shorter, finer, or coarser than the norm or that contain substantial amounts of contaminants. Lines may switch during the course of classing if what at first appeared to be the majority turns out not to be. A classer's skill lies not only in assessing fleeces quickly and accurately, but also in creating lines which separate out varying qualities of fiber without splitting the clip into unmarketably small lots. As Ian repeatedly stated, "it's not about how clever you are at splitting things up; it's about putting like with like."

The decision of where to differentiate "fine" from "medium" is determined partly by current market conditions: price breaks, currency exchange rates, and worldwide supply and demand. Classers consider the reactions of buyers and the mechanics of milling equipment. A fleece

Figure 2.3.4 Sorted lines and bales
© *Jennifer Hoover*

may technically meet the specifications of the A line but be "unappealing" or "not very stylish" and hence downgraded to the coarse line. Fleeces with different characteristics may be placed together in a line because they will process similarly when blended together in the mill. All these factors are considered in a matter of a few seconds as classers sort several hundred fleeces per day.

The characteristics of the fleeces at hand are primary among classing considerations, but the history of the flock (especially changes in breeding programs) and conditions of the surrounding region are also relevant. Classers also work with an eye toward where the wool eventually lands, in auction and textile mills.

For each physical characteristic, Ron and Ian demonstrated multiple ways of sorting through sight and touch. Ian prefers to class in short sleeves because the insides of his forearms are more sensitive than his hands; Ron demonstrated a new trick he had learned, pulling a lock between two fingers to gauge its fineness. In this process, the two experts were sharing skills with each other as much as instructing their novice trainee. While classers develop personal repertoires of sensory tests unique to their bodies, the location of training also shapes a classer's practice. Ian noted that classers trained in the US tend to rely on visual cues to determine fiber fineness, whereas in New Zealand he had learned that the crimp styles of the locally predominant merino sheep can fool the eye. Instead, he learned to identify fiber by feel: "My old butterfingers tell me."

EMPLACED SKILLS

A classer's skills develop within a particular locality and also contribute to representation of that locality within the larger system of wool production. Anthropologist Cristina Grasseni (2009) cautions, however, against an essentialized, static link between skill and place, noting that "local" skills circulate with the movement of migrant craftspersons, and that skill is constituted in the mutable constructs of social relationships and memory. For wool growers, the display of skill occurs through the sale of their clips. Growers', shearers', and classers' skills are also recognized through conversation (including gossip) among industry professionals as they move through the geographical and seasonal circuits of the shearing cycle.[5] Reputation and economic recognition can combine, as manufacturers are increasingly purchasing entire clips in order to produce specialty lines with traceable supply chains.

In Dominy's (2000) account of wool growing, shearing converts the congealed taskscape of wool into a portable form, and tactile evaluation of wool is simply a means by which buyers "read" the wool to assess its value. But the practices of shearing and classing also contribute to wool's value. A less-skilled shearer can devalue an otherwise high-quality fleece by cutting too far from the skin, thereby reducing staple length—or too close, thereby introducing contaminants in the form of skin tags. A classer's skill in setting the lines can also enhance or reduce the economic value of the clip. Place thus becomes expressed in wool in ways that can be measured through classing, while classing simultaneously informs how local wool-producing places are represented in the wider textile system.

CONCLUSION

Starting from an initiative that enacts "the local" in opposition to the exploitative practices of global "fast fashion," we have paradoxically ended up focusing on a rapid-fire practice at the heart of the global wool market. Yet this focus has afforded a detailed view of the entangled exchanges between the local and the global (and the material and the social) through which place is created.

Classing demands of, and instils in, the classer a highly localized knowledge of seasonal vegetation cycles, climate conditions, sheep breeding histories, and flock management practices. At the same time, classers make decisions based on global market conditions and manufacturing capabilities of (usually) distant mills. These distant and abstract forces, realized in the sorting and assigning of monetary value to wool, in turn shape the local landscape by altering ranching and shepherding practices. Just as sheep range across the landscape, wool circulates (in physical and conceptual form) along meandering routes across multiple disciplinary domains.

We have traced these routes from the oligopticon of the wool classer's table, at which converge local environmental conditions, national certification standards, and the manufacturing capabilities of mills in the US and China (not to mention the bodies of sheep and humans). A different vantage point—the shearing board, wool auction, or mill—would open onto another network of trails leading to a different, and perhaps even contradictory, conclusion. Within the metaphor of the knot, such contradiction is acceptable—even welcome, as tension and friction between contradictory forces are what holds a knot (actually, all textiles) together (Ingold 2015; Pan 2014). Susan Kaiser (2015) argues that the metaphors with which we describe systems of production, distribution, and consumption shape the ways we are able to analyze and change those systems. The knot metaphor allows sustainable fashion projects framed as "local" to open up to more complex and shifting enactments of locality.

As Fibershed's work evolves, it is engaging more explicitly with this more open sense of place. An emerging certification for "climate beneficial wool" aims to develop textile supply chains traceable to ranches practicing carbon sequestration protocols, combining a focus on locality with concern for global climate change. Struggles to secure funding for new mill construction have broadened that project as well. In order to demonstrate demand for expanded small- and mid-scale milling capacity, local fiber advocates must also work to strengthen the existing national wool processing infrastructure. We contend that such moves from local to national and global scales are not hypocritical, or transitional phases that must be gone through in order to return to a truly local sense of place, but are how place operates: through the entanglement of the local and the global.

NOTES

1. Unless otherwise cited, references to Fibershed's work are drawn from the organization's website (www.fibershed.com) or talks at the annual symposium (videos available on the website).
2. https://uppercanadafibershed.ca/what-is-a-fibershed/about/
3. This formulation reminds us of Elizabeth Wilson's (2003) description of clothes as "congealed memories of the daily life of times past" (1).
4. Even sheep with white wool but darker skin are separated out as potential sources of contamination. The segregation of sheep according to wool/skin color brings up the question of race within wool processing, a topic warranting more in-depth consideration than we can provide here. White fiber is preferred in commercial production because it can be dyed uniformly in large-scale lots; however, Libby Robin (1999) also notes the role of outwardly dirty but inwardly "pure" white merino fleece as a symbol of Australian white free-settler identity during the colonial period. Other scholars trace the development of political racism out of practices of animal breeding (Da Cal 1992) and enactment of colonial narratives of white supremacy in agricultural shows (Anderson 2003).
5. Many shearing crew workers, from unskilled "roustabouts" who sweep the shearing floor to experts like Ian, are themselves international

migrants; thus highly localized knowledge simultaneously circulates along regional and transnational routes.

REFERENCES

Anderson, K. (2003), "White Natures: Sydney's Royal Agricultural Show in Post-humanist Perspective," *Transactions of the Institute of British Geographers*, 28(4): 422–41.

Bieg, A., R. Burgess, D. Kahn, E. Axelrod, J. Kassan, M. DeLonge, and L. Wendt (2014), *Fibershed feasibility study for a California wool mill*, retrieved from http://www.fibershed.com/wool-mill-vision/

Da Cal, E. U (1992), "The Influence of Animal Breeding on Political Racism," *History of European Ideas*, 15(4–6): 717–25.

Dominy, M. D. (2000), *Calling the Station Home: Place and Identity in New Zealand's High Country*. New York: Rowman & Littlefield Publishers, Inc.

Grasseni, C. (2009), *Developing Skill, Developing Vision: Practices of Locality at the Foot of the Alps*. New York: Berghahn Books.

Gray, J. (1999), "Open Spaces and Dwelling Places: Being at Home on Hill Farms in the Scottish Borders," *American Ethnologist*, 26(2): 440–60.

Hebrok, M., I. G. Klepp, and T. S. Tobiasson (2012), *Valuing Norwegian Wool*, Oslo.

Ingold, T. (2000), *The Perception of the Environment: Essays on Livelihood, Dwelling and Skill*. New York: Routledge.

Ingold, T. (2007), *Lines: A Brief History*, New York: Routledge.

Ingold, T. (2010), "Bringing Things to Life: Creative Entanglements in a World of Materials." Manchester: National Centre for Research Methods.

Ingold, T. (2015), *The Life of Lines*. New York: Routledge.

Kaiser, S. B. (2013), "Introduction: Place, Time and Identity—New Directions in Critical Fashion Studies," *Critical Studies in Fashion & Beauty*, 4 (1&2): 3–16.

Kaiser, S. B. (2015), "Mixing Metaphors in the Fiber, Textile, and Apparel Complex: Moving Toward a More Sustainable Fashion System," in J. Hethorn and C. Ulasewicz (eds), *Sustainable Fashion: What's Next?*, 2nd ed., 139–64. New York: Fairchild Books, Inc.

Khan, M. J., A. Abbas, M. Ayaz, M. Naeem, M. S. Akhter, and M. H. Soomro (2012), "Factors Affecting Wool

Quality and Quantity in Sheep," *African Journal of Biotechnology*, 11 (73): 13761–66. Doi:10.5897/AJBX11.064.

Latour, B. (2005), *Reassembling the Social: An Introduction to Actor-Network-Theory.* Oxford and New York: Oxford University Press.

Law, J., and A. Mol (2008), "The Actor-Enacted: Cumbrian Sheep in 2001," in L. Malafouris and C. Knappett (eds), *Material Agency,* 57–77. Boston, MA: Springer US.

Massey, D. (1991), "A Global Sense of Place," *Marxism Today*, pp.24–29.

Pan, N. (2014), "Exploring the Significance of Structural Hierarchy in Material Systems: A Review," *Applied Physics Reviews*, 1(2): 1–31.

Pawson, E., and H. Perkins (2013), "Worlds of Wool: Recreating Value Off the Sheep's Back," *New Zealand Geographer*, 69(3): 208–20.

Peterson, H. H., G. M. Hustvedt, and Y.-J. Chen (2012), "Consumer Preferences for Sustainable Wool Products in the United States," *Clothing and Textiles Research Journal*, 30(1): 35–50.

Rebanks, J. (2015), *The Shepherd's Life: Modern Dispatches from an Ancient Landscape.* New York: Flatiron Books.

Robin, L. (1999), "Fleecing the Nation," *Journal of Australian Studies*, 23(62): 150–58.

Serres, M. (2008), *The Five Senses: A Philosophy of Mingled Bodies,* trans. M. Sankey and P. Cowley. New York: Continuum.

Trejo, H. X. (2014), *Exploring the New York Slow Fashion Value Chain: Local Animals, Fibers, and Knitwear.* Ithaca, NY: Cornell University.

Wilson, E. (2003), *Adorned in Dreams: Fashion and Modernity.* New York: I.B. Tauris.

CHAPTER 2.4

A SPOTLIGHT ON: PRELOVED (CANADA)

Doris Treptow-Kovacs, Savannah College of Art and Design, USA

Canadian brand Preloved is a pioneer in upcycling used garments ("knits") in order to create fashionable new styles. The brand was founded in 1995 by Julia Grieve, a former international model. She opened a vintage clothes store on Queen Street West, in Toronto, Canada. Some garments were "altered slightly," as Grieve describes, by changing buttons or shortening length to appeal to the modern taste. What started as one-of-a-kind creations were then developed into size-graded patterns and she started to employ design students to work on the cutting and matching of the used knits into new garments.

The brand gained publicity when celebrities like Anne Hathaway, Kate Hudson, and Julia Roberts started sporting some of their creations, and boutiques in North America, Australia, Europe, and Japan started carrying their merchandise. Larger apparel retailers became interested in the Preloved concept and style and the brand has been featured at Anthropologie, The Hudson's Bay Company, Beams Japan, Roots, and over 400 independent boutiques.

Julia partnered with Chak Cheng, from WS and Co, one of the biggest Canadian apparel manufacturers, which allowed Preloved access to manufacturing expertise and production at industrial scale. Preloved rents a 2,000-square-foot space inside at WS and Co., which houses its garment-sorting operation, design studio, showroom and photography studio.

Preloved sources its sweater knits from Canadian rag houses that collect donated and disposed-of garments. The process is labor intensive and has several touch points. Julia explains that a touch point is counted each time a vintage garment is handled. Clothes are screened for damages, such as holes and stains. They are also screened for panel sizes, since garments that are built of small panels, or those that are small in general, are more difficult to be used in the reconstruction of apparel items. These might still be used for the production of childrenswear, accessories, and home décor lines designed at Preloved.

Unsuitable cast-off products find multiple destinations: some are donated to other designers that upcycle through reconstruction, while others have been donated to the school system to be used for children's arts and crafts projects. Any remaining cast-off products are returned to the rag houses that have their own recycling programs.

The garments that are selected to be processed at Preloved then go through a washing phase that also functions as another point of quality control.

Figure 2.4.1 Preloved employee sorting used garments for reconstruction
Image reproduced courtesy of Rimba Muharram

"If the garment gets damaged in the wash, we will not use it in production," explains Grieves.

Working with the vintage garments poses a design challenge. The sample design expresses the desired balance of colors and textures sourced from salvaged sweaters or dress shirts by the designer. But how is that balance supposed to be replicated in scale production when the source materials are assorted? Preloved has developed guidelines for each design they produce, which considers what colors or patterns may be bundled. A trained team of Preloved employees sorts through the salvaged garments and determines the color and pattern combinations for each piece to be produced. For example, the "Miss Ellie" sweater is a staple item in the Preloved product mix. Achieving consistency is possible only if the strict guidelines are observed in order to "mass produce one-of-a-kind clothes," as described by Grieve.

To provide a consistent look to the merchandise of large orders, Preloved started to incorporate "deadstock" fabrics (left-over bolts of fabrics from other brands). This move allowed the brand to mass produce garments that did not depend entirely on the combinations of salvaged small pieces, but still included them as accents to garments that were cut from the bolts. Grieve explains: "If you're selling to large retailers like Holt Renfrew, they don't like the term 'assorted.' The buyer kind of needs to know what she's going to get. So, we're able to blend in some new fabrics that can keep the body the same, but add bits of recycled pieces to it so it can show the uniqueness." Bolts of deadstock fabric are acquired from other brands that manufacture at WS and Co., other contractors, or fabric wholesalers in Canada.

The garments bundled by the Preloved team are placed on a cart which is wheeled down for cut and sewing a few yards away. The textile waste generated by the cut and sew process is used in home décor throws, pillows and slippers that employ smaller pieces. Recycling and disposal of scraps is managed by WS and Co.

Grieve's celebrity status is a supporting factor on the promotion of Preloved. The brand and its founder have a strong intertwined online presence. She is the host of Ion Life television

Figure 2.4.2 Julia and models at a runway show
Image reproduced courtesy of George Pimentel

channel show "Diva on a Dime," has participated on "Project Runway Canada," and has a segment on "Entertainment Tonight Canada." The *PrelovedToronto* YouTube channel features a series of videos entitled "Being Julia," with weekly videos on style tips.

REFERENCES

Eco Fashion Talk (2013), Preloved. Available online at: http://www.ecofashiontalk.com/2013/06/preloved/ (accessed April 3, 2017).

Interview with Julia Grieve via Skype on February 23, 2017.

Preloved by Julia (n.d.). Available online at: http://prelovedtoronto.blogspot.com/p/about-preloved.html (accessed April 3, 2017).

Yoneda, Y. (2009), "Sustainable Style: Preloved's Recycle Vintage Couture." Available online at: http://www.ecouterre.com/sustainable-style-preloveds-recycled-vintage-couture/preloved34/ (accessed April 3, 2017).

SUSTAINABLE FASHION IN CANADA
Unpacking the Spaces and Practices of "Made in Canada"

Taylor Brydges, Stockholm University, Sweden

INTRODUCTION

The fashion industry is one of the most wasteful industries in the world, falling just behind the petroleum industry (Ecowatch 2015). As clothing has evolved from a durable good to a daily purchase through the advent of fast fashion (trendy, low-cost clothing produced by global fashion brands), production and consumption of fashion products have drastically increased. 80 billion new pieces of clothing are consumed every year; a 400 percent increase in just two decades (The True Cost 2017). Reinach (2005: 47) defines fast fashion as "a generic term that covers various types of products and brands: from simple, cheap items of clothing sold on street market-stalls, to proper brands such as Laltramoda (which also traces its beginnings back to the market-stall) and, above all, brands like Zara and Mango—both Spanish and both partially produced in China—to H&M, the legendary Scandinavian company, which is the fastest of them all." A number of factors

have been attributed to the globalization and speed of fashion production, including new supply chain management systems, the expansion of the fashion calendar to include new seasons, and the rise of trend-driven styles (Agins 1999; Tokatli 2008; Bhardwaj & Fairhurst 2010; Taplin 2014). Fast fashion has become extremely popular with consumers, and growth in this market segment continues to outpace the rest of the fashion industry (Quartz 2016).

However, local alternatives are also becoming increasingly relevant in the consumer marketplace. For example, in recent years, slow fashion has become a growing movement in the fashion industry. Slow fashion is defined by Fletcher (2007) as: "a different approach in which designers, buyers, retailers and consumers are more aware of the impacts of products on workers, communities and ecosystems." Slow fashion is based on principles of sustainability, social responsibility, and transparency (Clark 2008), with related movements including upcycling and the use of smart textiles (Ainamo 2014) and ethical fashion (Joergens 2006).

This essay shares insights on the state of sustainable fashion in Canada. A key finding of this research, comprised of interviews with independent fashion designers and key informants in the Canadian fashion industry, was the decision of independent fashion designers to emphasize quality and sustainability through the decision to design, produce, and retail their collections locally. These strategies are defined by the label "Made in Canada," which is a prominent aspect of many independent fashion designer brands. Canada is experiencing a revival of "Made in Canada" production, with designers carving out new paths to production and consumption in the fashion industry (Delap 2017). This is particularly interesting, given the fact that while "Made in Canada" is increasingly synonymous with quality, the country does not have a history of garment manufacturing in the same way as countries such as Italy or the United Kingdom (Crewe 2013).

To better understand these processes in the contemporary Canadian fashion industry, this chapter will unpack the motivations and practices behind the "Made in Canada" label. While it will be demonstrated that there are a number of significant challenges facing independent fashion designers, it will also be argued that the Canadian case provides insights as to how to build a more sustainable fashion industry.

METHODOLOGY

This chapter draws on eighty-seven semi-structured interviews with members of the Canadian fashion industry; fifty-four independent fashion designers and thirty-three key informants. A diverse range of designers, in terms of age, gender, experience, background, education, location, and career stage were interviewed. Key informants included executives and managers from the industry (such as fashion weeks, PR and consulting firms), professors and deans of fashion education institutions, and government representatives. Following the work of Valentine (2005), an interview guide was utilized in order to promote consistency across interviews and prompt discussion. Interviews covered a range of questions, including the educational and/or previous employment experiences, motivations for entering the fashion industry, their design and decision-making process, and their experiences in the Canadian fashion industry more broadly.

STRUCTURE OF THE CANADIAN FASHION INDUSTRY: THE INDEPENDENT FASHION DESIGN SECTOR

In Canada, there are relatively few firm-based employment opportunities for those who want to work as fashion designers. Rather, a key pathway to employment for aspiring designers is for them to become entrepreneurs and start their own fashion label. As a result, the overwhelming majority of fashion design businesses in Canada are small firms of one to four employees (Statistics Canada 2013). The vast majority of independent fashion design businesses could be classified as one of the following firm structures: either a business focusing on a particular product niche (such as leather goods, rainwear, scarves, or jewelry) or a business that offers a "traditional" menswear or womenswear line offering two collections a year following the established fashion calendar (spring/summer and fall/winter).

Apparel Manufacturing in Canada

When developing this study, it was not a requirement that a designer manufacture their clothing in Canada. Rather, this was a key empirical finding that emerged through interviews. Of the fifty-four designers interviewed, forty-six manufactured their collections exclusively in Canada, four chose to use a combination of domestic and international manufacturers, and four designers manufactured their collections exclusively outside of Canada.

In Canada, the apparel manufacturing industry employs approximately 20,000 people (Statistics Canada 2017), with approximately one-half of all national garment production taking place in Quebec and 30 percent in Ontario (Contenta 2013). In recent years, a number of factors—including trade liberalization, the offshoring of production and restructuring in the fashion retail landscape more broadly—have all weakened the sector (Statistics Canada, 2017). As a result, employment in apparel manufacturing, domestic imports and gross domestic product have all declined in recent years (Statistics Canada 2017).

However, Statistics Canada has identified the shift toward the production of high-end, research and design-intensive garments as a key opportunity for the domestic apparel industry. In order to meet these demands, the sector must address its skilled labor shortage (Statistics Canada 2017). A number of new initiatives are aiming to fill these gaps, including the George Brown college Fashion Exchange factory in Toronto's Regent Park neighborhood, as well as the college's new graduate certificate program on Sustainable Fashion, both of which seek to meet the need for increased manufacturing capacity, knowledge transfer, and physical infrastructure in the local industry (Vasil 2017).

Interviews with independent designers revealed two dominant strategies for manufacturing locally: to either work with an existing local manufacturer or establish a studio space where production could take place (see: Figure 2.5.1). If one of these options was not feasible, interviews revealed it was also common—particularly for designers operating on a smaller scale—to either work out of their home and/or recruit freelance seamstresses via online platforms.

THE MOTIVATIONS BEHIND "MADE IN CANADA"

This section will explore the rationale behind the decision of independent fashion designers to forgo producing their collection abroad, and instead manufacture locally. While "Made in Canada" is a label on clothing, it is also part of an ethos and lifestyle that designers strongly believe in. For example, many of the independent fashion designers interviewed were committed to selling not only style but a more conscious way to consume and live (Fletcher 2007; Clark 2008). It was common for designers to remark on the fact they did not want to create "just" another fashion brand, and in particular, a fast fashion brand. Rather, they were much more interested in being closely connected to design, manufacturing, and retailing of their products.

Here, quality and craftsmanship were important themes. A commitment to local, high-quality production was connected to the objective of creating a safe and equitable working environment. Because designers were closely involved in the manufacturing processes of their garments, they were acutely aware of the immense amount of skill and physical labor that goes into making a garment. As a result, designers emphasized the

Figure 2.5.1 Comrags on Dundas West Street West in Toronto, Canada
An example of a design studio and manufacturing facility above their flagship retail shop. Comrags was established in 1983.
Photograph courtesy of the author

importance of offering fair wages, a safe working environment, and standard working hours.

In many instances, manufacturing at smaller scales would take place in the home or studio of a designer, while larger orders are filled through working with an established garment manufacturing facility typically in Ontario or Quebec. Importantly, it should also be stated that

for many designers, manufacturing abroad is an option, particularly if they want to produce at higher volumes. Designers often described that producing at a higher volume would mean sacrificing quality and/or their design aesthetic. For example, at larger volumes, it would not be cost-efficient to implement intricate patterns or complex design. On the other hand, local manufacturers would have much lower minimum orders, which not only allows independent fashion designers to be more flexible and agile in adjusting to meet consumer demand but also affords greater control over the design process.

The Challenges and Opportunities of Selling "Made in Canada"

While independent fashion designers have positioned themselves as a high-quality, higher-cost and more sustainable alternative, there are also a number in a retail market that is extremely polarized. In recent years, the retail landscape in Canada has been defined by two key trends. First, there has been an influx of high-end department stores and luxury brands, and second, there has been an expansion (albeit not always successful) of discount retailers into the Canadian market (Karabus 2015). As a result, the middle of the market is rapidly shrinking, with wealthy consumers trading "up" and consumers in regions of slower economic growth trading "down" and

Figure 2.5.2 A sandwich board in West Queen West, Toronto, Canada
Photograph courtesy of the author

shopping at discount or low-cost retailers (Karabus 2015).

In this context, independent fashion designers must place themselves somewhere within this constricted retail landscape. Many find themselves operating within a niche segment of the market, as their prices are noticeably higher than discount brands, but still considerably lower than global luxury brands. A key strategy to compete is to create unique retail environments where consumers can learn about the clothing and the processes and people that went into making it. As owning a standalone brand boutique is often a challenge for independent brands, independent fashion retailers are a key space in the retailing of "Made in Canada." Here, designers and retailers can work together to curate the customer experience, such as facilitating the building of personal relationships and knowledge exchange (Leslie, Brydges & Brail, 2015). In these spaces, designers can emphasize their accountability as business owners and/or manufactures and highlight the various sustainability principles behind the brand.

As a result of these high quality and sustainable local manufacturing processes, independent fashion designers stand by their clothing. For example, Figure 2.5.3 below is a note from the cash register of an independent fashion retailer

Figure 2.5.3 A retailer guaranteeing Canadian goods in Blyth, Canada
Photograph courtesy of the author

offering a longer guarantee/warranty on Canadian-made merchandise that is not applied to items that were manufactured abroad.

However, a key challenge facing designers still remains whether they can convince consumers to invest in "Made in Canada" clothing. For example, Beard (2008) argues that while a growing number of consumers are indeed aware of the ways in which fast fashion is made, many consumers have become accustomed to purchasing inexpensive clothing on a regular basis. Designers often revealed their frustration that on the one hand, consumers are increasingly aware of human and environmental costs of fast fashion, but on the other hand, ultimately it is the price that is the key determining factor in choosing whether or not to purchase an item.

Despite this challenge, "Made in Canada" is still part of a strategy to define a brand as an alternative—or "antidote"—to fast fashion (Leslie, Brail & Hunt, 2014). Ensuring the production of a quality garment is central to the value proposition of many independent fashion brands in Canada. In an interview, one designer compared her small business of three employees to a prominent fast fashion brand, stating that if you want to compete it is not enough to merely be the most creative designer. However, where her business *could* compete is through producing high-quality garments and operating in a higher-price market segment. Similarly, another designer described the process of educating the consumer on factors such as the cost of fabric and other aspects of the production process that are reflected in the cost of a "Made in Canada" garment (see also: Leslie, Brydges & Brail 2015). The notion of investment in clothing—often described as thinking about clothing in terms of the "cost per wear" of a particular garment—was central to many "Made in Canada" brands.

Finally, a relatively new development in the Canadian fashion industry is the rise of non-profit organizations aimed at raising consumer awareness of the sustainability challenges facing the fashion industry. At the same time, a number of these organizations also have developed mandates whereby they are advocating and supporting home-grown sustainable fashion design talent. For example, Fashion Takes Action runs a Canadian sustainable fashion award competition that showcases leading sustainable fashion designers, while INLAND is a bi-annual curated pop-up shop that brings together ethical fashion designers from across the country in intimate settings where consumers and designers have the opportunity to interact. As a result, the push for sustainability in the fashion industry is no longer coming solely from fashion designers, but is now also amplified by the voices of other influential actors.

CONCLUSION

This essay has provided an examination of the practices behind the implementation of sustainable fashion principles by independent fashion designers in Canada. Independent fashion designers have made the decision to position themselves in a niche sector of the fashion industry, forgoing the mass market appeal of their garments in favor of local, quality production and smaller collections, summed up by the label "Made in Canada." Contemporary independent fashion designers are redefining what it means to be a Canadian fashion designer and are building the reputation of Canadian fashion as synonymous with quality and sustainability. As a recent article in the *Toronto Star* proclaimed, "Made in Canada is Cool Again" (Delap 2017), which suggest that the sustainable fashion movement in Canada is indeed growing, slowly but surely.

However, it is important to not overly romanticize the "Made in Canada" strategy, as it is indeed an uphill battle for many independent fashion designers. While movements such as slow fashion are gaining momentum and awareness, these are still largely niche markets. Indeed, in North America, many consumers have become accustomed to being able to purchase large volumes of clothing at low costs. For independent fashion designers, operating in the sustainable fashion niche market is also highly precarious due to the difficulty of accessing consumers and generating new business, as well as challenges for growth within this niche and the Canadian fashion industry more broadly.

Independent fashion designers are continuing to develop strategies to strengthen and grow their businesses. Despite these challenges, the case of "Made in Canada" production provides an alternative model of a fashion industry that offers a more socially responsible and sustainable form of fashion, where locally embedded fashion communities, built on respect for those who make our clothes, are possible. Indeed, there is considerable potential for the Canadian fashion industry to be an example of the ways in which to create a domestic fashion industry that is more positive for people and place. However, much of this potential is currently untapped. There is a need to recognize the fashion industry in Canada as a creative industry and for investment in this sector. The current policy situation and lack of investment in the fashion industry leaves many independent fashion designers struggling to stay in business (Brydges & Pugh 2017). The fashion industry in Canada holds the potential to support the entrepreneurial endeavors of independent fashion designers, which could spill over to related sectors such as garment manufacturing, retail, and place-branding.

ACKNOWLEDGEMENT

Extracted from Brydges, T. (2017) "*Made in Canada*": *Local production networks in the Canadian fashion industry*, The Canadian Geographer / Le Geographe canadien. Reprinted with permission from John Wiley & Sons.

REFERENCES

Ainamo, A. (2014), "Rethinking Textile Fashion: New Materiality, Smart Products, and Upcycling," *Swedish Design Research Journal*, 12 (2): 53–60.

Agins, T. (1999), *The End of Fashion*. New York: William and Morrow Company.

Beard, N. D. (2008), "The Branding of Ethical Fashion and the Consumer: A Luxury Niche or Mass-market Reality?" *Fashion Theory,* 12(4): 447–67.

Bhardwaj, V., and A. Fairhurst (2010), "Fast Fashion: Response to Changes in the Fashion Industry," *The International Review of Retail, Distribution and Consumer Research,* 20(1): 165–73.

Bowen, G. A. (2009), "Document Analysis As a Qualitative Research Method," *Qualitative Research Journal*, 9(2): 27–40.

Brydges, T., and R. Pugh (2017), "An 'Orphan' Creative Industry: Exploring the Institutional Factors Constraining the Canadian Fashion Industry," *Growth and Change*, Early View.

Clark, H. (2008), "SLOW + FASHION: an Oxymoron— or a Promise for the Future . . .?" *Fashion Theory*, 12(4): 427–46.

Contenta, S. (2013, May 27), "Made in Canada: How globalization has hit the Canadian apparel industry," *The Toronto Star*. Available online at: https://www.thestar.com/news/insight/2013/05/27/made_in_canada_how_globalization_has_hit_the_canadian_apparel_industry.html

Crewe, L. (2013), "Tailoring and Tweed: Mapping the Spaces of Slow Fashion," in S. Bruzzi and P. Church Gibson (eds), *Fashion Cultures: Theories, Explorations and Analysis*. London: Routledge.

Delap, L. (2017, September 23), "Fashion designers are making manufacturing in Canada cool again," *The Toronto Star*. Retrieved from: https://www.thestar.com/life/fashion_style/2017/09/23/made-in-canada-is-cool-again.html

Ecowatch. (2015), "Fast Fashion is the Second Dirtiest Industry." http://www.ecowatch.com

Fletcher, K. (2007), "Slow Fashion," *The Ecologist*. Available online: http://www.theecologist.org/green_green_living/clothing/269245/slow_fashion.html

Joergens, C. (2006), "Ethical Fashion: Myth or Future Trend?", *Journal of Fashion Marketing and Management: An International Journal*, 10(3): 360–71.

Karabus, A. (2015), "Canadian retailers are increasingly facing stronger headwinds," *Retail Insider*. Available online at: http://www.retail-insider.com/retail-insider/2015/8/headwinds (accessed August 17, 2015).

Leslie, D., S. Brail, and M. Hunt (2014), "Crafting an Antidote to Fast Fashion: The Case of Toronto's Independent Fashion Design Sector," *Growth and Change*, 45(2): 222–39.

Leslie, D., T. Brydges, and S. Brail (2015), "Qualifying Aesthetic Values in the Experience Economy: The Role of Independent Fashion Boutiques in Curating Slow Fashion," in A. Lorentzen, K. Topso Larsen, and L. Schroder (eds), *Spatial Dynamics in the Experience Economy*, 88–102. New York: Routledge.

Quartz. (2016), "One chart shows how fast fashion is reshaping the global apparel industry." Available online at: https://qz.com/825554/hm-zara-primark-and-forever-21-one-euromonitor-chart-shows-how-fast-fashion-is-reshaping-the-global-apparel-industry/ (accessed November 30, 2016).

Reinach, S. (2005), "China and Italy: Fast Fashion Versus Prêt à Porter—Towards a new culture of fashion," *Fashion Theory*, 9(1): 43–56.

Statistics Canada (2013), "Canadian Business Patterns 'Other Specialized Design Services.'" Available online at: http://www.statcan.gc.ca/daily-quotidien/130205/dq130205d-eng.htm

Taplin, I. M. (2014), "Global Commodity Chains and Fast Fashion: How the Apparel Industry Continues to Re-invent Itself." *Competition & Change*, 18(3): 246–64.

The True Cost (2017), The True Cost Movie. Available online at: https://truecostmovie.com/

Tokatli, N. (2008), "Global Sourcing: Insights from the Global Clothing Industry—The Case of Zara, a Fast Fashion Retailer," *Journal of Economic Geography*, 8(1): 21–38.

Valentine, G. (2005), "Tell Me About. . .: Using Interviews as a Research Methodology," in R. Flowerdew and D. Martin (eds), *Methods in Human Geography: A Guide for Students Doing a Research Project*. Upper Saddle River, NJ: Prentice Hall.

Vasil, A. (2017, April 21), "George Brown launches sustainable fashion program to capitalize on 'reshored' manufacturing," *NOW Magazine*. Available online at: https://nowtoronto.com/api/content/932dd468-26c5-11e7-89be-0aea2a882f79/

A SPOTLIGHT ON: PRATT INSTITUTE/BROOKLYN FASHION + DESIGN ACCELERATOR
"Keeping the Cart Attached To the Horse"

Deb Johnson/Pratt Brooklyn Fashion + Design Accelerator, USA

When it comes to asking the industry about the environmental and ethical impacts of technology on fashion, it is rather like standing in an echo chamber.

Innovators aren't considering sustainability when they are thinking about integrating new technologies into textiles. Think of innovation as a horse that takes off when it gets excited by a brash new idea. In the mad dash for the new, sustainability inevitably is left behind to be considered at a later date, if at all. In today's world we must consider the consequences of these new ideas, new materials, and new uses from the beginning. In the existing slowness of the apparel industry to adopt new technologies I see a real opportunity to change the existing innovation paradigm and to design really "smart" garments and functional textiles from the outset.

Pratt Institute | Brooklyn Fashion + Design Accelerator (Pratt/BF+DA) is committed to keeping the sustainability "cart" attached to the innovation "horse" as the industry advances. As garments and textiles get connected to the Internet, or nano-materials change simple yarns into microbial factories that interact with the body, or thread becomes a rechargeable power source, fabrics take on a new dynamic. The purpose of the garment adds a critical factor in determining environmental trade offs. For example, if I make a sweater less recyclable but the product reduces stress for someone in hospice, is it worth it? The BF+DA's philosophy is to consider the complete life cycle of all products and make keen decisions about the use of materials and manufacturing methods and thoughtfully consider the product's usefulness.

The last step is to design for when a product reaches end-of-life by asking the question: how can it be recycled, upcycled, or redefined?

To take on these challenges requires bringing together multiple perspectives. A sweater isn't just a sweater anymore and requires collaborative innovation teams that can think with a systems approach as ideas emerge. This means effectively tapping the knowledge of engineers, designers, coders, manufacturers, and social scientists. At the BF+DA we are assembling digital, manufacturing equipment, as well as sustainability resources and creating a place for this unique systems-centred design approach to emerge.

The Pratt/BF+DA has a unique combination of design power, the ability to design for manufacture, and the capacity to prototype and manufacture in small runs. We are leveraging this with other knowledge provided by a curated group of academic and industry partners that occupy pre-competitive, swing space for research. Collectively we are developing a new language and models to this systems-based approach for responsible, R&D and design.

In our ongoing project, TEK-TILES has assembled over thirty graduate and undergraduate students from twelve universities, that represent design, material science, textile engineering, design ethnography and Computer Science. Over ten weeks we connected the teams with access to our advanced manufacturing lab. The results have been remarkable—yielding new materials and potential products. Most importantly, the team assessed and reviewed the environmental impacts of their ideas as they were designing them and at the end of the week gathered together over "Pizza, Beer, and Ethics" to consider the implications of technology. These conversations were critical, thought-provoking discussions that looked square on at the consequences of our research—keeping the cart attached to the horse.

Sustainable technology isn't all about putting electronics into garments. Digitalization is quickly changing the industry from 3D virtual draping and design tools, to digital patternmaking and cutting, to body scanning that will allow for guided customization, replacing prêt-à-porter

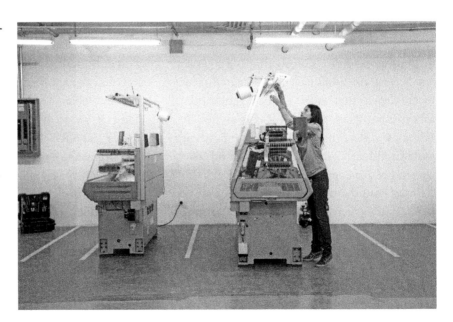

Figure 2.6.1 Kelly Puertas, Pratt Institute/BF+DA Knitwear Director, readying a wholegarment Shima Seiki knitting machine in the p.Lab
Image reproduced courtesy of Deb Johnson, Pratt Institute's Brooklyn Fashion + Design

Figure 2.6.2 Signal bicycle jacket created by Pratt Institute's BF+DA TEK-TILES team
Image reproduced courtesy of Deb Johnson, Pratt Institute's Brooklyn Fashion + Design

Figure 2.6.3 The TEK-TILES team at Pratt Institute's BF+DA
Image reproduced courtesy of Deb Johnson, Pratt Institute's Brooklyn Fashion + Design

with automatized bespoke production on demand. These technologies will shift the amount of waste in the design process and manufacturing process, which can only be a good thing. However, there is a potential backlash to consider. The battle cry of Fashion Revolution's "Who made my clothes?" may be overshadowed by the reduction in jobs as robots take over garment production. This is a growing area for concern across many job sectors. Sustainability of jobs is becoming an important consideration within the value chain.

....

How will we redefine "work" in the twenty-first century?

EUROPE PART 3

CHAPTER 3.1

SUSTAINABILITY AND GARMENT LONGEVITY IN THE UK HIGH STREET

Alison Gwilt, University of South Australia, Australia
Alana James, Northumbria University, UK

INTRODUCTION

Through a circular economy lens, this essay explores the ways in which UK producers and consumers can extend the life of high street fashion garments. In the United Kingdom, the sale of mass-produced fashion products has typically been the domain of the high street retailers. Traditionally, items sold in this market are designed for aesthetic appeal, and they are frequently constructed from inexpensive materials that keep the items affordable and (easily) replaceable. However, despite enticing consumers with lower price points the UK high street has been in rapid decline, with retailers encountering decreasing profits and country-wide store closures. Although UK consumers are still purchasing fashion products, over recent years their shopping preferences, needs, and demands have changed.

In this essay we explore the notion of circularity as an alternative to the linear production and consumption model that currently dominates the UK high street. We highlight some of the new business concepts and industry initiatives that are supporting UK producers and consumers to transform their perception and behavioral patterns toward the creation and use of fashion products. Further, we reflect on how engaging with circularity may be able to provide new opportunities for the UK high street.

THE UK HIGH STREET

The UK has an established relationship with fashion, where British design and manufacture is recognized internationally for quality and innovation in the industry. Brands such as Burberry remain steeped in British identity, with their iconic checked fabric being known globally as a symbol of its heritage. Other brands such as Vivienne Westwood and Paul Smith continue to strive forward with innovative, contemporary design while evoking nostalgic memories of a vibrant manufacturing scene, seen decades earlier.

Historically, the UK manufacturing industry was a hive of activity, representing the iconic style, creative design, and quality production for which Britain had become renowned. However, in more recent times, this view of British fashion has changed somewhat with the UK high street rapidly in decline, giving way to alternative shopping methods, a change in consumer needs, and an emerging market sector, all of which have contributed to a decrease in sales, footfall, and the popularity of the traditional shopping high street. Since the recession in 2008 there has been a knock-on effect in the profitability of high street stores, with forecasts expecting a 22 percent decline in the number of stores on the UK high street between 2013–18. A further 100,000 stores are predicted to close between 2020–30, contributing further to the decline of the traditional shopping high street (Milt 2015).

There are many challenges facing this cornerstone of British fashion, where an adaption of opening hours, local provisions and product offerings is needed. The change in purchasing behavior of the UK consumer can be evidenced as early as the 1960s with the emergence of the supermarkets, which compromised the sustainability of local, independent stores in the town center. This new approach to shopping provided the consumer with convenient alternatives, offering many types of goods under one roof, often with amenities such as toilets and cafes to further appeal to the customer. Today, supermarkets offer a vast range of products, services, and amenities including free parking, travel agents, and even tanning shops. Included within this diversification of goods is fashion, with all four of the large supermarkets now offering fashion collections in-store. This emergence of fashion within supermarkets has developed a new market sector within the industry, further contributing to the value sector.

The ever-evolving market is moving rapidly toward online purchasing as a more convenient method of shopping, with customers not even needing to leave their homes. The growth of Internet sales is again having a huge impact on the UK high street, with 16.8 percent of all UK sales currently being made online (Milt 2015). This is said to increase to approximately 40 percent by 2030 with a growing number of consumers turning to the Internet to purchase goods in preference to the local in-store alternatives. This too is evident across the fashion sector where online retailers are said to be stripping the shirt from the back of high street clothing stores. However, online purchasing is not remaining static either, with retailers such as Amazon now offering one-hour delivery slots in central London. Former retail correspondent, Graham Ruddick, believes that this approach is destroying the difference between online and in-store purchasing, with almost instantaneous delivery closing this gap.

With the increase of online and out-of-town shopping, iconic British high street brands are taking a hit in not only sales but also their presence on the high street altogether. Marks and Spencer (M&S) for example, synonymous with British culture, has experienced a decline in clothing sales year on year, with their online sales also suffering an 18 percent drop in 2016 (Bradshaw 2017). This was emphasized further with clothing sales declining a further 5.9 percent in the first three months of 2017 (Wood 2017). British Home Stores (BHS) is another example of a household British brand that was once a booming business. The company fell into administration in 2016, losing a total of 11,000 jobs (Ruddick et al. 2016). More recently the British clothing brand Jaeger, which during its heyday had dressed celebrities such as Audrey Hepburn and Marilyn Monroe, entered administration in April 2017. These examples begin to paint the picture currently seen in the UK market, as retailers do not keep pace with the changes and challenges facing the future of the high street (Neate 2017).

In addition to the high street, the fashion industry has also been changing, with an increasing emphasis on the lower, value end of the market sector. The emergence of the fast fashion business model has developed in response to consumer demand of large quantities of cheap clothing in preference to fewer pieces at a higher quality. The speed that these items are brought to market is also alarming, with catwalk-inspired pieces being delivered to store in just six weeks in some cases. This increase in speed puts immense pressure on the fashion supply chain, risking social and environmental compromise. The desire from consumers for such fashion collections demonstrates the dramatic change in purchasing behavior, where society is in favor of a more disposable system in preference of a circular, sustainable fashion industry.

When considering the bigger picture, however, it is the real core issues affecting the fashion industry that need to be addressed. The speed of consumption and the consumer's preference of cheap, mass-market product purchased at convenience is eliminating the traditional shopping high street as we know it. The development of the internet and online shopping needs to be incorporated within the fashion business model not just seen as the enemy. However, it is also the responsibility of high street stores to offer the customer something they cannot get elsewhere through experiential design. The atmosphere and service the consumer experiences in-store needs to be the appeal in differentiating online and in-store purchasing, regaining the appeal of the UK fashion high street.

THE UK FASHION CONSUMER

The recession in the UK in 2008 has acted as a catalyst for the change in consumer purchasing behavior across the consumer goods sector. The average consumer is now purchasing larger quantities of cheaper goods as a direct response to the impact on their personal finances. However, the need to feel they are purchasing as they did prior to the recession sees consumers resorting to cheaper goods from the lower value sector of the market. This too is true in fashion, where the development of the fast fashion business model facilitates the consumer's need in clothing, with stores such as Primark and supermarket collections responding directly. The low value market sector in fashion has been likened to McDonald's: cheap, fast, mass-produced, hassle-free, and reliant on social or environmental exploitation (Ritch & Schroder 2009). However, this consumer model of purchasing large quantities of cheap clothing brings new challenges to the fashion industry. Due to the volume and low cost of the garments being purchased, the consumer not only takes relatively little care of the clothing, but they are also more inclined to dispose of it relatively easily. This throw away culture is of concern and has much larger implications with regards to the environment during the disposal process.

When considering the broader context of these issues, it can be observed that the fashion life cycle remains linear and lacks the opportunity for circularity or longevity. The fast fashion business model is the very antithesis of sustainability with neither the garment itself nor the processes involved in the production, use, or disposal considering the implications for the future. The need to engage the consumer in sustainable values has the potential to change attitudes and consequently purchasing behavior, but there are several challenges currently preventing further engagement. First, the average fashion consumer has relatively little knowledge regarding the sustainable implications of the production of garments. This lack of knowledge and awareness is said to be preventing further consumer engagement, leaving them unable to make an informed decision.

The role taken by industry also contributes to the engagement of consumers with sustainability, with accessibility and availability of responsible products also playing a part. On the average fashion high street, there is little responsible clothing available for the consumer to purchase, and where this does occur, it is often in segregated collections or certain product lines. An example of this would be the Conscious Collection by H&M that promotes the use of recycled polyester fibers in the production of selected garments. However, this segregation can often send mixed messages to the consumer, highlighting only further the lack of engagement with sustainable values with the remainder of the garments in store. That said, these initiatives do play a role in the knowledge and awareness levels of consumers, bringing to their attention the possibilities for further circularity in the production of fashion.

The current consumer purchasing model also presents not only the type of consumption as an issue but also the speed of consumption and the consequential lack of value in clothing. How to create this value remains a challenge, relying on the consumer having the ability to be empathetic toward the environmental and social impact in the fashion supply chain. The creation of empathy assumes knowledge and awareness of sustainability on behalf of the consumer and as previously discussed these levels are also positioned as a challenge. The engagement of the consumer with responsible practices in fashion remains a complex and ongoing problem. There are several unanswered questions being posed that need to be addressed systematically in order to create real change. This development also relies on the engagement of several key stakeholders, including the consumer and retailer, in a united approach toward a phased approach to change.

FASHION AND THE CIRCULAR ECONOMY IN THE UK

Across the UK a wide range of fashion brands and retailers, non-governmental organizations (NGOs) and consumer activist groups have been raising awareness to the impacts of clothing. Within the industry there is now a greater awareness of cleaner and more efficient processes, an effort to engage with responsible manufacturing, and an understanding of the need to promote improved consumer behavior. Increasingly, a number of UK fashion brands are partnering with ethical manufacturers, or working with Fairtrade farmers and growers. Moreover, many designers are now sourcing fabrics and materials from textile companies that use low impact processes, or utilize textile waste as "food" for new product lines (Black 2012). While more radical waste-saving approaches, such as zero waste patternmaking, are still in their infancy in the industry, large companies are quickly beginning to "close the loop" by capitalizing on new developments in fiber-to-fiber recycling technology.

Although efforts have been made, in some quarters of the industry, to reduce impacts across the design and manufacture of clothing products, there has been a slower engagement in capitalizing on the use of design-led approaches to influence improvements during the use of a garment. In part this is because efforts have been put on improving the business-as-usual current linear system, which as the Ellen MacArthur Foundation (2017) argues has seen the industry divert its attention away from "… taking an upstream, systemic approach to tackling the root cause of the system's wasteful nature directly, in particular low clothing utilization and low rates of recycling after use." Approximately 350,000 tonnes of discarded clothing is sent to landfill in the UK and much of this waste is generated because consumers frequently discard clothing early, even if a product is still functional (WRAP 2012). However, consumers can actively help extend the lifetime of a garment if attitudes and practices toward clothing care improved, then, according to WRAP (2012, 2013a), the environmental footprint of clothing could be reduced.

Despite a number of major UK brands and retailers visibly promoting their sustainability credentials, there is still a reliance on using poor-quality materials and manufacturing processes for trend-driven fashion products in the UK high street. At the same time it is known that the decisions made during the development of a garment can affect the product's longevity; a garment's physical durability is compromised when low-quality textiles and processes are used, while the aesthetics of fashion can quickly "date" as subsequent seasonal collections emerge (Gwilt & Pal 2017). Additionally, consumers incorrectly assume that a designer-branded product with a high price point correlates with an extended garment durability.

While it is argued that brands and retailers need to explore approaches that extend the lifetime of garments, longevity has to be considered in terms of both the physical and empathetic qualities. And this needs to be considered in relation to the consumer's expectations, which is complex. Consumers are usually satisfied if a garment continues to function well during its use, but they tend to be indifferent as to whether the product should last for any longer than this (Cox et al. 2013). This perspective, however, should not distract brands and retailers from making good, responsible decisions about their products. The opportunity for the fashion industry in a circular economy is to not only extend the physical life of garments for as long as possible to keep materials in circulation, but also to encourage a change in the attitudes and practices that consumers have toward clothing lifetimes. The challenge for the UK fashion industry is to achieve these aims and remain economically positive while operating in a highly competitive environment.

HOW CAN THE LIFE OF MASS MANUFACTURED GARMENTS BE EXTENDED?

In a circular economy, the fashion industry, as the Ellen MacArthur Foundation (2017) sees it, should strive to ensure that "… clothes, fabric, and fibres are kept at their highest value during use, and re-enter the economy after use, never ending up as waste." While this alternate model for a "new textiles economy" is intended to sit alongside a linear fashion system that utilizes approaches focused on reducing negative impacts, the circular vision for fashion is "… one that is restorative and regenerative by design and provides benefits for business, society, and the environment" (2017).

Currently there is a motivation within the UK industry to investigate not only the "speedier" fiber-to-fiber recycling approaches, but also the "slower" routes to extending the life of clothes. Through a circular economy lens newly developed garments can be designed for an increased active life as they become "fit for purpose," desirable to consumers, and developed for longevity (Claxton et al. 2015; Gwilt & Pal 2017). In the UK, value-clothing retailer Tesco, through its F&F label, has been working in conjunction with the NGO Waste and Resources Action Programme (WRAP) on how to enhance the durability of affordable garments. Moreover WRAP has run similar exploratory trials with other UK brands and retailers including ASOS, John Lewis, and Ted Baker. Although it is difficult to ascertain how much of this work has trickled into the products sold in-store, it is, however, a step in the right direction. It is important to note that the mechanisms through which the life of garments can be extended may be approached from different perspectives, and we discuss some of these methods in the following examples.

Creating Garments for Longevity

A concern that is frequently voiced about the proposition to extend the garment lifetime is that there is no economic incentive for producers to move away from manufacturing large volumes of clothing. However, this perspective ignores new potential business models for fashion brands, which instead may focus on ". . . quality, durability and services, such as repair" (Oxborrow 2016).

In the UK, designer Tom Cridland[1] established a menswear fashion brand with the intention of developing garments designed to last for thirty years (Figure 3.1.1). While Cridland's range of T-shirts, jackets, and trousers are intentionally aesthetically classic, the garments are physically robust because of the decisions made during development; garment materials and construction methods are selected for their durability. If a product suffers a failure within thirty years of purchase, the item is repaired or replaced for

Figure 3.1.1 The "30 Year" menswear collection from UK designer, Tom Cridland
Image reproduced courtesy of Tom Cridland

free, although such occurrences are typically infrequent for Cridland's brand (Henderson 2017). The garments retail at a higher price point than lesser quality comparable products, but in providing an extended garment lifetime Cridland's products may be considered, in the long term, as good value for money in terms of price per wear.

Engaging Consumers: "Love Your Clothes"

The NGO WRAP works with the clothing and textiles industry, academic research, government,

Figure 3.1.2a WRAP's "Love Your Clothes" campaign aims to encourage people to value and make the most of their clothes
Image reproduced courtesy of Andrew Gilbert, WRAP UK

Figure 3.1.2b Textile researcher Angharad McLaren creatively upcycles and darns garments for the "Love your Clothes" campaign
Image reproduced courtesy of Angharad McLaren and Jack Stott, Local Editor at John Lewis Aberdeen

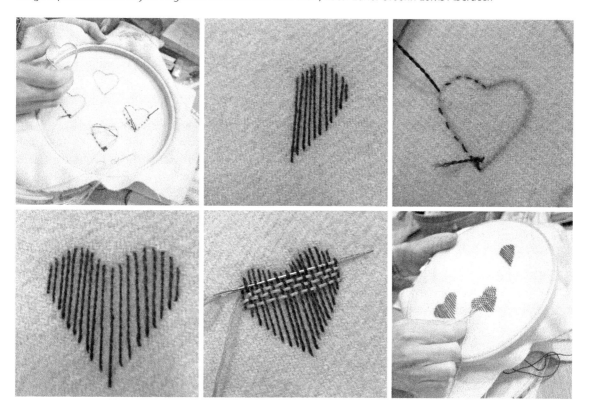

and local communities to support economic and environmental action. Of the many initiatives established by WRAP, the "Love Your Clothes"[2] (Figure 3.1.2a) campaign was developed to help organizations influence behavioral change among consumers. Resource advice is provided online on garment care and repair (demonstrated in Figure 3.1.2b), remanufacturing methods, and recycling / reuse ideas. Consumers are also actively encouraged to "get involved" by posting quick tips, video clips, and blog posts. While the campaign aims to support consumers to extend the life of their clothing, it also seeks to educate consumers in making better purchasing choices by highlighting the durable attributes that are typically found in different clothing types.

WRAP holds a unique position in that it works to support producers and retailers to engage with strategies that help extend the lifetime of clothing, while encouraging consumers to actively participate with clothing choices. "Love Your Clothes" is successfully raising awareness to the need for consumers to value what they wear, and yet at the same time it attempts to fill a void that has emerged between producers and consumers since the growth of fast fashion in the UK high street.

Proposing Services, Not Making Products

The UK high street has typically been the home for department stores, large international fashion brands, and domestic fashion labels and retailers who rely on selling (large) volumes of clothing to increase profits. In recent years there has been a wave of small, niche companies and entrepreneurs that have turned to provide fashion services in place of products, which as Oxborrow (2016) notes is a challenge if we consider fashion as a large scale business. But the success of fashion services may lie in

> … providing added sales value through deeper customer satisfaction and loyalty can compensate for lost unit sales. Add to this income from services, such as mending or leasing, and reduced waste from over-production and markdowns, and a smaller industry could perhaps be just as profitable, but more sustainable.

"Walk the Wear"[3] (see Figure 8, plate section) is a UK-based online clothes subscription service. Created by Zoe Partridge, the company allows subscribers to hire a specific number of designer items a month, selected from over 700 products kept in the company's library. Subscribers can visit the workshop space or choose online, and they are delivered in twenty-four hours. While hire agencies often lease items for a short period of time, Walk the Wear subscribers can lease garments for a month (or longer), or swap articles earlier for other styles, and garment returns and cleaning is included in the subscription fee. While the concept of hiring clothes is not new, the company differs in that it works with some of the newly emerging "luxury" ethical and sustainability design labels to make fashion accessible and—starting from £60 per month—affordable to high-fashion-conscious consumers. While Partridge does not claim to place sustainability at the forefront of the business, it importantly highlights to fashion consumers— the people so often criticized in the sustainable fashion literature—that products do not need to be owned, and that there are economic and "experience" benefits to sharing products.

CONCLUSION

Fashion brands and retailers on the UK high street have not on the whole exploited the opportunity to create longer-lasting garments or provide / support fashion service initiatives. Typically fashion consumers are not aware of the materials or production methods used in the industrial system, nor are they aware of the range of approaches that can be used to extend garment lifetimes. At the same time the mainstream UK fashion system is generally made up of profit-driven businesses that are dependent on a seasonal cycle of producing and on selling large quantities of clothing to meet economic returns. However, in the examples discussed in this essay there are clearly new avenues within which the UK high street brand or retailer can explore approaching the extension of garment lifetimes.

If the UK high street fashion brands and retailers envisaged longevity integrated within the business strategy, and embraced different business models, then perhaps consumers may be encouraged to change their consumption behaviors. But there are a number of factors that need to be considered when designing garments and services for longevity. For example, there has to be a greater awareness for the role of design and production in addressing design aesthetics; size and fit concerns; and providing greater durability. Moreover consumers need further support through enhanced communication and after sales services (WRAP 2013; Gwilt & Pal 2017). Additionally, in moving toward extending the garment lifetime, it will be imperative to emphasize "longevity" as a valuable clothing attribute, and reposition "disposable" garments as undesirable (Gwilt & Pal 2017).

NOTES

1. www.tomcridland.com/
2. www.loveyourclothes.org.uk
3. www.wearthewalk.co.uk/

REFERENCES

Black, S (2012), *The Sustainable Fashion Handbook*. Thames and Hudson: London.

Bradshaw, J. (2017), "Online retail booms as high street struggles," The *Daily Telegraph*, January 8, 2017. Available online at: http://www.telegraph.co.uk/business/2017/01/08/online-retail-booms-high-street-struggles/ (accessed June 19, June 2017).

Claxton, S., T. Cooper, H. Hill, H., and K. Holbrook (2015), "Opportunities and challenges of new product development and testing for longevity in clothing," in *Proceedings of the PLATE 2015 conference*. Nottingham: Nottingham Trent University.

Cox, J., S. Griffith, S. Giorgi, and G. King (2013), "Consumer Understanding of Product Lifetimes," *Resources, Conservation and Recycling*, 79: 21–29.

Ellen MacArthur Foundation (2017), "A new textiles economy: Redesigning fashion's future." Available online at http://www.ellenmacarthurfoundation.org/publications (accessed January 8, 2018).

Gwilt, A., and R. Pal (2017), "Conditional garment design for longevity," in *Proceedings of the PLATE 2017 conference*. Delft: TU Delft. Available online at: https://www.diva-portal.org/smash/get/diva2:1166835/FULLTEXT01.pdf (accessed January 7, 2018).

Henderson, P. (2017), "Meet Tom Cridland, the fashion designer whose clothes last 30 years," *GQ* magazine, October 6, 2017. Available online at: http://www.gq-magazine.co.uk/article/meet-the-fashion-designer-whose-clothes-last-30-years (accessed January 6, 2018).

Milt, D. J. (2015), "2030: The Death of the High Street," Parcelhero Industry Report: Brentford.

Neate, R. (2017), "Jaeger collapses into administration putting 680 jobs at risk," The *Guardian*, April 10, 2017. Available online at: https://www.theguardian.com/business/2017/apr/10/jaeger-goes-into-administration (accessed: June 20, 2017).

Oxborrow, L. (2016), "A circular economy is about more than clothes," The *Conversation*, November 21, 2016. Available online at: https://theconversation.com/a-circular-fashion-economy-is-about-more-than-clothes-68787 (accessed December 17, 2017).

Ritch, E., and M. Schroder (2009), "What's in Fashion? Ethics? An Exploration of Ethical Fashion Consumption as Part of Modern Family Life."

Available online at: http://www.northumbria.ac.uk/
static/5007/despdf/events/era.pdf (accessed
September 24, 2010).

Ruddick, G., S. Butler, and N. Fletcher (2016), "BHS
collapses into administration as rescue deal fails," The
Guardian, April 25, 2016. Available online at: https://
www.theguardian.com/business/2016/apr/25/
bhs-heading-for-administration-as-rescue-deal-fails
(accessed June 20, 2017).

Wood, Z. (2017), "M&S profits dive by nearly two-thirds
as clothing sales slide," The *Guardian*, May 24, 2017.
Available online at: https://www.theguardian.com/
business/2017/may/24/m-and-s-profits-clothing-
sales-restructuring (accessed June 20, 2017).

WRAP (2012), "Valuing Our Clothes: The True Cost of
How We Design, Use and Dispose of Clothing in the
UK." Banbury: WRAP. Available online at: http://
www.wrap.org.uk/sustainable-textiles/valuing-our-
clothes%20

WRAP (2013), "Design for Longevity: Guidance on
Increasing the Active Life of Clothing." Available
online at: http://www.wrap.org.uk/sites/files/wrap/
Design%20for%20Longevity%20Report_0.pdf
(accessed July 17, 2017).

WRAP (2017), "Improving the durability of denim
jeans." [Online]. Available at: http://www.wrap.org.
uk/sites/files/wrap/FF%20case%20study.pdf
(Accessed on February 21, 2018).

CHAPTER 3.2

A SPOTLIGHT ON: SUSTAINABLE FASHION IN THE NETHERLANDS

Mariangela Lavanga, Erasmus University Rotterdam, NL

The Netherlands is at the forefront of sustainable development and the circular economy. Numerous Dutch-based civil-society organizations and consultancies—MADE-by, Fair Wear Foundation, Circle Economy, Clean&Unique, Marieke Eyskoot, and W.Green, to name just a few—have been active in helping companies and designers to go green while at the same time increasing consumer awareness about sustainability. When looking at the role of the government, it is worthwhile mentioning the "Green Deal" approach that came into being in 2011. Green Deals are mutual agreements between the Dutch government, companies, civil organizations, and other parties to remove barriers and accelerate the transition to a sustainable economy. For example, the Natural Fibres Green Deal is a pilot project to stimulate the cultivation of hemp for the textile industry. More recently, in July 2016, a wide coalition of Dutch fashion brands, government agencies, unions, trade and civil-society organizations have signed the Agreement on a Sustainable Garment and Textile Sector. The aim is to increase sustainability within the international garment and textile supply chain, especially with respect to improving working conditions and reducing environmental pollution.

Dutch education institutions have also an important role in fostering future designers and entrepreneurs to embrace sustainability in all its aspects: from integrating sustainability in their curricula to organizing symposia (e.g. "Beyond Green" by the Amsterdam Fashion Institute, "What's Next? The Future of the Fashion Industry and Pioneers in Fashion: Better and Greener" by Erasmus University Rotterdam, Creating 010, and Het Nieuwe Instituut) and running projects that focus on sustainable material and (local) production processes (e.g. Going Eco, Going Dutch, and Closing the Loop by the Centre of Expertise Future Makers). The future generation of designers can ultimately act as a Trojan horse that triggers change from the inside out of the fashion system.

When looking at Dutch independent fashion designers and other smaller fashion companies, we could argue that more or less all of them are going green. For them, it is easier to control and green the supply chain not only given their smaller size but also their ability to be more flexible in terms of production volume, process, and distribution. They incorporate sustainability in their business models and, in doing so, they stand out from the crowd, carving out a unique niche in the hyper competitive fashion industry. Three interrelated main trends can be distinguished in their approaches to sustainability:

1. clean materials and recycling;
2. craftsmanship and timeless design;
3. hi-tech processes and smart textiles.

The brand MUD Jeans tackles social and environmental sustainability. It has a network of factories that ensures fair working conditions, and it aims at reducing environmental pollution and waste. MUD Jeans mostly uses BCI (Better Cotton Initiative), organic and recycled cotton (see Figure 3.2.1). It works with a loan system, where consumers can lease a pair of jeans (€7.5 per month) that can be repaired for free; after one year, consumers can decide whether to keep the jeans or replace them with a new pair. The old jeans will be upcycled and turned into a cool vintage item. When the jeans cannot be upcycled any further, the material is recycled and used to produce a new pair.

Craftsmanship and designing with sustainability in mind (timeless design, zero waste) are priorities of an increasing amount of Dutch independent fashion designers, such as Monique van Heist, Elsien Gringhuis, Mevan Kaluarachchi, Joline Jolink, Margreeth Oolsthorn, and Barbara Langendijk. They tackle not only environmental and social sustainability, but also cultural sustainability, for example by preserving artisan culture. Elsien Gringhuis (see Figure 9, plate section) only uses natural textiles and highly innovative patterns to reduce waste; she produces everything in the Netherlands and she does not develop new collections every season but designs a basic collection that she calls "Books." A number of styles, so-called "Chapters," then complement these "Books" regularly. It is a similar idea to the continuous collection "hellofashion" by Monique van Heist and the "Wardrobe" collection developed by Mevan Kaluarachchi.

Figure 3.2.1 Cropped Mimi model by MUD Jeans. Reproduced courtesy of MUD Jeans, from their Lookbook 2016
Image reproduced courtesy of Urte Kundrotaite

The Textile Lab within the Textile Museum in Tilburg has been particularly important for designers that use high technology and smart textile, for example Conny Groenewegen, Pauline van Dongen, Martijn van Strien, Marina Toeters, and Karin Vlug. In the Textile Lab they are able to experiment with different techniques and yarns and co-create with in-house product development and technical experts. Conny Groenewegen developed and produced the "01 Collection" for her new label Electric Co within the Textile Lab. The designs are produced on demand and in limited edition, employing 3D knitting with wool bio-fur yarn and recycled polyester monofilaments (see Figure. 3.2.2).

A critical mass of civil-society organizations, government initiatives, education institutions, large and small companies in the fashion and textile industries are clearly paving the way for a fashion revolution in the Netherlands.

CHAPTER 3.3

SUSTAINABILITY IN THE TEXTILES AND CLOTHING FASHION INDUSTRY
An Ongoing Study in Portugal

Ana Cristina Broega, University of Minho, Portugal

INTRODUCTION

The waste from fashion is a problem that has significantly increased due to the growth of "fast fashion," pushed by increasing efficiency in production, logistics, and marketing, all of which encourage consumers to buy more clothes and discard them quickly. Despite the aesthetic requirements of today's customers, design has an urgent ethical obligation to incorporate sustainability in the decision-making process. This will make a positive contribution to the global environmental, social, and economical agenda.

The challenge for professional designers is twofold: they must meet increasingly complex requirements of a changing society, and at the same time aim to achieve sustainability throughout the entire product life cycle. Such challenges are exacerbated by a lack of sustainability competency among designers, as well as other barriers including the poor externalization of sustainability costs, and a lack of both customer awareness and effective legislation. In this chapter I present an overview of sustainability practices in the Portuguese Fashion Industry (Textiles & Clothing) starting with a brief characterization of the sector, followed by perspectives of sustainable consumption practices in Portugal. Finally I will share some examples of successful brands demonstrating good practice in working within a framework of sustainable strategies.

The examples discussed in this chapter are based on small-business models that are closely linked to fashion design products. They present a focus on the choice for more sustainable materials, with many brands adopting organic, recyclable and/or biodegradable, and/or cruelty-free options. An alternative approach is related to upcycling, which extends the life cycle of materials and/or garments through redesign. Many brands, organizations, and companies play on the values of "ethical fashion for sustainability" which is based on "social and cultural responsibility" (attempts to work for social development—conducted mainly by artisans—by means of the contribution they make to improve the quality of life of those involved, for cultural, economic, and social enrichment). At an industrial level, environmental sustainability is the most discussed and prioritized. However, the promotion of Fairtrade or fair work practices, with the aim of creating professional training and opportunities for local communities that ensure good working conditions, while respecting the environment and prevailing cultures, is also valued in this sector.

In conclusion, I highlight the need for improved brand communication. Portuguese brands that adopt good sustainable practices need to communicate their values in a transparent and systematic way. It is not enough to make an effort to become sustainable in practice; it is necessary to know how to communicate these values.

THE TEXTILE AND CLOTHING INDUSTRY IN PORTUGAL

The Textile and Clothing Industry (TCI) in Portugal is one of the most significant business sectors at national level, and accounts for roughly 17 percent of gross value added (GVA) and 19 percent of employment in the country's manufacturing industry. It contributes up to 10 percent of total national exports and 8 percent of manufacturing industry turnover (APT 2016).

According to data from the Portuguese Textile and Clothing Industries Association (APT) Directory 2016, the Portuguese textile industry produces €6.4 billion and generates a turnover of €6.8 billion, of which €4.8 billion are the result of export activity. It exports to more than 180 countries around the world, corresponding to about 10 percent of all sales of Portugal abroad

and a net balance in the national transactions balance of more than €1 billion, thereby clearly playing an important strategic role in the Portuguese economy (APT 2016).

The sector comprises approximately 6,000 corporations and 5,600 individual companies, which employ roughly 130,000 direct workers (mostly located in Northern Portugal in cities such as Porto, Braga, Guimarães, and Famalicão; the roles in these locations represent 20 percent of employment in the national Textile and Clothing Industry) (APT 2016).

The Portuguese Textile and Clothing Sector has made remarkable progress in restructuring during the last few years, and has evolved to provide a multi-faceted activity, which is based on creativity, scientific, and technological knowledge. The development of innovative textiles with varied functionalities and high performance, as well as the use of sustainable eco-processing technologies, are already a reality in the Portuguese fashion and the textile industry. The development of technical fibers and yarns has contributed to the establishment of new frontiers in the use of sustainable fashion products, as well as functionality, safety, well-being and comfort. At the same time Portugal continues to maintain "private label" industrial activities with a significant level of sophistication and the highest level of product and process engineering. It should also be noted that the Portuguese TCI comprises mainly small- and medium-sized enterprises (SMEs) that have a strong family and traditional structure and are well known for their flexibility, rapid response, know-how, and innovation.

In anticipating differentiation and innovation, the TCI in Portugal has invested in the development of its own brands, including the "Made In Portugal" retail concepts and products, while simultaneously working in its traditional markets, such as the United States and Central Europe, as well as emerging markets such as the United Arab Emirates, Nordic countries, Japan, Singapore, and Eastern Europe. In line with international trends, the ATP—in partnership with the Citeve[1]—launched the Green Textiles Club project, which aims "to promote the competitiveness of SMEs in the Textile and Clothing Sector through the creation of a club of sustainable companies, to exchange experiences, define common strategies for the sector, promote the SteP[2] certification and the incorporation of quality and risk management (ISO 9001: 2015), with a view to the sustainable development of companies" (APT 2017). Many textile companies have joined this project (APT 2017), most of which operate in the private label system.

SUSTAINABLE CONSUMPTION IN PORTUGAL

In Portugal, as throughout Europe, a structured discourse on the protection of the environment and human rights is taking place. Many consumers now make sure to check the label in clothes as part of their purchasing decisions in order to learn more about the garments' origin and composition (Moutinho 2013). Signs of change in terms of consumption and the sustainability of textiles and clothing were first felt with the rapid growth in secondhand stores and markets: these range from the well-established Feira da Ladra, a popular street market where antiques of all types—tiles, ceramics, clothing, footwear, and other handicrafts—are sold, to the most recent alternative designer craft markets, such as Feira da Buzina, LX Market, or the Feira das Almas in Lisbon, and the flea market or Feira da Vandoma in Porto.

Simultaneously many secondhand vintage clothing stores started to emerge. In Lisbon, for example, one might visit The Other Face of the Moon (Outra Face Da Lua,[3] established in 2005), the Trunk Shop (Loja Baú,[4] 2009), the Viúva Alegre (2010), or the Ace of Spades (Ás de Espadas, 2010). Chocking Pink, (Rosa Chock,[5] 2006) and Quartier Latin-Vintage Luxury Store[6] (2010) can be found in an affluent area of Porto. But Portuguese consumers have also reviewed their behavior toward fashion sustainability by reflecting on the way in which they purchase clothes, and have begun to opt for reused items (re-created or co-created with new components), or by donating or exchanging products (Morais et al. 2011). Although this trend was significantly accelerated by the post-2013 economic crisis, it is here to stay.

The reuse and transformation of old garments by giving them a second life is strongly valued in Portugal (Broega et al. 2016; Broega and Fernandes 2016), as evidenced by the proliferation of restore/repair shops and transformation of clothing throughout the country. A new wave of dressmakers and local machinists has also spread nationally.

Even the most high-profile fashion designers, such as Dino Alves, direct their creations to more sustainable creative systems. The "Clothing Hospital: S.O.S. Dino Alves,"[7] is one example. Created by the designer the service aims to recover old (vintage) garments, and give them a new, more contemporary look, thereby increasing the life cycle of materials, in an upcycling operation. According to the designer, this service differs from that of the traditional seamstress by the "Operation Surprise Service concept, which implies that the customer does not know in advance what will become of the old garment" when delivering the item for re making.

This statement can also serve as a motto for social entrepreneurs, who have given rise to the

Figure 3.3.1 Vintage for a Cause
Image reproduced courtesy of Helena Silva

creation of Sewing Clubs, as is the case of "Vintage for a Cause" (see Figure 3.3.1), a social sustainability project that promotes interaction and companionship for woman aged over fifty via the redesign of vintage garments. Meetings are held in a convivial space that functions as occupational therapy for women who are no longer in an active professional life, but who need motivation to engage with the wider community. The project works in collaboration with prestigious Portuguese designers like Katty Xiomara, who contributes her knowledge and skills voluntarily to help the teams transform the old clothes. Everything is created with existing materials and often bringing together elements from two items can result in a completely different individual piece. The final results are unique vintage pieces, which are sold at markets and stores. Each product gets a hand-embroidered tag that is accompanied by a short text, which tells the story of the piece, where it came from, who transformed it, and invites the future owner to share online the next phases of the garment's life.

The project was created as part of a postgraduate degree in Social Entrepreneurship that brought together mentors Helena Silva, Isabel Fontes, and Márcia Coelho. In 2013 a pilot project started as a course with ten people who did not know how to sew. The aim was to improve their social inclusion, explains Helena Silva. The business model is scheduled for replication in other cities in the country in 2019. According to Helena Silva, the project has led to the discovery of "… another advantage of this eco trend: by giving a new hypothesis to the used clothes, ordinary women become improbable creators, recycling their lives too" (Silva 2017).

Also within the scope of social sustainability, ethical fashion contributes to the social integration of African migrants in Portugal. This is certainly the case for the Lisbon-based African Fashion Association (AMA), which was founded in 2014 by designer Sofia Vilarinho. It is a non-profit cultural and social organization that works on enabling "creative synergies between Portugal and Africa," by creating intervention projects with the African immigrant community in the Portuguese capital. The Association says that:

> African immigrant tailors live and work in conditions of great vulnerability (social and economic) and when they arrive in Lisbon, they do not find effective infrastructures that enhance their talent, promote education and inclusion for the generation of employability. These professionals survive with scarce resources, and are often forced to work in other fields of activity, including building construction and live in mostly on the threshold of poverty in a situation of illegality and without any social protection
>
> AMA 2015

Thus, the AMA is presented as a platform for the support and sharing of information, knowledge, and innovation, as well as social, cultural, and professional valorization for fashion designers, namely designers and tailors of African origin. Its mission is "to promote Sustainable Fashion in order to give visibility to African designers in Portugal," always from a sustainable, ethical, and socially responsible perspective. And in particular, the association sets out to foster positive social inclusion through empowering talents for socio-cultural development and affirmation (AMA 2015).

These are examples of the national panorama in terms of social sustainability that are mainly supported by state organizations, but there are also brands that aim at independent financial sustainability as well as social and environmental sustainability.

SUSTAINABLE BRANDS IN PORTUGAL

There are still relatively few sustainable brands in Portugal, as the fashion sector works almost exclusively under the "Private Label" regime. However, some young brands are already making their name heard, working within a green or Fairtrade approach, or both, as this section outlines.

Ecolã Portugal

Some positive examples can be found in some of Portugal's more rural areas, such as the Serra da Estrela. Known for its sheep population and grazing land, Serra da Estrela was once the backdrop of intense industrial wool production, but over the years has struggled to survive the vicissitudes of the textile industry. Now, however, a local textile fashion industry has been reborn that prizes the natural riches of the region, combining the art and the knowledge of the old weavers with contemporary design, in order to create high-quality original works. In this rural environment only the small artisan and family-run companies can survive. This is the case for Ecolã Portugal (Ecowool Portugal), a company founded in 1925 in the town of Mateigas. Its small size and flexibility have allowed it to survive; working in a traditional way, the company uses slow shuttle looms with the natural wool of the region that, due to its texture, only allows the manufacture of carded yarn for use in blankets or "burel"[8] fabric. The brand carries out the whole range of wool processing; shearing, preparing, spinning, weaving, and production of the final wool product, for a range of men's and women's clothing, accessories, and blankets. The company states that: "The genuine colors of wool identify our brand. The respect for the natural elements [is] deeply related to the Portuguese mountain lifestyle." It also argues that "The human factor is the main element, high standards being our commitment. Our aim is to pass on the art of our craft to future generations" (Ecolã 2017). Ecolã sells all products at its facilities in Manteigas, where one can also observe the entire production process.

Burel Factory

In 2010 in the same city of Manteigas the Burel Factory (Figure 3.3.2) was established, led by Isabel Costa (former administrator of a large Portuguese economic group) and her husband, both of whom had fallen in love with the region. Their project is, according to Isabel, "special, unique and sustainable, with Portuguese soul and feet well settled in the mountain" that inspires her. The Burel Factory aims to "combine design with tradition with unique, colorful and contemporary pieces" (Costa 2017). It works with the resources and local knowledge in *burel*'s manufacturing to "reinvent the value of the region's riches and show the world an ancient art, but [one that is] suited to modern times" (Costa 2017). The project began with the manufacture of *burel*, but quickly took on a wider scope. Today it creates original, contemporary-looking pieces

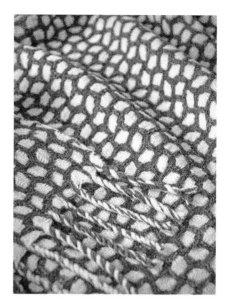

Figure 3.3.2 Burel Factory
Image reproduced courtesy of Romev Lebres

that can be found in houses, offices, hotels, and companies as carpets, cushions, wall coverings, backpacks, bags, and even a cover for Microsoft® Surface Tablet. The Burel Factory products are designed by Portuguese designers such as Sara Lamúrias (from the brand Aforest Design), whose work has always been linked to the ecological textiles and to the valorization of the artisan.

Both the Burel Factory and Aforest Design were recently awarded prizes at the Biennial of Design Iberoamericana 2016, as design company and designer[9] of the year, respectively. The Burel Factory shop allows customers to see in-house production processes and meet designers, so that they can develop their own piece during their visit.

These two companies together have greatly contributed to the sustainable development of the Manteigas region by promoting industrial tourism and opening the doors of their factories and museum to guided daily tours in English.

Elementum

In 2008, the Portuguese designer Daniela Pais founded Elementum, a brand with the vision to change the way we make and wear clothes. It is based on the idea that luxury has migrated to a more emotional level, questioning current models of consumption. It is a sustainable fashion brand, built on the zero-waste concept, and using only natural materials such as organic cotton (GOTS certified), linen, and reused cotton. The prints are exclusively created with natural pigments. The woolen knit fabric is used in the natural shade of the fiber. "Working with high-quality materials allows good fit and beautiful appearance," argues Daniela (Elementum 2008). The designs are timeless, multi-functional, and trans-seasonal offering a range of expression and

identity that fits the swiftly changing contexts of today's fashion world. During the production process, minimal cuts are made to the fabric, meaning that garments are seamless and fluid, so that end-users can maximize the use of the clothes. The garments can be worn in a variety of ways—as tops, dresses, tunics, vests, and scarves—and can be adapted by customers as they wish every day. However, each item has a QR code linked to a video that shows users how they could wear the piece, if they need some inspiration, or if they are unsure about how to actually wear or arrange a piece as (for example) a scarf, shirt, or dress. The brand is sold in several stores around the world, as well as online (Elementum 2008).

Textile sustainability in Portugal has also been extended to accessories and decoration, as is the case of Sukupira.

Sukupira

Portugal's efforts in the area of sustainability is already working across borders and extending to other Portuguese-speaking countries (PALOP[10]), as is the case for fashion brand Sukupira Conscious Wear (see Figure 10, plate section). Inspired by the Sucupira market in the city of Praia (Cape Verde), this city is also where the productive part of the company is dedicated to clothing and fashion accessories with a marked ethnic and ethical identity. The project started in Cape Verde, but has already been extended to S. Tomé & Príncipe, where fashion accessories are manufactured. According to co-founder Sara Gouveia, Sukupira is a fashion brand with sustainable concerns, which appeals for trade solidarity and a more conscious consumer society. "We represent the meticulous work of seamstresses living in the city of Praia (Cape Verde) and in São Tomé (São Tomé & Príncipe). They draw, cut and sew the garments with care and dedication" (Gouveia 2017). The brand uses a co-design approach, readapting models to a more contemporary reading so that Sukupira brings together a set of exclusive pieces with vibrant, joyful, and unique patterns. This project was created by three volunteers working for an NGO in Praia—Sara Gouveia, Catarina Reis, and Inês Lages—who, on seeing the vibrant designs on the local, traditional fabrics, saw a business opportunity for "the creation of a transatlantic social economy, which would create bridges between Portugal and these two countries, and even between Cape Verde and S. Tomé and Príncipe, which are very close in identity and culturally, countries that need our [Portuguese] presence and action to improve their living and working conditions" (Gouveia 2017).

Chic by Choice

Small lifestyle changes are beginning to emerge in Portugal, and the results of these will only be complete and visible within two or three generations. That said, they are leading toward the dematerialization of products through Sustainable Product-Service Systems (S.PSS). An example of this can be seen in the Portuguese international brand Chic By Choice,[11] a European luxury clothing rental company, which allows the rental of products from the best brands on e-commerce platforms for only a fraction (15 percent) of their original price and includes transport, cleaning, and small repair services. The company's success is in part due to the management of Lara Vidreiro (with co-founder, Filipa Neto), who at just twenty-three raised €520,000 worth of investment for the business in 2014. It came at a time of internationalization, when the company entered the UK and German markets (where it now has 85 percent of its clothes rental business). In July 2015, the company purchased its German competitor Laremia, and in just over two years, Chic By Choice has managed to establish itself as the leading clothing rental platform, operating in more than thirty countries in Europe and with exponential monthly growth. Currently the team is made up of twenty people, spread across its offices in London and Lisbon. In 2016 the brand was recognized as the best fashion start-up at European level by that year's Europe Start-up Conference & Awards.

FINAL CONSIDERATIONS

Changing mindsets is never easy; it requires a lot of awareness and resilience to make genuine progress toward sustainable consumption. Bringing sustainability into the clothing, footwear, and fashion accessories sector involves multiple factors, and this can make it difficult for some fashion products to be made 100 percent sustainable. Moreover, due to a lack of knowledge, consumers can find it hard to know when a product or brand is sustainable. Certain consumers choose not to buy items labeled as sustainable, in protest against the lack of alternatives or the fear of being fooled by "greenwashing" marketing campaigns (Moutinho 2013). At the same time, there is a growth in developing spin-off start-ups, which are directed toward youth entrepreneurship that leads to the implementation of change, giving birth to new projects that are leveraged by new alternative and sustainable business models in the textile and fashion arenas (Broega and Fernandes 2016; Jordão et al. 2016). In the realm of social entrepreneurship, committed entrepreneurs and designers aim to give social and economic power to artisan makers, and therefore their local communities, which is also helping traditional techniques to survive.

The policy priorities in the sector, when they exist, are essentially focused on the environmental area (using Community Financial Aid, the 2020 Framework Program), and on the social area, where attention is given to those who have suffered in the toxic production of raw materials such as textiles, clothing, and fur treatment (Jordão et al., 2016).

Many brands try to reverse environmental damage by looking for organic or more environmentally friendly products, while trying to reduce water waste. Some hope to keep all their processes—from fiber sourcing to final product—within their national borders, in order to reduce their ecological footprint. Some more radical brands are avoiding animal products, and are searching for new, alternative materials—eco-polymers or often organic vegetable fibers, say—to replace skins and hair, and sometimes even also wool and silk. Sustainability may also be prioritized in the design of clothing products, when for example a garment is customizable, and can be adapted to various situations, or even to several different users within the concept of "one-fits-all" or with "zero-waste" modulations. Already many viable examples exist of brands reusing discarded materials, giving them a second life, based mainly on the principles of upcycling.

One can certainly say that sustainability, in its various dimensions, has already started in Portugal, although it is still very much early days. However, one major challenge lies in the difficulty that Portuguese companies and brands have in *communicating* their sustainability values and principles. This is because it is not enough just to be sustainable; it is also necessary to show this stance not only by a business's product range, but also its brand position. And this can only be achieved by focusing on a strategic communication plan for sustainability (in a wide range of media including social media) that can and should also have an educational role for consumers.

NOTES

1. www.citeve.pt/
2. www.oeko-tex.com
3. www.aoutrafacedalua.com
4. www.lojabau2mao.com
5. http://rosachockvintage.blogspot.com
6. www.quartierlatin.pt
7. www.dinoalves.eu/hospital.html
8. One of the oldest fabrics in Portugal, handcrafted from wool since the eleventh century. It was traditionally used to make jackets and coats for the shepherds of Serra da Estrela.
9. www.aforest-design.com/work.html
10. Portuguese-speaking African countries.
11. https://chic-by-choice.com/pt_pt

REFERENCES

AMA (ASSOCIAÇÃO MODA AFRICANA EM LISBOA; 2015), *Corporate social responsibility*. Available online at: http://www.ama-lx.com (accessed May 20, 2016).

APT (2016), *Annual Report Directory 2016*. Available online at: http://www.atp.pt/fotos/editor2/diretorio%20 ATP%202016.pdf (accessed March 1, 2017).

APT (2017), *Green Textiles Club Project*. Available online at: http://www.atp.pt/gca/index.php?id=497 (accessed March 1, 2017).

Broega, A. C., and C. Fernandes (2016), "Creating a Business Model from the Traditional to Global Fashion: Guimarães Embroidery," *Proceedings of the International Conference on Sustainable Smart Manufacturing, S2 2016*, FAU, Lisbon, Portugal. Available online at: http://hdl.handle.net/1822/43372 (accessed March 9, 2017).

Broega, A. C., M. O. Santos, and B. O. Soares (2016), "Reuse of Clean Waste from the Fashion Industry in Sustainable Design Development with a Focus on Social Responsibility," *Proceedings of the 16th AUTEX World Textile Conference, AUTEX 2016*, Ljubljana, Slovenia. Available online at: http://hdl.handle. net/1822/43392 (accessed March 9, 2017).

Carvalho, C. (2017), author interview with Catarina Carvalho, CEO of Darono Interior Design (www.darono.pt/), Porto, February 17, 2017.

Costa, I. (2017), author interview with Isabel Costa, CEO of Burel Factory Company (https://burelfactory.com/en/), Manteigas, March 17, 2017.

Ecolā (2010), Ecolā Portugal website. Available online at: https://www.ecolaportugal.com/pt/home (accessed May 20, 2016).

Elementum (2008), brand website. Available online at: http://luxuryistohavesimplethings.com (accessed February 23, 2017).

Gouveia, S. (2017), author interview with Sara Gouveia, co-founder of Sukupira Conscious Wear (www.sukupira.org/), Lisbon, March 28, 2017.

Jordão, C., A. C. Broega, and S. B. Martins (2016), "O empreendedorismo sustentável e a geração de valor no reuso de tecidos do setor têxtil. Estudo de caso do banco de tecido de reuso de São Paulo," Atas do 12º Colóquio de Moda – 9ª Edição Internacional, Unipê-Centro Universitário de João Pessoa, JP – PB, Brazil, September 2016. Available online at: http://hdl.handle.net/1822/43399 (accessed February 9, 2017).

Morais, C., C. Carvalho, and A. C. Broega (2011), "A design tool to identify and measure the profile of sustainable conscious fashion costumer," *Proceedings of the 11th AUTEX World Textile Conference AUTEX 2011, Mulhouse, France*. Available at: http://hdl.handle.net/1822/14928 (accessed March 28, 2017).

Moutinho, S. R. F. (2013), "Fast Fashion or Slow Fashion? The New Consumer and the New Conception Culture," MSc dissertation, University of Minho, 2013.

Silva, H. (2017), author interview with Helena Silva, the mentor of Vintage for a Cause (http://vintageforacause.pt/en/), Porto, April 19, 2017.

A SPOTLIGHT ON: VIGGA.US
Sharing Baby Clothes in a Sustainable Product-Service System

Vibeke Riisberg, Design School Kolding, Denmark

VIGGA is a Danish subscription service that offers the leasing of baby clothes from size newborn up to two years, delivered in intervals that match the growth of children.[1] Vigga and Peter Svensson, who developed the concept inspired by the circular economy, launched the company online in January 2015. The website states that: "VIGGA is founded on the conviction that we may care better for our blue planet if we share with each other and reuse all we can."

VIGGA operates as a sustainable product-service system that is considered one of the most promising solutions to over-consumption because its focus is on fulfilling the customers' needs rather than selling a product (Mylan 2015). This type of business model challenges ownership as well as traditional consumption and use patterns by (for example) offering limited personal choices, reducing the need to go shopping, and, in this case, promoting the sharing of clothes. For the company, controlling logistics at all levels is of great importance. Production—

located in India and Lithuania—is planned and carried out in collaboration with a sourcing company that monitors the supply chain and guarantees all certifications. Packaging and the status of subscriptions are handled in-house and controlled by a computer program that secures delivery of the correct garments to each subscriber, in terms of both size and any gender preference. A chip inside the garment controls the stock of each style in its different sizes—a system developed in collaboration with the laundry.

Customers can choose between three basic packages with differing amounts of items—small (eight), medium (sixteen), or large (twenty-four)—for the price of 299, 369, or 449 DKK per month respectively.[2] The collection is designed by VIGGA with a recognizable aesthetic profile supported by the website layout, colors, and styling of photos. All fabrics are made in organic GOTS-certified cotton and the look of the collection is slowly shifting as worn-out models

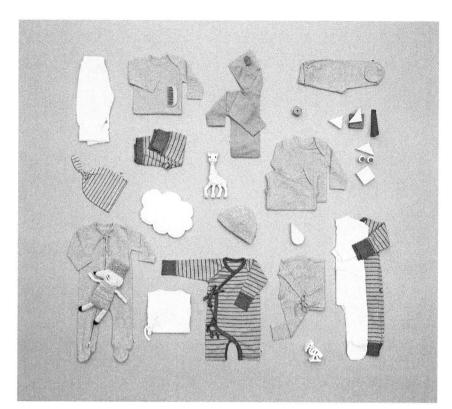

Figure 3.4.1 Unisex clothing package for newborns
Image reproduced courtesy of VIGGA™

are replaced with new ones. The newborn package is unisex and comes in muted tones and white, whereas the rest of the range gradually adds more colors and patterns as the child grows. When the baby is one month old, the subscriber can choose between different packages for girls and for boys; these selections can either be made by VIGGA or the customers themselves.

Subscribers receives their packages by post in special bags that may also be used to return the clothes; in the case of size newborn the clothes should be returned after one month, sizes 56–62 after two months, size 68–74 after three months, and size 80–92 after six months. If the size dispatched does not fit the baby it was intended for, the subscriber can contact the company at any time and request to keep the clothes longer or change to a different size. When the clothes are

returned they are cleaned by a professional laundry service that is certified with the Nordic Swan eco-label and which adheres to strict hygiene standards. The clothes are carefully inspected before being circulated again and, if necessary, repaired. After being sent to between five and eight subscribers, clothes that are still usable but look too worn are donated to a children's home, upcycled (made into toys, for example), or handed in for recycling.

In addition to promoting subscriptions online Vigga Svensson arranges events where the collection is displayed, and the idea behind the brand is introduced and explained. This informal dialog prompts further a deep understanding of user needs, which in turn helps the company to improve the concept and develop new items. Newsletters and frequent updates on social media

Figure 3.4.2 Boy's garment size 74 and girl's garment size 86
Image reproduced courtesy of VIGGA ™

invite the users and potential subscribers to post comments and pictures. These activities are part of forming a mutual trust and establishing a feeling of community and responsibility which is key to keeping the clothes in good condition and a prerequisite for them to circulate as long as possible (Petersen & Riisberg 2017).

NOTES

1. This article is based on research and fieldwork carried out by the author and Trine Bruun Petersen 2014–16.

2. The concept is constantly developing, and in spring 2017 maternity clothes, hand-knitted baby items in organic wool, beach- and outerwear collections, in collaboration with Patagonia, were launched.

REFERENCES

Mylan, J. (2015), "Understanding the Diffusion of Sustainable Product-Service Systems: Insights from the Sociology of Consumption and Practice Theory," *Journal of Cleaner Production*, 97: 13–20.

Petersen, T. B., and V. Riisberg (2017), "Cultivating User-ship? Developing a Circular System for the Acquisition and use of Baby Clothing," *Fashion Practice, The Journal of Design, Creative Process & the Fashion Industry*, 9(2).

VIGGA.us A/S Official website. Available online at: http://www.vigga.us/#bornetoj-pa-en-ny-made (accessed March 22, 2017).

SETTING OUT ON A JOURNEY TOWARD SUSTAINABLE LUXURY IN SPAIN

Elena Salcedo Allende, far & sound and Istituto Europeo Di Design, Barcelona, Spain

INTRODUCTION

Starting Point: Defining the Concept of Sustainable Luxury

In order to contextualize the following research we need to understand how luxury is shifting its meaning toward sustainability. That shift is occurring in response to a changing business climate (Curry and Peck 2014), which itself has been influenced by current environmental and social challenges (resource scarcity, environmental deterioration, and increasing poverty), as well as by the resulting changes in consumer behavior.

Consumers, according to The Futures Company's Global MONITOR Study, have begun to look beyond price and brand name (PR Newswire 2010). As Na and Lamblin summarized in the *Making Futures* journal (2014: 429–36), consumers are:

1. Becoming **more responsible** and vigilant in their purchases, seeking more information about a particular product, and weighing pros and cons in terms of avoiding lower-quality goods and wasting time and money.
2. Becoming **more resourceful,** valuing manual and craft skills as a means to both pleasurable hobbies and practical money-saving repairs.
3. Learning to **better prioritize** and assess what they truly "need," favoring the richness of a happy life and well-being.
4. Joining **networks of narrower and shared interests**, drawing from one another the values of and means to leading more responsible, vigilant, resourceful, and well-prioritized lives.

Na and Lamblin (2014) explain in detail how this shift in consumption patterns indicates a desire for a new kind of luxury (sustainable luxury) that distances itself from the traditional luxury markers of prestige, visibility, and exclusivity, while still maintaining and even reemphasizing the central valuation toward pleasurable and meaningful high-quality products. This shift in consumption patterns and purchase drivers provides the context within which sustainable luxury can be more fully understood.

This new type of luxury is what Bendell and Kleanthous define as sustainable luxury (2007: 2): "Sustainable luxury is a new type of luxury whose deeper values are fully embodied in the sourcing, manufacture, marketing and distribution of products and services. Authentic luxury brands are those that provide the greatest positive contributions to all affected by their creation and that identify their consumers as having the means and motivation to respect both people and the planet."

To conclude, it is impossible to speak today of luxury without integrating the notion of sustainability into the equation just as it is impossible to speak about successful twenty-first century businesses that do not embrace this principle. One sentence, in my view, summarizes this concept well: "Brands used to be about desired identity. But the next generation of brands will be about desired society." (Tom LaForge, Coca-Cola, in Curry and Peck 2014: 31).

AIM OF RESEARCH AND RESEARCH METHOD

Following this contextualized approach of defining the concept of "sustainable luxury," we move on to answer how entrepreneurs can set out on a journey that balances the ecological, economic, and social dimensions of sustainable luxury. For this question, the journey toward sustainable luxury will be examined through one case study that will be analyzed to identify the key elements in their vision and business strategies, and from that outline a rough guide for future entrepreneurs. The research method comprised in-depth interviews with company founders. These interviews raised interesting questions about the way these founders think about their customers and their markets, about their innovation processes, and about their workforce. The data was compiled following qualitative research analysis.

The first step was categorizing the data into four blocks:

1. Company mission
2. Commitment to sustainability
3. Management policy
4. Value creation

The second step was interpreting meanings and identifying elements (ways of designing and managing businesses) that led to the final step of synthesizing the results.

CASE STUDY: TEIXIDORS

Teixidors[1] is an initiative that includes products of high quality, in terms of craftsmanship, materials, and durability, that are made to last for a long time by people who enjoyed making them. Teixidors was created to generate employment for people with learning difficulties, with the overall aim of helping them live a normal life, and uses handmade fabric to facilitate this goal. With this initial idea in mind Teixidors has created a unique business model built around the cooperative system and offers the market a high-quality product that generates well-being for all the agents in the value chain, including, of course, the end user.

Teixidors represents a thriving, growing business that has already gone through the first stages of uncertainty and proved its viability. The company's main data and figures are summarized in Table 3.5.1.

TABLE 3.5.1

TEIXIDORS' MAIN DATA AND FIGURES.

	*2016 DATA
YEAR OF ESTABLISHMENT	1983 (34 YEARS OLD)
COLLECTION SIZE (NUMBER OF REFERENCES)	1.000 REFERENCES (+5% GROWTH PLANNED FOR NEXT YEAR)
PRICE RANGE	70€-950€
NUMBER OF EMPLOYEES & COLLABORATORS	43 EMPLOYEES
NUMBER OF RETAILERS	2 OWN STORES IN SPAIN 350 EXTERNAL RETAILERS IN 35 COUNTRIES •SPAIN (39% TOTAL SALES) •USA (20% TOTAL SALES) •FRANCE (6% TOTAL SALES) •GERMANY (4% TOTAL SALES) •JAPAN (4% TOTAL SALES) •BELGIUM (8% TOTAL SALES) •OTHERS (19% TOTAL SALES)
YEARLY REVENUES	2012: 650.000 € 2013: 869.019€ 2014: 831.416€ 2015: 969.768€ 2016: 852.508€
NET PROFIT (%)	NON PROFIT BUSINESS
SALES GROWTH FORECAST (%)	+15% IN TWO YEARS
STAFF GROWTH FORECAST	+2 EMPLOYEES
RETAILERS GROWTH FORECAST	N.A.

The next section will examine Teixidors' attempts to balance the ecological, economic, and social dimensions of sustainable luxury.

Teixidors' Founders

The architects of this project are Marta Ribas, a social worker specializing in psychiatry, and Juan Ruiz, a technical engineer. Marta had the intial idea to select a project that would create jobs for people with learning difficulties. Work-therapy at that time provided only low-quality jobs, and Marta and Juan were eager to look for something more creative, something of better quality that could also provide a living. With these two elements in mind, they started working on their idea and stumbled on the world of textiles where they saw possibilities and later looked for a business component.

In 1983, they decided to move to Terrassa, a medium-sized city of 200,000 people situated 29 km from Barcelona and known for its important textile history, which was at its height in the nineteenth century but, like the rest of Europe's textile centers, had suffered the consequences of globalization. Terrassa welcomed them with open arms to create an original yet unusual project: social integration using wood looms in a cooperative setting.

Figure 3.5.1 A Teixidors Product: Gobi Poncho Gobi (50 percent yak wool, 50 percent ecological merino wool).
Photography: Emilio Lecuona

Company Mission

From the very beginning, the Teixidors project has been committed to generating well-being and focusing on the social economy. It seeks to achieve:

- Well-being for people with learning disabilities, supporting them and creating specialized and integrated work for them, in this case hand-weaving.
- Well-being for agents in the supply chain, generating added value together.
- Well-being also for discerning consumers, satisfying their desire for a unique product of exceptional quality.

Commitment to Sustainability

Teixidors looks to nature for inspiration and as a model. It only uses natural materials. The core of Teixidor products is top-quality natural fibers such as wool, ecological wool, linen, or cashmere.

Care of raw materials is key to ensuring the quality of high-end products. The following examples illustrate the way in which Teixidor understands this important aspect.

Transparency

"Teixidors requests all its suppliers to abide by environmental rules in their treatment of water and use of dyes and additives." One example is their linen supplier. These days the best quality flax is grown in northeast France. Teixidors sources its linen from Masters of Linen, the only French spinning company that has not moved its production to Asia and is certified by OEKO-TEX Standard 100.

Traceability

"Teixidors guarantees the traceability of its products. At every stage, it knows where the raw material comes from and what processes have been used to make the thread." An example is the fabric made from yak wool. This fiber is sourced from a cooperative of nomadic farmers in the

Khangai mountains of central Mongolia. In this remarkable yet fragile ecosystem, the yaks live in harmony with nature. The shepherds include yaks in their flocks to manage the pastures in a sustainable way and reduce the risk of desertification. Baby yaks are combed by hand to get the fine under-hair, which then becomes a Yak "duvet," known for its softness, warmth, and strength. This unique natural fiber helps to preserve the country's rich nomadic tradition while providing the members of the cooperative with a stable income and means to plan for the future.

Authenticity

"Knowing the source and handling of the raw material is a fundamental part of the company's commitment to quality, while helping to add authenticity and consistency to its textiles." One example of authenticity is the story of Macomerinos, Teixidors' merino wool supplier. Manu and Corine are a farming couple who are passionate about their work and have managed to raise the quality of their merino sheep herd to the point where they produce one of the finest wools in Europe. It is a type of wool that normally could only be found in Australia or New Zealand, but Teixidors has found it in the south of France, only a few kilometers from their home base.

Teixidors and Macomerinos also share an interest in product traceability, as stated by Manu, one of the Macomerinos founders: "We are a small company and we need to ensure the traceability of our wool—it's our product. For that reason, we pay a lot of attention to its destination. Many people want to buy our wool. We prefer to work with Teixidors for one simple reason: they add value to our wool. Teixidors has a unique and wonderful story. The people behind the project make it strong and sound. When

someone buys a Teixidors product, he/she is buying a little piece of heart, of our heart and of all the weavers, a great heart!"

The collaboration between Teixidors and Macomerinos includes the values of proximity, traceability, and sustainability from the lamb's birth to the final sale, and that wool is the foundation of Teixidors' 100 percent ecological collection. Without using any synthetic dyes, the collection's base color is the color of the wool itself. Any touches of color are achieved using natural plant dyes (rubia tinctorum, birch leaves, cochineal, Brazilwood, logwood, indigo, and onion skin among others) thanks to the work of Cornelia Blümi, a Swiss artisan who has settled in Penedes. All the items in the collection are woven by hand, so energy consumption is practically zero.

Management Policy
Artisanal production process

The commitment to quality and to a totally artisanal production process involves two things: limited production; and control and direct management of most of the value chain.

Recognizing this fact, Teixidors encourages continuous experimentation using design combined with technique, taking advantage of its size to do things that bigger industry cannot.

As a result, when we talk about Teixidors' processes, we need to talk about the people and the skills behind each process:

- fabric: looms and weavers
- carding: hands and wool carder
- finish: washing, industrial ironing, and finisher
- final product: sewing machine and machinists

At the end of the process, the result is fabrics that speak for themselves.

**Figure 3.5.2 Teixidors'
employees at work**
*Image reproduced courtesy
of Teixidors. Photography:
Pensandoenblanco*

Cooperative structure

Among the unique characteristics that make
Teixidors different is its business structure, the
cooperative. It is a formula that can sound
anachronistic but which serves to outline a
different work environment, one that is much
more democratic and integrated, for all the
partners in the enterprise. The top governing
body of the cooperative is the members' assembly.
Even so, the management team makes daily
decisions and strategic plans.

Every two weeks, information is passed along
so that everyone (members and employees) stays
informed and can discuss the main points in
what might be considered an informal members'
meeting, in which, as the founder puts it, they
always look for common sense to reign. "In a
normal cooperative, no one imagines that
illogical decisions will be made, but here there is
a risk because of the special makeup of the
cooperative. For that reason, we have to be
constantly teaching and communicating."

Building the brand

At the point at which it was decided strategically
to compete at the high-end international level,
Teixidors' product started to rub shoulders with
well-known and prestigious brands. The only way
to survive was to invest not only in a fine product,
but also in building a brand.

In the framework of creating a brand, Teixidors
defines some of its values:

- Legitimacy, from more than thirty years in
  business
- Credibility, which creates the expectation of
  continuity
- Emotions, generated by the stories behind
  how the products were made
- Country of origin: confronted with a global
  marketplace, valuing a historic textile center
  such as Terrassa (Barcelona)
- Innovation that distances its product from the
  typical industrially made ones

Value Creation

Naturally Teixidors does not want to, nor can, compete on price, but it certainly can compete on value. Teixidors' value rests on the quality of its product, quality that has been created in a different environment. The value that differentiates Teixidors lies in that environment, in the human story behind the quality of the product. This story is the foundation of the emotional connection with the consumer, but also with all the other agents in the value chain (farmers, herdsmen, distributors, design studio, and so on) that curiously, in connecting with Teixidors, are jointly creating this story. For many years, only the quality of the product was trumpeted in Teixidors' communications. No public reference was made to the social aspect of its work.

The evolution of the marketplace toward valuing companies with a different vision has turned the decision of Teixidors to support a workforce with learning disabilities into an opportunity to communicate value.

RESULTS

Teixidors is unique, and uniqueness is what has served them best to approach this idea of sustainable luxury. A summary of the attributes of Teixidors is shown in Table 3.5.2.

But beyond these unique attributes, I have identified some elements that can guide other initiatives when it comes to defining their own unique strategy.

These elements are:

1. The company was open and prepared for a radical shift to sustainability.
2. Their leaders incorporated their personal beliefs and values into their business.
3. The brand shows who they are by the people, the elements, and the stories they choose to surround themselves with.

Ready for a Radical Shift to Sustainability

To understand the idea of a radical shift to sustainability I would like to revisit an inspiring

TABLE 3.5.2

TEIXIDORS' SUSTAINABLE LUXURY ATTRIBUTES.

MISSION	Generate well-being for all the agents in the value chain, including of course the consumer
COMMITMENT TO SUSTAINABILITY	**Environmental commitment** •Care of raw material through guaranteeing transparency, traceability and authenticity **Social commitment** •Generate jobs that bring together people with disabilities with the common goal to live a normal life, using fabric made by hand to achieve this
MANAGEMENT POLICY	•Preserve the artisanal production process •Cooperative business structure •Building a brand
VALUE CREATION	**Value for all agents in the chain:** •Quality product made in a different environment •Connection through human story behind product

quote from Yvon Chouinard, the owner and founder of Patagonia Inc. and one of the main promoters of sustainable fashion:

> In whatever organization, the desire for quality and sustainability has to go beyond the products themselves … extending to the way in which we address the following question: How are things and how should they be? Everything starts with the attitude of embracing change instead of resisting it and assumes that if we look hard enough we can find a better way of doing things.
>
> Chouinard 2006: 144

From these words, I draw the idea that sustainability is a direction, not a destination. Sustainability is a never-ending journey that starts with one's attitude: being open to changing the way things are done.

At Teixidors, the founders were open to changing the way things were done and/or seen. The journey began by defying the status quo and asking a disruptive question: is it possible to generate well-being by doing creative, quality work-therapy? We also see a specific focus in the way they negotiated the transition, in that they opted for a *radical* transition. The concept of radical transition comes from adapting a framework created by Davila et al. (2006: 15), who designed a matrix (Table 3.5.3) to classify different types of innovation (incremental, semi-radical, and radical) based on two axes of change: business model; and technology. The authors explain that changes in the business model refer to how a company creates, sells, and provides value to its customers. On the other hand, technological changes relate to the supply of products and services, the processes, and the

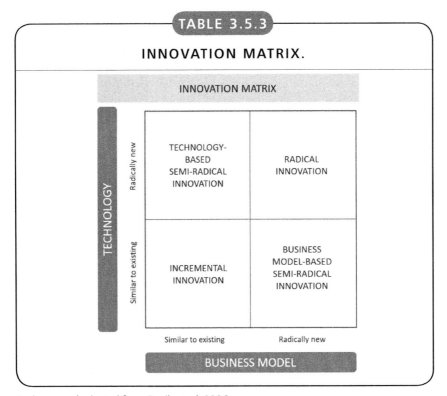

TABLE 3.5.3

INNOVATION MATRIX.

Redrawn and adapted from Davila et al. 2006

technologies that make them possible. The nature of the innovation will be determined by analyzing whether or not the technology and/or the models are an improvement on the prevailing general practices in the sector.

Just as Carreras and Sureda (Rodríguez Blanco et al. 2012) created a framework of innovation for NGOs, I have adapted that framework to create one for transition to sustainability with the same end: to classify the types of transition to sustainability. In adapting this model to transition to sustainability, we understand that the business model is the same as the management model of the value chain. On the other hand, the technological changes relate to changes in the product development process. The result of the adaption can be seen in the Table 3.5.4.

The nature of the transition relates to whether or not the proposal to improve the product development processes and/or management models is an improvement on the prevailing general practices in the sector (Salcedo 2014: 24).

Incremental transition in most cases tends to be a reactive transition; in other words, a response to external factors (legislation, pressure from NGOs and civil society, market demand, and so on.) As an example of incremental transition, we could take the collections made of organic cotton

---

TABLE 3.5.4

TRANSITION TO SUSTAINABILITY MATRIX (SALCEDO, ADAPTED FROM DAVILA ET AL.'S INNOVATION MATRIX (2006)).

MATRIX OF TRANSITION TO SUSTAINABILITY

PRODUCT DEVELOPMENT PROCESS		Similar to existing	Radically new
	Radically new	PRODUCT-BASED SEMI-RADICAL TRANSITION	RADICAL TRANSITION
	Similar to existing	INCREMENTAL TRANSITION	MANAGEMENT MODEL-BASED SEMI-RADICAL TRANSITION

VALUE CHAIN MANAGEMENT MODEL

that the big fast-fashion chains are introducing. The product is very similar to what is already available: only the fabric has been changed (organic cotton for conventional cotton), a small improvement in the product, but the business model is the same. We label it incremental rather than semi-radical based on the product, because semi-radical transition implies a significant modification, and the example above does not correspond to a significant modification in the product development process. Semi-radical transitions make significant modifications in one of two categories—the management model or the product—but not at the same time. Finally, radical transition, which tends to involve a significant change in both the organization's management model and product, has the potential over time to change the rules of the game in a sector.

In analyzing Teixidors, we have established how their founders proposed to improve the present system through the product development process and management model. Table 3.5.5 summarizes these improvements.

I would not suggest that Teixidors has changed the fashion market or the general way clothes are being purchased. In other words, their transition has not had a disruptive effect. But, in my view, initiatives like Teixidors are instigating changes to models of leadership, management, and consumption that could lead to big fundamental changes in the sector.

Incorporating Leaders' Personal Beliefs into Businesses

In Teixidors, the founders have been leaders who knew how to integrate their personal values into their businesses. The values we have identified that could direct us to a sustainability paradigm are:

- Confidence
- Transparency
- Collaboration
- Long-term vision
- Shared values
- Respect for slowness
- Optimal size

Lastly, Table 3.5.6 shows us how Teixidors integrated these values into their businesses.

As Michael Porter and Mark Kramer have explained, "companies had spent too long simply extracting value from their suppliers, workers and the communities in which they operated, and needed to share value with them instead, if they wished to ensure their survival" (Curry & Peck 2014: 8).

TABLE 3.5.5

SIGNIFICANT CHANGES AT TEIXIDORS.

SIGNIFICANT CHANGE IN PRODUCT DEVELOPMENT PROCESS	•Raw material selection process, based on transparency and traceability •Artisanal and slow production process (handmade by people with disabilities)
SIGNIFICANT CHANGE IN VALUE CHAIN MANAGEMENT MODEL	•Internalize processes to guarantee product quality and small production volumes •Continuous training and education to guarantee collective decisionmaking •Proximity of raw material to production •Selection of team, associates, suppliers on the basis of shared values

TABLE 3.5.6

INCORPORATION OF LEADERS' VALUES INTO BUSINESSES.

CONFIDENCE	•Process of selecting suppliers and associates
TRANSPARENCY	•Process of selecting raw materials •Process of internal communication and jointly deciding strategy
COLLABORATION	•Collaborating with suppliers in product development process
LONG-TERM VISION	• Commitment to the suppliers, workers and distributors •Continuous education
SHARED VALUE	•Well-being of all the agents in the value chain
RESPECT FOR SLOWNESS	•Process of obtaining materials and their production •Process of manual production
OPTIMAL SIZE	•Growth in accord with production capacity and thus aligned with original company mission

Brands Show Who They Are By the People, the Elements, and the Stories they Choose to Surround Themselves with

Teixidors' value proposition is based primarily on the story behind their products. These stories are jointly written by various authors. As Curry and Peck have said: "The 21st century organization will tend to be more porous, with more blurred boundaries with suppliers, staff and customers" (Curry & Peck 2014: 15). What would Teixidors be without Macomerinos?

Selecting companions on the road to sustainability (workers, suppliers, distributors, associates, consumers, etc.) is key when it comes to planning a brand and creating the story behind the product. If we make a comparison with the film industry, the brand/story would be the film and the companions the cast. On this point, I was interested in analyzing the criterion for "casting" to see if I could identify a focus when it came to selecting actors for the film. And in doing so, I discovered Teixidors has an understanding of excellence and look for the same understanding in all their companions. How do they define excellence? Teixidors defines excellence based on the following factors: the joy of caring and making conscious decisions; thinking like an artisan and commitment to exploring.

The joy of caring

All the actors want to look after resources, materials, people/animals, and spaces. They pay attention to time as well, the time that processes need, and encourage a return to the natural speed of things. All the actors appear to share Carl Honoré's idea that "Slowness allows us to be more creative at work, to have better health and be able to connect with pleasure and with others." (Honoré 2005). As Na and Lamblin have said: "The craft ethos offers solutions to environmental and ecological issues, stemming from its concern for natural resources and the use of traditional and locally sourced materials and embodies slowness; that is, more thinking and a greater awareness of how things are made and how craft processes impact the environment" (2014: 429–36). Thus, excellence is a question of conscious choice and discipline. In Teixidors' case, making conscious decisions starts with the individual, moves onto the team, transforms the organization and, in the long run, can alter a system.

Thinking like an artisan

As Na and Lamblin define craft ethos, thinking like an artisan means emphasizing high quality—more specifically, high quality that fits the right purpose. "As a bulwark against obsolescence and mass-production, the craft ethos aims to satisfy needs, not demand; bringing pleasure, rather than waste" (2014: 429–36). As Richard Sennett puts it: "Thinking like an artisan means moving

from a linear vision with a beginning and preconceived end to a circular metamorphosis in which thinking and doing happen at the same time. You draw and do, and the drawing is constantly revised until you feel it has been well done … a balance between perfection and the practical" (2008: 63). As the table below shows, this idea of experimentation and repetition appears to be, in Teixidors' case, a good tool for innovation (Rodríguez et al. 2012: 95).

CONCLUSION

Every company is unique and the strategy that will best serve it to move toward the idea of sustainable luxury is also unique, and can be understood as: "a new type of luxury whose deeper values are fully embodied in the sourcing, manufacture, marketing and distribution of products and services" (2007: 2), as Bendell and

Figure 3.5.3
Guidelines toward sustainable luxury
Diagram courtesy of the author (Salcedo 2016)

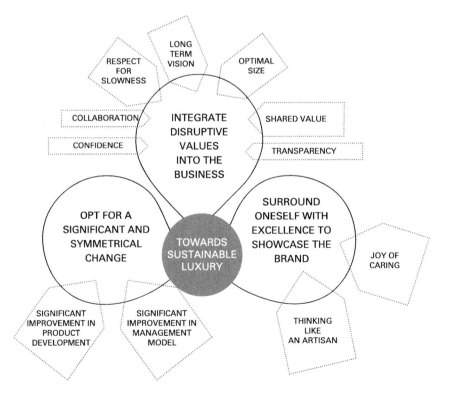

Kleanthous define it. The exercise of analyzing Teixidors shows us some elements that can guide other initiatives when it comes to defining their own unique strategy to sustainable luxury. With these elements, we could start to build a "Draft guide of how to shift to sustainability" whose script is summarized in Figure 3.5.3 opposite.

This draft guide aligns with Curry and Peck's key guidelines to succeed in today's business world (2014: 36):

1. Organizational culture is more important than strategy.
2. Intrinsic values are becoming more important than extrinsic values, for both customers and employees.
3. Connection is the key to both driving down cost and driving up customer engagement.

This is the perfect starting point to work in the future on a "Definitive guide of how to shift to sustainability."

NOTES

1. www.teixidors.com

REFERENCES

Bendell J., and A. Kleanthous (2007), *Deeper Luxury: Quality and Style When the World Matters*. London: World Wildlife Fund.

Chouinard, Y. (2006), *Let My People Go Surfing: The Education of a Reluctant Businessman*. New York: Penguin Books.

Curry, A., and P. Peck (2014), "The 21st Century Business: Planning for Success in a Changing World." The Futures Company. Available online at: http://thefuturescompany.com (accessed February 20, 2015).

Davila, T. M., J. Epstein, and R. Shelton (2006), *Making Innovation Work: How to Manage It, Measure It and Profit from It.* Wharton School Publishing New Jersey.

Honoré, C. (2005), "Hemos perdido la capacidad de esperar," in Imma Sanchís (ed.), *La Vanguardia*, Barcelona (Grupo Godó, in press). Available online at: http://www.xtec.cat/~fserra22/docs/arts/honore-lentitud.pdf (accessed April 1, 2017).

Na, Y., and M. Lamblin (2014), "Sustainable Luxury: Sustainable Crafts in a Redefined Concept of Luxury from Contextual Approach to Case Study,". In: *Making Futures*, Vol. 3, ISSN 2042–166. Plymouth College of Art: Plymouth, UK.

PRNewswire (2010, Sept. 29), "Consumers Have Begun to Look Beyond the Recession Era Focus on Price." Available online at: http://www.prnewswire.com/news-releases/according-to-the-futures-companys-2010-global-monitor-study-consumers-have-begun-to-look-beyond-the-recession-era-focus-on-price-103992108.html (accessed April 1, 2017).

Rodríguez Blanco, E., I. Carreras, and M. Sureda (2011–12), "Innovate for Social Change. From Ideas to Action." ESADE-PwC Social Leadership Programme, p 19.

Salcedo, E. (2014), *Moda ética para un futuro sostenible.* Barcelona: Gustavo Gili Publishing.

Sennett, R. (2008), *The Craftsman.* New Haven, CT: Yale University Press.

World Commission on Environment and Development: "Our Common Future." Available online at: http://www.un-documents.net/our-common-future.pdf (accessed April 1, 2017).

CHAPTER 3.6

A SPOTLIGHT ON: TEXTILE-LED SUSTAINABLE INNOVATION OF SURFACE COLORATION AND PATTERNING FOR SPORTSWEAR

Laura Morgan, Loughborough University, UK
Faith Kane, Massey University, New Zealand
John Tyrer, Loughborough University, UK
Jinsong Shen, De Montfort University, UK

INTRODUCTION

Advances in textile design and technology often underpin innovation in fashion. This is in part due to textiles being the fabric of fashion, but also to the natural intersection of design and science that occurs through textile practice (Kane & Philpott 2016). Our understanding of sustainable innovation is informed by Stevels' (1997) description of four "levels" of innovation, as shown in Table 3.6.1. We aim to demonstrate the potential for innovation across all four levels, based

TABLE 3.6.1

STEVELS' LEVELS OF SUSTAINABLE INNOVATION (MORGAN 2016, FROM STEVELS 1997:10).

Level 1	Incremental improvements	Level 1
Level 2	Re-design of existing products and systems	
Level 3	Functional sustainability designed into products from outset	
Level 4	Systems: changing modes of production or consumption	Level 4

on five principles of sustainability for textile design outlined in Table 3.6.2.

INNOVATIVE LASER-BASED TEXTILE SURFACE DESIGN TECHNIQUES

This case study describes the ability to use laser processing as a digital tool in order to reduce resource consumption in textile-surface coloration, patterning, and three-dimensional surface modulation via targeted and direct-to-garment methods, for aesthetic and performance enhancements. The work was undertaken through phases of creative exploration of materials and processes, alongside systematic scientific inquiry, textile testing, design development, and design review.

Peri-dyeing: A Laser Surface Coloration Technique for Textile Design

A laser-based dyeing technique, named as Peri-dyeing, was developed to enable surface design of textile substrates (Morgan 2016). In this technique, the dye diffusion and reaction take place at the point of interaction between the laser and textile material, providing water and chemical efficiency through targeted "on the spot" dyeing. This technique can provide multi-color surface-design opportunities, drawing parallels with digital printing capabilities. Advancements of Peri-dyeing include micro-precision capabilities, as well as double sided, non-contact, and direct-to-garment processing on textured textiles and finished garments, as shown in Figure 3.6.1.

The commercial potential of the technique was demonstrated through industry validation of prototype samples and textile testing that met

Figure 3.6.1 Visualization of print designs for direct-to-garment Peri-dyeing
Image reproduced courtesy of Laura Morgan

with international ISO standards. Peri-dyeing showed the potential to enable digital design innovation and customization in the manufacture of finished textile goods with potential sustainability benefits through reduced energy, water, and chemical consumption.

Laser-Molding: Surface Patterning with Three-dimensional Effect

A second technique was developed by utilizing the photothermal properties of a CO_2 laser for three-dimensional molding and texturing of materials

(Morgan 2016). The technique allowed designs to be "set" on synthetic fabrics using the laser, resulting in accurate surface textures and three-dimensional design features on the surface of the cloth, as shown in Figure 3.6.2(a–d). The laser-molding technique offers ease of pattern change for manufacture through digital generation of designs, negating the use of additional materials or waste products such as physical molds or thread for stitching. In addition, the mono-materiality of the textile remained intact, providing sustainability benefits for potential ease of recycling.

CONCLUSION AND REFLECTIONS

The sustainability benefits of the techniques developed in relation to Stevels' four levels of innovation and against five principles of sustainability are summarized in Table 3.6.2.

As listed in Table 3.6.2, the study points to the potential to reduce chemical, water, and energy use in textile coloration and surface patterning and the opportunity to design for cyclability through a mono materials approach as defined by Goldsworthy (2012), for modifying textural properties of textiles. The ability to add customized, direct-to-garment features were highlighted by industrial partners as advantageous benefits of the laser textile techniques for sportswear. As such, the study points to the opportunity to apply the techniques within the changing landscape of retail.

Evolving online retail spaces allow for more responsive modes of production, providing an alternative to commonplace bulk production.

Figure 3.6.2 Laser-molded polyester: a) molded and Peri-dyed circle pattern; b) block repeat circle pattern; c) pleated squares; d) large-scale 3D molding
Image reproduced courtesy of Laura Morgan

a)

b)

c)

d)

TABLE 3.6.2

POTENTIAL ADVANTAGES OF LASER TEXTILE DESIGN FOR SUSTAINABLE SPORTSWEAR (MORGAN 2016).

Sustainability Principle	Laser Textile Design Technique Advantages	Stevels Level
Material Choices	• Effective processing on mono-materials • Improved processing allowing more sustainable material choices	Level 1
Energy and Water reduction	• Dry processing for laser-moulding • Energy and water efficient coloration and patterning • Combining production stages	
Chemical reduction	• Improved dye performance- minimized dye chemicals • Laser-moulding requires no chemicals	
Waste Reduction	• Targeted, digitally engineered design • Non-contact, Direct-to-garment processing • No molds, screens, mechanical parts to replace. • Agile manufacture, responsive supply, less surplus stock	
Sustainable Systems	• Mass customization and personalization opportunities • Close to market or local production opportunities • Production-on-demand systems	Level 4

Being digitally driven, the laser techniques developed in the study create potential for production-on-demand systems that move toward shorter textile production runs or direct-to-garment processing, where close-to-market customization opportunities can facilitate late-stage design decisions to suit regional markets. In addition to reducing over-supply and subsequent waste, this could engage the customer in a transparent process.

As exemplified with laser processing in this case study, advances in digital techniques for textiles provide potential to innovate across multiple levels of sustainable innovation and a move toward more efficient, agile modes of garment production.

ACKNOWLEDGEMENTS

The authors would like to thank the UK Arts and Humanities Research Council (AHRC contract number: AH/J002666/1) and industrial partners Speedo and Camira for their support toward the Lebiotex Project, a collaborative venture between Loughborough University and De Montfort University. The Lebiotex Project Website can be found at www.dmu.ac.uk/laserenzymetextiles

REFERENCES

Goldsworthy, K. (2012), http://www.kategoldsworthy.co.
uk/design-cyclability/

Kane, F., and R. Philpott (2016), "Textile Thinking: A
Flexible, Connective Strategy for Concept Generation
and Problem solving in Inter-disciplinary Contexts,"
in T. H. J Marchand (ed.), *Craftwork as Problem
Solving: Ethnographic Studies of Design and Making.*
Abingdon: Routledge.

Kane, F., L. Morgan, K. Akiwowo, and J. Tyrer (2015),
"Textile Design Research: From Chemistry to
Craft Towards Sustainable Design Innovation,"
The Value of Design Research, 11th International
European Academy of Design Conference,
April 22–24, 2015, Paris, http://www.
europeanacademydesign.co.uk/

Morgan, L. (2016), "Laser Textile Design: The
Development of Laser Dyeing and Laser Molding
Processes to Support Sustainable Design and
Manufacture," PhD Thesis, Loughborough University.

Stevels, A. (1997), "Moving Companies Towards
Sustainable Design Through Eco- Design:
Conditions for Success," *Journal of Sustainable
Product Design*, 3 (October 1997), The Centre for
Sustainable Design.

ASIA (WESTERN, CENTRAL, SOUTH CENTRAL, EASTERN)

PART 4

CHAPTER 4.1

FASHIONING SUSTAINABILITY IN HONG KONG AND CHINA

Gloria Wong, Hong Kong Polytechnic University
Benny Ding Leong, Hong Kong Polytechnic University

INTRODUCTION

Hong Kong has been a pioneer in the garment and fashion industry since the 1970s, and later became a key investor and influencer of apparel and mass fashion in the Pearl River Delta region and China. The Hong Kong clothing industry faces a litany of issues with regard to sustainability due to the environmental pollution rampant in China. This manifests itself in the production process and environment, where working conditions are poor and labor rights are undermined. Consumers globally contribute to the issue by blindly following trends and prioritizing desires over needs, causing the fashion industry to respond using unsustainable practices, leading to the rise of fast fashion since the 1980s (Ghemawat & Nueno 2003). In China particularly, consumers' lack of awareness regarding environmental and ethical issues, as well as their reluctance to wear used clothing, has compounded the issue and allowed unsustainable practices to prevail. Despite this, Hong Kong's globalized environment and exposure to Western influences have put the issue of sustainability at the forefront of business. For instance, in the

1980s, Hong Kong-based international label Esprit pioneered its own ecological line using organic cotton and its naturally-derived color dyes for garments. Prominent textile company, Esquel, has its own fields in Xinjiang growing organic cotton for its brands. Many other companies like Li & Fung and Fenix abide by the tenets of sustainability when it comes to sourcing, overseeing manufacturing, and minimizing their logistics' carbon footprint. The Pearl River Delta region has also received the benefits of Hong Kong's sustainability movement due to its geographical proximity to Hong Kong and its role as a special economic zone in China, resulting in swift socioeconomic development over the past thirty years. This essay will reveal the extent to which this region faces more challenges than the rest of the world, and subsequently how prominent companies implement environmental strategies and management policies to address these issues while maintaining their geographical competitiveness. Most importantly, we highlight how emerging fashion companies and non-governmental organizations (NGOs) respond with various design strategies, moving toward sustainability.

CURRENT DEVELOPMENT OF FASHION INDUSTRY IN HONG KONG AND CHINA

With a projected consumer spending of over US$440 billion by 2018 ("Fashion Retail Opportunities in China" n.d.), China is now the leading market of apparel and fashion in Asia. At the same time, due to rises in costs and unstable demand in international markets, most fast fashion manufacturers and retailers are turning their attention to the developing China and consequently Hong Kong. There are now more than 10,000 garment brands and 22,000 manufacturers in China ("Casual Wear" 2016) which mainly comprise Hong Kong-based/-originated, China-based/-originated and global players. Among them, the dominant players are mostly fast fashion and casualwear manufacturers and retailers established over many decades.

Notable global players, such as Zara, H&M, Uniqlo, C&A, and GAP[1] Giordano,[2] Belle International,[3] Esquel Group,[4] High-Fashion International,[5] Baleno, I.T., and Jeanswest, were founded mainly in between the 1960s and 1980s. Lastly, the most popular China-originated brands are Metersbonwe,[6] Heilan,[7] Septwolves,[8] Semir,[9] TONLION, and Cabbeen. While they serve mainly the mass local markets, they are also the youngest establishments among their global and regional competitors, as they were founded mostly after the 1990s.

In recent years, along with rising labor costs and the aggressive expansion of the global causal-wear brands on the Chinese mainland, an increasing number of Hong Kong and mainland retailers and manufacturers have been shifting toward higher value-added (i.e. improved-design, custom-made) items to enhance differentiation and upmarket recognition (HKTDC 2017). Strategies include adoption of radio frequency identification (RFID), enterprise resource planning (ERP) and big data technologies to enable production and logistic efficiency for responsive orders and lower prices (HKTDC 2016; Niinimäki and Hassi 2011) or widening market reach to capture the predictive sales of US$180 billion by 2018 via e-tailing ("Fashion Retail Opportunities in China" n.d.).

REGIONAL ENVIRONMENTAL PROBLEMS AND THE CSR PRACTICES OF SELECTED COMPANIES IN THE REGION

As "the world's factory" of textiles and garments, there are more than 100,000 garment factories in China, producing over half of the world's fabric—over 80 billion meters yearly—and holding a record of 43.6 billion garments exported in 2012 alone (SACOM 2015). Meanwhile, positioned perfectly as the southern gateway of China, Hong Kong acts as a global sourcing and trading hub of garments. For example, Hong Kong-based manufacturers Esquel Group and High-Fashion International have made use of geographical proximity as well as cheap labor and resources on the mainland to turn themselves into global suppliers for a number of retail giants including Zara, H&M, Uniqlo, NEXT, and Mango. While both Hong Kong- and China-based garment suppliers and manufacturers serve major apparel brands, and form highly efficient supply-networks within and outside China, the planned obsolescence of "fast-fashion" practices continues to accelerate and spread. To meet unrestrained demands, casualwear retailers have shortened the ordering cycle, with new designs being made up and distributed in just weeks (Wei & Zhou 2011). The factory workers employed by Chinese suppliers are forced to work excessively long overtime shifts in order to meet tight delivery times, or to carry more of the risks of managing stock (SACOM 2016).

China is now bearing the heavy social and environmental costs of such development, particularly from textile waste and subsequent pollution. For instance, fabric dyeing and finishing process alone swallows over 2 billion tons of water and consumes about 110 million tons of coal yearly (Wei & Fang 2015). As a result, roughly two-thirds of China's cities suffer from water scarcity, and water from a quarter of its key rivers is not potable. Furthermore, about 80 percent of its cities has failed to meet national pollution standards. Such pollution has caused millions of premature deaths in China annually (Albert 2016).

In response to the worsening environmental and social consequences of fast-fashion practices, major Hong Kong- and China-based fashion companies have been trying to act and adopt Corporate Social Responsibility (CSR) practices in their operations. To make it easier to review the current CSR practices of those major and leading apparel manufacturers and retailers, we have sampled, studied, and evaluated nine representational companies—Metersbonwe, Heilan, Septwolves, and Semir from mainland China, and Esprit, Giordano, Belle, Esquel, and High-Fashion from Hong Kong—based on their scale and popularity. We adopted a case-study approach to collect data from secondary sources include sustainability reports from Esprit (2016), and Esquel Group (2014)[10]; CSR reports from Metersbonwe (2015), Septwolves (2016), and Semir (2013); ESG reports from High-Fashion

International (2016); annual reports from Giordano (2015), Belle (2016), Metersbonwe (2015), Heilan (2016), Septwolves (2016), and Semir (2016); corresponding company websites and the CSR hub[11] websites.

....

Based on our analysis, the selected companies have adopted five common measures in responding to the social and environmental challenges of their operations as follows:

1. *Sustainable products.* Ensure product quality and safety, and promote the use of eco-materials. Companies such as Esprit and Esquel are active in adopting organic cotton, natural cellulose, and natural-dyed fibers, but most of the Chinese companies selected for the study have less clarity about their products' sustainable quality.

2. *Ethical sourcing.* Enable suppliers to operate cleanly, safely, and ethically according to local laws and regulations. Nearly all companies conduct some degree of auditing and training for their suppliers. Esprit, Giordano and Esquel appear to be very enthusiastic and thorough in this aspect.

3. *Environmental protection.* Enforce the reduction of environmental impacts from the production to retailing aspects of operation. Apparently, all selected companies are willing to pursue eco-friendly measures throughout their supply chains to minimize their environmental footprint, while China-originated companies pay attention predominantly on the production-end of their operations.

4. *Social philanthropy.* Embark on programs of donation funding local projects and encouraging employees to serve local communities. Mainland companies are

comparatively high-profile in social initiatives related to disaster relief, local charity, and education initiatives. Hong Kong-based companies have extended their social programs to fund micro-loans, social welfare projects, and healthcare for local farmers, children, and youngsters.

5. *CSR transparency.* Ensure regular updating and reporting of CSR practices to the general public and key stakeholders. In this respect, Esprit, Esquel, Metersbonwe, and High-Fashion International are extremeley willing to share detailed CSR practices via specific reports and web pages.

In fact, sustainable measures and related corporate strategies are also encouraged by some NGOs and industry associations in China. Greenpeace's "Detox My Fashion" campaign encourages manufacturers and brands to promise an action plan for employing chemical consultants to tackle current problems by upgrading machinery and production methods to produce non-toxic textiles. The Zero Discharge of Hazardous Chemicals (ZDHC) Foundation has been formed by the companies operating within the textile industries to conduct research into chemical alternatives, develop audit protocols, and provide training on implementation of zero-hazardous standards. The China Textile Information Center (CTIC) is the newest associate contributor, and advocates that Chinese companies engage in the hazardous chemicals control movement as well. To conclude our evaluation, a concise summary of the CSR performance of the selected companies is listed in Table 4.1.1.

As an initial conclusion, CSR practices adopted by all aforementioned Hong Kong- and China-based manufacturers and retailers are ostensibly "half-hearted": while some sustainable production issues are addressed, these companies have engaged less with sustainability on the consumption side, such as conscious garment care and clothing "reduce" and "reuse," and have instead boosted consumption via seasonal sales, free gifts, and buy-one-get-one-free campaigns online. Given that the fast fashion trend is amplified by the rapid growth in sales of clothing over the Internet, with over 72 percent of the Chinese consumers preferring to purchase clothes in this way, fashion has now become the biggest e-commerce category in China (Cobbing & Vicaire 2016; HKTDC 2017). Companies *can* play a role in promoting sustainable consumption, but have not yet done so.

TOWARD SUSTAINABLE FASHION PRACTICES

According to Greenpeace (Cobbing & Vicaire 2016), approximately 1,400 T-shirts are thrown away every minute in Hong Kong. The average Hong Kong consumer has seventy to 100 garments in his or her wardrobe, fifteen items of which are worn less than three times. It is evident that environmental issues corresponding to fashion consumption are prominent in Hong Kong and China. Before formulating solutions for a more sustainable environment, it is necessary to pin down the root problems.

First, Chinese consumers perceive second-hand goods and sustainability differently from Westerners. Most Chinese people, especially the older generation, considers wearing used clothing from the deceased as a taboo associated with bad luck, evil spirits, and possession. Second, wearing secondhand or recycled products is connected with poverty, as these items are often regarded as "shabby" clothing. Third, China's economic surge since the 1980s has elevated the poor to the

TABLE 4.1.1

COMPARISON OF PROFILES AND CSR PRACTICES OF SELECTED APPAREL MANUFACTURERS AND RETAILERS OPERATING IN HONG KONG AND/OR CHINA.

Company (Date of Establishment)	Market Segment	Brands Owned (Client /Licensed Distribution)	Scale of Business: Turnover (year)	production volume/unit (yearly)	Employees (indirect)	Markets (quantity)	No. of outlets	Outlets (China)	E-tailing (%)	Sourcing: No. of Supplier/ factory	China (%)	Others (%)	CSR Practice*: PR	SU	EM	EN	CO	CU	CSR Transparency: Sustainability Indices	Report specific/ online	** CSR RATING
China-originated Company																					
Metersbonwe Group *** (1995)	young fashionable, casual apparels for men, women and children	Meters/bonwe, ME&CITY, moomoo, AMPM, CH'IN, Bango: (Chris Christy)	~0.91 bn (2015)	~100 million	9420 (NA)	China (NA)	~3,700	~3,700	NA	300 factories	~90%	~10%	1.5	1.5	3	2.5	2.5	0	0	3	1.75
Heilan Home Co. Ltd. *** (1988)	men's casual fashion and apparel	HLA, EICHITOO, SANCANAL, Heirika	2.46 bn (2016)	~600 million	40,000 (NA)	China (31 regions)	5,243	5,243	~35%	270 suppliers	100%	0%	2	1.5	3	1	2.5	0	0	1.5	1.44
Septwolves industry *** (1990)	men's high-end casual wear and children apparel	swissmen, SWKIDS (CANALI, Versace, George Jensen)	0.38 bn (2016)	47 million	2,495 (NA)	China (NA)	3,855	3,855	~34%	NA	100%	0%	1.5	1	2	1	2	0	0	1	1.06
Semir Clothing *** (1996)	children wear, youthful casual apparel	Semir, Balabala, MianColor, ...minette, Mongobobi, U.T.B, etc. (it MICHAA, Sonobonbi, Marc O'Polo)	1.37 bn (2015)	~140 million	2,353 (150,000)	China (31 regions)	~4,000	~4,000	NA	>100 suppliers	100%	0%	2	1.5	3.5	2.5	3	1.5	1	2.5	2.19
Hong Kong-originated Company																					
Esprit Holdings (1968)	casual fashion, footwear, accessories	Esprit	2.3 bn (2016)	~110 million	8,000 (~360,000)	Germany, Europe, China, Asia Pacific, etc. (40 countries)	7,093	1,112	23.3%	NA	28.9%	71.1%	2	3	3.5	3	3	1.5	2.5	4	2.81
Giordano International Holdings (1981)	men's, women's and children's basic, fashion apparel and accessories	Giordano, Giordano Ladies, Giordano Junior, BSX, Beau Monde.	0.69 bn (2015)	NA	>8,000 (NA)	Greater China, Asia Pacific, Middle East, America. (40 countries)	~2,400	962	>16%	NA	NA	NA	2	2.5	3	2.5	2.5	1	1.5	3	2.25
Belle International Holdings (1987)	footwear, handbags, sportswear, and accessories	Belle, Teenmix, Tata, Staccato, Senda, Millie's, Mirabell, etc. (CAT, Clarks, FitFlop, Hush Puppies, Nike, Adidas, PUMA, Converse, Tim berland, etc.)	5.9 bn (2015)	~40 million	119,061 (NA)	China, Hong Kong, Macau, Taiwan, etc. (34 regions)	21,017	20,873	NA	5 factories	100%	0%	1.5	1.5	2.5	1.5	1.5	0	0	1.5	1.25
Esquel Group *** (1978)	casual and upmarket men and women apparels.	PYE, Determinant (GAP, Kohl's, NIKE, Marks & Spencer, Giordano, Boteno, Tommy Hilfiger, Ralph Lauren, etc.)	1.3 bn (2016)	110 million	~57,000 (NA)	USA, Europe, China, Japan, others	NA	NA	NA	195 suppliers	84%	16%	4	3	3.5	3.5	3	3	2.5	4	3.31
High Fashion International *** (1976)	women's and men's leisure fashion, sportswear, neckties, home textile products	Theme, August Silk, Axellecboste, Cluny selfes, C8, CSR (ZARA, Mango, Nina, DKNY, Missy's, L.C. Penney, Mark & Spencer, Target, Nordstorm, etc.)	0.31 bn (2016)	>40 million (garments/ meters silk)	~7,000 (NA)	Greater China, India, Russia, Iran, Vietnam, Indonesia, Mongolia, others	~2,500	~2,000	NA	5 key suppliers	100%	0%	1.5	2	2.5	2.5	2.5	1.5	1	2.5	2.00

* KEY for the CSR Practice:

PR (Product) – Ensure products quality with high safety and health standard for consumer, as well as enforcing sustainable materials utilization of products and packaging.

SU (Supply) – Enable suppliers and/or partner factories to operate cleanly, safely and ethically via practicing regular auditing, assessment to uphold labour rights.

EM (Employee) – Enforce proper corporate culture which fosters business ethics, work-life balance, career developing and talent retention.

EN (Environment) – Exercise restriction of hazardous chemicals, reduction of water consumption and GHG emissions, while promoting renewable energy in production and retail practices.

CO (Community) – Embark on social initiatives together with NGOs and/or governmental bodies to foster positive and sustainable development for local communities and vulnerable groups.

CU (Customer) – Engage customer to minimize environmental footprint through the practices of conscious garment care, recycle and/or reuse.

(RATING RANGE: 0= NIL   1= Barely Adequate   2= Adequate   3= Satisfactory   4= Good   5= Outstanding)

** CSR RATING:

The ratings for the selected companies are averaged from the eight items under the 'CSR Practice' and 'CSR Transparency' sections of the table. These ratings are reference from authors' review of [1] company's reports, websites, literature, and [2] the ratings of the 'CSR HUB' website. The rating are not meant to be judgmental but as a reference for discussion only.

*** CSR Ratings of this company CANNOT be found at the 'CSR HUB' website.

Table courtesy of Gloria Wang and Benny Ding Leong

"newly rich," leading Chinese people to crave luxury, and thus over-consumption. Furthermore, there has been a lack of education regarding the importance of sustainability until very recently.

Solving current environmental issues is undeniably arduous, but independent eco-fashion brands and education can play a role in shifting consumer perceptions in a way that large-scale business is unable or unwilling to do. Financially, eco-fashion brands are facing challenges since most of the sustainable strategies could barely generate enough revenues to keep them afloat. In Hong Kong, high rental costs further exacerbate the problem, while in China, banks are reluctant to loan initial capitals to enable small new brands to start up. As a result, financial support in the form of favorable terms and policies from government or other private funding sources is the most direct measure. For example, the Hong Kong government provides a Recycling Fund of HK$1 billion dollars to subsidize programs regarding sustainability; an eco park has also been established for waste recycling and environment engineering.

Meanwhile, education is of key importance. In fact, some NGOs have initiated sustainable education campaigns such as Detox campaign by Greenpeace, and a roundtable forum by Beijing Fashion Collective. Redress (Figure 4.1.1) is commendable for its efforts to organize the EcoChic Design Award, an annual international fashion design competition promoting sustainability to the young fashion designers and the general public. It has also developed training packs for lecturers around the world. Moreover, some brands and NGOs are collaborating among themselves to run crossover activities, such as charity bazaars, conduct workshops, and organize seminars, such as the "ANCARES" upcycling project by Angus Tsui (Figure 4.2.2), and "The 365 Challenge" by Redress. The Green Ladies & Green Little charity shops selling used clothing have cleverly created a chic ambience for the shops, employ voluntary celebrity spokespeople, and organize educational tours. All of these activities help to arouse public awareness of sustainability, and hopefully will change even the older generation's negative perception of wearing used clothing.

Figure 4.1.1 Redress organizes the EcoChic Design Award, a worldwide competition promoting sustainability
Image credits: left, Redress, center, Redress, right, Tim Wong for Redress, designer Kevin Germanier, styling Denise Ho

Figure 4.1.2 Angus Tsui's "ANCARES" project provide experiential workshops regarding sustainable design
Image reproduced courtesy of Tsui Yat Sing for Angus Tsui

CASE STUDIES: EMERGING INDIVIDUAL SUSTAINABLE FASHION BRANDS AND NGOs IN HONG KONG AND CHINA

Independent sustainable brands can be catalysts for positive change as their innovations may change consumer mindsets. In order to find out more about ongoing attempts to combat this issue, a number of sustainable fashion brands and NGOs were interviewed and studied, and the results are outlined in this section. With reference to Niinimäki and Hassi's (2011) value-creation table, the eco-brands and NGOs were selected for inclusion if they had adopted some sustainable strategies, including production-driven strategies like sourcing, technology, upcycling, recycling, and reusing; if they had adopted socially driven strategies like Fairtrade and ethical practice; if they employed culturally driven strategies like

tradition preservation and embedding cultural elements; and if they used customer-experience-driven strategies like emotional value, customization, experience design, and co-creation, as well as consumption-driven strategies like high-quality material and finishing, durability, and timeless/classic/slow design.

Table 4.1.2 summarizes many of the brands adopting a combination of various sustainable strategies. In contrast with hazardous fast-fashion practices, some are advocates of slow fashion (Brown 2010; Niinimäki & Hassi 2011), which emphasizes both quality and ethical values, and aims to extend the product life span (Blackburn 2009; Blanchard 2008). For instance, they produce high-quality, durable, and classic products and offer a post-purchase maintenance service. If we take NEEMIC as an example, their products focus on meaning, comfort, quality, and timeless design. They believe sustainability is a business opportunity instead of an obstacle. Similar strategies can be found at ICICLE, which offers

TABLE 4.1.2

SUSTAINABLE DESIGN STRATEGIES OF EMERGING FASHION BRANDS/NGOS IN HONG KONG AND CHINA.

CATEGORIES	Production Driven			Social Driven		Cultural Driven		Customer Experience Driven				Consumption Driven			
Sustainable Design Strategies	Sustainable Sourcing	Sustainable Technology	Upcycle Recycle Reuse	Fair Trade	Ethical Practice	Tradition Preservation	Cultural Elements	Emotional Value	Customization	Experience Design	Co-creation	High Quality	Durability	Timeless Classic	Slow Design
Brands															
NEEMIC	Y		Y									Y	Y	Y	Y
Angus Tsui	Y	Y	Y	Y		Y	Y		Y		Y	Y	Y	Y	Y
EARTH.er	Y		Y	Y	Y	Y	Y			Y	Y			Y	Y
WOUF	Y	Y			Y	Y	Y	Y	Y	Y					
ICICLE	Y	Y										Y		Y	Y
LastbutnotLeast			Y					Y			Y				
FFIXXED STUDIO	Y		Y						Y			Y	Y		Y
FINCH			Y									Y			Y
Classic Anew		Y	Y	Y		Y	Y								
Fabrick Lab				Y	Y	Y	Y								
Summerwood		Y		Y		Y	Y								
Indigo 11.50						Y	Y	Y		Y	Y				
Lamina	Y	Y			Y							Y		Y	Y
TPASSION	Y	Y			Y							Y			
NGOs															
Love Multi-culture				Y		Y	Y								
Green Ladies			Y		Y					Y					Y
Redress	Y		Y							Y					
Greenpeace		Y			Y										

Table courtesy of Gloria Wang and Benny Ding Leong

pared-back and classic designs that promote the harmony between humans and nature. Likewise, Earth.er does not follow trends, but instead offers less diversification, with a special focus on which materials it uses, some of which have been upcycled. Angus Tsui uses high-quality materials and a combination of sustainable strategies to create edgy yet still timeless items.

Emotional value is another important element of the strategies. Product attachment helps to promote an emotional link between a person and an object that eventually helps to extend the product life span. Fashion items can be enhanced by various means, such as customization and co-design. For example, a customer might contribute opinions regarding the design and the fit that are specific to him/her. This provides personal meaning and stimulates emotional bonding. Angus Tsui provides unique design with a tailor-made service for customers. Last-but-not-Least provides tailor-made upcycled products with customer involvement, for example, by upcycling a mother's wedding dress for her daughter. The dress is thus embedded with the love from one generation to the next, imbuing it with great meaning, emotional value, and bonding. Another example can be found in WOUF (see Figure 13, plate section) where customization takes the form of each knitted item originating from the customer's pet. The hairs are sustainable, animal-friendly fiber. More importantly this product is precious to the customer since it embodies a strong emotional attachment and the lifelong bonding between the customer and the pet.

Enhancing customers' experience is another strategy strengthening emotional value. Consumers may gain better understanding and improved knowledge of sustainability with a special shopping experience. This will engender positive feelings toward brands that adopt Fairtrade and environmentally friendly strategies.

Basics for Basics emphasizes Fairtrade initiatives that benefit communities in India. Meanwhile, instead of an air-conditioned store environment, EARTH.er purposefully offers a glass of cool water to customers. Customers may be puzzled by this gesture and ask for the rationale behind it, giving the business the opportunity to pass on sustainability-related insights.

Benefiting from massive scales, fast fashion can be manufactured with low costs and at high speed, prompting the death of traditional craft techniques that requires time and manual skills. Urbanization also contributes to the problem, as younger people eschew craft skills (Paulicelli & Clark 2009), like the time-intensive handmade production of ethnic clothing and natural dyeing processes. This is exactly what the environmental activists and eco-brands are concerned about. Hence some brands aim to preserve tradition and ethical production, to encourage people to reflect on current global practices of mass production. For example, EARTH.er used a traditional dyeing method from Thailand in which all pigments are natural materials. Indigo 11.50 offers not only the products made by traditional natural dyeing methods, but also workshops at which people can try out indigo dyeing processes for themselves. The Fabrick Lab started "UN/FOLD" to work with the Shui ethnic minority in Guizhou, China. They employ batik textile techniques to make scarves. This subsidizes the livelihood of the Shui people, and allows their traditional handicrafts to be preserved. In addition to traditional techniques preservation, upholding cultural elements (Davis 1994) is another merit of eco-brands. For example, Classic Anew is committed to promoting Chinese customs; it gives a modern twist to the traditional cheongsam style, while Angus Tsui applied origami in his "Somewhere in Time" collection. In terms of ethical practice, Lamina creates

animal-friendly products that are PETA-approved vegan and donates a proportion of its profits to animal-welfare organizations such as Hong Kong Dog Rescue and the Cat Society of Hong Kong.

Furthermore, some eco-brands employ sustainable sourcing and technology in their green production strategies. They utilize organic materials, upcycled wastes, natural dyes, and non-toxic ingredients for the textiles production and employ advanced cutting and printing methods for garment production (Blackburn 2009). For instance, Angus Tsui uses 100 percent organic cotton, upcycled materials, and production offcuts for his collection. He also applies zero-waste cutting and digital printing to reduce fabric and chemical waste. NEEMIC (Figure 4.1.3) adopts all natural materials, such as organic linen and silk, for fabricating their garments. They import GOTS-certified cotton from Turkey and ramie from Yi Hongbo's Summerwood, which is eco-friendly, grown in Hunan province, hand-woven, and dyed with local herbs. New sustainable developments in

Figure 4.1.3 NEEMIC uses organic certified (GOTS) linen fabric imported from Turkey; hand-woven ramie fabrics from Yi Hongbo's Summerwood with fabric dye derived from local plants and herbs; and upcycled jeans collected at vintage shops and recycling stations
Images reproduced courtesy of Hans Galliker, NEEMIC

Hong Kong include "local-for-local" digital production, which focuses on applying cutting-edge textile with sustainable technology while benefitting the local community. TPASSION employs local skilled workers, fashion and graphic designers to create naturally dyed organic cotton using eco-digital printing technology.

CONCLUSION

It is encouraging to discover the growing number of good practices for fashion sustainability in China and Hong Kong. Although the textile and garment industry has started to develop the awareness of environmental issues and willingness to improve, environmental issues still present a major challenge within the region. As Gwilt and Rissanen (2011) stated, the situation should be improved through education, promotions, and regulations by activists and government. Hence it is of profound importance that activists continue their advocacy to government, industry, customers, and the general public of all ages. Through the joint efforts of all stakeholders in the long run, this environmental issue should be resolved, and we will see a promising move toward sustainable fashion in Hong Kong and China.

NOTES

1. www.esprit.com/company
2. http://corp.giordano.com.hk
3. www.belleintl.com/index.php?file=en
4. www.esquel.com/en/index1.html
5. www.highfashion.com.hk/
6. http://corp.metersbonwe.com/Index/Company
7. www.heilan.com.cn/
8. www.septwolves.com/index.php
9. www.semirbiz.com
10. http://sustainability.esquel.com/2016/
11. www.csrhub.com

REFERENCES

Albert, E. (2016), "China's Environmental Crisis," *CFR Backgrounders*, January 18. Available online at: http://www.cfr.org/china/chinas-environmental-crisis/p12608 (accessed April 17, 2017).

Belle Annual Report FY15/16 (2016), Belle International Holdings. Available online at: http://210.6.198.19/cache/www.belleintl.com/uploads/2016/08/261758216260.pdf?ich_args=1b2b6d8e5ea521cb61464b2e5443a1d1_1_0_0_11_a40221ba52814cbaf42ff5458745a4297531cb0997b8f237e942546cc6434a54_b711c1539bb6c2fe25f469059531dcd9_1_0&ich_ip= (accessed April 17, 2017).

Blackburn, R. S., ed. (2009), *Sustainable Textiles: Life Cycle and Environmental Impact*. Boca Raton, FL: CRC Press.

Blanchard, T. (2008), *Green is the New Black: How to Change the World with Style*. New York: William Morrow.

Brown, S. (2010), *Eco Fashion*. London: Laurence King Publishers.

Casual wear market in China still has a huge market potential (2016), Daxue Consulting, March 4, Available online at: http://daxueconsulting.com/casualwear-market-in-china/ (accessed April 18, 2017).

Cobbing, M., and Y. Vicaire (2016), "Timeout for Fast Fashion," Greenpeace e.v. Available online at: http://www.greenpeace.org/international/Global/international/briefings/toxics/2016/Fact-Sheet-Timeout-for-fast-fashion.pdf (accessed September 18, 2017)

Davis, F. (1994), *Fashion, Culture, and Identity*. Chicago and London: The University of Chicago Press.

Esprit Sustainability Report FY15/16 (2016), Esprit Holdings. Available online at: http://www.esprit.com/press/sustainabilityreport/GRI201516.pdf (accessed April 17, 2017).

Esquel Group Sustainability Report (2014), Sustainable Integration. Available online at: http://sustainability.esquel.com/2014/Esquel-Sustainability-Report-2014.pdf (accessed September 17, 2017).

Fashion Retail Opportunities in China (n.d.), Pure London, Available online at: http://www.purelondon.com/files/pure_china_brochure.pdf (accessed 17 April 2017).

Ghemawat, P., and J. L. Nueno (2003), "Zara: Fast Fashion," *Harvard Business School's Case*, 9-703-497.

Giordano Annual Report (2015), Giordano International Holdings. Available online at: http://corp.giordano.com.hk/files/financial_reports/2015-12-31%2000.00.00.3381/e0709_160303_ARFV.pdf (accessed April 17, 2017).

Gwilt, A., and T. Rissanen, eds (2011), *Shaping Sustainable Fashion: Changing the Way We Make and Use Clothes*. London: Earthscan Ltd.

Heilan Annual Report (2016), Heilan Home Co. Available online at: http://www.sse.com.cn/disclosure/listedinfo/announcement/c/2017-03-11/600398_2016_n.pdf (accessed April 17, 2017).

High Fashion ESG Report (2016), Available online at: http://www.highfashion.com.hk/wp-content/uploads/2017/07/ESG_design_20170725_Chinese_final_smallest.pdf (accessed September 18, 2017).

HKTDC (2016), 'China's Garment Market', *Hong Kong Trade Development Council*, July 12. Available online at: http://china-trade-research.hktdc.com/business-news/article/China-Consumer-Market/China-s-Garment-Market/ccm/en/1/1X000000/1X002L72.htm (accessed April 18, 2017).

HKTDC (2017), "The Clothing Industry in Hong Kong," Hong Kong Trade Development Council, July 25. Available online at: http://hong-kong-economy-research.hktdc.com/business-news/article/Hong-Kong-Industry-Profiles/Clothing-Industry-in-Hong-Kong/hkip/en/1/1X000000/1X003DCL.htm (accessed April 18, 2017).

Metersbonwe Annual Report (2015), Meterbonwe Group. Available online at: http://disclosure.szse.cn/finalpage/2016-04-25/1202228125.PDF (accessed April 17, 2017).

Metersbonwe CSR Report (2015), Meterbonwe Group. Available online at: http://www.cninfo.com.cn/cninfo-new/disclosure/fulltext/bulletin_detail/true/1202228105?announceTime=2016-04-25 (accessed April 17, 2017).

Niinimäki, K., and L. Hassi (2011), "Emerging Design Strategies in Sustainable Production and Consumption of Textiles and Clothing," *Journal of Cleaner Production*, 19(16): 1876–83.

Paulicelli, E., and H. Clark, eds (2009), *The Fabric of Cultures: Fashion, Identity and Globalization*. Abingdon: Routledge.

SACOM (2015), Investigative Report on the Working Conditions in UNIQLO's China Suppliers [report]. Available online at: http://sacom.hk/wp-content/uploads/2015/01/2014-UNIQLO-Investigative-Report_final_20150109.pdf (accessed April 17, 2017).

SACOM (2016), "Reality Behind Brands' CSR Hypocrisy: An Investigative Report on China Suppliers of ZARA, H&M, and GAP" [report]. Available online at: http://sacom.hk/wp-content/uploads/2016/07/Full-report.pdf (accessed April 17, 2017).

Semir Annual Report 2015 (2016), Semir Clothing. Available online at: http://www.semirbiz.com/investorsshowdetail/433.html (accessed April 17, 2017).

Semir CSR Report 2012 (2013), Semir Clothing. Available online at: http://www.semirbiz.com/investorsshowdetail/343.html (accessed April 17, 2017).

Septwolves Annual Report (2016), Septwolves Industry. Available online at: http://www.cninfo.com.cn/finalpage/2017-04-01/1203245167.PDF (accessed April 17, 2017).

Wei, J., and J. Fang (2015), "New Report: China's Sustainable Fashion Leaders Save $14.7 Million Annually Through Major Cuts in Water, Energy & Chemical Use," NRDC, April 14. Available online at: https://www.nrdc.org/media/2015/150414 (accessed April 17, 2017).

Wei, Z. X., and L. J. Zhou (2011), "Case study of online retailing fast fashion industry," *International Journal of e-Education, e-Business, e-Management and e-Learning*, 1(3): 195–200.

A SPOTLIGHT ON: SUCCESSFUL STRATEGIES AND CORE STRENGTHS OF THE SELF EMPLOYED WOMEN'S ASSOCIATION
Learning Milestones toward Building Sustainable Fashion Organizations

Goutam Saha, Darniya Roy, Harsha Rani, National Institute of Fashion Technology, India

With over 2 million members, the Self Employed Women's Association (SEWA) is the largest society of informal workers in the world and India's biggest non-profit organization (Chen 2006). SEWA's success in dominating national and international textile, handloom, and handicraft markets, and thereby expanding its reach into Pakistan, Nepal, Bangladesh, Afghanistan, and Sri Lanka, has positioned SEWA as a leading sustainable fashion organization in South Asia and led to its winning both national and international accolades. SEWA's success strategies,

design intervention, and core strengths are briefly highlighted here to showcase an organization that has achieved much for sustainable fashion production in South Asia, and to provide a few guidelines for those associations who might also want to be successful in the region. SEWA caters to global and national brands as well as direct to Indian consumers, and also provides training to artisans from leading national institutions of design, technology and management. SEWA has also built independent multi-facility centers. These are places for designing and manufacturing

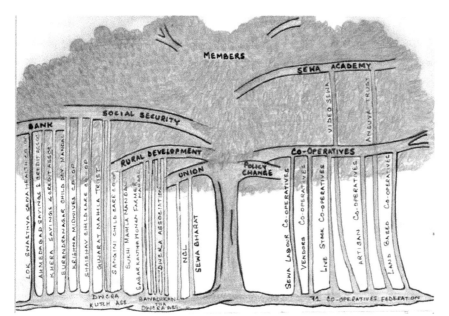

Figure 4.2.1 SEWA tree (inspired by the picture available on SEWA's website)
Image reproduced courtesy of Ms. Darniya Roy

garments and forming a rich embroidery pool, as developed by several artisan communities and their indigenous embroidery techniques.

DESIGN INTERVENTION STRATEGIES

Hansiba is the in-house brand of SEWA, and represents India's timeless embroidery skills. Marginalized women artisans, whose families have often been through difficult times, make every single item in Hansiba's line. The brand is unique in a number of ways: first, products are all hand embroidered; second, 65 percent of sales go directly to the artisans; third, artisans are shareholders and suppliers of the company. SEWA also started the Hansiba Museum, which is owned and maintained by these skilled female craftworkers to preserve and protect traditional embroidery from growing industrialization.

Sewa Kalakruti is a retail brand promoted by the Gujarat State Women's SEWA Cooperative

Figure 4.2.2 Chain stitch embroidery
Image reproduced courtesy of Ms. Tanya Sahney

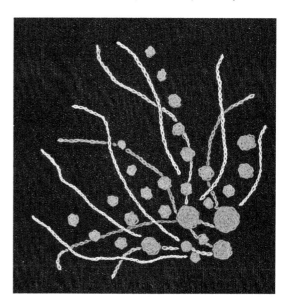

Federation. Its objective is to give the artisans an ideal business environment along with an interface via which they can directly market their products to customers. As with Hansiba,

A SPOTLIGHT ON: SEWA 145

65 percent of Kalakruti's revenue from products sold goes directly to the artisans (STFC 2017).

SEWA'S CORE STRENGTHS

The Ability to Organize Members

SEWA follows three levels of staffing away from its headquarters. A District Coordinator is supported by Team Leaders who are supported by Organizers. Women, in the latter two roles, talk to village councils about SEWA and recruit female representatives to work on a stipend basis. These women become members of the trade group and are encouraged to participate in cooperative or other activities within that trade through a Spearhead Team formed with two Staff Organizers and eight active women volunteers. SEWA trains these women in managerial skills, and also gives them increased responsibilities as well as opportunities for more income for the women, their families and community. Some of them also reach senior positions at SEWA.

Associating Vision and Values in Business Operations

SEWA's clarity on prioritizing self-employed poor women's well-being is reflected in their operations. Some of the principles from the Gandhian belief system that they follow include truth, non-violence, integrating all faiths and people, promoting local employment, and self-reliance. The culture and values of egalitarianism, inclusion, and participation are promoted by addressing each other as "brother" or "sister," conducting all meetings in a highly participatory manner, and not firing any SEWA staff member, but rather adjusting their work to match their talent. The highest-paid SEWA employee earns no more than three times than of the lowest-paid SEWA worker.

Flexibility

The organizers at SEWA are guided by "how to" principles rather than narrow "what to do" guidelines, which promotes natural experimentation and innovation. Staff members and organizers have a commitment to inquiry and fact-finding, and they value objectivity. Such flexibility helps SEWA to adapt and grow easily while keeping the principles of the organization intact. This made SEWA a "learning organization" long before this term came to management vocabulary.

Leadership

Ela Bhatt, the founder of SEWA, created leaders at the grassroots of the organization. Her vision and idealism inspired a cadre of professional women to join and stay with SEWA. These professionals have in turn created a culture of participative management that reduced the social distance between managers and mentors. The "one term post" rule allows a regular rotation of office-holders and decentralization of power. There is a less chance of loss of continuity as the core management team is very stable. SEWA makes a conscious effort to find and develop new leaders from working women (Blaxall 2004).

SEWA's relentless focus on artisans' full employment, social security, and self-reliance has positioned SEWA as a leading sustainable fashion organization in South Asia.

REFERENCES

Blaxall J. (2004), "India's Self-Employed Women's Association (SEWA): Empowerment through Mobilization of Poor Women on a Large Scale," Scaling Up Poverty Reduction: A Global Learning Process and Conference Shanghai, 2014.

Chen, M. (2006), *Self-Employed Women: A Profile of SEWA's Membership*. Bhadra, Ahmedabad: SEWA Academy.

STFC (Online) Available online at: http://www.sewatfc. org (accessed March 27, 2017).

COLLABORATIVE CONSUMPTION FOR SMALL- AND MEDIUM-SIZED FASHION ENTERPRISES IN SOUTH KOREA

Eunsuk Hur, University of Leeds, UK

INTRODUCTION

Sustainability in the fashion industry is challenging due to numerous problems, which entail both complex production and consumption processes in a global context. Over the past decade, clothing consumption patterns have changed considerably, influenced by the disposable fast fashion phenomenon. In recent decades, the need to incorporate sustainability in business practices in the fashion industry has become increasingly clear. The concept of a "circular economy" (CE) has been promoted to highlight the need to find an alternative approach for recovering or regenerating resources for the maximum value of a garment's life (WRAP 2016). This concept has attracted increasing attention because of the need to reduce waste and optimize resource productivity while achieving a competitive advantage and reducing the negative environmental effects of clothing production and consumption (WRAP 2016). The demand for sustainability in business practices and creative ways of promoting sustainability has thus grown in many organizations.

This essay focuses on alternative approaches to revitalizing the economy as well as consideration of the environmental and social impacts of clothing on the sharing economy when purchasing, using, and disposing of clothes with a more circular approach. First, this essay offers a brief background of the South Korean fashion industry and the challenges involved in sustainable production and consumption in the fashion industry in South Korea. Second, it provides an overview of collaborative consumption (CC) in fashion and discusses various drivers of CC in South Korea. Third, the essays provides two case studies of social enterprises that facilitate CC in South Korea.

OVERVIEW OF THE SOUTH KOREAN FASHION INDUSTRY

South Korea has one of the world's fastest-growing economies. The textile- and fashion-related industries have made a significant contribution to the country's growth. Clothing consumption in South Korea has been increasing since 1960 and was responsible for over 40 percent of total textile and clothing exports in 1970 (cited in Jin and Moon 2006). However, the Korean textile- and fashion-related industries are currently losing their competitive advantages due to challenges resulting from increased production and labor costs, as the industries are still heavily reliant on labor-intensive manufacturing processes. Since the early 2000s, Korean Textiles and Apparel (T&A) has progressively concentrated on value-added design activities, focusing on design, marketing, branding, innovation, and creativity (Ha-Brookshire & Lee 2011).

Similar to western high street retailers such as ZARA and H&M, current Korean fashion companies quickly produce a high volume of low-priced garments, which has led to changing consumer consumption patterns. The significant volume of textile and garment waste has progressively increased over the past decade in South Korea. The Ministry of Environment of Korea (2013) estimated that the textile and garment waste in the country was 54,677 tonnes in 2008, and this increased by 17 percent to 64,075 tonnes within two years (Kim & Kim 2016). According to the United Nations Comtrade Database (2013), South Korea is the fourth largest used clothing exporter, following the US, UK, and Germany. Korea exported more than US$364 million of used garments overseas in 2013 (Rodgers 2015). The existing secondhand clothing supply chain system is unsustainable in the global context. Due to the arrival of cheap, imported secondhand clothes, the local textile and garment industries in developing countries have fallen significantly.

In response to the global sustainability movement, great pressure has been placed on the fashion industry by the government and the public to integrate sustainability. The Korean government has recently implemented a "Green Growth" initiative, aiming to encourage businesses to incorporate sustainability into their business activities. The major green fashion movement is often focused on the utilization of eco-materials (e.g. organic, biodegradable, recycled materials), eco-marketing, and the upcycling of products. Na and Na (2013) conducted 396 case studies of Korean fashion companies to examine how Korean fashion and textiles companies are incorporating sustainability into their business practices. Their research shows that Korean apparel companies commonly use three major strategies for addressing issues of sustainability: 36.9 percent use eco-materials such as natural or recycled or biodegradable fibers, 58.6 percent focus on eco-marketing to reshape their brand images, and 4.4 percent focus on the reuse of the garments through remodeling and upcycling processes. Fashion companies commonly use organic materials and green marketing to promote their green product ranges.

On the consumption side, there is a growing interest in green products in South Korea. World research (2005) showed that 58 percent of South Korean consumers are interested in green products and 76 percent would like to purchase them even though the price is slightly higher than similar products (cited in Sung & Kincade, 2010). Korean fashion companies are striving to meet consumer needs related to the current green movement. However, they are still in the very early stages of implementing sustainability in their business practices and have mainly focused on eco-product developments as part of their relatively short-term business strategies. There has been a lack of exploration of the Product-Service System (PSS) and how materials and garments can be utilized in different ways. Furthermore, the various production and consumption issues call for alternative business models and the creation of new product, process, and service systems. In particular, young enterprises are looking for new production and consumption processes.

APPROACH TO SUSTAINABLE FASHION AND COLLABORATIVE CONSUMPTION

The term "collaborative consumption" is also referred to as the "sharing economy." Felson and Speath (1978) defined CC as one or more individual exchanges or consumptions of a product or service through a process of social engagement activities with one or more users. Bostman and Rogers (2010) defined CC in a broader context, encompassing various exchange activities including "sharing, bartering, lending, trading, renting, gifting and swapping" in peer-to-peer marketplaces. In turn, Belk (2014) argued that this definition is *too* broad. For example, a gift that directly transfers ownership and CC occupies "a middle ground between sharing and marketplace exchange, with elements of both." He argued that CC requires people to coordinate the acquisition and distribution of a good or service. Thus, he proposed a definition of CC as "people coordinating the acquisition and distribution of a resource for a fee or other compensation" (Belk 2014).

Although there are various definitions and interpretations of CC, its major purpose is to facilitate a more collaborative and sustainable society through a shared economy in the social system (Heinrichs 2013). The social-engagement process enables the sharing or acquisition of products and services, ideas, knowledge, and talent, skills, etc. It also helps in the reuse of resources and facilitates alternative material consumption in various ways by shifting individual ownership to shared ownership or short-term rentals promoting individual participation (Belk 2014). This allows fashion businesses to co-produce the values of their products or services with consumers.

Botsman and Rogers (2010) suggested that CC supports alternative consumption activities by alleviating hyper-consumption and reducing environmental impacts. They offered comprehensive classifications of collaborative consumption types including PSS, Redistribution of Market (RM), and Collaborative Lifestyle (CL). First, PSS allows an organization to provide products as services rather than selling the goods in the marketplace. In this case, consumers do not have ownership of the products but are able to temporarily access them. Thanks to the advancement of internet technology, the sharing economy is gaining popularity. The internet provides access to knowledge and allows idea sharing using the Web 2.0 communication system. Second, RM enables users to purchase pre-owned goods by exchanging money (i.e. eBay) or swapping products. Fashion companies also promote and incentivize the return and reuse of secondhand products through various campaigns. For example, M&S and Oxfam launched the Shwopping partnership, as a result of which 20 million items were collected to promote the redistribution, reuse, and recycling of unwanted garments.

Third, CL is based on sharing or exchanging intangible assets, including rental space (i.e.

AirBnB), skills or ideas (i.e. Kickstarter), crowdsourcing design (i.e. Threadless), and crowdfunding fashion projects (i.e. Betabrand). Collaborative lifestyle services are commonly associated with the optimization of intangible product usage and consumer experiences, such as personal styling services and co-creative product and service systems using crowdsourcing and peer-to-peer marketplaces.

There are various motivations for participating in CC. Hamari et al. (2016) suggested that CC has positive impacts on environmental issues (environmental value) through the utilization of resources. Second, participation in CC offers enjoyment of the activity through engagement of the local community (hedonic and social value). Third, CC makes it possible to maximize economic value by supporting maximum connectivity in the community. One of the most positive indicators for participating in a CC event is its economic value. However, Hamari et al. (2016) showed that ecological consumption or environmental concerns are not directly associated with participation in CC. Their research suggests that strictly emphasizing sustainability issues does not directly lead to a positive attitude toward CC. Similarly, Roux and Guiot (2008) indicated that the major consumer motivation for purchasing used items is based on economic and hedonic values. Consumers that purchase secondhand goods are mainly price-sensitive and looking for treasures or bargains.

THE RISE OF COLLABORATIVE CONSUMPTION IN SOUTH KOREA

The concept of CC gained considerable attention in South Korea during the global financial crisis that began in 2008. The social and economic issues related to the crisis encouraged people to reduce their family expenditure. Today, the idea of CC has moved more toward the social value of creating positive relations among various communities by optimizing resource usage instead of wasting resources in the consumption process.

In the last few years there has been a progressive increase in the number of small and medium-sized businesses focusing on CC to support sustainable development in South Korea. The city of Seoul launched the "Sharing City" in September 2012, and this concept of sharing spread to its urban policies in the public and private sectors. The purpose of this strategy was to mitigate various social issues by supporting local businesses and promoting civic engagement through the "shared use of both public and private resources" (Share Hub, 2016).

This sharing economic platform allows the public and businesses to distribute and access products and services to promote sustainable development. Share Hub (sharehub.kr) is aiming to facilitate the sharing of products and services, intellectual skills and ideas, and lifestyles. The main philosophy behind sharing activities is to support a better environment, encourage economical and conscious consumption, and provide opportunities for people in society as a whole.

A sharing website developed by the Seoul government in 2013 has been widely promoting education, books, products, media, travel, art, cars, government, spaces, experiences, knowledge, and skills. The Seoul Metropolitan Government (SMG) designed and supported seventy-seven sharing services from 2013 to 2016, covering a range of similar topics. This project facilitates cultural and economic sharing that connects the government, citizens, and businesses. As a result, public sharing in Seoul has nearly quintupled

Figure 4.3.1 Seoul Metropolitan Government (SMG) sharing economy services
Image reproduced courtesy of ShareHub Korea

since 2014 (from 326,426 citizens in 2014 to 1,556,069 in 2016) (ShareHub Korea 2016).

The SMG has educated citizens through various seminars and conferences and has organized campaigns with social sharing enterprises by networking with diverse CC- and sharing economy-based organizations.

The Open Closet

The Open Closet (www.theopencloset.net) is a non-profit organization that facilitates social innovation and tackles an important social issue. The company supports poor young jobseekers in order to minimize unemployment and social

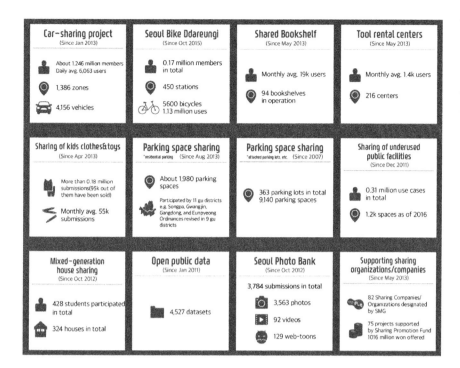

Figure 4.3.2 SMG's sharing polices and their achievements
Image reproduced courtesy of ShareHub Korea

Figure 4.3.3 The Open Closet social enterprise business model
Image adapted from The Open Closet (2017)

inequality. The company's business model is based on a CE model, particularly focusing on the post-consumption process.

According to *The Korea Herald* (2015), the youth unemployment rate in South Korea is continuously increasing and is currently at its highest level in fifteen years. The Open Closet supports young people who are searching for jobs by helping with the economic burden of purchasing formal suits for their job interviews. The company serves young people who are socially and culturally marginalized or vulnerable, and who wish to find employment. One of its projects is targeted toward unemployed women in Korea, attempting to overcome sexual discrimination in the male-dominated South Korean society. The Open Closet was launched in 2012 and accumulated more than 2,251 donators' and 11,838 renters' stories in three years.

The background of the operation process involved building a strong relationship with donors and lenders by encouraging active participation in the CC of suits by providing their personal stories. People donate their secondhand business suits along with their personal stories to the website. The Open Closet then cleans and repairs the suits and rents them to jobseekers at fairly low prices. Those who rent the clothes then return the items along with their personal stories.

The Open Closet argues that it is not just another rental company: it aims to build a cultural movement that helps young people. The company shares the stories behind the sharing. This creates a new type of relationship between the donors and users. More than 100 stories can be related to a single suit. The sharing process itself creates very strong social bonds. The Open Closet seeks to provide a feasible solution for specifically targeted user groups and a specific product type. The company identified the gap in the general economic and CC systems in Korea—the ambiguity regarding what is shared and how the sharing occurs. The Open Closet believes that sharing all clothes is not particularly feasible, so they reduced the number of options and focused on specific needs rather than trying to address

Figure 4.3.4 Lenders and donors share stories related to their clothing
Image reproduced courtesy of The Open Closet

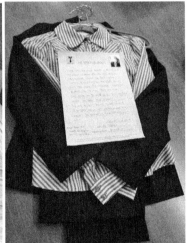

Figure 4.3.5 The Open Closet's repairing process and showroom
Image reproduced courtesy of The Open Closet

everything at once. The company's mission statement involves sharing formal clothing and thereby providing value to society.

The Business Model Canvas (BMC) (Osterwalder & Pigneur 2010) is widely used by various enterprisers because it addresses the key areas of the activities involved in building a business structure. The model consists of the nine principal building blocks that comprise the four major areas of a business. The four main activities include customers, offer, infrastructure, and finances. Based on the nine building blocks of the business model canvas, Table 4.3.1 describes The Open Closet's business model.

The Open Closet's average target customers are mainly twenty to thirty years of age, but the company serves individuals from fourteen to seventy who are looking for formal clothing. Approximately eighty consumers visit the showroom office daily, and around 50,000 people have used the service since 2013 (*The Seoul Economic Daily* 2017). The company's revenue stream is based on clothing rental services. The costs include renting the showroom office, staff salaries, maintenance, and promoting the business. The company was initially supported by individual clothing donors but is now receiving donations from organizations and fashion design companies.

TABLE 4.3.1

THE OPEN CLOSET'S BUSINESS MODEL.

The 9 building blocks of the BMC	Description
Customer segments	Jobseekers or those who wish to wear formal or business suits and shoes.
Value proposition	Formal clothing rental company based on second-hand business outfits for interviews or special occasions. Company promotes economic, social and environmental sustainability.
Channels	Company website acts as a clothing sharing platform and provides showroom space for visitors.
Customer relationships	Building community support through social media. Focus on the satisfaction of the clothing donors and users and address their needs. Connecting and supporting citizens and organising consultancy programs or campaigns for young people who wish to find a job.
Revenue streams	Users pay an affordable rental fee and use crowdsource funding (i.e. GlobalGiving) for donations.
Key resources	Formal clothing, storage space, online interface and various volunteers.
Key activities	Repair and upcycle garments and shoes for other users. Attract individual, community and organisational donors. Promote and spread its business idea using various media to motivate active participation. Form online and offline communities.
Key partnerships	Other non-profit organisation platforms to obtain funding. Collaboration with designer brands and other organisations.
Cost structure	Non-profit organisation that maintains its business based on individual and organisational donations.

Table courtesy of Eunsuk Hur

Kiple

Kiple (www.kiple.net) is a peer-to-peer collaborative consumption platform that enables users to share children's products that are still good quality but no longer used. The company was established in 2011, and people currently share more than 204,000 products. Children generally grow very quickly and consequently a child's clothes can only be worn a few times due to sizing issues. This online platform allows users to buy and sell secondhand or recycled children's products with a relatively low exchange cost in order to reduce parents' economic burden and optimize resource usage.

The owner of Kiple noted that the starting of their business was very smooth as there were few collaborative consumption business models available for kids' clothes. However, Kiple identifies several weaknesses of their initial business model to sustain their organization for long term future. First, an existing peer-to-peer (P2P) sharing service often inflicts a lot of inconvenience on consumers as they are required to upload each product image and the product's information online. Second, the majority of consumers shared kids' products as a bundle but the product qualities were often not consistent. They realized that a single product return method was also required for each product. Third, some users had barriers when purchasing products in their initial business model, which was completely based on the P2P sharing platform. If someone does not share products, they could not use the Kiple service. Finally, their P2P model was based on a low profit structure per transaction and the cost often increased due to a frequent P2P delivery process (Lee 2013).

After several improvements to the existing P2P business model, Kiple is now able to offer a more effective collaborative consumption service. When users send secondhand clothes to Kiple, they select good-quality products. Depending on the products' levels of quality, condition, and brand, they provide 50–80 percent of Kiple "money," which is a virtual currency, and obtain membership points. The ranking money system is based on the product's quality that is categorized as follows: Best—provides 80 percent of Kiple money; Better—70 percent of Kiple money; and Good– 50 percent.

Figure 4.3.6 Kiple's social enterprise business model
Image adapted from Kiple (2017)

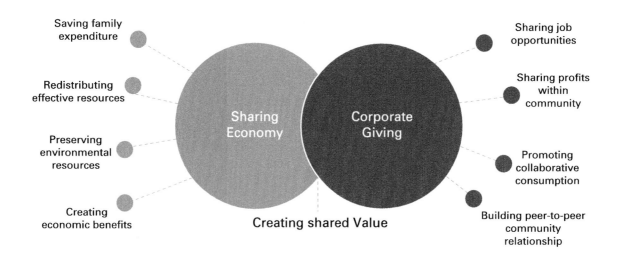

Saving family expenditure

Redistributing effective resources

Preserving environmental resources

Creating economic benefits

Sharing Economy

Corporate Giving

Creating shared Value

Sharing job opportunities

Sharing profits within community

Promoting collaborative consumption

Building peer-to-peer community relationship

Plate 1 Contextura upcycling (Chapter 1.1)
Photo by Pedro Fonseca, model Jake Bisinela

Plate 2 12na at Malmö Festival (Chapter 1.3)
Image reproduced courtesy of Maria de las Mercedes Martinez

Plate 3 Pamela Cavieres Jewelry (Chapter 1.3)
Author pieces: Pamela Cavieres, visual artist. Author photography: Damián Wasser

Plate 4 Ana Livni design (Chapter 1.4)
Model: Stefania Tortorella. Photographer: Rafael Lejtreger. Make-up: Inés Silvera. Hair: Roberto Tajes;
Direction and design: atelier Livni-Escude

Plate 5 Feel Croquis (Chapter 1.6)
Image reproduced courtesy of Margarita Yepes Montoya

Plate 6 The Miss Ellie sweater (Chapter 2.4)
Image reproduced courtesy of Rimba Muharram

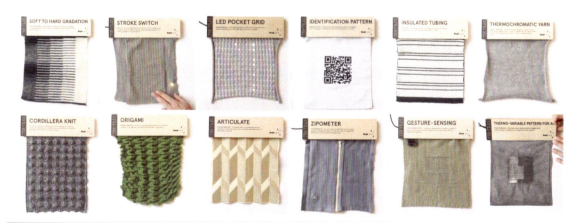

Plate 7 A TEK-TILES sampler (Chapter 2.6)
Image reproduced courtesy of Deb Johnson, Pratt Institute's Brooklyn Fashion + Design

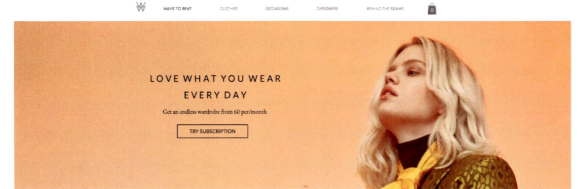

WEAR the WALK

MEMBERS

WAYS TO RENT   CLOTHES   OCCASIONS   DESIGNERS   BEHIND THE SEAMS   0

LOVE WHAT YOU WEAR
EVERY DAY

Get an endless wardrobe from 60 per/month

TRY SUBSCRIPTION

HOW SUBSCRIPTION WORKS

CHOOSE

WEAR

ROTATE

Plate 8 UK clothing rental company, Wear the Walk (Chapter 3.1)
Image reproduced courtesy of Zoe Patridge, founder, Wear the Walk

Plate 9 Inspired by the sky-Shadow, Elsien Gringhuis (Chapter 3.2)
Image reproduced courtesy of Tse Kao (Casa De Kao Photography)

Plate 10 Sukupira—Conscious Wear (Chapter 3.3)
Image reproduced courtesy of Sarah Girão Mendes Gouveia

Plate 11 Newborn, girl size 56 and boy size 68. *Photo © VIGGA* (Chapter 3.4)
Image reproduced courtesy of VIGGA™

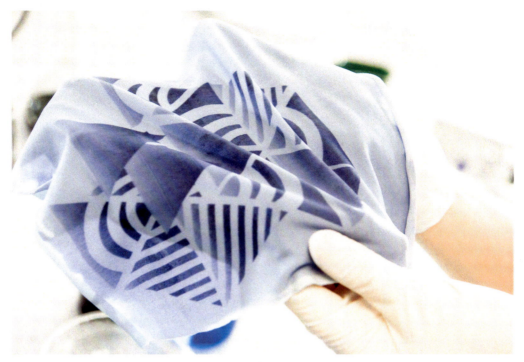

Plate 12 Peri-dyed textile surface design (Chapter 3.6)
Photography: Emilio Lecuona

Plate 13 WOUF designs (Chapter 4.1)
Image reproduced courtesy of Margaret Lok

Plate 14 Sequin and threadwork (Chapter 4.2)
Image reproduced courtesy of Ms Tanya Sahney

Plate 15 House of Lonali look book, image e. (Chapter 4.4)
Image reproduced courtesy of Lonali Rodrigo

Plate 16 Başak Cankeş, from 2015/16 Doors collection (Chapter 4.5)
Image reproduced courtesy of Başak Cankeş

Plate 17 Spools of yarn, Tasmania (Chapter 5.1)
Image reproduced courtesy of Karina Salijak

Plate 18 Elisa Jane Carmichael, *Saltwater footprints, shades of blue* (Chapter 5.2)
Image reproduced courtesy of Elisa Jane Carmichael

Plate 19 A local Vietnamese worker adds decorative details to an Ipa Nima bag (Chapter 5.3)
Photograph by Esther Huang Huiai with thanks to Christina Yu, Ipa Nima

Plate 20 Garment workers travelling to work in the factories in Phnom Penh (Chapter 5.5)
Image reproduced courtesy of Montesano Casillas

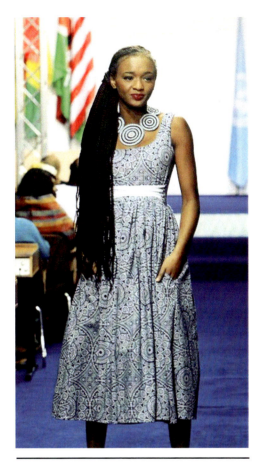

Plate 21 A casual dress with African prints
(Leteisi) from Botswana, African Fashion
(Chapter 6.3)
Image reproduced courtesy of Botho Chalebgwa

Plate 22 African attire. *Image reproduced courtesy of Shalom, Letwin, Mercy, and Thandiwe, Solusi University*
(Chapter 6.4). *Image reproduced courtesy of Zembe Thandiwe, Shalom Machanyangwa, Prisca and Letwin Hunyenyiwa*

Plate 23 Emirati women. *Image reproduced courtesy of Charney Magri* © charneymargri.com (Chapter 6.5)

Plate 24 Emirati weaving. *Image reproduced courtesy of Charney Magri* © charneymargri.com (Chapter 6.5)

TABLE 4.3.2

KIPLE'S BUSINESS MODEL.

The 9 building blocks of BMC	Description
Customer segments	Customers are mainly parents, and consumers are children.
Value propositions	This method of e-commerce provides users purchasing and selling second-hand children's clothing through peer-to-peer collaborative consumption.
Channels	E-tailing business and social media.
Customer Relationships	Providing sharing closet platform and connecting sellers and buyers for children's recycled products and create memberships.
Revenue Streams	Consumers purchase second-hand children's clothing.
Key Resources	Maintain storage spaces, an online interface and service management team.
Key Activities	Quality control management for second hand goods. Form peer-to-peer online and off-line community relationships between buyers and sellers. Promote and spread its business idea using various media types to motivate active participation.
Key partnerships	Partnerships with sharing oriented business.
Cost structure	Parents can sell and purchase their kids' products using the credit points.

Table courtesy of Eunsuk Hur

Neither sellers nor buyers can exchange actual money for selling and purchasing the products.

Kiple encourages users to categorize product types based on children's clothing, books, toys, and baby products, among others. They provide clear guidelines on which items of clothing can be shared. Users can enjoy shopping using Kiple money and share stories that are pertinent to the clothing. The purchasing and selling process is very simple and user-friendly. Existing secondhand trading services are often very time-consuming, but Kiple only requires the user to complete a simple pick-request form, and a courier will then collect the items at a convenient time. Users can search for a product based on age, gender, season, colors, product type, and brand name. The company adopted the circular economy model and shares stories about the products. The major building blocks of Kiple's business model are shown in Table 4.3.2.

DISCUSSION

Collaborative Consumption (CC) can provide an alternative consumption process through utilizing effective resources via redistribution of products or increased serviceability of the products. The Open Closet uses the Product-Service System of CC through renting formal suits. In this case, the amount of usage per garment will be significant. As the product is primarily used for special occasions, the rental service is very convenient.

This approach is mainly focusing on maximization of the positive consumer experiences during the post consumption process through supporting the online and offline community of jobseekers. The finding of the research shows that the specialized product ranges, and the targeted consumer groups, are significant factors for operating a collaborative consumption business rather than trying to offer all product ranges in non-segmented markets. Open Closet consumers mostly prioritize the social and economic values as a sustainable alternative solution. The sharing experiences help to maximize the emotional attachment of the rented product as each piece of clothing contains a unique sentimental story. Open Closet optimizes the various social activities, collaborating with other organizations in order to promote social integration with outcasts.

Kiple offers secondhand children's clothing via the redistribution of used products. The usage intensity per garment will be less optimal than the PSS model but children's clothing is used in a specific period and is more relevant to the redistribution markets (RS) model. Small- and medium-sized social enterprises are often at greater risk of business failure than larger entities, and there are various barriers involved in facilitating collaborative consumption. Kiple quickly responded to consumer needs and updated its business model for more effective services in the P2P-based sharing marketplace.

In the last few years, the perception of secondhand goods in South Korea has changed significantly thanks to vintage clothing trends. Younger consumers are slowly taking more interest in secondhand clothing, but there are still niche markets and various challenges involved in collaborative the consumption process and secondhand clothing market sector. According to Kim and Kim (2013), younger consumers tend to have more negative perceptions toward secondhand clothing as they are used to purchasing fast-fashion products. However, their research identified that people who had experience of purchasing used garments have more a positive perception of secondhand goods.

CONCLUSION

This chapter discusses the opportunities and challenges involved in collaborative consumption in the South Korean market. Both Open Closet and Kiple have successfully implemented the social enterprise model, and have specifically targeted social issues while concentrating on product type for differentiation. The CC movement has been transforming our production and consumption process through networking and building P2P communities. In particular, Web 2.0 online technology enables users to participate in collaborative consumption processes including purchasing, wearing, maintaining, sharing, and updating clothing until the end of each item's life cycle. Implications of the research is that management of the consumption process and customer experiences are significant in maintaining the long-term future of sustaining a collaborative consumption business. The secondhand service design system as an area of academic research is still in its early stages; there potentially exists an opportunity to build alternative customer-to-customer (C2C) businesses and a shared economic system that has a positive impact on environmental and social elements.

ACKNOWLEDGEMENTS

The author gratefully acknowledges The Open Closet and the Korea Creative Commons for providing their images and sharing their valuable experiences.

REFERENCES

Belk, R. (2014), "You Are What You Can Access: Sharing and Collaborative Consumption Online," *Journal of Business Research*, 67: 1595–1600.

Botsman, R., and R. Rogers (2010), *What's Mine Is Yours: The Rise of Collaborative Consumption*. Harper Business: New York, NY.

Felson, M., and J. Speath (1978), "Community Structure and Collaborative Consumption," *American Behavioral Scientist*, 41: 614–24.

Ha-Brookshire, J., and Y. Lee (2011), "Firm capabilities and firm size: The case of Korean apparel manufacturers," International Journal of Fashion Design, Technology and Education, 4(1): 59–67.

Hamari, J., M. Sjöklint, and A. Ukkonen (2016), "The Sharing Economy: Why People Participate in Collaborative Consumption," *Journal of the Association for Information Science and Technology*, 67(9): 2047–59.

Heinrichs, H. (2013), "Sharing Economy: A Potential New Pathway to Sustainability," GAIA, 22(4): 228–31.

Jin, B., and H. C. Moon (2006), "The Diamond Approach to the Competitiveness of Korea's Industry: Michael Porter and Beyond," *Journal of Fashion Marketing and Management*, 10: 195–208.

Kim, D., and M. Kim (2013), "Perception, Purchase Behaviours of and the Buying Motives Toward Second-hand clothing products," *The Research Journal of the Costume Culture*, 21(3): 324–37.

Kim, C. S., and K. R. Kim (2016), "A Case Study Comparing Textile Recycling Systems of Korea and the UK to Promote Sustainability," *Journal of Textile and Apparel, Technology and Management*, 10(1).

Kiple, (2017), Kiple Homepage, Retrieved from http://www.kiple.net

Lee, M. (2013), "Kiple: Sharing economy through kids clothing." Available online at: http://platum.kr/archives/7067

The Korea Herald (2015), "Youth unemployment rate in Korea reaches highest in 15 years." Available online at: http://www.koreaherald.com/view.php?ud=20150726000328

Na, Y., and D. K. Na (2015), "Investigating the Sustainability of the Korean Textile and Fashion Industry," *International Journal of Clothing Science and Technology*, 27(1): 23–33.

Osterwalder, A., and Y. Pigneur (2010), *Business Model Generation: A Handbook for Visionaries, Game changers, and Challengers*. Hoboken, NJ: John Wiley & Sons.

Rodgers, L. (2015), "Where do your old clothes go?", BBC News. Available online at: http://www.bbc.co.uk/news/magazine–30227025

Roux, D., and D. Guiot, D (2008), "Measuring second-hand shopping motives, antecedents and consequences," *Recherche et Applications En Marketing* (English Edition), 23(4): 63–91.

Sheth J. N., N. K. Sethia, and S. Srinivas (2011), "Mindful Consumption: A Customer-centric Approach to Sustainability," *Journal of the Academy of Marketing Science*, 39: 21–39.

Sung, H.W., and D. H. Kincade (2010), "Typology of Korean Eco-sumers: Based on Clothing Disposal Behaviors," *Journal of Global Academy of Marketing*, 20(1): 59–69.

Share Hub (2016), Sharing City Seoul Homepage, Retrieved from http://english.sharehub.kr/

The Open Closet (2017), The Open Closet Homepage. Available online at: https://theopencloset.net/

The Seoul Economic Daily (2017), The Open Closet interview. Available online at: http://www.sedaily.com/NewsView/1ODHTTFAJR

WRAP (2016), "WRAP and the circular economy." Available online at: http://www.wrap.org.uk/about-us/about/wrap-and-circular-economy

CHAPTER 4.4

A SPOTLIGHT ON: EXAMPLES OF SUSTAINABLE FASHION IN SRI LANKA

Sumith Gopura, University of Moratuwa, Sri Lanka
Alice Payne, Queensland University of Technology, Australia

The Sri Lankan (SL) apparel industry has evolved over the past four decades to move from basic apparel assembly to original design manufacturing, and accounts for approximately 40 percent of SL's total exports. Major manufacturers such as MAS, Brandix, Hirdaramani, and Hela Clothing provide design and manufacturing solutions for global brands such as GAP, Marks and Spencer, and Victoria's Secret (Khattak et al. 2017; Lopez-Acevedo & Raymond 2016). Since 2000, the SL government and apparel industry have sought to establish the industry reputation as a provider of "garments without guilt," through world-class environmentally friendly factories committed to ethical and high-quality apparel manufacturing (Loker 2010; Ruwanpura 2015). Although the industry has high levels of workers' health and safety, questions remain in the challenges that the SL industry has faced in recent years around providing living wages and securing appropriate labor conditions (e.g. Ivy Park scandal) to workers in apparel manufacturing (Read 2017).

With fashion design education introduced in SL in the early twenty-first century, SL designers hold key positions in the export apparel industry, and many others have established their own independent labels. A number of independent designers draw on SL heritage in craft skills. Examples include Darshi Keerthisena who works with batik, and Kasuni Rathnasuria who works with handloom and Beeralu lace; both have had their work showcased at SL Design Festival and Colombo Fashion Week. However, these crafts skills are rarely used in the export apparel manufacturing context as they are not suited to mass-production capabilities.

Due to the availability of infrastructure, SL's large-scale manufacturing factories are mainly based in the western part of the country, particularly in the Colombo suburbs. For this reason, workers have migrated from rural areas to the city, creating social and economic glitches as the apparel manufacturing zones are densely populated and high in living expenses. Over 90 percent of employees in the sector are female and the average labor turnover is approximately 60 percent per annum. The industry loses many female workers to foreign employment, or they

Figure 4.4.1 Pamunuwa street market offering trims and accessories for sale
Image reproduced courtesy of Tharundu Aluthge

Figure 4.4.2 Pamunuwa street market textiles for sale
Image reproduced courtesy of Tharundu Aluthge

stop working after marriage. The category of young male employees has also seen higher labor turnover as many move out of the apparel industry and into driving taxis, in the local terms "three wheelers," which require no special skills and provide flexible working hours. Therefore, retaining skilled labor is an important issue which the apparel industry has sought to address through attractive wage schemes, creating self-esteem around the job, and providing workers with benefits such as health cover and a wide range of professional development programs.

From the environmental perspective, the scale of production leads to tons of waste materials, including excess textile offcuts and rejected apparel. This waste may be incinerated as an energy source, or else be stored and obsoleted to protect brands' intellectual property rights before being released to the local market. Pamunuwa is one of the main street markets in the country with bargain textile and apparel shops that trade in pre-consumer textiles. As the export apparel industry caters to a vast array of overseas brands,

from formal wear, casual wear to active wear, Pamunuwa is a treasure trove of fabrics, trims, and accessories that can be used in the local context, albeit limited to the availability on shelves. Pamunuwa attracts small- and medium-local business owners, independent designers, and fashion students for their inspirations and raw material needs.

HOUSE OF LONALI

House of Lonali is a sustainable brand that uses the export apparel industry's textile waste as the basis for design. House of Lonali was established in 2012, led by Lonali Rodrigo, a fashion graduate from Academy of Design SL. Lonali aspires to care for the planet through fashion and style, upcycling discarded fabrics and trims from the SL export

Figure 4.4.3 House of Lonali shoes

Images reproduced courtesy of Lonali Rodrigo

apparel industry through the unique relationships she has built up with the factories. Her collections cleverly incorporate the odd-shaped offcuts into her patternmaking, developing fresh and youthful designs with intriguing paneling and drape. In some instances, she makes appliqué styles from the offcuts to recover defect fabrics used in her collections, and also offers a collection of shoes made from waste. Lonali's work proposes a model for sustainable collaboration between large-scale and small-scale industry in SL.

REFERENCES

Khattak, A., N. Haworth, C. Stringer, and M. Benson-Rea (2017), "Is Social Upgrading Occurring in South Asia's Apparel Industry?" *Critical Perspectives on International Business,* 13(3): 226.

Loker, S. (2010), "The (R)Evolution of Sustainable Apparel Business: From Codes of Conduct to Partnership in Sri Lanka." Paper presented at the Ethical Fashion Symposium, Sri Lanka Design Festival.

Lopez-Acevedo, G., and R. Raymond, eds (2016), *Stitches to Riches?: Apparel Employment, Trade, and Economic Development in South Asia.* New York: World Bank Publications.

Read, B. (2017), "Start preparing for the rise of the conscious consumer." Available online from: http://www.just-style.com (accessed May 11, 2018).

Ruwanpura, K. N. (2015), "Garments without guilt? Uneven labour geographies and ethical trading—Sri Lankan labour perspectives," *Journal of Economic Geography,* 423–446, https://doi.org/10.1093/jeg/lbu059.

CHAPTER 4.5

SUSTAINABLE ANATOLIA
Craft-Centered Design in Turkey

Şölen Kipöz, Izmir University of Economics
Duygu Atalay, Beykent University, Turkey

INTRODUCTION

Anatolia, historically a transitional region, and a bridge between Europe and Asia, has inherited a great deal of craft tradition. Through a renewed appreciation of its autochthonously sustainable qualities in Anatolia, Turkey has been able to develop a craft-based design approach toward sustainability. In search of a sustainable fashion culture, the slow fashion movement, which is fed by the craft traditions of Turkey, has evolved due to the emergence of a reaction against stereotypical fast fashion. Through a reappreciation of local crafts, Turkish designers are challenging the Eurocentric, standardized, global workings of fashion design. They have begun to highlight the need for quality over quantity, diversity over monoculture, the use of local materials and crafts, as well the importance of employing local expertise to create a fairer production process. Reinterpretation of traditional crafts as a design method has been embraced not only by designers, but also by communal craft circles. Many of these designers and communities regard the concept of craft as an agent of anti-consumerism or slow production. This essay concentrates on the story

of sustainability in Turkey within the context of craft, and provides an introduction and examination to Turkish designers and the communities as case studies, which have adopted sustainable design identities, based on the creative impulse of craft.

INDUSTRY CONTEXT IN TURKEY'S FASHION SECTOR

Turkey has transformed itself from a leading clothing supplier to Europe in 1970s into an international actor thanks to its well-established manufacturing industry. The same period also witnessed the development of a Turkish ready-to-wear industry and the emergence of local brands. As a reaction to the negative consequences of global economy and stereotyped design identity, Turkish haute couture designers developed a cultural response, based largely on the incorporation of Anatolian motifs into contemporary clothing designs. Following the swing toward nationalist politics of the 1980s, in the following decade designers were able to make

Turkish fashion visible in the global market due to the elimination of customs barriers. In addition, new national strategies supplying local design as a value-added business paved the way for a cultural design identity, which allowed designers to incorporate Anatolian values, traditional crafts skills, and materials in their collections. The creation of this contemporary design identity was also supported by the establishment of the Turkish Fashion Designers Association, which has adopted a vision of creating an internationally recognized Turkish fashion movement, and also the "Turquality" project (2005), an accreditation system for Turkish brands.

Despite these institutional attempts to transform Turkey into a country known for its design, the formation of a sustainable fashion culture was hindered by the mismatch between the extensive industrial production capacity and the rather small-scale creative potential of the designers. This problem was exacerbated by the difficulty of merging industrial production with creative design, and the general lack of workers with appropriate craft knowledge. Furthermore, local crafts faced extinction due to the rapid development of the ready-to-wear industry, and the rate of local migration from villages to metropolitan cities. These factors delayed the formation of a sustainable culture, even though Turkey is located in an autochthonously sustainable geography, equipped with archaic wisdom in various manual skills.

THE ROLE OF CRAFT IN REVALUING THE "LOCAL"

The practice of crafting represents an inherent resistance to the commodity-oriented capitalist system. Crafting is summed up by Sennett (2008:

145) with the phrase "desire to do a job for its own sake." The very mirror image of the rapid circulation of global fashion cycles, which focus on constant change, craft represents a slow activity, because "after all you can only consume as much as, and as fast as, the craft person can produce" (Fletcher and Grose 2012: 149). Recently craft shifted from its individualistic and domestic role into the public domain as a collective agent of social change. By allowing the active involvement of non-designers in the creative process, craft has become instrumental in the coalescence of community members, through the meanings and symbols it communicates (Atalay 2015).

The valorization of craft culture in design allows the use of local knowledge connected to a local system, thus creating a socially responsive design process, providing locals with a source of income (Manzini 2010: 10). This income gives rise to the "distributed economy," in which the global system is comprised of a network of local systems, providing an alternative to standardization, centralization, and identical products (Clark 2008: 430). Historically rooted productive local institutions and communities create a trust based on personal contact, as well as a strong sense of local pride and attachment (Hall 1992: 319 in Clark 2008: 432). Revaluing local crafts not only facilitates the preservation of cultural identity, but also reactivates collective memory, bringing a sense of belonging and attachment to community values. Handmade products in time-tested designs enable the use of *tacit knowledge*, which is passed on from artisan to apprentice, and can only be sustained within close-knit communities. An accumulation of such wisdom, transferred between generations (Kipöz 2015: 120), has the potential to lay the foundations for community well-being and intergenerational equity. Nevertheless, it is important to apply and reinterpret traditional and local crafts in regard to the contemporary cultural needs, which necessitates the integration of traditional and modern designs.

USE OF CRAFT IN CREATING A TURKISH DESIGN IDENTITY

A craft-integrated mode of fashion design has emerged within the ideals of modernization and the westernization of Turkey, as a part of the education and professionalization of young women, through Applied Arts Institutes for Girls. Education in these institutions sets out not only to empower women and create a female labor force for the national economy, but has also allowed the nation's cultural identity to be preserved through the application of Turkish textile crafts (Akşit 2005). Some of these women studied at European colleges, and subsequently became "educated dressmakers," and formed a female labor force that could develop a clothing manufacturing culture and promote the ideals of westernization. While most created their personal styles through the adoption of European fashions, a minority showed a preference for a more "Turkish" look, which emanated from an ethnic style inspired by Anatolian culture and the resurgence of local values, cultural heritage, and interest in a mythic past. This movement had various effects on three generation of designers. While the first two generations adopted a more individual haute couture design process in utilizing and preserving local crafts, the third generation promoted Turkish style internationally, and developed a collective Turkish fashion movement through the Fashion Designers Association (MTD), which was established in 2006 with the aim of positioning Istanbul as a "Fashion Design Territory."

CRAFT-CENTERED DESIGN

Turkey developed a craft-centered design approach toward sustainability, generating two major roles for designers. In the first, designers act as craftspeople, emphasizing the quality of designs, tradition, and workmanship; in the second, they collaborate with craftspeople to strengthen communities and local cultures, playing a facilitating role.

Designer As Craftsperson

In this role, the designer adopts an artisanal and holistic approach to the life cycle of garments across the entire design and production processes. Following this route, rather than the linear process of fashion design, was meant to create a successive cyclic approach by promoting the role of a "maker," thus overcoming the wastefulness generated by the separation of these steps in the production process hitherto (McQuillan 2011: 85). The "designer as craftsperson" approach is in line with the Bauhausian term of "the whole (wo) man"; knowledge is based on craft, practice, and understanding of societal aspects. Designers become specialists "equipped with the clarity of feeling and the sobriety of knowledge" (Gropious & Moholy-Nagy 2010: 556).

When an independent designer unites the role of designer and craftsperson into one entity, the design output of the process is more likely to be artistic and intuitive. For example, some of the Turkish haute couture designers in the 1980s developed a personal style, inspired by a particular craft skill and know-how in the fabrication of the garments at small-scale fashion houses. Among these, designer Zühal Yorgancıoğlu (*b*. 1926), who was initially educated at the Institute of Applied Arts before attending art school in the United States, reflects this personal approach by drawing on her embroidery skills. She uses various embroidery techniques to embellish graphically applied Turkish motifs borrowed from Ottoman and Anatolian culture. In developing a quasi "Turkish rococo" style, she uses floral motifs with silver and gold threads, mostly with techniques such as *hesap işi, sarma, dival işleri, kafes işi, a*nd appliqué. Her use of appliqué in particular has a specific importance as a sustainable design practice, as she incorporates discarded and or aged fabrics and embroideries into new designs, through the practice of upcycling. She has tried to ensure the survival of these materials by reusing and revaluing them and respecting their former uses, stating: "I am trying to give a new life to old and ancient embroideries which over time have come to resemble rags." Anatolian patterns are applied in her designs through special techniques such as *taş köprü* and *tel kırma* on hand-woven textiles from the Ödemiş-Birgi, Buldan, and Kızılcabölük areas in the Northern Aegean region of Turkey (Kipöz n.d.).

Another second-generation designer, Esin Yılmaz (1944–2011), also made use of hand-woven fabrics, such as silk *bürümcük*-crinkled fabric, and golden and silver *tel kırma* motifs from the Ödemiş-Birgi region in contemporary designs developed from mythological legends and folkloric influences. Her natural dyes were derived from a range of sources, including damson fruit, cinnamon stems, different types of wood, and bunches of grapes. She characterized her remarkable simplicity and modest design approach as follows; "The voices of the past, the sounds and colours of Anatolia should not scream loudly in design; they have to whisper" (Kipöz 2011).

Figure 4.5.1 Esin Yılmaz, hand-woven silk pleated dress
Image reproduced courtesy of Sabah Şardağ

Other designers from the same generation who incorporated their expertise through the application of Turkish crafts into contemporary designs include Cemil İpekçi, Ayla Eryüksel, Vural Gökçaylı, Bilge Mesci, and Gönül Paksoy. Gönül Paksoy in particular—with an academic background in chemical engineering—has implemented a fully sustainable process through her innovative style based on the use of hand-woven natural fibers and dyes, and the repurposing of her own discarded materials including brocade, raw silk crêpe, and silk velvet. Her own design process involves upcycling these materials into new products. She has created a harmonious reflection of past and future, described as "timeless simplicity," that is strongly influenced by Anatolian Dervish culture. Paksoy creates combinations that have a way of "enfolding you, of carrying you away, of making you feel nearer to your roots, your culture" (Akgün in Paksoy 2007: 27). In her experimental journey of work(wo)manship, she creates "fabric collages" (Paksoy 2007: 31). Rejecting the use of mounted sleeves, she instead makes garments easily reversible and able to be transformed; for example she used two coats to create a single outfit.

A notable figure among emerging fourth-generation designers is Başak Cankeş, founder of

Figure 4.5.2 Gönül Paksoy, hand-woven caftan
Image reproduced courtesy of Gönül Paksoy

the Bashaques label. After graduating from in 2010 from the Fashion Design Department of Izmir University of Economics, she studied at Central Saint Martins in London. She opened her own art/fashion store in Alaçatı—a resort near İzmir—in 2014 and presented her first collection in Istanbul Fashion Week the following year. Her collections merge art and fashion as she collaborates with artists and crafters, creating pieces that she defines as "wearable art." Her 2016 collection, entitled "Door," in particular reflected the inspiration she took from travelling in Catalonia—and especially from the patterns in Gaudi's oeuvre. Her work has helped to shift the trajectory of Turkish fashion toward a more crafted and artistic approach. In collaboration with internationally recognized Turkish textile artist Fırat Neziroğlu, Cankeş transformed these inspirations into intricate decorative appliqués, knits, crochets, and prints infused with a variety of materials such as silk, leather, knitwear, wool, and cotton. By incorporating crafts into design, Cankeş has managed to balance wearability with unique artistic quality by creating outfits that appeal to the high street and a youthful audience (Cankeş n.d.).

Textile designer Ayfer Güleç has put the 3,000-year-old Turkish craft of felting at the center of her design methods. Güleç creates delicate combinations of felt with other ecologically sound materials, such as silk and cotton, in the style of colorful collage work, ensuring a personalized item for each customer through designs that are almost impossible to reproduce. After witnessing a decrease in felt-making, she decided to hold regular workshops in her atelier, "Women's Production House," in Seferihisar, located in Aegean Turkey. She emphasizes the importance of a traditional master–apprentice relationship in promoting innovation and creativity, and aims to prevent the extinction of this historical craft (Ovacık & Gümüşer 2016).

As well as their common emphasis on craft culture and skill in traditional craft techniques, these designers all work in small-scale ateliers that are accessible to their consumers. In this way, they challenge two of the biggest negative aspects of conventional fashion design system: consumers' alienation from products; and designers' alienation from consumers. For consumers, this direct contact creates an emotional connection, thus rendering the product more meaningful. Clark points out that handmade items, including those from haute couture ranges, not only offer individualized fit and appearance, but also provide customers with a sense of attachment, due to the stories and origins that increase their emotional value (Clark 2008: 441). She also underlines that only small-scale businesses can provide this transparent mode of production, by providing greater cultural and material value (Clark 2008: 435).

Designer Working with Craftspeople

In recent years, capital has been attracted by industrial production strategies that operate alongside "handicrafts." The communal craft circle has the ability to produce a community through production and distribution of an object (Bratich & Brush 2011: 234). Cardoso (2010: 330) argues that in order to survive in the face of overt consumerism, craft must embrace community and shared interaction, as a collective experience. Due to its collaborative nature, craft provides a sense of belonging to a local culture, which in turn engenders a sense of responsibility and trust (Clark 2008: 434). Designer-integrated craft communities can prevent the extinction of traditional craft techniques, thus generating new bonds and strengthen existing ones.

An outstanding example of such collaboration is Argande, a unique fashion brand associated with a social responsibility project in Turkey, founded as part of the "Innovations for Women Empowerment in the South-eastern Anatolia Project (SAP) Region" in collaboration with United Nations Development Programme. Argande launched its first collection in 2009 and now a large proportion of each season's production of 3,500–6,000 items are stocked in seventeen branches of MUDO, a major Turkish retailer. With the support of the Swedish International Cooperation Development Agency, Argande provides employment for approximately 145 disadvantaged local women, promoting fair working and production. Revenue from sales is paid directly to the producers, and the company also contributes to the local economy by using fabrics native to South-eastern Turkey (Argande n.d.). The designs are created by leading contemporary Turkish designers and coordinated by Hatice Gökçe (b. 1973), part of the third generation of designers. She is one of the founding members of the Fashion Designers Association with Özlem Süer, Arzu Kaprol, Ümit Ünal, Bahar Korçan, and Hakan Yıldırım.

Argande is a model for social sustainability, and shows social capital can be accumulated through fashion, and how that capital can be transformed into a potential source of societal well-being. The project also represents an initiative for reviving regional traditional crafts, by, for example, reactivating looms for weaving local Kutnu fabric, thus providing income for the local community due to demand generated by Argande's new collections. This type of equitable production creates a transparent and cyclical relationship between the supply chain processes in the fashion sector, and allows a fair exchange between producer and consumer. Rather than sweatshop exploitation, there is a close collaboration between designers and craftspeople, particularly through designers' visits to the

Figure 4.5.3 Argande 2016/17, by Aslı Jackson; the dress draws attention to traditional "Kutnu" fabric
Image reproduced courtesy of Hatice Gökçe

region. The project also encourages gender equity by empowering women economically and socially. Furthermore, Argande's feminized production approach validates the notion of "skill" as a mode of tacit knowledge and provides an intergenerational transfer of expertise, as well as promoting collectivity and collaboration between designer and community (Kipöz 2016).

Another notable designer–crafter collaboration is "Leather Age Anatolia," created by Hatice Gökçe, a key figure in the Argande story discussed earlier. Known as a pioneering figure who has challenged the conventional Turkish patriarchy, Gökçe developed this project in association with the Association of Turkish Leather Brands and local craftsmen in İstanbul. The inspiration for the collection of sixteen leather artistic outfits comes from eight ancient Anatolian civilizations—Hittite, Lydian, Arzawan, Phyrgian, Ionian, Urartun, Assyrian, and Trojan—and presents an epic vision infused with a sense of mystery of the past, combined with contemporary skills, and interpreted in pattern and texture on leather. Inspired by Anatolia's history, Gökçe creates an organic bond with the future guided by knowledge of the past. This involves adapting traditional approaches of crafts(wo)men to facilitate innovative and unconventional design possibilities. Thus, the ephemeral structure of the fashion industry is resisted through an appreciation of timeless design. At the same time, the project expresses a unique language by showing great respect for the process, through increasing the visibility of the details on each processed leather surface. That involves "spending more effort with the designs" with the sense of "charging each single moment." The collection aroused international interest at its first presentation at İstanbul Modern Art Museum in 2014, followed by appearances in Peking (2014), Shanghai (2015), and finally, at Milan Fashion Week (2015).

Another example of collective womanly production is Çöp(m)adam, founded in 2008 by Tara Hopkins, an American living in Ayvalık (in Northern Aegean Turkey) and sponsored by Sabancı University and Unilever. The project—which can be broadly translated as "Garbage Ladies"—refers to female crafters who transform garbage through upcycling, recycling, and reuse into "cool, fashionable, useful, and fun" accessories. Apart from providing a designerly solution to the waste problem, Çöp(m)adam has provided over 400 women with employment, fair wages, and a good working environment. As a result, these women are able to sustain their families and

Figure 4.5.4 Trojan woman and man from "Leather Age Anatolia" by Hatice Gökçe., 2014

Image reproduced courtesy of Hatice Gökçe

communities, increase their self-confidence, and are credited for their work on the product package (Çöp(m)adam n.d.).

Nazlı Çetiner Serinkaya is a young textile artist who specializes in colorful and playful knitwear in the form of classic handmade clothing for adults and children which she distributes through her brand Mandalina Rossa. Following her belief in sustainable living without mass production, Nazlı also coordinates and contributes to social projects aimed at facilitating consumer participation, through activities such as DIY design instructions and collaborative workshops. By taking on various roles in her work—from illustrator to embroiderer, knitter, gardener, and tailor—she emphasizes her close connection with nature, which she believes "is diminishing with industrialism." One major project is a tribute to people trying to live in harmony with nature through traditions, rituals, and respect, for which she developed a series of drawings to raise awareness to our roots and identities with image references inspired mostly by 1970s *National Geographic* magazines (Mandalinarossa n.d.).

CONCLUSION

Like many other developing and capitalized countries, Turkey has experienced the devaluation and extinction of local crafts and skills, despite the Anatolian legacy of autochthonously sustainable qualities. Due to the differences in size of operations between industrial production and the creative design profession, a craft-centered design approach has been limited to small-scale slow design business models, which mainly work through either designers themselves acting as craftspeople or by working in collaboration with them. Both approaches have the potential to overcome the problem of alienation among consumers, products, and designers through establishing a non-hierarchical communication, which creates greater trust in the relationship between artisans and designers. Moreover, it allows the valorization of local values, work(wo)manship, tacit knowledge, and skill-sharing between members of the community, consequently increasing awareness of the product life cycle among consumers.

Despite the labor-intensive character of the current industrial system of fashion manufacturing,

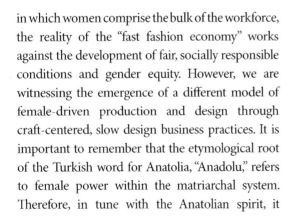

Figure 4.5.5 Nazlı Çetiner Serinkaya, cementing the bonds between mothers and daughters with knitted sweaters
Image reproduced courtesy of Nazlı Çetiner Serinkaya

in which women comprise the bulk of the workforce, the reality of the "fast fashion economy" works against the development of fair, socially responsible conditions and gender equity. However, we are witnessing the emergence of a different model of female-driven production and design through craft-centered, slow design business practices. It is important to remember that the etymological root of the Turkish word for Anatolia, "Anadolu," refers to female power within the matriarchal system. Therefore, in tune with the Anatolian spirit, it is appropriate to challenge the gender-biased patriarchal understanding. In conventional design discourse, design is associated with creativity, exchange value, professionalism, and masculinity, in contrast to craft, which is associated with the traditional, use value, the homemade, and femininity (Baydar 2015; Buckley 1989). It appears that this intergenerational community of women has become a remarkably influential voice in the promotion of an ethical and socially responsive production and consumption cycle.

REFERENCES

Akşit, E.E. (2005), *Kızların. Sessizliği: Kız Enstitülerin Uzun Tarihi / Silence of the Girls: Long Story of Women's Institutes*. İstanbul: İletişim.

Argande (n.d.), About Us, viewed May 14, 2015, <http://www.argande.com/>

Atalay, D. (2015), "Women's Collaboration for the Enhancement of Craft Culture in Contemporary Turkey," *Craft Research*, 6(2): 223–39.

Baydar, G. (2015), "Arayüzler: Tasarım, Zanaat ve Toplumsal Cinsiyet"/ "Interfaces: Design, Craft and Gender," in Ş. Kipöz (ed.), *Sürdürülebilir Moda/ Sustainable Fashion*, 89–99. İstanbul: Yeni İnsan Publisher.

Bratich, J. Z., and H. M. Brush (2011), "Fabricating Activism: Craft-Work, Popular Culture, Gender," *Utopian Studies*, 22(2): 250–52.

Buckley, C. (1989), "Made in Patriarchy: Toward a Feminist Analysis of Women and Design," in V. Margolin (ed.), *Design Discourse: History, Theory, Criticism*, 251–62. London: University of Chicago Press.

Cankeş, B. (n.d.), "Collections." Viewed March 15, 2017, <http://www.bashaques.com/the-door/>

Cardoso, R. (2010), "Craft versus Design: Moving beyond a Tired Dichotomy," in G. Adamson (ed.), *The Craft Reader*, 321–31. Oxford and New York: Berg.

Clark, H. (2008), "Slow + Fashion: an Oxymoron—or a Promise for the Future?" *Fashion Theory*, 12(4): 427–46.

Ç(ö)pmadam (n.d.), "About Us." Viewed March 10, 2017, <http://www.copmadam.com/about-us/what-we-do/)>

Gropius, W., and L. Moholy-Nagy (2010), "Manifesto of the Bauhaus" and "Education and the Bauhaus," in G. Adamson (ed.), *The Craft Reader*, 554–58. Oxford and New York: Berg.

Kipöz, Ş. (2016), "Sürdürülebilir Moda: Bir Oksimoron mu?" / "Sustainable Fashion: Is it an Oxymoron?" Paper presented at Social Good Summit, İstanbul.

Kipöz, Ş. (2015), "Kuşaklararası Sürdürebilirlik ve Dişil Bilgeliğin Aktarımı" / "Intergenerational Sustainability and Transferring the Female Wisdom," in Ş. Kipöz (ed.), *Sürdürülebilir Moda / Sustainable Fashion*, 113–23. İstanbul: Yeni İnsan Publisher.

Kipöz, Ş. (2011), "Bir Moda Perisinin Ardından"/"In Pursuit of a Fashion Angel," Original title: May 7, 2011, *Yeni Asır* Daily Newspaper, İzmir.

Kipöz, Ş. (n.d.), Biography of Zuhal Yorgancıoğlu. Available online at: http://zuhalyorgancioglu.com.tr/ (accessed March 15, 2017).

Mandalinarossa (n.d.), "About" section of website, available at: http://portfolio.mandalinarossa.com/about (accessed March 10, 2017).

Manzini, E. (2010), "Small, Local, Open, and Connected: Design for Social Innovation and Sustainability," *The Journal of Design Strategies: Change Design*, 4(1): 8–11.

McQuillan, H. (2011), "Zero-waste Design Practice. Strategies and Risk Taking for Garment Design," in A. Gwilt and T. Rissanen (eds), *Shaping Sustainable Fashion. Changing the Way We Make and Use Clothes*, 83–97. London: Earthscan.

Ovacık, M., and T. Gümüşer (2016), "Geçmişten Günümüze Keçe: Ayfer Güleç İş Modeli Üzerine Bir Analiz" / "Felt from Past to Present: An Analysis on Ayfer Güleç's Bussiness Model," *Yedi: Sanat, Tasarım ve Bilim Dergisi*, 15(1): 155–71.

Paksoy, G. (2007), "Gönül Paksoy: Zamansız Sadelik"/"Gönül Paksoy: Timeless Simplicity." İstanbul: Rezan Has Müzesi.

Sennett, R. (2008), *The Craftsman*. New Haven, CT and London: Yale University Press.

CHAPTER 4.6

A SPOTLIGHT ON: REDRESS
A Case Study of a Sustainable Fashion Initiative Influencing Consumption Practices in Hong Kong and Asia

Anne Peirson-Smith, City University of Hong Kong, Hong Kong

Redress, a Hong Kong based NGO, was founded in 2007 by CEO Christina Dean, with the aim to "promote environmental sustainability in Asia's fashion industry" (Redress 2017a). To achieve this, Redress implements promotional strategies and tactics, involving events that encourage sustainable fashion activities oriented to the consumer rather than the product.

Figure 4.6.1 Redress pop-up secondhand clothes sales event, Hong Kong, November 2017
Image reproduced courtesy of Redress/Hong Kong Photography Studio

Figure 4.6.2 The 3% Garment Waste Mountain, June 16, 2011, Star Ferry, Hong Kong
Image reproduced courtesy of Anne Peirson-Smith

SOCIAL MARKETING CAMPAIGNS

Redress initially focused on the theme of waste reduction, as surveys and focus groups indicated that Asian and European consumers related to this message. The role of industry is highlighted in terms of pre-consumer waste generated in the garment production process with a focus on upcycling solutions at production level, while examples of post-consumer waste are illustrated in the disposable mentality of throwaway garments.

"Triggering events" are used by Redress to raise awareness such as the campaign using photo-worthy techniques based on the grounded example of an installation of post-consumption garment waste featuring "The 3% Mountain." This comprised a six-meter-high clothes pile representing just 3 percent of the average textile waste going into Hong Kong's landfill daily. Reminiscent of an art installation, this powerful message was well covered in local, regional, and global media and by bloggers.

CONSUMER ORIENTATION AND INVOLVEMENT

Consumer focus and involvement is heightened using social media commentary on practical ways that consumers can remedy this issue inside their own wardrobes.

Redress ran a "15/30 The Capsule Wardrobe Project" challenging the consumer to wear and share images of fifteen clothing items over a thirty-day period with a moratorium on clothes shopping for one month in order to promote conscious wardrobe management and responsible clothing-waste reduction. Participants in this online project were also encouraged to customize existing outfits and donate unwanted clothes to recycling banks.

Clothing care partner, Miele, a German domestic appliance manufacturer, organized a series of "Keep Caring Clothing" events for the sale of unwanted clothing and issued a series of top tips on sustainable consumer care in a booklet and fridge stickers exhorting consumers in affective language to "Recycle, swap, resell, or donate unwanted clothes—keep them in the fashion loop and out of landfills." Redress also worked with Esprit when developing the "R Cert" certification system for textiles used in garment production making them traceable across the supply chain and demonstrating that companies have reused their waste using a minimum 20 percent of recycled fibers.

COLLABORATIVE OPPORTUNITIES

Stakeholder engagement includes: government departments (CreateHK); opinion-formers (Orsola de Castro); ambassadors (Amber Valetta, Bonnie Chen); designers (Diane von Furstenberg, Barney Cheng); textile and garment manufacturers (Laws group, Nam Fung group); retailers, schools, and universities (London College of Fashion, Parsons New York); media representatives (*HongKong Tatler*, WGSN); corporations (Cathay Pacific, UPS, Uber); fashion business members across the supply chain (Shanghai Tang, Esprit). Sustainability-oriented NGOs, such as China Water Risk and Friends of the Earth, are also involved. In addition to featuring in "The True Cost" film, Redress commissioned a feature length documentary, "Frontline Fashion" (Redress 2017d).

The EcoChic fashion competition launched in 2011 encourages young designers to create and showcase collections based on minimal textile waste using techniques such as upcycling. Award-winners gain placements with industry partners and with the affordable luxury brand and social impact business, BYT.

Figure 4.6.3 Hong Kong designer Lu Lu Cheung's "Eco Couture" dress and hat made for Redress using faulty garments from current collection. Redress on the Runway show, May 20, 2011, Hong Kong
Image reproduced courtesy of Anne Peirson-Smith

Figure 4.6.4 Australian designer Amit Ayalon's "Eco Couture" dress and hat made from Envirosac bags. Redress on the Runway show, May 20, 2011, Hong Kong
Image reproduced courtesy of Anne Peirson-Smith

RE-ADDRESSING THE CULTURAL–COMMERCIAL DYNAMIC

Figure 4.6.5 The Forever Better with Miele fashion show event sponsored by Miele, Waterfront, June 16, 2011, Hong Kong
Photograph by Anne Peirson-Smith

Involvement with designers to utilize regionally produced materials and local skilled labor in order to reclaim and rebalance the local commercial fashion and cultural ecology is core to the Redress mission. In addition to a high-profile fashion show and exhibition at Harvey Nichols intended to raise consumer awareness and encourage upcycling, Redress HK invited fifteen of Hong Kong's most prominent designers, including Johanna Ho and Dorian Ho, to recreate a fashion piece from used clothing launched at the "Forever Better Fashion Show" party sponsored by Miele. Attended by over 300 guests, including media, the pieces were exhibited with a limited-edition charity retail collection at Harvey Nichols. The reach of the Redress initiatives now extend beyond Asia, so that young designers—regardless of location—can be part of the EcoChic competition highlighting the universality of the sustainable fashion challenge.

CONCLUSION

Although transforming fashion design, practice, and consumption is an enormous challenge, it is not a quick fix and for any systemic change to be effective it should be incremental and a conscious multi-dimensional social marketing collaborative effort. This includes consumer awareness and engagement, clear objectives, directive core messages, collaborative stakeholder support, social diffusion, and leadership modeling aligning with local value systems. To effect sustainable change impacting on lives and lifestyles, designers and consumers both have to re-address their design and consumption practices inside the seams of the system rather than from the eco fringes.

REFERENCES

Redress (2017a), *Redress: Our Story*. Available online at: https://hannah-lane–9cal.squarespace.com/about/story/ (accessed March 1, 2017).

Redress (2017b), *Redress: Our Work*. Available online at: https://hannah-lane–9cal.squarespace.com/our-work/ (accessed March 2, 2017).

Redress (2017c), *Dress [with] Sense*, London: Thames & Hudson.

Redress (2017d), *Frontline Fashion*. Available online at https://hannah-lane–9cal.squarespace.com/frontlinefashion (accessed March 2, 2017).

SOUTHEAST ASIA AND OCEANIA

PART 5

CHAPTER 5.1

SUSTAINABLE FASHION IN AUSTRALIA
Raw Fiber, Fast Fashion, and New Localism

Alice Payne, Queensland University of Technology, Australia

Tiziana Ferrero-Regis, Queensland University of Technology, Australia

INTRODUCTION

Australia has a high-consuming customer base accustomed to purchasing low-cost imported clothing, resulting in high volumes of waste. At the same time, Australia is a primary producer of natural fiber: it is the world's largest exporter of Merino wool, and third-largest exporter of cotton. Yet local textile manufacturing is almost non-existent, with the bulk of raw fiber exported and the majority of clothing imported. This hollowed-out manufacturing base presents as a challenge to progressing a connected, local, and sustainable fashion system within the country. This essay examines the designers, entrepreneurs, and retailers working against the odds to promote a sustainable "local" fashion system via different strategies that vary between fledgling reshoring projects that make use of local raw fiber, and the shortening of supply chains for heightened transparency. The practices we discuss highlight the inherent ambiguities of seeking to establish a local sustainable system in a country such as Australia. Local production systems are unlikely to supplant and replace the current globalized systems of fashion production without seismic shifts in the wider economic reality of the industry. However, the subtle resurgence of locally-made points to a desire from both the consumer and producer to have greater connection with a product's origins.

BACKGROUND

"Sustainable fashion" is a tricky expression, but in this essay we use the term to encompass all fashion practices aspiring toward more socially responsible and environmentally conscious modes of production and consumption. Many environmental and social sustainability issues confronting fashion industries worldwide are compounded by globalized, opaque production systems. It is a fact that fast fashion has changed the fashion paradigm, accelerating production and consumption. The dramatic increase of fast fashion manufacturing in low-wage countries, at the cost of human lives and severe environmental impacts, has led to incremental shifts toward improving conditions through the combined efforts of non-governmental organizations, unions, governments, and industry. Today, sustainable and/or ethical fashion have entered large global companies' boardrooms. Corporates that include sustainable practices and supply chain transparency in their Corporate Social Responsibility (CSR) see their market value increase. In this context, the concerns regarding social and environmental sustainability in fashion are comparatively recent in Australia. Despite the fact that sweatshop scandals—in both Australia and abroad—have hit the local market since the 1980s, throughout the 2000s the local fashion retailers who dominated the market did not undergo the same scrutiny as their North American and European counterparts.

Globalization is seen as the single strategic economic driver to the rise of corporatism, and integration and flows of humans, capital, societies, cultures and communication (Appadurai 1996; Hewart & Verdier 2013). Globalization has given rise to a complex set of issues that include environmental degradation and exploitation of human capital in regions in which wages are low and regulation lax. However, the incremental delocalization of labor from Western countries to low-cost countries (LCCs) has prompted a turn toward localism. In opposition to globalization, localism has emerged as a positive discourse of resistance to what is perceived as a dehumanizing economic and economic system. Thus, localism is seen as the human response to environmental disaster and health and safety issues of workers. In addition, the International Monetary Fund

(IMF) sees anti-globalization sentiments rising in view of Western countries wanting to maintain high quality and traditions in manufacture, typically in value-add products, such as food and luxury fashion, that are part of the country's tradition in artisanship, locally made or locally grown. Anxiety is also increasing in regard to the escalation of the flow of immigration (Department of Industry, Innovation and Science 2016, 24).

Localism has mobilized many strategic discourses aimed at reconstituting "key sites of social organisation and engagement" (Featherstone et al. 2012: 177). Glocalization, a mix between producing locally and selling globally, redefines business across boundaries with a local flavor; importantly, it attempts to bring together cosmopolitanism with self-governance. Reshoring, in contrast to outsourcing, is a term that has gained currency in recent years especially in the United States and Europe, following the 2008 global financial crisis and the dramatic decline of employment in the manufacturing sector in Western countries (Ashby 2016). In supply chain management terms, outsourcing to LCCs requires a careful balancing of many risks, such as the potential for supply chain interruptions, the stability of a country's labor cost, and its government's trade policies, as well as the country's political, social, and environmental record (Ellram et. al. 2013: 17). Although reshoring may often be a company's response to managing these risks as well as offering opportunities for enhanced speed-to-market (Johnsen et al. 2014), reshoring as an idea has become central to the narrative of localism.

PRODUCING FASHION IN THE WIDE BROWN LAND

Australia is a wealthy, highly urbanized nation with a small population clustered chiefly along the east coast of the continent. As a post-industrial knowledge economy, Australia's manufacturing capacity has reduced in all sectors, with education the country's third largest export in 2015, and over 70 percent of the economy based on services (Australian Government 2015). Alongside, the mineral and agricultural industries operating in the vast interior of the continent represent the bulk of the country's exports (Department of Industry, Innovation and Science 2016: 25). However, these industries are suffering a decline due to the current low level of capital investment, while the services sector continues to grow. The Australian economy is slowly shifting toward the knowledge economy while continuing to relinquish low-paid jobs in manufacturing. A sewing-machine operator is seen as a low value-add employment, while prototyping and working in Research and Development (R&D) is considered as high value.

Over the past twenty years, the largest social sustainability concerns in Australian fashion have been around the plight of local garment workers. From the 1980s, the Textile Clothing Footwear (TCF) industries entered a steep decline, with local manufacturing jobs moving offshore. Local design teams still design for the Australian context, but manufacturing is chiefly located in Asia, with China, Bangladesh, and Vietnam as key sourcing hubs. To protect the remaining Australian garment workers, the government-funded organization Ethical Clothing Australia (ECA) was founded in 2009, in partnership with local TCF unions and industry (*Ragtrader* 2009; Benmedjdoub 2010). ECA seeks to ensure employers are compliant with Australian law, and consumer-facing swing tags signal that the garment is made onshore and without worker exploitation.

Several fabric production facilities remain in Australia, for example Australian Textile Group,
which manufactures fabrics for industrial work wear and the military, and Hedel Holdings which manufactures jacquard fabrics for soft furnishings (Do 2017). Networks of ready-made garment makers and factories remain, thirty-two of which are accredited to ECA (ECA 2018), but the number of total clothing manufacturing operations continues to decline annually (Magner 2017b). As of 2016 there were only 17,310[1] people employed in the Australian clothing manufacturing industry, but in stark contrast, there are over 130,000 people employed in clothing retail locally (Magner 2017c). While clothing retail continues to grow, local clothing manufacturing declines at a rate of 3 percent annually (Magner 2017b). These figures clearly represent the economic pattern in which Australia is a consumption-oriented country, rather than a manufacturing one.

The entry of international fast fashion retailers into the Australian market from 2010 onwards altered the local industry dynamics still further, as greater competition saw a rush of local retailer closures, and also brought greater scrutiny of brands' corporate social responsibility. Concurrently, the release of the first Baptist World Aid *Australian Fashion Report* (Nimbalker et al. 2013) provided a score card of local retailers' CSR performance and supply chain transparency, revealing a cursory examination of Australian retailers' websites. In particular, the document pointed to a dearth of sustainability reporting. Since the first report, this situation has changed; retailers are responding to the negative publicity from the *Australian Fashion Report* by demonstrating transparency through actions such as publishing factory locations on their websites (Nimbalker et al. 2017).

Like many wealthy, high-consuming nations, Australia's decline in manufacturing mirrors a rise in textile waste, as low-priced imported clothing has led to higher clothing consumption and hence disposability. Fast fashion revenue grew at a colossal 21 percent annually in the period 2012–17, with growth anticipated to remain over 10 percent for the next five years (Magner 2017a). Growing consumption of low-priced, fashionable clothing has resulted in higher volumes of post-consumer waste, with consumers retaining garments, on average, for just three months (*Ragtrader* 2014). In Australia, the bulk of textile waste is handled through networks of charitable organizations, with some independent for-profit businesses also involved in collection. Charities report being swamped in donated clothing items, many of which are not fit for resale, whether locally or on the export market (Leggatt-Cook et al. 2016). An estimated 500,000 tonnes of textile waste are sent to landfills each year, or twenty-three kilograms per person per year. However, this does not account for the used textiles that are exported, even at a loss to charities, or the textiles that are ragged.

PRODUCING RAW FIBER

Turning from the downstream impacts of fashion production, Australia's upstream industries of cotton and wool are major providers of raw inputs for the apparel value chain. Both the wool and cotton industries in Australia are technologically advanced agricultural industries seeking to ensure sustainable and traceable commodities for sale in global markets. The closeness to Asia, where the majority of textile production is located, is a strategic advantage for growers, allowing speed to market with only twelve to twenty-five shipping days.

In terms of cotton production, Australia produces a relatively small crop (3 percent of global cotton production) but remains a significant southern hemisphere producer, meaning Australian cotton is seasonally available when other growths (e.g. Indian or United States cotton) are unavailable. Australian cotton has established a reputation for high-yielding, high-quality upland cotton, with environmental practices assured by the industry-wide on-farm management system, Best Management Practices (BMP) (CA and CRDC 2014). BMP is aligned to the global standard of the Better Cotton Initiative (BCI). Innovations in seed technology have resulted in Australian cotton reducing insecticide inputs by 89 percent over the past ten years (Cotton Australia 2017). Globally, cotton production is under close scrutiny from retailers, governments, and non-government organizations (NGOs), with issues around water management, chemical use, and social issues such as child and indentured labor of highest concern (SEEP and

Figure 5.1.1 Australian charity collection bin
Image reproduced courtesy of Alice Payne

FAO 2015). The environmental issues in particular are areas that the Australian cotton industry has actively sought to address, largely through research and development into local on-farm practices, but also internationally through work with BCI and the Department of Foreign Affairs and Trade (DFAT) to share best practices with other cotton-growing countries (DFAT 2018).

After cotton, wool is the world's second most popular natural fiber, and Australia is the world's largest supplier. It is widely acknowledged that Australia produces the best quality woolen fiber, namely fine and superfine Merino wool. This is due to the superior know-how of growers in breeding the best quality of sheep for the production of the finest Merino wool. For this reason, Australia has traditionally been able to export 90 percent of its wool production (ABS 2003). However, the incremental dismantling of manufacturing over the post-war period has led to the disappearance of mills and yarn spinners. Simultaneously, by the 1990s, due to competition from man-made fibers, the progressive fall of wool prices and unethical animal practices such

Figure 5.1.2 Round modules of Australian harvested raw cotton
Image reproduced courtesy of Alice Payne

as mulesing, the Australian wool industry took a dive.

Recent demand by fashion designers globally has increased interest in wool as a viable and versatile fiber for fashion. Despite the fact that wool is a more expensive fiber to process than cotton (ABS 2003), the high price paid for the finest Merino wool such as 13 and 14 micron has initiated a new profitable phase. As a natural fiber, pure wool is fully recyclable and biodegradable.

This context sees the Australian fashion industry in a strange slump in which raw fiber production is booming, and garment retail is booming, but in the middle, local capacity for manufacturing is denuded. Alongside, Australian consumers generate post-consumer textile waste to a greater extent with little capacity for it to be handled locally. Given the economies of scale, and the closeness to Asian manufacturing hubs, it would appear that this fragmented approach to fashion production is here to stay. In this context, a corporate social responsibility approach would see large operators work with their supply chain to ensure sustainable and transparent manufacturing approaches that are environmentally sound and socially ethical. Yet other ways are possible, and a number of companies at varying scales are seeking to re-energize the local supply chains to suggest other ways of working.

LOCAL STORIES AND LOCAL MAKING

In this section, we explore the ways in which Australian companies and designers promote sustainable fashion through new ways of re-embracing ideas of "local." The philosophy underpinning a desire for local production can be traced to the Slow Movement, beginning with its origins in 1980s Italy as a campaign operating in another paradigm from the growing corporatization of food culture. The Slow Food Movement, founded in mid–1980s by Carlo Petrini, renewed the idea of making food from local produce, in opposition to the introduction of American fast food chains such as McDonald's franchises. The movement gained wide traction particularly because artisanal practices linked to local traditions of food production were under threat by European policies, perceived as homogenizing. On the contrary, the Slow Food Movement advocated networks of small-scale producers that create products deeply rooted in place and culture, nourishing a community and acting as a philosophical counterpoint to the deceptive ease and anonymity of globalization. Within the international division of labor, products are made half a world away and arrive with no story, hiding the exploitation that may have occurred in their making.

Cotton Stories

Slow as in speed of production and consumption may be one aspect, but another is how the slow philosophy aligns to locally-made, and the benefits this may have in developing traceable supply chains. The Australian high street retailer Jeanswest, owned by Hong Kong-based Golden Sun, has worked to align a story of Australian-made goods to Australian fiber. Their Homespun collection, first released in 2015, includes garments and accessories manufactured locally, with ECA accreditation. Recent collections utilize Australian-grown cotton and local manufacturing, marketing the quasi-sun-faded, vintage-look T-shirts as "the quintessential Australian summer staple," a message that aligns the local material origins of the product with an intangible image of Australian-ness (Jeanswest 2018).

A number of Australian mass-market retailers have embraced utilizing Australian-grown cotton in their garments. Retailers including Target, Kmart and Bonds have seen an opportunity for niche lines made with local Australian cotton, which although processed offshore, presents value to Australian consumers through the link to supporting Australian farmers. This kind of local branding is common around the world and is tied to a resurgent nationalistic pride, as we have seen with the Italian Slow Food Movement. The resistance to international free trade agreements and European policies has both positive and negative merits and political implications. However, in the context of sustainable fashion, the most important aspect of a local declaration lies in the opportunity for traceability. Knowing the origins of a product is the first step toward making assurances that the inputs and processes undertaken in a garment's production are ethical and environmentally sustainable. For instance, in the case of cotton, as of November 2017, 276 brands and retailers from around the world have pledged to eliminate Uzbek cotton due to child-labor concerns (Sourcing Network 2017).

At the small-scale end, entrepreneur Meriel Chamberlin has worked hard to re-establish locally spun cotton yarn from Australian-grown cotton, woven and knitted locally. Working with one of the very few commercial spinners still in operation, Chamberlin developed a range of woven and knit textiles in local cotton, highlighting the local sustainable story, even though local in the Australian context means "on the continent." She established her business, Full Circle Fibres, after seeing potential for a highly niche product that spoke to the growing interest in food miles, drawing on paddockto-plate thinking, in which buying local becomes both a statement and an action in ethical consumption.

Wool Stories

Within the wool industry, the concept of traceability to farm level has gained traction. In a context of growing concerns for fashion waste and human exploitation, some Australian wool growers have started to commit to transparency by shortening the supply chain. Several wool growers that belong to the Australian Superfine Wool Growers Association are attempting new business models that can be classified under the rubric of glocalism. These models refer to direct connections with Australian designers, transparency on textile manufacturers and garment producers abroad, and bypassing auctions and wholesaling of the raw fiber.

An active area in sustainable farming practices that exclude mulesing has recently emerged north of Hobart, in Tasmania. Here the glocalism concept can be clearly articulated. It refers to the collaboration between superfine wool producer Simon Cameron and men's suit designer Matt Jensen from MJ Bale (Breen 2017). This direct connection means that wool can be singularly traced to the grower, as Simon Cameron sends his bales directly to the Italian woolen mill owned by Vitale Barberis. As discussed earlier, the lack of local infrastructure and know-how for processing high-quality wool textiles from fine merino wool means that the bales must still be sent to North Italy for spinning and weaving. The fabric is then sent to Japan, where suits are manufactured. The direct link between the grower and the designer ensures transparency to a certain level along with values of quality and sustainability. Similar practices of single origin wool traceability are rearticulating and mobilizing a new way to look

Figure 5.1.3 Tasmanian sheep farm and shearing shed
Images reproduced courtesy of Tiziana Ferrero-Regis

at localism and globalization in conversation, instead of in opposition.

Another local business working with wool is Seljak Brand. Seljak Brand's model of recycled and recyclable wool blankets intertwines the issues of textile waste, local fiber, and locally made goods into a brand philosophy aligned with the vision of a circular economy. The company, a collaboration between sisters Karina and Sam Seljak, produces woolen blankets in the last vertically integrated wool mill in Australia. The mill, based in Tasmania, weaves the blankets from a blend of wool offcuts to produce a waste-to-resource product

Figure 5.1.4 Karina inspecting the spinning machine at the mill
Image reproduced courtesy of Karina Seljak

Figure 5.1.5a Seljak Brand blankets
Image reproduced courtesy of Karina Seljak

Figure 5.1.5b Seljak Brand blanket label
Image reproduced courtesy of Alice Payne

(Figures 5.1.4–5). The blankets are 70 percent Merino wool, and blended with polyester, alpaca, mohair, and cotton offcuts (Seljak Brand 2018). The recapturing of local waste, from local wool, and manufactured onshore, is a critical component to the brand's story, demonstrating the potential for waste to resource production from the materials at hand.

LOCAL AND TRANSPARENT, LOCAL AND AUTHENTIC

We have discussed several examples that have been engaging with alternative ethical and economic practices that raise questions around localism. At this point, we need to return to the discussion of globalization. As Appadurai (1996) well demonstrates, globalization cannot be taken as an all-encompassing monolithic system of economic, political, and economic exchange. Returning to the concept of "glocalism," for Australian fashion, returning to local production at scale may be currently impractical. However, the principles of shortening supply chains, reshoring, disrupting business models, and creating disjunctures are all ways to intervene in the global fashion system and create not only pragmatic solutions, but also rearticulations of narratives of localism and locally made goods.

The concept of local can have measurable benefits for environmental sustainability, aligned with the concept of food miles and thus leading to a lower carbon footprint, as measured through Life Cycle Assessments (LCAs). However, sustainability is multi-faceted, and LCAs are only one mechanism for its measurement. In fashion, the story matters as much as the supply chain, and therefore localism is as much immaterial story as material traceability through to fiber production. In the examples above, these narratives construct the idea of "Australian made" as a way to imagine collective aspirations of sustainability and authenticity through the known origins of a product. In particular, in this essay, the "made in Australia" concept touches on two primary resources—cotton and wool—that are iconic for the Australian economy, and that have been and still are part of the Australian psyche (with wool in particular). The wool and cotton industries have been able to reconstruct a narrative of pride around raw fibers that are no longer only based on farming, but which present ideas of belonging to a new form of citizenship centered on ethics and sustainability.

CONCLUSION

In conclusion, both large-scale retailers and independent brands have sought to capitalize on tracing the origins of their goods to highlight Australian-made items, or in reshoring elements of production to tell this story. In this context, "local" and "sustainable" may go hand in hand. These varied approaches to reinvigorating connections between local fiber, manufacturing, and marketing connect to fashion and sustainability in two main ways. First, traceability is embedded as a core concept, and one having inherent value in addressing many of the sustainability issues that have plagued fashion and apparel production. Second, the idea of local becomes a powerful narrative that communicates to Australian consumers the value of traceable, ethical supply chains. The promise of local therefore lies as much in promoting the necessity of traceability to a product's origins, as it lies in storytelling.

NOTE

1. Employment figures calculated from Magner (2017b; 2017d).

REFERENCES

Appadurai, A. (1996), *Modernity at Large: Cultural Dimensions of Globalization.* Minneapolis: University of Minnesota Press.

Ashby, A. (2016), "From Global to Local: Reshoring for Sustainability," *Operations Management Research*, 9:3–4, 75–88, DOI 10.1007/s12063-016-0117-9.

Australian Government (2015), *The Value of International Education in Australia*, Australian Government Department of Education and Training, prepared by Deloitte Access Economics. Available online at: https://internationaleducation.gov.au/research/research-papers/Documents/ValueInternationalEd.pdf (accessed February 11, 2018).

Benmedjdoub, A. (2010), "Homeworker rights to get fashion-forward," *Ragtrader*. Available online at: http://www.ragtrader.com.au/archive/homeworker-rights-to-get-fashion-forward (accessed January 29, 2010).

Cotton Australia (2017), "Biotechnology and cotton." Available online at: http://cottonaustralia.com.au/cotton-library/fact-sheets/cotton-fact-file-biotechnology (accessed September 18, 2017).

Cotton Australia (CA) and Cotton Research and Development Corporation (CRDC) (2014), *Australian Grown Cotton Sustainability Report*: Cotton Australia and Cotton Research and Development Corporation. Available online at: http://crdc.com.au/sites/default/files/pdf/Cotton Sustainability Report_Exec Summary.pdf (accessed January 12, 2017).

Department of Foreign Affairs and Trade (DFAT) (2018), "Improving access to global cotton markets for farmers in Pakistan." Available online at: http://dfat.gov.au/aid/who-we-work-with/private-sector-partnerships/bpp/Pages/improving-access-to-global-cotton-markets-for-farmers-in-pakistan.aspx (accessed January 12, 2017).

Department of Industry, Innovation and Science (2016), Australian Industry Report. Available online at: https://www.industry.gov.au/Office-of-the-Chief-Economist/Publications/AustralianIndustryReport/assets/Australian-Industry-Report-2016-Chapter-2.pdf (accessed January 12, 2018).

Do, K. (2017), "Synthetic and Natural Textile Manufacturing in Australia," IBISWorld Industry Report C1310. Available online at: http://clients1.ibisworld.com.au.ezp01.library.qut.edu.au/reports/au/industry/default.aspx?entid=1862 (accessed February 12, 2018).

ECA (2018), "Manufacturers." Available online at: http://ethicalclothingaustralia.org.au/manufacturers/ (accessed February 12, 2018).

Ellram, L. M., W. L. Tate, and K. J. Petersen (2013), "Offshoring and Reshoring: An Update on the Manufacturing Location Decision," *Journal of Supply Chain Management*, 49(2): 14–22.

Featherstone, D., A. Ince, D. Mackinnon, K. Strauss, and A. Cumbers (2012), "Progressive Localism and the Construction of Political Alternatives," *Transactions of the Institute of British Geographers*, 37: 177–18, doi:10.1111/j.1475-5661.2011.00493.x.

Leggatt-Cook, C., N. Grevis-James, J. Wilson, S. Batchelor, and V. Hall (2016), *Does your donation count or cost? Understanding donating and dumping behaviours and their impacts for Queensland charities*. Available online at: https://www.ehp.qld.gov.au/waste/pdf/donation-count-or-cost.pdf (accessed September 16, 2016).

Hewart, J.Y., and L. Verdier (2013), *Economic Globalization: Origins and Consequences*. Paris: OECD Publishing, http://dx.doi.org/10.1787/9789264111899-en (accessed March 15, 2015).

Jeanswest (2018), "Homespun short sleeve vintage tee." Available online at: https://www.jeanswest.com.au/en-au/clearance/men/tops-&-tees/short-sleeve-tees/homespun-short-sleeve-vintage-tee-muc-01378.htm/Washed-Cobalt/MUC-01378-01 (accessed January 8, 2018).

Johnsen, T. E., M. Howard, and J. Miemczyk (2014), *Purchasing and Supply Chain Management: A Sustainability Perspective*. Abingdon and New York: Routledge.

Magner, L. (2017a), *Fast Fashion in Australia*, IBISWorld Industry Report OD4172, http://clients1.ibisworld.com.au.ezp01.library.qut.edu.au/reports/au/industry/default.aspx?entid=4172 (accessed September 12, 2017).

Magner, L. (2017b), *Women's and Girl's Wear Manufacturing in Australia*, IBIS World Industry Report C1351b. Available online at: http://clients1.ibisworld.com.au.ezp01.library.qut.edu.au/reports/reportdownload/default.aspx?rcid=61&rtid=101&eid=139 (accessed February 12, 2018).

Magner, L. (2017c), *Clothing Retailing in Australia*, IBIS World Industry Report G4251. Available online at: http://clients1.ibisworld.com.au.ezp01.library.qut.edu.au/reports/au/industry/default.aspx?entid=407 (accessed November 30, 2017).

Magner, L. (2017d), *Men's and Boys' Wear Manufacturing in Australia*, IBIS World Industry Report C1351a. Available online at: https://ezpauth.library.qut.edu.au/secure/ticket/index.php?a=generateticket&o=ticket&url=http%3a%2f%2fclients1.ibisworld.com.au%2freports%2freportdownload%2fdefault.aspx%3frcid%3d61%26rtid%3d101%26eid%3d139 (accessed November 30, 2017).

Nimbalker, G., C. Cremen, and H. Wrinkle. (2013), *Australian Fashion Report*. Sydney: Baptist World Aid Australia.

Nimbalker, G., J. Mawson, H. Lee, and C. Cremen (2017), *Australian Fashion Report*. Sydney: Baptist World Aid Australia.

Ragtrader (2009), "Pacific Brands blinded by backlash," *Ragtrader*. Available online at: http://www.ragtrader. com.au/archive/pacific-brands-blinded-by-backlash (accessed January 12, 2017).

Ragtrader (2014), "Let's get wasted," *Ragtrader*. Available online at: http://www.ragtrader.com.au/news/ let-s-get-wasted (accessed September 18, 2014).

Ragtrader (2016), "Jeanswest gets accredited," *Ragtrader*. Available online at: http://www.ragtrader.com.au/news/ jeanswest-gets-accredited (accessed January 12, 2017).

SEEP and FAO (2015), "Measuring Sustainability in Cotton Farming Systems: Towards a Guidance Framework." Available online at: https://www.icac. org/getattachment/Home-International-Cotton-Advisory-Committee-ICAC/measuring-sustainability-cotton-farming-full-english.pdf (accessed January 12, 2017).

Sourcing Network (2017), "Company Pledge Against Forced Labor in the Cotton Sector of Uzbekistan." Available online at: https://www.sourcingnetwork. org/uzbek-cotton-pledge (accessed December 28, 2017).

CHAPTER 5.2

A SPOTLIGHT ON: SUSTAINABLE AUSTRALIAN INDIGENOUS FASHION

Jennifer Craik, Queensland University of Technology, Australia
Kathleen Horton, Queensland University of Technology, Australia

Australian Indigenous inspirations and motifs have been common in fashion design and textiles, but the design of contemporary fashion and sculptural forms by Indigenous artists is relatively new (Maynard 2001; Craik 2016). This spotlight explores Australian Indigenous fashion through the work of two emerging Australian Indigenous creatives, Elisa Jane Carmichael and Grace Lillian Lee, who constitute an exciting new development in sustainable fashion practice.

The distinctive fashion aesthetic of Indigenous designers embraces a mix of visual culture, performance, and objects that is both "tradition-based and blazingly new" (Rothwell 2016). This embodies the re-discovery and re-connection by fashion designers with their cultural heritage, thereby reviving Indigenous cultural and community expression of identity and heritage. Equally, it re-connects Indigenous people with their land and spiritual inspirations by using traditional, natural, and found materials in the creation of their artistic works including textiles, fashion, and sculptural forms. The common element of Carmichael's and Lee's work is

hybridity. Both Lee and Carmichael draw on multiple aesthetic codes, combining traditional and aesthetic references that achieve sustainable fashion expressions in innovative multi-dimensional forms.

A descendant of the Quandamooka people of North Stradbroke Island in Queensland, Carmichael works among Indigenous textile artists who use traditional techniques in innovative applications (Hamby 2010). Her inspiration is the spiritual connection with her homelands and people. She uses a combination of found materials, natural elements, and cotton twine to embellish cotton fabric that is digitally printed with the designs of her paintings. Through techniques of looping, twining, and coiling, Carmichael makes the cording that forms her garments.

Her exhibition, *Weaving Past Present and Futures* (2016), was comprised of six sculptural forms of everyday contemporary dress. The vibrancy of the palette and the tactile quality of the garments is a nod to the delight Carmichael takes in fashion as a creative form. Her works contribute to an intergenerational history of

Figure 5.2.1 Elisa Jane Carmichael, *Saltwater Footprints*, yellow net, coil stitch top, and bushfire jacket (2017)
Image reproduced courtesy of Elisa Jane Carmichael

Figure 5.2.2 Grace Lillian Lee, *Acceptance*. Model: Hanz Ahwang
Image reproduced courtesy of Greg Semu

Figure 5.2.3 Grace Lillian Lee, *Shimmer*. Model: Kris Branchins
Image reproduced courtesy of camera artist: Carly K

weaving practices that have survived the impact of colonialism, making them both a hybrid cultural form and political statement.

Lee, who is based in Cairns in Far North Queensland, sees her work as establishing a cultural dialog between traditional practices and contemporary cultural contexts. In her weaving practice, Lee applies traditional techniques to make dramatic body sculptures. In a more commercial application, Lee also uses these techniques to make a range of woven neckpieces. Lee's collaboration with Mornington Island Art Designs (MIArt Designs) resulted in a range of striking fashion garments and accessories.

Lee's work has been a centerpiece of the fashion performance at the annual Cairns Indigenous Art Fair, which brings together emerging First Nation communities, fashion designers, textile artists, and models. A far cry from traditional market-driven fashion shows, the visual and emotional impact of these performances resonates with local communities and arts audiences alike and raises the profile of Indigenous creatives from across Australia. Indigenous fashion is gaining legitimacy due to its sustainability in ethical, environmental, consumerist, and cultural terms. Carmichael and Lee are part of an emerging generation of young creatives who are developing robust transformative practices that are building cultural dialogs and sustaining Australia's First Nation's cultures through fashion.

REFERENCES

Carmichael, E. J. (2016), "How is Weaving Past, Present, Futures," MFA diss., Queensland University of Technology, Brisbane, Australia.

Craik, J. (2016), "Australian Indigenous Inspirations as Exotica in Fashion," in A. Jansen and J. Craik (eds), *Modern Fashion Traditions*, 97–118. London and New York: Bloomsbury.

Hamby, L., ed. (2010), "Cross Cultural Exchanges in Craft and Design," *Craft + Design Enquiry*, 2. Canberra: Australian National University.

Maynard, M. (2001), *Out of Line: Australian Women and Style*, Sydney: UNSW Press.

Rothwell, N. (2016), "Cairns Indigenous Art Fair: Tradition from a Different Angle," *The Australian*, 19 July, p. 15.

CHAPTER 5.3

PRODUCING SUSTAINABLE FASHION
Made in Vietnam

Angela Finn, Royal Melbourne Institute of Technology University, Australia

INTRODUCTION

Vietnam has been discussed as "the next China" in terms of developing as a manufacturing economy. This essay provides an overview of the state of fashion in Vietnam and discusses the country's potential for developing sustainable and ethical production at an early stage in the development of a local fashion industry. The opportunity for Vietnam is to use sustainable design and manufacturing as a fast track to becoming a fashion leader within South East Asia. Such a strategy would put them ahead of rivals such as Cambodia and Bangladesh, where unsustainable practices are evident as developing social and environmental issues emerge. The current spectrum of different production methods range from the clothing factory, akin to the modern manufacturing system of large trading partners such as China and India, to custom tailoring workshops steeped in the traditions of the past French Imperialism of the late 1800s and mid–1900s. A range of approaches presented at the recent Fashion Colloquia 2016, hosted by RMIT University in Ho Chi Minh City,

provides the background to a discussion of an emerging fashion culture that is distinct to Vietnam. Individual cases are discussed as examples of best practice with the potential to develop a sustainable fashion industry, in terms of ethical production that supports local workers and provides opportunities for local investment, alongside the development of a fashion culture that is reflective of and responsive to the local environment.

BACKGROUND

The Socialist Republic of Vietnam is being hailed as "the next China" in terms of developing as a manufacturing economy (Freidman 2012). This presents industry and government with the unique opportunity to develop sustainable approaches to fashion manufacturing in tandem with the development of the local manufacturing industry. The aspirations for emerging designers to engage with designer fashion in Vietnam suggests an opportunity to promote local brands and designers as ethical and sustainable while still leveraging a commercial model that benefits the local economy. Learning from the past experience of other major manufacturing nations in the sector, such as China and Cambodia, will enable Vietnam to avoid replicating manufacturing models that are known to be unsustainable, and worse, those that result in long term economic, social, and environmental damage. Part of this potential is founded in the distinct characteristics of the clothing and textiles sector in Vietnam that have resulted from the combination of its history as a French colony combined with its more recent growth as a communist nation in the company of other major advancing communist nations, specifically China. The expectation within the global financial sector is that Vietnam will follow in the footsteps of China, in terms of developing a manufacturing industry to provide jobs for its citizens and growth for the national economy (Freidman 2012). However, recent evidence suggests that this change has already occurred, with textiles, clothing and footwear exports having almost doubled in the past five years resulting in Vietnam moving up seven places to become the fifth largest exporter of textiles and clothing, in terms of gross domestic product, in the world after China, India, Italy and Germany in listed order (WITS 2017). For clarity it should be noted that, by comparison, Chinese exports of textiles and clothing remain equal to the exports of the remaining top five countries combined (WITS 2017).

In line with, or perhaps even as a result of this increasing capacity for manufacturing, there is a new generation of Vietnamese fashion savvy locals that demonstrate a desire and determination to develop a local fashion scene and design economy as much as a making economy. Unlike larger countries in South East Asia, Vietnam has an opportunity to develop a designer fashion industry with the benefit of research into sustainable production and consumption. This is an opportunity that may have been missed with local manufacturing where major stakeholders, such as international brands investing in off shore production in Vietnam, invest in improvements to engage with rising consumer demand for their products that have been produced ethically and sustainably. Similarly, local workers are more aware of international standards relating to workers' rights, the living wage, and the power of workers involved in collective bargaining and with the right to form unions. Examples include country specific reports on labor in Vietnam from organizations including the International Labour Organization (ILO 2017). The development of innovative models of manufacturing that draw on local strengths, and are designed to match opportunities within the international fashion industry, may provide Vietnam with a means of standing out within the emerging marketplace. The main focus of the 2016 Fashion Colloquia Vietnam, "Producing Fashion—Made in Vietnam," hosted by RMIT University at its South Saigon campus in Ho Chi Minh City, was to explore the range of different approaches to "making fashion," from designing to mass manufacture. This essay proposes that the development of a "designing economy" alongside a "making economy" has great potential for a textiles and fashion industry that is sustainable.

TEXTILES AND CLOTHING IN VIETNAM

Understanding the history of Vietnam is essential to understanding that the country is distinctly different to its largest trading partners in the region. The legacy of French colonialism has directly influenced the development of clothing production in Vietnam, with dressmaking and tailoring being traditionally the method of purchasing garments (as opposed to ready-to-wear), which in turn has enabled the localization of fashion consumption. The traditions of making are centered on tailored forms rather than any local traditional style. The traditional Vietnamese dress, the *ao dai*, was developed in the eighteenth century to replicate French (Parisienne) fashion, unlike traditional Japanese or Korean dress that developed over centuries. This style of dress is still dominant in discussions of "fashion design" in Vietnam, as evidenced by the importance of designers such as Si Hoang who has made a career in designing *ao dai* as an extension of his training in fine art (Arnold 2016).

The Vietnam War extended from 1956 to 1975, following a period of social and political unrest that started in the 1940s. This had a devastating impact on the local population and on the development of popular culture and fashion within the region that still has relevance for the local fashion scene today. Trần Nguyễn Thiên Hương, Chairperson of Sunflower Media, which publishes the Vietnamese edition of *Harper's Bazaar*, recollects that as a child in the 1970s there was no fashion in Vietnam (Yen 2016). The local people dressed in basic garments made in drab colors and from unattractive fabrics. Necessity determined local clothing trends rather than anything resembling the kind of fashion exploding in world centers such as London and Paris. Since then, the emergence of a Vietnamese fashion scene has been aligned with the accepted activities that are characteristic of emerging fashion design economies such as Australia and New Zealand, among many others. These include the development of a dedicated fashion week in Vietnam, participation of fashion design graduates in international competitions and the increase of fashion education opportunities within the major city centers of Hanoi and Ho Chi Minh City (Designs on Fashion 2003). The local versions of key fashion publications, such as *Harper's Bazaar* and *Vogue*, are also good indications of an emerging fashion culture.

In addition to the indications of a return to fashion, there are other factors that contribute to the theory that Vietnam will emerge as a fashion leader within the region. Vietnam's population, approximately 90 million, is one of the youngest in the world with a median age of 28.5 years (World Bank Data 2017). The advantage is a young energetic workforce, a high level of engagement with technology and a current generation of university students, who are well traveled, speak English as a second language, and are looking to align their education with developing new careers for the future of Vietnam. Discussions at Fashion Colloquia 2016 helped to remind us that the aim of fashion students in Vietnam is the same as fashion students elsewhere in the world, namely to gain the skills and knowledge required to develop a career within the creative industries, as a fashion designer. Despite recent suggestions from a leading trend forecaster, fashion is not dead—far from it, in fact, and the conversation should move on to the rebirth of fashion after decades of repetition and formulated fashion responses that are the result of trend-based design processes. A significant risk can be found where the ability to imagine and make has become limited. The popularity of courses such as Fashion Merchandising or Fashion Product may lead to situations where "designers" are side-stepped in favor of big data mining to a point where new product is determined by market analytics, branding, and supply chain management or even artificial design intelligence. The advantage in Vietnam is a developing high-tech manufacturing capability *alongside* traditional and craft methods of production that are accessible to the emerging designer fashion industry. The connection between design and manufacturing has not been degraded by offshore production processes, but is at risk of being overlooked for its potential to develop as a sustainable industry by local and foreign investors as well as aspiring local designers and retailers due to its relatively small scale.

DESIGNER FASHION

The irony is that the move of manufacturing to Vietnam has been foreseen as an expected outcome of the transient nature of manufacturing as an outsourcing of labor to nations where the economy has developed to an ideal point of infrastructure without workers' rights or economic advantage that would level out market equity. The Chinese government supports a system that allows China to have a fixed (pegged) currency at up to 2 points below the US dollar. This means that the value of Chinese currency is not determined by supply and demand as it is in Australia where the AU dollar is "floated" against the US dollar. This is likely to have a direct impact on enabling modern slavery in the twenty-first century by keeping costs artificially low (*Wall Street Journal* 2010).

The undervaluation of Chinese currency means that companies are selling their services for less than their real value. The result is a slow, and potentially negative, wage growth for local workers, as imported goods become more expensive, effectively resulting in non-payment of wages (see *LATimes* 2015; ILO 2018). As workers want and expect fair working conditions, and fair pay, the advantages of outsourcing production offshore are lessened. It has taken a long time for those of us waiting for the tide to

turn in favor of local manufacturing, as a strategy toward sustainable fashion production, but recent evidence of reshoring is reassuring for local manufacturing industries. With this in mind, the challenge for Vietnam is to leverage existing research and avoid the cycle of becoming a manufacturing nation to replace China. In the most recent statistics of textiles and clothing producing countries (WITS 2018), textiles, clothing and footwear in Vietnam equate to approx. 3.6 percent of GDP which is on par with other established manufacturing countries such as India (4.89 percent), Italy (4.13 percent), Germany (3.93 percent), Bangladesh (3.73 percent) and Hong Kong (3.49 percent), well behind China at 35.99 percent. Early investment in design-led production would be an advantage to the nation. Encouraging immigration or temporary working visas for experts from nations such as Australia, or establishing residency programs where designers share design knowledge within the local fashion industry, would be a long-term advantage.

The opportunity for developing sustainable fashion in Vietnam is reliant on designing products that can provide socially responsive, rewarding, safe, well-paid work for local workers. Local brand Ipa Nima is a developing Vietnamese luxury brand that leverages local making skills, talent, and expertise to produce a viable product that is sold within Vietnam as designer fashion accessories but also exported to other markets. The business has combined the craftsmanship inherent in traditional making methods, such as beading and embroidery, with medium-scale manufacturing methods that rely on more modern production methods to offset the time involved in hand worked techniques. The Ipa Nima label was founded by Christina Yu in 1997 coinciding with the arrival of the first wave of luxury brands in Vietnam, the first of which was

Louis Vuitton—their first Vietnamese store opened in Hanoi that same year (Yen 2016). The strategy of developing a local luxury brand able to be sold at a premium price demonstrates the capability of local designers in Vietnam to develop sustainable fashion businesses that enable and support ethical and sustainable production. The quirky and memorable designs available under the brand are directly connected to the processes and craft-based making skills of the factory staff producing their designs (Ipa Nima 2016).

A similar case is the social enterprise Fashion4Freedom, founded by LanVy Nguyen and with creative input from UK designer Victoria Ho, who at the time of Fashion Colloquia was the Head of the Fashion Department at South Saigon Campus, RMIT University Vietnam. The philosophy is simple: to provide socially and culturally responsible supply chains by connecting artisans with the fashion industry through design. The company is promoting a supply chain model that claims to be "The first socially responsible, ethical and transparent supply chain in Vietnam" (Fashion4Freedom 2016). Rather than resell artisans' work in a traditional supply chain model, the business is involving local artisans in the process of contributing to the design and development of new footwear and accessories that appeal to the global fashion market. Their distinctive designs are based on the craft of pagoda wood carving that has been used to provide a distinct design feature to their signature "dragon shoes" from the Reincarnated Soles label under the umbrella of their Saigon Socialite brand. The products are available for sale through their website (Saigon Socialite 2016) as well as being showcased on coolhunting.com (Tauber 2014). This design practice is an example of how sustainable fashion might develop differently in Vietnam where designers, manufacturers, and retailers could benefit from the lessons learned in other places to structure enterprises that are set up for ethical and sustainable production at the outset.

A final method of developing sustainable fashion, and particularly sustainable fashion production, is one that can be the result of collaborations between talented local staff and offshore design-led businesses that choose to set

Figure 5.3.1 The Ipa Nima brand is built on distinctive product that leverages local craft practices and skills to produce distinct design aesthetics
Image reproduced courtesy of Esther Huang Huiai

Figure 5.3.2 The advantages of the Ipa Nima business model is to bring traditional craft techniques into the contemporary factory environment
Image reproduced courtesy of Esther Huang Huiai

Figure 5.3.3 The iconic "Reincarnated Soles" are an example of how local social enterprise Fashion4Freedom's focus on design consultancy is being used as a method of ensuring culturally and socially responsible supply chains in line with their business philosophy
Image reproduced courtesy of Fashion4Freedom

up their own workrooms in Vietnam. It should be noted that an early example of this model in collaborative production between Australia and China has been explored by fellow researcher Dr. Tim Lindgren in his own design business that operated between Shanghai and Brisbane (Lindgren 2014). An example of this model being used in Vietnam is the collaboration between Melbourne designer Matthew Roach and Van Ho Bao, who manages the production for Melbourne-based label P.A.R.C.A Equipment Co. in Vietnam (Phung 2016). The joint project offers a great opportunity for emerging designers such as Matthew, who was unable to grow the business due to limitations surrounding large production minimums required by other manufacturers, when he realized that a solution lay in working with Van Ho Bao to start their own production facility (Phung 2016). The collaborative model means that designers can be more directly connected to their supply chain, particularly the

pay and conditions of their garment workers, resulting in an increased likelihood of ethical business practices that are sustainable. It is early days for P.A.R.C.A Equipment Co., established in Summer 2013, and time will reveal the potential success for this type of fashion production to become a sustainable model.

FASHION INDUSTRY WORKERS

The growing fashion and textiles industry in Vietnam is currently fueled by the demand for low-cost production and is at risk of being reduced to being the "next China," where Western fashion companies have their stock produced for a largely mainstream fast fashion market (Freidman 2012). The most recent data indicates that textile and clothing production in Vietnam is increasingly vital to the national economy (WITS 2017). The question for industry and government in Vietnam is: does the replication of large scale clothing manufacturing systems mean the replication of worst practices associated with these systems? The existing body of research into sustainable fashion suggests that unsustainable and unethical business practices are often associated with clothing production, namely sweatshop conditions, low rates of pay, modern slavery, and unsafe workplace practices in terms of machinery and chemical processing (see Fletcher 2014). Likewise, the low-tech, often craft-based, workers are equally exposed to exploitation in the name of fashion. This can be as a result of fashion trends that leverage inexpensive decorative processes within supply chains that lack complete transparency for example. Vietnam has the advantage of learning from the mistakes of the past and avoiding the worst aspects of becoming the next manufacturing nation by being proactive and informed in its methods of producing fashion.

The opportunity for aspiring fashion designers in Vietnam is to develop their own design industry and develop product for the local fashion market as well as for export, in turn providing further opportunities for local manufacturers and entrepreneurs. In terms of production, Vietnam may also build on specialist manufacturing capabilities rather than replicate a large-scale fashion production system that has developed in countries such as Bangladesh and India who are among the top five producing countries at present (WITS 2017). The advantage for Vietnamese garment workers is the growing maturity of internationally recognized organizations that lobby local governments and industry to develop policy that stipulates sustainable and ethical practices for local garment workers. In particular, the Fair Wear Foundation (Fair Wear Foundation Vietnam 2017) is one such organization that is directly engaged with the clothing, textile, and footwear industry in Vietnam to develop a local approach that could see Vietnam avoid the phase of sweatshop production, or at least shorten its existence by supporting early education schemes for local workers. Reporting on the activities and raising awareness about acceptable working conditions and safety standards is likely to give Vietnam an edge as global fashion labels become more in tune with consumer demands for transparent supply chains and assurance that production of their garments has been ethical. Organizations such as Fashion Revolution (Fashion Revolution Vietnam 2017) are gaining support, and institutions such as RMIT University Vietnam (RMIT Vietnam 2017) are raising awareness of sustainable design and production practices through activism and education. This is further evident in the work of intergovernmental

organizations, such as the World Bank and United Nations, that utilize top-down approaches to facilitate and support workers' rights and work toward ensuring safe and fair working conditions. There are also examples of best practice from other sources, such as the "Garments without Guilt" initiative (SGS 2018), that have relevance to improving outcomes for local Vietnamese fashion and textiles workers.

THREATS TO THE LOCAL INDUSTRY

Threats to local fashion designers and brands are being realized through the expansion of Western fashion labels and brands into the Vietnamese fashion marketplace. The perception of European and American jeanswear labels as designer fashion brands, as identified through studies such as Lee and Nguyen (2017), is interesting given the culture of dressmaking and tailoring that remains dominant within centers such as Ho Chi Minh City and Hanoi. This is more prevalent in the villages of Vietnam that specialize in craft forms aligned with methods of traditional making that have been the result of French colonialism in the eighteenth and nineteenth century. Christina Yu and Anna Vo both identified in their comments at Fashion Colloquia Vietnam that an additional risk is the lack of opportunity for emerging designers to showcase their work, alongside a dearth of opportunity for emerging designers to work in the industry before attempting to establish their own brand (Phung 2016). The government of Vietnam has demonstrated its willingness to support the emerging industry with initiatives such as Vietnam International Fashion Week (Fashion Week Vietnam 2017) and by allowing production of the popular TV network program Project Runway (Project Runway Vietnam 2017), which at the time of writing has run for three seasons (projectrunway.com.vn). Momentum has been building and positivity surrounding the proposed Trans Pacific Partnership (TPP) was evident and discussed by many of the fashion industry guests at Fashion Colloquia Vietnam (Fashion Colloquia Vietnam 2016). However, the more recent collapse of the TPP will have had a devastating effect on the local fashion industry but even without US involvement the deal may go ahead in a different format. Alongside fashion design and fashion productions collaborations, such as the examples included in this essay, the potential for fashion research projects between fashion in Vietnam and Australia has begun. An example of this nature is demonstrated in the Wool Innovation project presented at Fashion Colloquia Vietnam (Ha 2016), a further demonstration of how collaborative models for producing sustainable fashion have emerged and will continue regardless of agreements such as TPP.

CONCLUSION

This essay has provided an overview of how sustainable fashion design models might be realized in Vietnam at a stage where the opportunity exists to actively design a large-scale manufacturing system. Cases such as Ipa Nima demonstrate a possibility for manfacturing luxury goods in Vietnam as an alternative to developing luxury production for Western companies. Alternatives such as Fashion 4 Freedom aim to develop sustainable supply chains as a catalyst to connecting fashion design, through ethical and sustainable principles, to artisanal practices inherent to the local culture. Finally, joint proprietors Matthew Roach and Van Ho Bao are exploring the possibilities of collaborative and connected design and production model that spans two countries:

Australia and Vietnam. Early joint research projects explore the possibilities of establishing raw materials and processing alongside emerging manufacturing markets as a part of producing sustainable fashion. These examples showcase just three possibilities for sustainable fashion design and production here. However, the local culture of making and different approaches to business, including the important potential of socially constructed business models, is only beginning to be understood in terms of a local fashion industry.

The principal risk for Vietnam's emerging fashion industry is that it might become a service industry that is focused on producing products designed for foreign markets by foreign designers. Part of the rights of passage for any country in terms of developing fashion is to develop a distinct fashion culture through design. As one fashion student put it at the plenary session to the 2016 Fashion Colloquia, "Producing Fashion—Made in Vietnam," fashion students in Vietnam are not going to university to learn how to make fashion for other people! They want to know how to design their own fashions, just like everywhere else in the world. It is aspirational to believe that Vietnam can achieve a sustainable and ethical fashion design and manufacturing industry overnight; this outcome is reliant on a multitude of internal and external factors. However, equally, the journey to developing such an industry does not have to follow the same evolutionary process for each new instance or geography. The point here is that sustainable approaches are not mutually exclusive. Developing a local designer fashion industry can take place alongside the development of a sustainable and ethical manufacturing industry. The design economy and the making economy are ideals that can be developed in tandem. This is the opportunity for the emerging fashion and textiles sector in growing economies such as Vietnam.

ACKNOWLEDGEMENTS

The author would like to acknowledge the organizers of and participants in Fashion Colloquia 2016 "Producing Fashion: Made in Vietnam" for sharing their knowledge and expertise, and engaging in critical discussions around the potential for Vietnam as an emerging fashion center. The insights shared here are a result of active participation in this event and the knowledge gained from travelling to Vietnam and working with the fashion program team at RMIT University Vietnam.

REFERENCES

Arnold, M. (2016), *Dressed to Impress*. Available online at: www.oivietnam.com/2016/05/dress-to-impress (accessed August 14, 2017).

Australian War Memorial (2017), *Vietnam War 1962–1975*. Available online at: www.awm.gov.au/articles/event/vietnam (accessed August 14, 2017).

Designs on Fashion (2003), *Vietnam Investment Review*. Available online at: https://search-proquest-com.ezproxy.lib.rmit.edu.au/docview/201509407?accountid=13552 (accessed August 17, 2017).

Fashion4Freedom (2016), *Fashion for Freedom—Our Philosophy*. Available online: http://www.fashion4freedom.com/#philosophy (accessed October 10, 2016).

Fair Wear Foundation Vietnam (2017), *Fair Wear Foundation Vietnam*. Available online: https://www.fairwear.org/country/vietnam (accessed August 14, 2017).

Fashion Colloquia Vietnam (2016), *Producing Fashion: Made in Vietnam Fashion Colloquia*. Available online at: https://www.rmit.edu.au/events/all-events/conferences/2016/july/producing-fashion-made-in-vietnam (accessed August 14, 2017).

Fashion Revolution Vietnam (2017), *We Are Fashion Revolution Vietnam*. Available online at: www.fashionrevolution.org/vietnam (accessed August 14, 2017).

Fashion Week Vietnam (2017), *Vietnam International Fashion Week 2017*. Available online at: www.vietnaminternationalfashionweek.vn (accessed September 15, 2017).

Fletcher, K. (2014), *Sustainable Fashion and Textiles: Design Journeys*, London: Taylor and Francis. Available online: https://ebookcentral.proquest.com/lib/RMIT/detail.action?docID=3061180 (accessed February 7, 2018).

Friedman, A. (2012), *Sourcing Horizons: Looking Beyond China*, 8–9. New York: Fairchild Fashion Media.

Ha, H. (2016), "Fashioning New methods of Production in Vietnam." Available online at: https://www.rmit.edu.vn/news/fashioning-new-methods-production-vietnam (accessed December 10, 2016).

Ipa Nima (2016), *Welcome to Ipa Nima*. Available online at: ipa-nima.com.

International Labour Organization (ILO) (2017), *International Labour Organization Statistics*. Available online at: http://www.ilo.org/dyn/lfsurvey/lfsurvey.list?p_lang=en&p_country=VN (accessed February 7, 2018).

International Labour Organization (ILO) (2018), *International Labour Standards on Wages*. Available online at: http://www.ilo.org/global/standards/subjects-covered-by-international-labour-standards/wages/lang--en/index.htm (accessed February 7, 2018).

LA Times (2015), "Why China's devaluation of the Yuan Matters So Much." Available online at: http://www.latimes.com/business/la-fi-china-devalues-yuan–20150811-htmlstory.html (accessed February 7, 2018).

Lee, J., and M. Nguyen (2017), "Product Attributes and Preference for Foreign Brands Among Vietnamese Consumers," *Journal of Retailing and Consumer Services*, 35: 76–83.

Lindgren, T. (2014), *Fashion in Shanghai: The Designers of a New Economy of Style*. Available online at: https://primo-direct-apac.hosted.exlibrisgroup.com/primo-explore/fulldisplay?docid=TN_trove_thesis189970698&context=PC&vid=RMITU&search_scope=Books_articles_and_more&tab=default_tab&lang=en_US (accessed June 8, 2017).

Phung, H. (2016), "Experts discuss challenges facing Vietnam's Fashion industry," RMIT University

Vietnam. Available online at: https://www.rmit.edu.vn/news/experts-discuss-challenges-facing-vietnams-fashion-industry (retrieved October 16, 2016).

Project Runway Vietnam (2017), *Project Runway Vietnam*. Available online at: http://www.projectrunway.com.vn (accessed October 16, 2016).

RMIT University Vietnam (2017), *About RMIT Vietnam*. Available at: https://www.rmit.edu.vn/about-rmit-vietnam (accessed December 10, 2017).

Saigon Socialite (2016), *Fashion for Freedom Saigon Socialite*. Available online at: https://www.etsy.com/shop/Fashion4Freedom (accessed October 10, 2016).

SGS 2018, "Garments without Guilt." Available online at: http://www.sgs.com/en/sustainability/social-sustainability/social-responsibility-sr/garments-without-guilt (accessed February 7, 2018).

Tauber, N. (2014), "Saigon Socialite Shoes." Available online at: http://www.coolhunting.com/style/saigon-socialite-shoes (accessed October 10, 2016).

Wall Street Journal (2010), "How China Manages Its Currency—An Explanation for Humans." Available online at: https://blogs.wsj.com/marketbeat/2010/06/21/how-china-manages-its-currency-an-explanation-for-humans/ (accessed August 8, 2017).

World Bank Data (2017), *Population total Vietnam*. Available online at: https://data.worldbank.org/indicator/SP.POP.TOTL?locations=VN (accessed August 8, 2017).

World Integrated Trade Solution (WITS) (2017), *Textiles and Clothing Exporting Countries*. Available online at: http://wits.worldbank.org/visualization/detailed-product-analysis-visualization.html (accessed August 14, 2017).

World Integrated Trade Solution (WITS) (2018), *Textiles and Clothing Exporting Countries*. Available online at: http://wits.worldbank.org/visualization/detailed-product-analysis-visualization.html (accessed February 7, 2018).

Yen, H. (2016), *RMIT News—Twenty Years of Vietnamese Fashion*. Available online at: https://www.rmit.edu.vn/news/twenty-years-vietnamese-fashion (accessed December 17, 2017).

CHAPTER 5.4

A SPOTLIGHT ON: SPACE BETWEEN
Fashion Activism in New Zealand

Jennifer Whitty, Massey University, New Zealand

As in most developed Western countries, people in New Zealand are buying more clothes than ever before (Statistics New Zealand 2016) the majority of which are imported. This accelerated consumption pattern is exemplified by the linear "take, make, and waste" model, which has influenced consumer culture to consume and discard clothing at their earliest convenience. Kate Fletcher (2016: 85) believes that in order to foster a climate for change, we must first come fully to terms with the realities of our current fashion context to locate ourselves in our actual condition. In an attempt to interrogate these issues and base ourselves fully in the actual NZ fashion condition, the practice-based enterprise/research project Space Between was established by the researchers Jennifer Whitty and Holly McQuillan in 2015. Its aim is to explore and disrupt the space between the components of the linear system inherent within industry, consumer culture, and education with the aim of creating a more expansive, inclusive circular mode of operation. It is focused on fostering innovation developing micro-fashion business models to provide a new vision and practice for fashion in a twenty-first century context.

Space Between offers a thoughtful new way to design, make, and use locally produced fashion. Being situated in New Zealand's leading creative tertiary institution has been key to its formation, as Massey University is focused on addressing "wicked problems" and places an importance on knowledge transfer from research/enterprise. The innovation takes the form of design-led

Figure 5.4.1 Fashion= fast+cheap+throwaway? Graphic design: Whitty (2016)
Image reproduced courtesy of H. McQuillan and J. Whitty

TAKE, MAKE AND WASTE

| PRE CONSUMPTION PHASE **TAKE & MAKE** | SHOP

POINT OF PURCHASE | POST CONSUMPTION PHASE **USE/WASTE** |

RAW MATERIAL EXTRACTION
RESEARCH AND DESIGN
GARMENT MANUFACTURING
PACKING AND DELIVERY

PRODUCT USE AND MAINTENCE
OPTIONAL RECYCLING AND REUSE
FINAL DISPOSAL

Figure 5.4.2 Take, Make, and Waste
Image reproduced courtesy of J. Whitty

Figure 5.4.3 Fundamentals range on Space Between website, 1st life and 2nd life
Image reproduced courtesy of J. Whitty and H. McQuillan

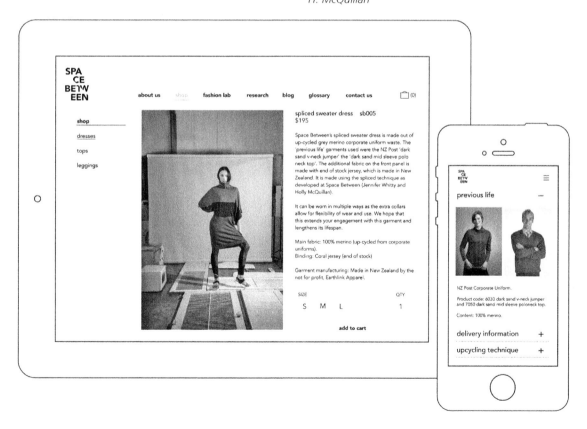

activism as described by Alastair Fuad-Luke (2009), oriented toward addressing sustainability issues such as resource depletion, consumption, and production. It asks whether we can we find a sustainable balance between the design, manufacturing, and consumption of garments by reducing the speed, volume, and impacts of "waste-ready" global consumerism? It does this by adopting new systems thinking (Niinimaki 2013) with an agenda to address issues of waste and bring about "positive change" in industry, by examining the product-service system to transform negative consumption and production patterns.

The impetus to rethink waste and apply circular economy principles was reinforced by the strategic cross sector partnership with New

Figure 5.4.4 Space Between home page with an example of the Fundamentals range
Image reproduced courtesy of J. Whitty and H. McQuillan

Zealand Post Group, a state-owned enterprise, and its corporate manufacturer, Booker Spalding. In 2012 NZ Post (2015) identified that a vast number of their used uniforms—approximately 9,000 every year—were in a workable condition, but were being downcycled or exported to Papua New Guinea to be disposed of. NZ Post estimates that New Zealand's twenty largest organizations whose employees have uniforms use 860,000 garments (approx. 430,000 tonnes) per annum. The vast majority of these uniforms end up in landfill.

The Fundamentals range (Whitty and McQuillan 2015), demonstrates solutions for the industry's waste stream (post-consumer corporate uniforms) in the form of a capsule limited edition remanufactured collection designed by Space Between designers made by EarthLink (2015), a not-for-profit which opens the door to employment for many people with health and social barriers. This minimal-impact range and accompanying wholly transparent system unlocks the latent qualities of undervalued resources through a circular economy approach. The series of upcycling or remanufacture processes, design strategies, and three upcycling techniques—the conjoined, spliced, and pieced—could be applied to any given garment. In order to encourage micro-cooperative practices through social innovation to occur, all information about the manufacturing methods and techniques are open to access, adapt, remix, and share via the website and other social media channels.

Space Between advocates for an expanded view of fashion which makes a strong assertion for the potential of working collaboratively in a multi-dimensional capacity. Space Between provides a "safe" space for testing and developing ideas with a direct link to the market as they explore new platforms for fashion; bridging the physical and digital realms of creating, producing, thinking, and distributing clothes.

REFERENCES

Earthlink Incorporated (2015), Available online at: http://www.earthlink.org.nz / (accessed February 8, 2017).

Fletcher, K. (2016), *Craft of Use: Post-Growth Fashion*, 85. Abingdon and New York: Routledge.

Fuad-Luke, A. (2009), *Design Activism: Beautiful Srangeness for a Sustainable World.* London and Sterling, VA: Earthscan.

Niinimaki, K. (2013), *Sustainable Fashion: New Approaches.* Aalto University publication series. Available online at: https://www.taik.fi/kirjakauppa/images/57175badb573d97c59ec6a99ecc1011c.pdf (accessed June 10, 2016).

NZ Post (2015), "Sustainable solutions sew new life into NZ Post uniforms." Available online at: https://www.nzpost.co.nz/about-us/media-centre/media-release/sustainable-solutions-sew-new-life-into-nz-post-uniforms (accessed March 19. 2016).

Statistics New Zealand (2016), *Consumption goods continue upward trend in January.* Available online at: http://www.stats.govt.nz/browse_for_stats/industry_sectors/imports_and_exports/consump-goods-up-trend–16.aspx (accessed March 10, 2017).

Whitty, J., and H. McQuillan (2015), "Space Between." Available online at: www.spacebetween.ac.nz (accessed July 10, 2016).

FASHION PRACTICES IN CAMBODIA

Contrasting Paradigms Between the Export Apparel Industry and Small–medium Enterprises in Cambodia

Lauren Solomon, Queensland University of Technology, Australia

INTRODUCTION

As a key site of twenty-first-century fashion production, the garment industry in Cambodia provides a source of employment for hundreds of thousands of workers. Employing over 646,000 workers, the apparel sector amounts to 78 percent of the country's market exports (International Labour Organization 2016: 9). Cambodia has attracted some of the world's largest fashion multi-nationals, including H&M, Marks & Spencer, Nike, Adidas, Levi's, Zara, Gap, Kmart, and C&A. In the early 2000s, the International Labour Organization (ILO) promoted Cambodia as a responsible place of manufacturer, through their Better Factories Cambodia (BFC) compliance monitoring program (International Labour Organization

2016; Oka 2016). Despite the continuation of the ILO's BFC compliance monitoring program today, international media (for example, Vice 2012) and Human Rights Watch (Kashyap 2015) have reported widespread industry exploitation. This chapter draws on primary data collected in May–June 2015 during fieldwork conducted in Phnom Penh, Cambodia, from industry stakeholders and emerging fashion and accessories small-to-medium enterprises (SMEs). Data were collected via first-hand observation and through a series of qualitative interviews conducted with garment workers, representatives of the Free Trade Union of the Workers of the Kingdom of Cambodia (FTUWKC), the ILO's Better Factories Cambodia (BFC) division, the Garment Manufacturers' Association of

Cambodia (GMAC), and individuals running SMEs, including Tonle, A.N.D., Smateria, and Fairsew. Secondary data are also utilized from academic and industry publications.[1]

This chapter explores the contrasting paradigms between large scale export garment production and small scale enterprises manifesting in Cambodia. By exploring how SMEs in Cambodia are operating in a fundamentally different way to the export apparel industry, this chapter provides a regional example of best practice. It firstly examines the emergence of the labor movement in the Cambodian garment industry. This examination intends to provide the context for key interconnected industry challenges, including industrial relations, production capabilities, and working conditions. Significantly, the industry features a lack of opportunity for women working in a highly gendered garment industry that cannot upgrade its production capabilities, meaning there is no opportunity for worker advancement. Next, non-governmental organizations (NGOs) and local initiatives that can drive incremental changes in the industry are discussed. The practices of a sample of SMEs are discussed, including: increasing worker's capabilities, addressing local social issues, and investing in the well-being of their workforces. This highlights the contrasting paradigms between SMEs and the garment industry in Cambodia.

LABOR MOVEMENT IN THE CAMBODIAN GARMENT INDUSTRY

Highly exploitative behavior in the global fashion industry has consistently sparked international outrage. During the 1990s, workers' rights abuses and sweatshop practices in the garment industry by multi-nationals became public knowledge (Arrigo 2013). Publicity of exploitative practices resulted in a backlash of consumer distrust and an erosion of corporate reputations (Arrigo 2013). While the anti-sweatshop movement was gaining momentum, Cambodia could be marketed as a responsible place of manufacture, as compliance with labor standards was linked to international trade agreements such as the Multi-Fibre Arrangement (MFA) and the Trade Agreement on Textiles and Apparel (TATA) (International Labour Organization 2016; Dasgupta, Poutianen and Williams 2011; Miller et al. 2009). The MFA and the TATA agreements meant that higher quotas could be achieved on the proviso that factories improved working conditions and abided by labor law (Ear 2013; Staritz & Frederick 2012). The establishment of the ILO Better Factories Cambodia program in 2001 assisted in monitoring labor standards, while the incentive-driven scheme (connecting quota allowances to labor conditions) was the first of its kind within the Asian region (Arnold & Shih 2010; Asuyama 2013; Dasgupta et al. 2011). The BFC program was considered extremely credible (Staritz 2010), yet Miller et al. (2009) argue that as export quota allocation was based on industry performance, factories could conceal breaches. And, with the incentive for improving of labor conditions removed at the conclusion of the TATA (2001) and MFA (2004) agreements, the garment industry was in a precarious state (Arnold & Shih 2010). Workers were starting to protest working conditions and low wages, by participating in a local labor movement.

Industrial Relations

Prior to the trade agreements ending, a labor movement was emerging in the Cambodian garment industry (Hughes 2007; Oka 2016). This was initiated by strikes at factories and a revision of the labor code in 1997 which included "worker's right to freedom of association" (Oka 2016: 649). Simultaneously, the first independent union within the garment industry in Cambodia—The Free Trade Union of the Workers of the Kingdom of Cambodia (FTUWKC)—was formed in 1996 (Arnold & Shih 2010). By 2004 the FTUWKC represented 40,000 workers (Hughes 2007). Collective activism from the union's president, Chea Vichea, forced the minimum wage to increase from "US $27 a month in 1996 to $45 a month in 2000" (Hughes 2007: 846). In the same year Vichea was assassinated due to his union activity (Say, General Secretary, Personal Interview, 10/06/2015). In addition to Vichea, several other local union leaders from the FTUWKC have been assassinated and many have been fired or officially "blacklisted" from the industry for fighting for fairer conditions (Say, General Secretary, Personal Interview, 10/06/2015). These accounts by Say revealed the danger union leaders face for speaking out about industry issues in the country.

Despite the risk associated with union activity and affiliation, there are over 1,000 unions in the Cambodian garment industry (Say, General Secretary, Personal Interview, 10/06/2015). Arnold and Shih (2010: 416) argue that because of the high number of unions, "effectiveness ... [is] questionable, leaving many unions weak, under-funded, competing with one another, and subject to corruption and political interference." In addition to these internal challenges between unions, union action regularly impacts and affects relationships with industry stakeholders. For example, in the first quarter of 2016 the Garment Manufacturer's Association of Cambodia (GMAC) reported that twelve strikes took place with over 44,000 working days lost

as a result (International Labour Organization 2016: 9). According to Bower from GMAC, unions regularly hold

> non-procedural strikes, because legally speaking they need to get the majority approval from the workers (sic) ... they also need to inform the factory seven days before it happens ... they just do the strike to put pressure on the factory *(sic)*, they know very well the situation, for example the factory is about to export or transport [the] product out, then they do the strike (sic).
>
> Bower, Legal and Labour Manager,
> Personal Interview, 08/06/2015

In contrast, Say from the FTUWKC claims that if the union does give notice for strikes, the factory management uses physical violence and verbal abuse to discourage them (General Secretary, Personal Interview, 10/06/2015). Therefore, industrial relations are a major challenge in Cambodia and cause ongoing tension between factory management, unions, and workers.

Production Capabilities

The Cambodian garment industry is highly gendered, with women making up "an estimated 90 to 92 percent of the industry's ... workers" (Kashyap 2015: 6). With minimal education, many women move into the Cambodian garment industry with few (if any) skills (Bonacich 2002; Hurley 2005; Natsuda et al. 2010). Garment workers interviewed in Phnom Penh explained that they were provided with only basic sewing training in the factories and their job consisted of repetitive work (Garment Workers, Personal Interview, 12/06/2015). As garment workers can produce only basic products, the industry is unable to upgrade from Cut, Make, Trim (CMT) production capabilities (Natsuda et al. 2010). The limited prospect of skills training, combined with the low capabilities of the workforce, means that opportunities for workers to progress internally and externally remain slim (Bower, Legal and Labour Manager, Personal Interview, 08/06/2015; Chan & Oum 2011). Cambodia's capacity in supplying production processes that go beyond basic CMT products is further hampered by the fact that Cambodia does not have an established textile industry and has "a very limited number of backward linkage industries" (for example labels, embroidery etc.) (Ear 2013; Hossain 2010: 11). Brands rely on importing materials and outsourcing any added-value processes to other countries (Natsuda et al. 2010). Additionally, management rent facilities and equipment to increase flexibility, mean that relocation is easy if they cannot maintain competitive advantage (Say, General Secretary, Personal Interview, 10/06/2015; Brooks 2015). Consequently, workers are under constant pressure to meet high production targets for factories to make a profit and remain competitive as the industry remains at the lowest end of the market.

Working Conditions

The limited capabilities of the workforce, combined with the inability of the industry to upgrade from CMT production, is directly impacting industry working conditions and causing tension between workers and management. For example, the pressure to meet production targets has been identified by Human Rights Watch as compromising workers' well-being (Kashyap 2015). According to a Human Rights Watch report:

> many workers from large factories directly supplying to international brands and small, subcontractor factories – complained that management pressure to meet production targets undermined their ability to take breaks to use washrooms, rest, or drink water (refer to Figure 5.5.1).
>
> Kashyap 2015: 8

Figure 5.5.1 Garment workers in a factory in Phnom Penh, 2018
Image reproduced courtesy of Montesano Casillas

Industry stakeholders revealed a matrix of issues that were effecting worker's well-being, including: the lack of safe transport (refer to image 2); nutrition; health; hygiene; poor working conditions and accommodation (Avery, Assessor/Advisor Manager, Personal Interview, 02/06/2015; Bower, Legal and Labour Manager, Personal Interview, 08/06/2015; Say, General Secretary, Personal Interview, 10/06/2015; Garment Workers, Personal Interview, 12/06/2015; Scott, Ex-Auditor, Personal Interview, 04/06/2015).

Poor industry conditions are exacerbated by the lack of investment in long-term infrastructure by multi-nationals using Cambodia as a site for CMT production. As an example, Avery from Better Factories Cambodia (BFC) noted that rented factories generally had lower compliance levels as managers were unable to alter existing factory buildings (Avery, Assessor / Advisor Manager, Personal Interview, 02/06/2015). In an industry plagued by poor working conditions, NGOs play an important role in advocating for fairer conditions for garment workers.

NGOs and Local Initiatives Addressing Industry Issues

NGOs have assisted in supporting the people working in the garment industry in many ways, such as their involvement in multi-stakeholder initiatives (MSIs), report writing, corporate partnerships and at a grassroots level. Collaborative governance through the emergence of MSIs attempts to mitigate some of the challenges of self-regulatory governance (for example Corporate Social Responsibility), by involving multiple stakeholders. This collaborative approach to governance aims to develop shared standards while fostering dialog between stakeholders (Jerbi 2012; Hughes et al. 2007; Tighe 2016). "Who Made My Clothes? A

Report from Cambodia" (Noggle & Stuart 2017) collected data from many garment workers, reporting insights of the industry from workers' perspectives. Telling stories of participants, this report gives workers a voice, while the international profile of Fashion Revolution allows for global dissemination. In recent years, corporate and NGO partnerships have become increasingly popular (Larsson et al. 2013: 270). "Who Made My Clothes? A Report from Cambodia" was funded by the C&A Foundation, an NGO linked to the multi-national fashion corporation C&A, showing an example of a corporate and NGO partnership (Noggle & Stuart 2017). In a similar vein GAP and Levi's have partnered with CARE Cambodia to implement social programs in factories, tackling some of the common social issues workers face (Project Profile: Personal Advancement and Career Enhancement 2014; Project Profile: Sewing for a Brighter Future 2014). At a grassroots level, there are several organizations which are working to advocate for, and advance, the rights of garment workers in Cambodia, including the Workers' Information Centre (United Sisterhood Alliance 2016) and The Solidarity Center (Solidarity Center 2018). By fostering dialog between stakeholders, allowing workers to share their personal experiences, addressing specific social issues of workers and through advocacy, these various initiatives can drive incremental change in the industry.

CONTRASTING PARADIGMS AND PRACTICES IN CAMBODIA

While export apparel production can improve incrementally, fieldwork illustrated how fashion production is emerging through fundamentally different modes of production in the one geographical location. In fact, the trajectory of the Cambodian garment industry can be connected to the rise of fashion SMEs in Cambodia that are addressing social issues prevalent in a country still recovering from decades of conflict and instability. The garment industry has had a positive impact on the Cambodian economy, significantly improving the Gross Domestic Product (GDP) (Ear 2012). As a result, Cambodia has become "one of the world's fastest-growing economies in the first decade of this century" (Unteroberdoerster 2014: 1). The World Bank (2009) has reported an increase in private-sector activity and Cain (2011) cites an increase in entrepreneurship activities in Phnom Penh. With the garment industry contributing to the rapid growth of Cambodia's economy and thus increasing local business activity, there is an emerging space for ethical and sustainable fashion brands to operate in. Globally, there is growing consumer interest in the practices of fashion brands operating in developing countries, stemming from industrial relations scandals, notoriously the 2013 collapse of Rana Plaza in Bangladesh, that killed more than 1,000 workers and injured 2,500 (see: Brooks 2015; Nimbalker et al. 2017; Siegle 2014). Catering to socially conscious consumers, SMEs in the fashion sector sell to the local tourist and expatriate market and export internationally to growing niche markets (Goldsmith & Carbonaro 2013). This section explores the contrasting paradigms between large scale multi-national garment production and the small–medium scale enterprises operating in Cambodia. Primarily, it draws on data collected during fieldwork with a sample of fashion and accessories SMEs in Phnom Penh, including Tonle (a zero-waste fashion and accessory brand), A.N.D. (a Fairtrade fashion and accessory brand), Smateria (a social enterprise), and Fairsew (a fashion manufacturer).

Skills Development and Training

A fundamental difference between the garment industry in Cambodia and this sample of SMEs is the capabilities of the workforce. Tonle, A.N.D., Smateria, and Fairsew have invested in improving the capabilities of their workforce. For example, Fairsew offers their employees regular training, and have a system of skill levels for workers (Murray, Director, Personal Interview, 03/06/2015). Using this system, workers at Fairsew can progress to more highly skilled roles in the organization once they reach the appropriate skill level (Murray, Director, Personal Interview, 03/06/2015). In addition to improving the capabilities of their workforce, this provides employees opportunities for career progression.

Observing finished products in the A.N.D. stores, it was clear that items were extremely well constructed, using high-quality finishes and designs that were more complex than basic CMT apparel. Bell from A.N.D. states that:

> people have come from factories to be interviewed … [however] they get quite frightened because our people can cut a pattern and sew a whole garment, they find when they come from factories they have very, very limited skills … [they] work in lines … [for example they] sew these two shoulder seams and that's all they do.
> Bell, Director, Personal Interview, 12/06/2015

Bell highlights the dearth of skills among garment workers, illustrating a large skill gap between typical Cambodian employees in this sector and A.N.D. employees.

Textiles Sourcing and Innovation

Skills development has also extended to textiles sourcing and innovation for these SMEs. For example, A.N.D. has taught traditional artisans to weave cotton ikat fabric using the handloom, which is then transformed into garments and accessories in their Phnom Penh workshop (Bell, Director, Personal Interview, 12/06/2015). With minimal cotton production in Cambodia, the cotton ikat created by A.N.D. is a unique product within the marketplace (Bell, Director, Personal Interview, 12/06/2015).

Additionally, Smateria has invested in embroidery machines, while Tonle screen-prints and dyes their own fabrics (Kerr, Director, Personal Interview, 05/06/2015). These investments allow these enterprises to achieve high-quality finishes and niche prints that subsequently adds value to their products, which are sold to the local tourist and expatriate market and exported internationally. Textile sourcing for each SME includes practices of reuse, recycling, and repurposing excess stock

and cut-offs from factories in Cambodia, which end up in the local marketplace (Bell, Director, Personal Interview, 12/06/2015; Murray, Director, Personal Interview, 03/06/2015; Kerr, Director, Personal Interview, 05/06/2015). With factories generating a large amount of textile waste in Cambodia, the export apparel industry has unintentionally created a local sourcing hub in Phnom Penh, which is used by local fashion SMEs. Tonle, Fairsew, and Smateria source textiles from the local marketplace, turning excess stock and waste materials into garments and accessories. For example, Smateria turns waste materials (nylon netting, scrap leather and plastic) into high-quality bags and accessories (Kerr, Director, Personal Interview, 05/06/2015). By turning a challenging environment in which to source and develop products into an opportunity to innovate and include sustainable practices, these SMEs have created products with niche market appeal. For example, as noted earlier, Tonle's workshop is zero-waste, which appeals to the environmentally conscience consumer.

Addressing Local Social Challenges

In addition to considering environmental sustainability in their practices, these SMEs are part of an emerging start-up culture in Phnom Penh that is addressing social issues prevalent in a country still recovering from many years of turmoil and uncertainty. For example, Smateria prioritizes working with women and provides on-site free pre-school and childcare which allows its employees a safe, accessible, and affordable solution to their familial responsibilities (Kerr, Director, Personal Interview, 05/06/2015).

Smateria also provides rice for its workers and is working toward creating a canteen to improve workers' nutrition (Kerr, Director, Personal Interview, 05/06/2015). Fairsew's all-female workforce receive healthcare, as part of efforts to improve their accessibility to medical services and overall well-being (Murray, Director, Personal Interview, 03/06/2015). A.N.D. offers

Figure 5.5.4 Children of Smateria's employees at the on-site pre-school, 2018
Image reproduced courtesy of Smateria

employment opportunities for a marginalized sector of Cambodian society, particularly people with disabilities, who create accessories and homewares that are sold in A.N.D. stores in Phnom Penh (Bell, Director, Personal Interview, 12/06/2015). These companies' practices demonstrated a connection to the people involved in their production processes and the welfare of their workforces. Their practices are fundamentally different to those typically prevalent in the garment industry, and provide an insight into how SMEs which support and provide opportunities for women and other marginalized sectors of the workforce can emerge at a key site of global twenty-first century fashion production.

CONCLUSION

Unable to move beyond CMT production and provide opportunities for skills development and industry progression for its highly gendered workforce, the garment industry in Cambodia is stagnant and often exploitative. The industry in Cambodia provides employment for many low-skilled workers and NGOs and local initiatives are assisting in advocating for fairer conditions and creating incremental change in the sector, yet grave industrial relations challenges persist. However, by improving the economy in Cambodia and creating avenues for textile sourcing, the Cambodian garment industry can be connected to the emerging market for fashion SMEs in Phnom Penh. Exploring practices within both the Cambodian garment industry and of a sample of fashion SMEs in Cambodia, this essay showcases how different paradigms of fashion production may emerge in the one geographical location. Significantly, this essay illustrates how SMEs in Cambodia are operating in a fundamentally different way to the export

apparel industry. By exploring how these SMEs are increasing workers' capabilities, addressing local social issues, and investing in the well-being of their workforce, this essay provides a regional example of best practice.

NOTES

1. Names have been changed to protect the privacy of interviewees.

REFERENCES

Arnold, D., and T. H. Shih (2010), "A Fair Model of Globalisation? Labour and Global Production in Cambodia," *Journal of Contemporary Asia*, 40(3): 401–24.

Arrigo, E. (2013), "Corporate responsibility management in fast fashion companies: The Gap Inc case," *Journal of Fashion Marketing and Management*, 17(2): 175–89.

Asuyama, Y. (2013), "Firm dynamics in the Cambodian garment industry: firm turnover, productivity growth and wage profile under trade liberalization," *Journal of the Asia Pacific Economy*, 18(1): 51.

Bonacich, E. (2002), "Labor's Response to Global Production" in Gary Gereffi, David Spener, and Jennifer Bair (eds), *Free Trade and Uneven Development: The North American Apparel Industry after Nafta*. Philadelphia: Temple University Press.

Brooks, A. (2015), *Clothing Poverty: The Hidden World of Fast Fashion and Second-hand Clothes*. London: Zed Books.

Cain, G. (2011), "Misruling Cambodia: Corruption is rife and dissent is stifled, as 'Cambodia's curse' shows. But entrepreneurs are giving the country some hope," *Wall Street Journal*.

CARE Cambodia (2014a), "Project Profile: Personal Advancement and Career Enhancement (P.A.C.E.)." Accessed 06.08.2015.

CARE Cambodia (2014b), "Project Profile: Sewing for a Brighter Future (SBF)." Accessed 06.08.2015.

Chan, S., and S. Oum (2011), Impact of Garment and Textile Trade Preferences on Livelihoods in Cambodia. Part of Oxfam America Research

Backgrounders Series, Kimberly Pfeifer (ed). Boston, MA: Oxfam America.

Dasgupta, S., T. Poutiainen, and D. Williams (2011), *From Downturn to Recovery: Cambodia's Garment Sector in Transition.* Phnom Penh, Cambodia: International Labour Organization, Country Office for Thailand, Cambodia and Lao People's Democratic Republic.

Ear, S. (2013), "Cambodia's Garment Industry: A Case Study in Governance," *Journal of Southeast Asian Economies,* 30(1): 91–105.

Goldsmith, D., and S. Carbonaro (2013), "Fashion and the Design of Prosperity: A Discussion of Alternative Business Models," in S. Black, A. de la Haye, J. Entwistle, R. Root, H. Thomas, and A. Rocamora (eds), *The Handbook of Fashion Studies: International Perspectives.* London: Bloomsbury Publishing.

Hossain, Z. (2010), *Report on Cambodian Textile and Garment Industry.* Nairobi: African Cotton and Textiles Industries Federation.

Hughes, A., M. Buttle, and N. Wrigley (2007), "Organisational Geographies of Corporate Responsibility: A UK-US Comparison of Retailers' Ethical Trading Initiatives," *Journal of Economic Geography,* 7: 491–513.

Hughes, C. (2007), "Transnational Networks, International Organizations and Political Participation in Cambodia: Human Rights, Labor Rights and Common Rights," *Democratization,* 14(5): 834–52.

Hurley, J. (2005), "Unravelling the Web: Supply Chains and Workers' Lives in the Garment Industry," in A. Hale and J. Wills (eds), *Threads of Labour: Garment Industry Supply Chains from the Workers' Perspective.* Malden, MA: Blackwell Publishing Ltd.

International Labour Organization (2016), *Better Factories Cambodia: Garment Industry 33rd Compliance Synthesis Report.* Geneva: International Labour Organization and International Financial Corporation.

Jerbi, S. (2012), "Assessing the Roles of Multi-Stakeholder Initiatives in Advancing the Business and Human Rights Agenda," *International Review of the Red Cross,* 94(887).

Kashyap, A. (2015), "Work Faster or Get Out: Labour Rights Abuses in Cambodia's Garment Industry." New York: Human Rights Watch.

Larsson, K., C. Buhr, and C. Mark-Herbert (2013), "Corporate Responsibility in the Garment Industry: Towards share value," in M. A. Gardetti and A. L. Torres (eds), *Sustainability in Fashion and Textiles: Values, Design, Production and Consumption.* Sheffield Greenleaf Publishing.

Miller, D., V. Nuon, C. Aprill, and R. Certeza (2009), "Business As Usual? Governing the Supply Chain in Clothing Post-MFA Phase-out—The case of Cambodia," *International Journal of Labour Research,* 1(1): 9–33.

Natsuda, K., K. Gotob, and J. Thoburn (2010), "Challenges to the Cambodian Garment Industry in the Global Garment Value Chain," *European Journal of Development Research,* 22(4): 469–93.

Nimbalker, G., J. Mawson, and H. A. Lee (2017), *The 2017 Ethical Fashion Report: The Truth Behind the Barcode.* North Ryde, New South Wales: Baptist World Aid.

Noggle, E., and G. Stuart (2017), *Who Made My Clothes? A Report from Cambodia, Garment Worker Diaries.* Ashbourne: Fashion Revolution.

Oka, C. (2016), "Improving Working Conditions in Garment Supply Chains: The role of unions in Cambodia," *British Journal of Industrial Relations,* 54(3): 647–72.

Siegle, L. (2014), "In Focus: One year after Rana Plaza, the world is still addicted to fashion: Disaster took 1,133 workers' lives, but garment trade is rewarded with a boom," *The Observer.*

Solidarity Center (2018), "Cambodia." https://www.solidaritycenter.org/where-we-work/asia/cambodia/

Staritz, C. (2010), "Cambodia's Clothing Exports: From Assembly to Full-Package Supplier," in C. Staritz (ed.), *Making the Cut: Low-income countries and the global clothing value chain in a post quota and post crises world.* Washington, DC: World Bank Publications.

Staritz, C., and S. Frederick (2012), "PART 2: Summaries of the Country Case Studies on Apparel Industry Development, Structure, and Policies: Cambodia," in Gladys Lopez-Acevedo (ed.), *Sewing Success? Employment, Wages and Poverty Following the End of the Multi-fibre Arrangement.* Washington, DC: World Bank Publications.

Tighe, E. (2016), "Voluntary Governance in Clothing Production Networks: Management Perspectives on Multi-Stakeholder Initiatives in Dhaka," *Environment and Planning A: Economy and Space,* 48(12): 2504–24.

United Sisterhood Alliance (2017), "Workers
    Information Center." Available online at: http://wic.
    unitedsisterhood.org/

Unteroberdoerster, O. (2014), *Cambodia: Entering a New
    Phase of Growth*. Washington, DC: International
    Monetary Foundation.

Vice (2017), "Cambodia Fashion Week." Available online
    at: https://www.vice.com/en_us/article/4w3me9/
    cambodia-part-1

World Bank (2009), *Cambodia: A Better Investment
    Climate to Sustain Growth—Second Investment
    Climate Assessment*: Washington, DC: World Bank
    Publications.

CHAPTER 5.6

A SPOTLIGHT ON: SUSTAINABILITY OF RENTING WEDDING DRESSES IN ASIAN REGIONS

Seoha Min, University of North Carolina at Greensboro, USA
Marilyn DeLong, University of Minnesota, USA

It is widely agreed that renting clothing is a good way to achieve sustainability, because the renting practice greatly encourages a decrease in clothing consumption. Among various products, wedding dresses can be categorized as garments that are exceptionally suited for rental. The rental-friendliness of the wedding dress mainly derives from the following two characteristics: the significant cost associated with high-end bridal wear; and its (expected) one-time usage. This is where renting a wedding dress becomes a highly attractive alternative from the bride's perspective. Studies show that brides in Asian countries, such as South Korea, China, Thailand, Taiwan, and Japan, have achieved sustainability through renting their wedding dresses within a well-established wedding package system (Edwards 1987; Min and DeLong 2015; Adrian 2003) and cultural characteristics of many Asian countries are deeply associated with this practice.

From the perspective of sustainability, wedding-dress rental is a desirable cultural ecosystem in itself. Min and DeLong (2015) interviewed eight Korean brides who rented a wedding dress for their nuptials and found that the brides were able to save significant resources in the consumer-decision process. Environmental resources were saved because renting results in less consumption of wedding dresses. Most brides in Korean regions tend to wear both a Western-style and traditional wedding dress on their wedding day (see Figures 5.6.1 and 5.6.2), so they often decide to rent both dresses in order to save economical resources. In addition, renting removes the burden of repairs or upkeep from individuals who might simply dispose of an item rather than maintain it. Renting can also allow the wearer the experience of wearing the dress, and still provide the functional and experiential aspects without the demand of ownership.

Figure 5.6.1 Western-style wedding ceremony in Korea
Image reproduced courtesy of Seoha Min

a)

b)

c)

Wedding dress rental is also well established in other Asian countries such as Japan, China, and Taiwan. This appears to relate to "face culture" in Asian regions. Here, "face" refers to a sense of self-respect in social contexts (Ting-Toomey 1994). Since many people will attend the wedding ceremony, it provides a great opportunity to display the prestige of the bride's family. Renting a gown thus makes it possible for brides in Asian regions to wear prestigious wedding dresses and gain face on their wedding days—despite a limited budget.

Figures 5.6.2a, b, and c Traditional wedding ceremony in Korea. After the western-style wedding ceremony (Figure 5.6.1), the traditional wedding ceremony takes place in a private room with the bride, the groom, and their families. Thus, the bride and groom need to change their attire into traditional wedding costumes. As a part of the ceremony, the bride and groom pour a traditional Korean alcoholic beverage into each other's glasses and drink it in the hope of securing the longevity of their marriage (Figures 5.6.2a and 5.6.2b). They also share jujube fruit as a symbol of love and prosperity (Figure 5.6.2c)
Images reproduced courtesy of Seoha Min

Furthermore, brides in Asian regions tend to rent wedding dresses because most of their friends and families have done the same (Min & DeLong 2015). This finding is deeply associated with the high conformity in Asian regions. Asian countries such as South Korea, China, and Japan are highly collective societies, wherein the "we" is more important than the "I" (Hofstede 2011). Since consensus and compromise are important in these countries, people tend to conform to societal practices. In general, introducing and promoting sustainable practice and system is a challenging task, as it requires a thorough cultural understanding of the target population. Nevertheless, once a sustainable practice becomes a social norm, the benefit is substantial as it greatly promotes sustainable behavior among the people. Asian brides, without intending directly to do so, have been saving environmental and economic resources by choosing to rent their wedding dresses rather than buying them (Min & DeLong 2015). Therefore, setting a sustainable social norm should actively be pursued, especially for those with collectivistic culture.

Renting a wedding dress is highly sustainable considering the cost as well as maintenance expenses of these gowns. Wedding-dress renting practices in Asian regions are greatly influenced and catalyzed by the cultural characteristics, such as face culture and high conformity to social standards. As such, understanding the culture is key to introducing and promoting a sustainable practice that can positively impact a society.

REFERENCES

Adrian, B. (2003), *Framing the Bride: Globalizing Beauty and Romance in Taiwan's Bridal Industry*. Oakland, CA: University of California Press.

Edwards, W. (1987), "The Commercialized Wedding as Ritual: A Window on Social Values," *Journal of Japanese Studies*, 13(1): 51–78.

Hofstede, G. (2011), "Dimensionalizing Cultures: The Hofstede Model in Context," *Online Readings in Psychology and Culture*, 2(1): 8.

Min, S., and M. DeLong (2015), "Exploring sustainability in Korean wedding package culture," *The International Journal of Social Sustainability in Economics, Social and Cultural Context*, 11(2): 61–72.

Ting-Toomey, S. (1994), *The Challenge of Facework: Cross-cultural and Interpersonal Issues*. Albany, NY: SUNY Press.

CHAPTER 6.1

A CASE FOR DESIGN-LED ENVIRONMENTALLY SUSTAINABLE FASHION DESIGN PRAXIS IN SOUTH AFRICA

Desiree Smal, University of Johannesburg, South Africa

INTRODUCTION

A study on environmental sustainability in the South African fashion and textile industry undertaken between 2012 and 2016 presented interesting findings. This essay reports on some of these findings by, first, considering some of the areas of scholarly survey that informed the data collection for the study; second, by explaining the research design; and, third, by providing an overview of three specific areas of significance the case study highlighted. The fundamental principle that underpins designers' decisions to consider environmental sustainability strategy as key to their business is based on an inherently personal, holistic, and meaningful worldview. This in turn informs their approach to design and manufacturing praxis as well the difficulty they face in implementing such a strategy.

FASHION AND TEXTILE INDUSTRY OF SOUTH AFRICA TODAY

The fashion and textile sector represents a significant component in manufacturing employment but has experienced approximately 50 percent job loss in recent years. Job loss and declining export markets pose a crisis in this sector of the South African economy (Van Zyl & Matswalela 2016: 371–88). The textile and fashion industry has the potential, due to its labor-intensive approach and the opportunities it offers for unskilled labor, to add meaningfully to the South African manufacturing economy. While the local textile sector lags behind those of Asian countries such as China, Indonesia, and Bangladesh, the clothing sector is characterized by high labor costs and a lack of technology (Van

Zyl & Matswalela 2016: 382). Like many similar industries globally, the local fashion and textile industry is vulnerable to cheaper imports (Chitrakron 2017). Approximately only 30 percent of locally sold clothing is manufactured locally, this being due in part to high import duties on textiles (Steyn 2014).

In a report completed for the South African Sustainable Textile and Apparel Cluster (SASTAC) in 2014 as part of an investigation into sustainability in the South African Textile and Apparel value chain, five particular issues are fore-fronted that contribute to, or impede growth in the South African textile and fashion industry (Mossgroup 2014). Although all five issues are of equal importance for development in the industry, the last issue specifically dealt with environmental sustainability. The report referred to environmental issues as the "poor cousin," as they did not necessarily feature as a primary concern to participants in the survey, with only 5 percent considering environmental issues to be of significance to the industry (Mossgroup 2014: 17). Even more concerning was the avoidance of taking responsibility for environmental sustainability in the industry (Mossgroup 2014: 19).

ENVIRONMENTAL SUSTAINABILITY: THE APPROACH AND THE STRATEGY

An overview of environmental sustainability from a business perspective suggests that a holistic approach is a key driver (Esty & Winston 2009; Berns et al. 2009; Ehrenfeld 2008). Berns et al. (2009: 3–6) suggest that companies that seem to be successful in the implementation of environmental sustainability do so from an economic point of view and acknowledge the importance of engaging with the entire value chain. The challenges presented indicate that an approach to environmental sustainability affects all operations of a company, impacts the value chain, considers all the stakeholders, and promotes effective collaboration (Esty & Winston 2009; Berns et al. 2009). Challenges that impede the above are knowledge of environmental sustainability and the communication of this knowledge. Environmental sustainability should be planned and its impact, although often intangible, constantly evaluated; also, the uncertainty of market conditions in which the approach to environmental sustainability needs to be implemented must be kept in mind. (Berns et al. 2009: 11). An open approach is needed to the challenges that it presents, as well as to the economic advantages environmental sustainability could offer.

Aspects of high importance that are highlighted include forming partnership, transparency, considering strategies for environmental sustainability, an emphasis on environmental stewardship in the value chain, and placing eco-values as core within the workplace (Esty & Winston 2009: 15, 57; Ehrenfeld 2008: 200–01). This is referred to as the "there-is-no-alternative" (TINA) approach, which requires not only that the ownership of environmental sustainable thinking be placed at the core of the business, but also that it become part of the core values for short- and long-term benefits (Esty & Winston 2009: 219–23). This places design, or re-imagining, as a pivotal aspect for establishing an eco-advantage (Esty & Winston 2009; Ehrenfeld 2008). Esty and Winston (2009: 101–21) present an economic strategy framework that is based on short-term aspects such as time, energy used, and cost of materials, and refer to it as an "eco-advantage building strategy," adapted by Smal (2016: 61) from Esty and Winston (2009), as reflected in Figure 6.1.1.

Figure 6.1.1 An eco-advantage strategy
Image reproduced courtesy of Desiree Smal

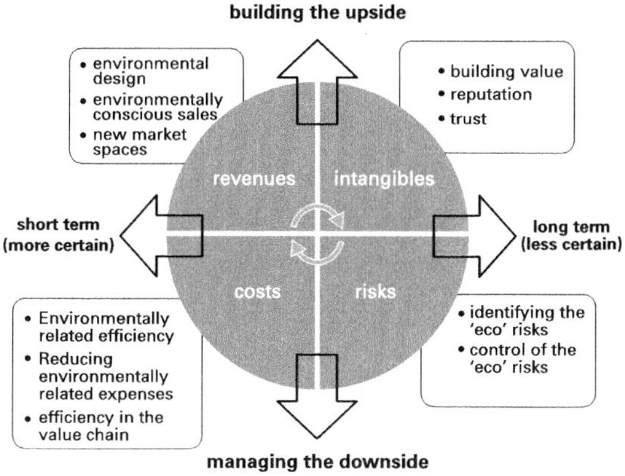

An important aspect that should be considered for *building the upside* is positioning consumer environmental needs above mere consumer needs and thus alludes to how design approaches environmental sustainability in product development (Esty & Winston 2009: 74). Brand positioning and communicating the environmental strategy, such as the environmental footprint of a product, to the consumer are considered a necessity in this strategy and relate to reputation of and trust in a brand (Esty & Winston 2009: 130–40). Areas that are considered in *managing the downside* are improving resources, productivity, and waste that can lead to cost effectiveness, reducing and controlling related eco-expenses, and managing environmentally driven risks by engaging with suppliers (Esty & Winston 2009: 105–20).

A HOLISTIC APPROACH TO ENVIRONMENTAL SUSTAINABILITY

The fashion and textile industry consists of a long and fragmented supply chain where influence from the design is becoming increasingly important. Fletcher and Grose comment that:

> Fashion at its creative best is one of the most powerful and direct expressions of personal aspirations, individuality and belonging. But the fashion industry also contributes to environmental and social degradation through pervasive advertising and short-term trends manipulating and exploiting people's innate needs for integration and differentiation, in order to drive fast retail cycles and ever-increasing growth in commercial production.
>
> Fletcher & Grose 2012: 138

The complexity of the industry adds to the challenge of implementing environmentally sustainable strategies. The most recognized and feasible approach is to develop renewable source material, using resources effectively and minimizing chemical impact while considering the carbon footprint of the product, regarding fair labor practices as an essential component, and reducing waste in the product life cycle during development stage (Fletcher & Grose 2012: 13). Environmental awareness and transparency in the entire value chain have increased and most of the above-mentioned processes fall into the pre-consumer phase (Black 2010: 253; Fletcher & Grose 2012).

Armstrong and LeHew (2011) argue that a paradigm shift in thinking about environmental sustainability in the fashion industry is needed as the industry is intrinsically in conflict with environmental sustainability. The authors suggest that while one should permit the consumer to maintain traditional consumption habits, there should also be an emphasis on transformation in current consumer culture (Armstrong & LeHew 2011: 41; Smal 2016: 122). Figure 6.1.2 provides a visual representation of the author's suggested framework which "focuses on efficient use of resources, effective practices and consumer utility, while conscientiously considering the needs of the consumer, and all of the above in relation to a holistic approach to environmental sustainability" (Smal 2016: 123). Levels one and two relate to pre-consumer processes, whereas levels four and five align to post-consumer processes that not only consider minimizing environmental impact, but also promote environmental well-being. In particular, design has the opportunity to become the change agent required to drive transformation in the industry as design decision influences all of the above (Smal 2016: 123–24).

In Figure 6.1.2 focus is placed on two opposing concepts, one being *maintain*, which includes pre-consumer processes that maintain traditional practices. Maintaining suggests eco-aligned practices that are based in energy efficiency, waste reduction, the addressing of waste usage, and the suggestion of alternate, more effective environmental practices. Both levels one and two in the framework are tangible issues and suggest improved production processes with regard to environmental impact. Design decisions made by the fashion designer during product development influence the above, yet these have little influence on the consumer, who is not necessarily knowledgeable about or concerned with the applied processes or systems. The opposing focus is on *transformation*, which suggests maintaining efficient and eco-considered practices as well as transformative approaches to consumption. In all levels of the framework the designer's decision centers around impact on the environment through efficiency in manufacturing and use, plus effective disposal of the product.

Level three, consumer consciousness, moves toward transformation, and builds on levels one and two and the methods contained within them. The objective in this level is to minimize environmental impact through careful product and process planning, and also to develop a product or process that adds value. Level four, environmentally sustainable lifestyle, requires that design leads the consumer, accentuating environmentally sustainable lifestyles in conjunction with an environmentally sustainable focus on products and systems. The result of such an approach is a broad view of all issues, thereby considering tangible and intangible aspects as well as adding value *up-stream* (pre-consumer) and *down-stream* (post-consumer) (Armstrong & LeHew 2011). Level four should therefore not be seen in isolation but rather as an extension of the previous levels; thus it not only ensures minimizing environmental impact through product, process and system, but also considers environmental well-being. In such an approach, design can activate change.

Figure 6.1.2 A shift in thinking
Image reproduced courtesy of Desiree Smal

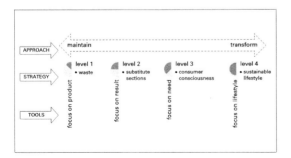

REFLECTIONS

The research strategy for the case study consisted of an extensive survey of scholarship that informed the development of a conceptual framework which guided the case in order to collect data, organize, analyze, synthesize, and report on the data (Babbie

& Mouton 2003: 120–30). Data gathering on the case, consisting of three active designer-manufacturers in South Africa, was achieved through seven in-depth interviews of designers and company management, analysis of thirty-two documents relating to the work of the three companies, as well as an analysis of their products within a particular time frame. Although the case study consisted of three purposively selected companies, which at the time of data collection publicly promoted environmental sustainability as core to their business approach and operational practices, it cannot be thought of as being representative of the entire South African fashion industry, but rather as a snapshot of current practice. Even if the case offers a mere glimpse into the fashion and textile industry, it does present interesting viewpoints on the successes and difficulties facing designers and manufacturers which use environmental sustainability as a key business strategy. The multi-method approach of data collection formed part of the analytical strategy of the case and added to its credibility. The analytical strategy for the case applied direct interpretation, including pattern matching and explanation building to allow for data saturation and thick description (Stake 1995: 78; Yin, 2009: 136–60). Three of the most prominent findings are presented in more detail in relation to the literature discussed.

HOLISTIC VIEW AND MEANING

The most prominent similarity of the companies studied in the case is that fundamental principles and an eco-aligned mindset informed the approach to environmental sustainability. The case revealed that certified organic, non-certified but organic components, and fabrics that could be considered friendlier to the environment, were most important to the companies. However, many of these components were not readily available in South Africa and therefore needed to be sourced from further away on the African continent, for example Madagascar or Mauritius, or from Europe. Rising costs, lack of resources, unsuitability of current eco-fabrics needed for trend-driven products, and lack of expertise were mentioned as obstructing the implementation of an environmentally sustainable approach, which align to the SASTAC report discussed at the start of the essay. However, despite these apparent difficulties, environmental sustainability was cited as a key driver of their business and corresponds to Esty and Winston's (2009: 282–3) suggestion that companies that are successful in applying environmental sustainability as a key driver for eco-advantage do so from a holistic vision and embed environmental stewardship as part of the core values of an eco-aligned mindset.

Aspects that emerged from the study which informed *building the upside* of the economic strategy suggested by Esty and Winston (2009) included incorporating consumer environmental needs in design (life cycle and praxis), brand positioning, developing an eco-defined marketspace, and corporate and brand reputation.

First, providing information to the consumer in order for them to make an informed buying choice was an integral part of the environmentally sustainable approach. Second, product life cycle seemed to be an important aspect; consideration of practices such as Fairtrade, fabric dyeing techniques that have the least impact, reducing waste, and reducing energy consumption were mentioned. A clearly defined eco-market space and need to consider environmentally sustainable constraints in product development

TABLE 6.1.1

THE ECO-ADVANTAGE MIND-SET.

Eco-advantage mind-set	Company 1	Company 2	Company 3
Taking a broader view	x	x	x
Considering stakeholders regarding the company's environmental performance	x	-	x
Basing environmental decisions on core values for short- and long-term benefits	x	x	x

Source: Desiree Smal.

was foregrounded. The importance of corporate and brand reputation for an eco-aligned business strategy was also mentioned. Therefore, all the aspects relating to *building the upside* overlapped with the findings of the research. Only two areas of *managing the downside* overlapped with what Esty and Winston (2009) consider important.

Reducing resources was an important approach to consider for environmental sustainability. One of the companies specifically referred to the abuse of resources that the fashion industry is known for. Engaging with suppliers in the value chain was very evident in the practice of two of the companies. It was apparent that the obstacles hindering these companies from operating with an environmentally sustainable approach outweighed the benefit and thus none of the three participants considered it to be an economic advantage and claimed high costs as an inherent barrier to environmental sustainability. What seemed to be the key driver was an essential personal belief in ethics, eco-consciousness and awareness of environmental sustainability and how these could be applied in the fashion industry in South Africa.

THE APPROACH TO PRAXIS

Armstrong and LeHew's (2011) framework informed the approach to praxis in each of the companies that participated in the case study, but differed slightly in each. Company One, the largest of the three participants, was clearly a volume-driven entity which, at the time of the research, was creating products for forty-nine own retail entities in the whole of South Africa. but manufactured none of the products within the borders of the country. The decision to take manufacturing and sourcing offshore was based on a problematic local manufacturing culture and lack of available resources and knowledge with regard to environmental sustainability in the South African textile and fashion industry. The offshore African companies provided superior expertise and knowledge that was required to obtain certified organic cotton, and companies that focused on Fairtrade were selected as manufacturers. Direct sourcing and close relationships ensured that the company knew what went into their products and could observe manufacturing processes and, despite offshore sourcing and manufacturing, keep a hands-on approach to this section of the value chain. The company showed a socially responsible approach to their own business practices too, which led to other socially responsible projects being undertaken by the company and its staff. An alignment of the data to the Armstrong and LeHew framework emphasized levels two and three.

Company Two took a holistic resource-driven approach as the availability of suitable environmentally sustainable fabrics was the starting point for all product development, which stemmed from a deep personal belief in contributing to the well-being of the planet. The driver for environmental sustainability for this company was clearly defined as sourcing suitable environmentally sustainable fabric as the main objective. This company also experimented with several different types of environmentally sustainable fabrics and focused on regional production. The second objective was to reduce waste through pattern development by, for example, aiming at zero waste, establishing carefully planned cutting processes, and donating waste fabric for the making of paper. Of equal importance was a focus on recycle/reuse/rework and repair. This company had several product lines, one of which was bridal gowns. In some cases, used or unsold wedding dress stock was used to develop new products and clients could also bring old/used garments to be repurposed into their newly designed wedding dresses. The company placed emphasis on quality and longevity and encouraged clients to bring products back for repair. Although sourcing fabrics was done nationally, imported fabric was also used, but all products were made in-house or regionally, aligning to Fletcher and Grose's (2012) suggestion of alternate approaches to a fashion business. In this company, level two showed as the dominant level.

Company Three's approach was that of being trend-driven as its product is classified as high-fashion. This company struggled with the unsuitability of environmentally sustainable fabrics and often imported, at high cost, fabrics considered environmentally sustainable. One of the environmentally sustainable foci of this company was to consider what to do with waste. Waste was either reconfigured into innovative accessory products or donated to non-profit organizations. Although the components used in the products could not always be considered environmentally sustainable, a focus of the owner-designer, a strong public advocate of ethical and environmentally sustainable practices, was consumer consciousness, facilitated by providing information and educating the public through interviews and articles on approaches to lifestyle with regard to environmental sustainability. As Fletcher and Grose (2012: 158) suggest, designers who are also communicators and educators can trigger new behavior. This company also focused on level two, thus level two being the dominant level, due to the recycling and manufacturing practices. Figure 6.1.3 presents the consolidated results, aligned to the Armstrong and LeHew model of all three companies (Smal 2016: 238).

Levels one and two comprised 67 percent with levels three and four combined comprising 33 percent, showing a predominance for maintaining

Figure 6.1.3 Consolidated result of all three companies
Image reproduced courtesy of Desiree Smal

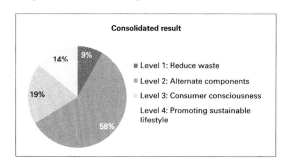

environmentally sustainable practices. Level two showed as predominant for all three of the companies; thus the findings showed that there is currently a prominent reliance on environmentally sustainable resources and processes.

THE KNOWLEDGE GAP AND THE DESIGNER

Two of the three companies indicated that the lack of consumer knowledge with regard to environmental sustainability in the textile and fashion industry was a major concern, whereas Company Three indicated a need to raise consumer awareness and consciousness as important. Paloma-Lovinski and Hahn (2014) indicate that the inability of the textile and fashion industry to address environmentally sustainable issues was due to designer inability to do so and could indicate a knowledge gap. In general, the designers of the three companies that participated in the case generally understood implementation of environmental practices well enough but were predominantly reliant on the use of environmentally sustainable resources. A more inclusive and holistic approach to environmental sustainability was needed by fashion designers. Fletcher and Grose (2012) argue that designers need to become knowledgeable about the technical issues of environmentally sustainable practices in order to implement environmentally sustainable fashion design praxis. The above places the issue of environmentally sustainable fashion design praxis as a key responsibility in fashion design education.

CONCLUSION

In a way, the findings align to the SASTAC report; however, in a world where the fashion and textile industry needs to be more environmentally conscious, environmental sustainability as a strategy for praxis could add immense value to the industry. As a fashion design educator, the need to close the gap in knowledge on environmentally sustainable fashion design praxis is imperative. What the research further highlighted is the need for an aligned approach to environmentally sustainable fashion design praxis. As one of the fundamental drivers seemed to be a personal approach to eco-consciousness and awareness, the Armstrong and LeHew (2011) framework discussed earlier needs an additional layer, which could be considered as the core driver for implementing environmentally sustainable strategies. The focus of this "layer" is therefore based on how companies think, how they are influenced and how their thinking and experiences shape action (Smal 2016: 249). An aligned environmentally sustainable fashion design (ESFD) framework (see Figure 6.1.4 below)[1] should consider the approach to education, economic strategies, the environment, the fashion consumer and industry support mechanisms.

Figure 6.1.4 Suggested framework for ESFD
Image reproduced courtesy of Desiree Smal

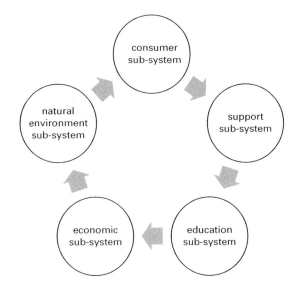

Not only is each section influenced by the other, but it also should inform the next; therefore there is a continuous process of know-how generated in one area becoming knowledge used in another. As gaining knowledge and imparting know-how requires transmission, communication through fashion design praxis could provide the specialist knowledge needed for the implementation of environmental sustainability by fostering an empathic approach to fashion design in such a way that it promotes eco-awareness and eco-consciousness, and, through environmentally sustainable fashion design praxis, induces and inculcates behavioral change (Smal 2016: 253–4). This interconnected and integrated framework should be the driver of a design-driven environmentally sustainable fashion industry.

NOTE

1. Based on the model presented by Carayannis et al. (2012) and explored by Smal (2016: 253).

REFERENCES

Armstrong, C., and M. LeHew (2011), "Sustainable Product Development: In Search of a New Dominant Social Paradigm for the Field Using a Sustainable Approach," *Fashion Practice*, 3 (1): 29–62.

Babbie, E., and J. Mouton (2003), *The Practice of Social Research*. Oxford: University Press.

Black, S. (2010), "Ethical Fashion and Ecofashion," in V. Steele (ed.), *The Berg Companion to Fashion*, 251–60. Oxford: Berg.

Berns, M., A. Townsend, S. Khayat, B. Balogopal, M. Reeves, M. Hopkins, and M Kruschwitz (2009), *The Business of Sustainability: Findings and Insights from the First Annual Business of Sustainability Survey and the Global Thought Leader Research Project*. Available online at: https://sloanreview.mit.edu/reports/the-business-of-sustainability. Accessed 18 March 2010).

Carayannis, E., T. Barth, and F. Campbell (2012), "The Quintuple Helix Innovation Model: Global Warming as a Challenge and Driver for Innovation," *Journal of Innovation and Entrepreneurship*, 8 August 1(2).

Chitrakron, K. (2017), *Business of Fashion*. Available at online at: https://www.businessoffashion.com/articles/global-currents/africa-vs-the-usa-a-secondhand-clothing-showdown?utm_source=facebook.com&utm_medium=socialshare&utm_campaign=bof (accessed October 18, 2017).

DTI (n.d.) *DTI*. Available online at: http://www.dti.gov.za/editmedia.jps?id=3062 (accessed February 4, 2015).

Ehrenfeld, J. (2008), *Sustainability by Design*. London: Yale University Press.

Esty, D., and A. Winston (2009), *Green to Gold: How Smart Companies Use Environmental Strategy to Innovate, Create Value, and Build Competitive Advantge*. Hoboken, NJ: John Wiley & Sons Ltd.

Fletcher, K., and L. Grose (2012), *Fashion & Sustainability: Design for Change*. London: Laurence King Publishing.

Mossgroup (2014), *The Material Issues Facing the South African Textile and Apparel Industry*. Available online at: http://mossgroup.co.za/wp-content/uploads/2014/09/Material-Issues-Report_Final_26Nov14.pdf (accessed December 8, 2014).

Paloma-Lovinski, N., and K. Hahn (2014), "Fashion Design Industry Impressions of Current Sustainable Practices," *Fashion Practice*, 6(1): 87–106.

Smal, D. (2016), *The Role of Environmental Sustainability in a Design-Driven Fashion Industry: A South African Case Study*. Available online at: http://cput.worldcat.org/title/role-of-environmental-sustainability-in-a-design-driven-fashion-industry-a-south-african-case-study/oclc/947084669&referer=brief_results (accessed July 2, 2016).

Stake, R. (1995), *The art of Case Study Research*. Thousand Oaks, CA: SAGE Publications.

Steyn, L. (2014), "Retailers wanting to cash in on trends quickly have thrown local clothing makers a lifeline," *Mail & Guardian*. Available online at: http://mg.co.za/article/2014-01-24-00-sa-cottons-on-to-fast-fashion (accessed March 11, 2015).

Thorpe, A. (2010), "The Designer's Role in Sustainable Consumption," *Design Issues*, 26(2): 3–15.

Van Zyl, G., and K. Matswalela (2016), "A Comparative Analysis of the Level of Competitiveness of the South African Clothing and Textile Tndustry," *Journal of Economic and Financial Science*, 9(2): 370–91.

Yin, R. (2009), *Case Study Research: Design and Methods*. 4th ed. Thousand Oaks, CA: SAGE Publications.

CHAPTER 6.2

A SPOTLIGHT ON: DEVELOPING SUSTAINABLE FASHION IN SOUTH AFRICA
Sustainable Cotton Cluster

Marsha A. Dickson, Huantian Cao
Martha Carper, University of Delaware, USA

The South Africa Sustainable Cotton Cluster (SCC) launched in 2014 with government funding. SCC integrates the cotton supply chain from farm through retail, facilitating balanced supply and demand, creating scalable solutions through partnerships among stakeholders, encouraging growth of small- and medium-sized enterprises, and ensuring traceability throughout the entire chain so that sustainability claims are supported and progress is measured (Sustainable Cotton Cluster 2015). After two years of operation, SCC had tested a pilot supply chain that produced cotton T-shirts and developed an innovative and award-winning information technology platform to trace cotton from the farms of South Africa to the retail floor. Cotton production had increased by 240 percent until dropping due to a devastating drought (Cotton SA 2016).

The authors engaged with SCC during its first two years, reviewing global standards for evaluating sustainability performance, conducting a sustainability workshop for industry stakeholders, and carrying out research to benchmark social and environmental management practices (Cao et al. 2017; Siron & Dickson forthcoming), examining global buyer interest in output from the integrated

Figure 6.2.1 South African cotton field
Image courtesy of Huantian Cao

Figure 6.2.2 South African cotton is naturally bright white
Image courtesy of Huantian Cao

supply chain (Dickson 2016), and investigating the role of South African retailers in creating demand for sustainable apparel and household textile products (Blissick et al. 2017). The research identified best practices and key environmental, ethical, and economic challenges in the cotton supply chain.

While early focus was on supplying the domestic market, SCC aspires for the country to become "the country of choice for sourcing selected sustainable cotton textile and apparel products" (Sustainable Cotton Cluster 2016: 13). This could be challenging. Global buyers indicated limited interest in sustainable products from the SCC due to the country's unfavorable geographic proximity to key consumer markets (Dickson 2016). An international retailer based outside the country, and operating retail stores in South Africa, was an unlikely partner because it adhered to a global sourcing strategy when stocking merchandise for their stores (Blissick et al. 2017).

Several recommendations were made for SCC; some key points noted are:

1. **Assist retailers in developing materials' selection processes and integrating sustainability considerations into product design.** Helping retailers understand the sustainability trade-offs between fibers could create greater demand for the products of sustainable supply chains.

2. **Consider the product categories produced.** An initial idea of the SCC was to produce cotton T-shirts, which could be a disaster given the high level of competition in this low-skill segment of the industry. On the other hand, household textiles could be a good choice; these often require 100 percent cotton for best performance and were often imported by South Africa's retailers.

3. **Expand the market with small, "sustainable" brands.** SCC could explore partnerships with emerging sustainable fashion brands in the United Kingdom, Europe, or Asia. Start-ups have difficulty finding suppliers that will provide space in

Figure 6.2.3 SCC cotton is tracked through the supply chain
Image courtesy of Huantian Cao

their factories for smaller orders and commit to the buyer's sustainability values.

4. **Value organized labor as a key stakeholder.** The SCC's ethical strengths have resulted from collective bargaining and provide a point of differentiation compared with many countries' labor relations. Ensuring that union representatives have a seat at SCC's table is valuable for sustainability branding and smoothing inconsistencies in compliance that are present across the industry.

5. **Tackle corruption and distrust with transparency.** Collaboration can be facilitated with transparent business operations, revealing the size of sustainability problems and supporting understanding of how to address them.

In conclusion, while this spotlight focuses on SCC, recommendations may be useful for other country-level initiatives focusing on sustainability as a competitive advantage and can provide a basis for future research.

ACKNOWLEDGEMENT

This research was funded by Sustainable Cotton Cluster.

REFERENCES

Blissick, M, M. A. Dickson, J. Silverman, and H. Cao (2017), "Retailer Extent of Involvement in Sustainability and Role in Creating Sustainable Apparel and Textiles from South Africa," *International Journal of Fashion Design, Technology and Education* (special issue on Sustainable Fashion Technology and Management 1).

Cao, H, C. Scudder, and M. A. Dickson (2017), "Sustainability of Apparel Supply Chain in South Africa: Application of the Triple Top Line Model," *Clothing and Textiles Research Journal*, 35 (2): 81–97.

Cotton SA (2016), "*Two Years of Achievements.*" Available online at: https://sustainablecottoncluster.wordpress.com/2016/04/11/two-years-of-achievements/ (accessed viewed March 27, 2017).

Dickson, M. A. (2016), "Drivers of Global Buyer Sourcing of Sustainable Apparel from a South African Supply Chain," *Proceedings of the International Textile and Apparel Association, Vancouver, British Columbia.*

Siron, L., and M. A. Dickson (forthcoming), "Benchmarking social upgrading and decent work in a South African sustainable cotton textile and apparel supply chain."

Sustainable Cotton Cluster (2015), "Our mission." Available online at: http://cottonsa.org.za/sustainable-cotton-cluster/mission-objectives/ (accessed March 227, 2017).

Sustainable Cotton Cluster (2016), "Cotton Industry Strategy and Plan." Available online at: https://sustainablecottoncluster.files.wordpress.com/2016/04/final-cotton-industry-strategy-and-plan-_18march16.pdf (accessed March 27, 2017).

CHAPTER 6.3

CHALLENGES PREVENTING THE FASHION INDUSTRY FROM IMPLEMENTING SUSTAINABLE PRODUCT SERVICE SYSTEMS IN BOTSWANA AND KENYA

Yaone Rapitsenyane, University of Botswana
Sophia Njeru, Machakos University, Kenya
Richie Moalosi, University of Botswana

INTRODUCTION

Unsustainable consumption caused by fast fashion has created a vicious circle that has led to a dramatic increase in material production and material consumption as well as carbon impact, water usage, and waste generation. This is a challenge currently facing the fashion industry in the era of global warming and climate variability. The fashion industry faces a myriad of environmental, social, economic, and ethical conundrums that demand innovative design-thinking approaches to address them without off-setting economic benefits. In most cases sustainable fashion design has largely focused on materials selection based on environmental

impacts throughout the clothing life cycle. In some instances, sustainable materials have a limited lifespan, due to low quality or poorly designed apparel that is worn only a few times before they are disposed of (Armstrong et al. 2016). The industry requires a more holistic and systemic thinking approach to sustainable design, to take account not only of how fashion is produced, but also of its consumption. Sustainable consumption will not be achieved by the work of a single entity, but through a collaborative innovation across the value chain and engaging consumers in a redefinition of value (Hutter et al. 2010).

Various alternatives have been explored to address this challenge, such as slow fashion, upcycling, restyling, and recycling. However, these approaches have not made any significant social and environmental improvements. This essay presents Sustainable Product-Service Systems (S.PSS) as a new, promising alternative to addressing sustainability challenges in the fashion industry in Botswana and Kenya. The goal of S.PSS is to be more competitive in the economy by satisfying consumers' social demands while still reducing consumption of material products through alternative scenarios of providing product-service solutions rather than product ownership, and offering services that have a low negative environmental impact (Armstrong & Niinimäki 2014; Briceno & Stagl 2006; Vezzoli & Manzini 2008; Manzini & Vezzoli 2003). However, for S.PSS to work, a cultural shift will be required to redefine consumer needs away from product ownership to accessibility and services. It is against this background that this essay assesses fashion designers' awareness and preparedness to embrace S.PSS in producing sustainable fashion in order to address some of the environmental, social, and economic challenges facing the society.

SUSTAINABLE DESIGN IN SUSTAINABLE FASHION

Fashion consumption and sustainability are often two opposing concepts. The former is a highly resource-intensive and wasteful practice, while sustainability frowns on wasteful consumption (Dissanayake & Sinha 2012). Fashion consumers have an insatiable desire for new garments, which prompts fashions to change (Horn & Gurel 1981). Constantly changing trends, affordable prices, and mass-production systems have led to unsustainable consumption behavior and disposal of waste products (Niinimaki 2012). Sustainability in the fashion business is still an emerging issue and Dissanayake and Sinha (2012) have recognized the importance of investigating how it could be achieved.

Sustainable fashion design should engage in cleaner production, and thus the creation of goods and services using processes and systems that are safe and healthy for workers, communities, consumers, and the environment; in addition, this production approach should be rewarding both socially and creatively for everyone involved. Sustainable consumption requires consumers to buy less, use products longer, and produce less waste (Armstrong et al. 2016). Sustainable fashion should strive to design products and services that are durable, mendable, easily biodegradable, and recyclable. The products' packaging should use minimal amount of materials and energy and change consumer mindsets through education. Workers should be valued and their work should be organized to conserve and enhance their efficiency, creativity, security, and well-being. All stakeholders engaged at any stage of the product life cycle, including workers and members of the community, should be respected and enhanced economically, socially, and culturally, as noted earlier, and valued in the decision-making process. When consumers purchase sustainable products they implement United Nations Sustainable Development Goal (SDG) 12 on responsible consumption and production, while a designer who creates the same products embraces SDGs 9 (industry, innovation, and infrastructure) and 13 (climate action) on sustainable production and take action to combat climate variability and its impact.

CO-CREATION PROCESS IN SUSTAINABLE FASHION

Co-creation is arguably a revolutionary design approach where many stakeholders are actively involved in the design process (Prahalad & Ramaswamy 2004). It involves redefining the way enterprises engage individuals, consumers, employees, suppliers, partners, and other stakeholders in bringing them into the value creation process and engaging them in enriched experiences. The emphasis for today's enterprises should be on creating a conducive environment where users' experience is central to value creation, innovation, business strategy, and leadership (Ramaswamy & Gouillart 2010; Zwass 2010). The process has, over the years, gained extensive popularity within the business community. For example, more companies are now using the co-creation process to learn and appreciate the needs of consumers so that new products and services can meet their needs effectively. Groups of stakeholders are involved to create a conducive environment for consumer engagement and collaboration. This cross-fertilization of ideas may be what is necessary to develop consumers' sense of ownership, loyalty, and trust toward the products and services developed, thus avoiding over-consumption, short usage time, and premature disposal of fashion products. Such products will carry symbolic meaning, and portray the consumer's values and identity (Niinimäki 2012).

SUSTAINABLE BUSINESS MODELS FOR SUSTAINABLE FASHION

Sustainable innovation business models support the argument for growth which is not based on high volumes of production, but rather on business sophistication led by design innovation in redefining what value means. Social innovation business models aim to maximize the impact of expenditure by solving social problems through new ideas that work at meeting transactions such as happiness, well-being, inclusion, and empowerment (Mulgan 2006; Phills et al. 2008). Service innovation business models aim at providing service-oriented differentiation, defining value in less tangible terms, especially in manufacturing companies, and more in intangible and dynamic services produced and consumed simultaneously (Neu & Brown 2005; Oliva & Kallenberg 2003). S.PSS innovation business models, also widely discussed alongside servitization (Morelli 2003; Baines & Lightfoot 2013), can be viewed as an integration of new product development and new service development (De Lille et al. 2012). By simultaneously addressing the product and service components of value creation, S.PSS aims to shift the business focus "from designing (and selling) physical products only, to designing (and selling) a system of products and services which are jointly capable of fulfilling specific client demands, while re-orienting current unsustainable trends in production and consumption practices" (Manzini & Vezzoli 2003: 851).

One business application of S.PSS in developing countries may be to act as a catalyst to facilitate the growth of the solution-based economy, bypassing the stage characterized by individual ownership of mass-produced goods in the transition toward a more advanced service economy (Manzini & Vezzoli 2000). The success of S.PSS hinges on its capability to provide human satisfaction through eco-efficient solutions (Vezzoli et al. 2014). S.PSS in the fashion industry includes services such as maintenance, renting, upgrading, redesigning, swapping, or lending. S.PSS may provide the industry with a mechanism to increase factors such as product quality and longevity and at the same time provide alternative consumption models that decrease unnecessary consumption and facilitate material recycling. This study discusses the potential for S.PSS implementation in the fashion industry by exploring its three archetypal models in a developmental context, namely Botswana and Kenya:

1. Product-oriented service: ownership of the product is transferred to the consumer and services—such as maintenance, customization, take-back, repair, or advice and consultancy—are provided to ensure the utility of the product over a given period of time.

2. Use-oriented service: offers product renting, sharing, pooling, leasing, lending, bartering, or swapping services and is characterized by a lack of personal ownership by the user. Therefore, the provider retains ownership as well as the responsibility for the product's upkeep.

3. Results-oriented: while ownership of the product is retained by the service provider, the consumer purchases the utility as an outcome based on their agreement with the provider, over a given period of time. For example, the consumer purchases the service of clean apparel delivered through an agreement per number of wash cycles until the apparel is returned for recycling.

RESEARCH METHOD

A single exploratory case study with multiple units of analysis was deemed appropriate for this research enquiry to allow proximity to the phenomena being researched (Dyer & Wilkins 1991), due to the informal nature of some businesses being researched. The units of analysis were businesses in the fashion industry in the developing economies of Botswana and Kenya. Ten purposefully sampled companies in Botswana, and eight in Kenya, participated in the study. Semi-structured interviews were used to collect data. The goals of the semi-structured interviews were to: find out what sustainability initiatives fashion practitioners undertook; determine how fashion practitioners translated sustainability initiatives into income-generating initiatives; identify opportunities in possible sustainability initiatives that could contribute to developing a S.PSS business model. Qualitative data were analyzed using thematic analysis (Braun & Clarke, 2006). The first step was to define the samples for analysis, develop a coding system which involved naming and grouping data into themes. That is, similar properties were grouped together to form a theme. "The crucial requirement is that the themes are sufficiently precise to enable different coders to arrive at the same results when the same body of material is examined" (Silverman 2001: 123).

FINDINGS

Participant Characteristics

The findings show that the majority of the Batswana fashion design companies interviewed were mainly new start-ups that had been in operation for three to five years, and which had fewer than six employees. However, in Kenya, the majority of companies were mature businesses that had been up and running for over ten years, and which employed fewer than twenty-five employees. Out of ten companies who participated in the Botswana study, only four had staff with relevant professional qualifications in fashion design and the rest came from other fields such as accounting, engineering, political science, etc. Of the eight companies interviewed in Kenya, four had staff with relevant professional qualifications in fashion design and the rest in other fields. Of all the eighteen interviews conducted in both countries, only two companies in Botswana had a vision and mission that recognized sustainable fashion design, e.g. "our mandate involves actively participating in the establishment of sustainable, vibrant and diverse fashion industry in Botswana" (BW10).

Knowledge Requirements for Applying S.PSS

The level of knowledge required to implement S.PSS in the fashion industry in both countries is lacking, which is expressed in interviewees' understanding of what S.PSS is and how they think they can benefit from it. In both countries, most perceptions of S.PSS express such characteristics as "a cohesive business system" (KE6), "conserving the environment and being socially conscious" (KE7), "essential end use function" (KE3), "... to use something without either buying it or owning it" (BW6), and "alternative socio-technical ideas that can provide end use functions" (BW5). Only a few participants were able to provide a more detailed description of S.PSS.

The Need for a Clear Strategy

Most participants' visions and missions were focused on ethical business practices, such as: "to provide employment for the disadvantaged members of the Kenyan society, especially single mothers" (KE8); "empower and mentor" (KE6); "empower young designers" (KE1); "consumer products ethically made in Botswana or customer and relationships focused" (BW6); "building lasting relationship with brands" (BW2); "products that appeal to local and international markets" (BW6); "... not to provoke customers negatively" (BW8); "our mandate involves active

participation ..." (BW10); "custom-made outfits ensuring customer satisfaction" (KE3) and " to provide good quality alluring lingerie for buxom women" (KE7). Even though there were nods towards innovation, there was no clear deliberate inclusion of sustainable business practices that pointed to the need to think of sustainability at a strategic level so that it would trickle it down to various business practices in the fashion houses.

The Approach to S.PSS Design

One positive practice that can benefit S.PSS design, and which was observed in the findings, was the user-orientedness of participants' practices. These were captured in most companies' missions/visions statements and directly reported as co-design and user-centered design approaches via which sustainable fashion could be achieved in Botswana and Kenya. Co-creation with clients, and catering for the needs of the marginalized customers such as the plus-sized and physically impaired, was suggested by all interviewees. This is a design-led approach with the capacity to direct solutions toward non-product ownership as producers/providers build a common understanding of solutions together with their customers.

The Need to Develop Green Markets

Almost all participants had combinations of markets varying from "high class, male, female, middle age" (KE2) to "high class/middle class/female' (BW7) but none indicated they had omitted green consumers and the elderly as their markets. This omission was observed in both Botswana and Kenya in terms of inclusiveness of interviewees' markets; e.g., "... all except green consumers"

(BW8), and "all except green consumers and the elderly" (BW9; BW10; KE5; KE8). The need to develop products for green markets is stark across both data sets. What participants consider as the benefits of sustainable fashion include reduction of waste disposal to landfills, developing durable products that are of good quality, and a reduced need to keep buying the same product.

Ethical and Social Considerations

There was an outcry around issues such as ethical business practices, reported mostly in Kenya, especially with regard to employees' working conditions and remuneration. Decency in how workers should be treated and rewarded is a major issue in the Kenyan fashion industry. The perceived benefit of a S.PSS business model is "workers mean more than production results" (KE6). A peculiar observation concerning ethical business practice was made that concerns the use of animal skin in making clothes; ". . . no use of animal fur and leather" (BW5). The company and its workers considered the use of animal fur and leather for making clothes as unethical.

Benefits of S.PSS in the fashion industry

Despite the challenges, several potential benefits of Sustainable Product Service Systems were reported by participants (Table 6.3.1). Although these benefits were based on the participants' relatively poor understanding of S.PSS and sustainable fashion, they relate to dematerialization, resource efficiency, and the systems-oriented attributes of S.PSS and sustainability.

TABLE 6.3.1

REPORTED BENEFITS OF S.PSS.

Botswana	Kenya
Employment creation	Employment creation
Cost savings	Cost savings
Income generation from waste material	Consistent supply of affordable resources
Strategic positioning	Strategic positioning
Increased market size	
Eco-friendly fashion pieces	

Table courtesy of Yaone Rapitsenyane, Sophia Njeru, Richie Moalosi

DISCUSSION

Despite the challenges, and in light of the perceived benefits of sustainability and S.PSS, potential S.PSS markets could be developed in terms of the three typical S.PSS models in both Botswana and Kenya. A buy-in approach could be initiated with clothing/apparel in both haute couture and ready-to-wear categories. Almost all participants produce clothing/apparel for various common markets except green markets and the elderly. High-end fashion (haute couture) could initially be a possibility in a use-oriented product lease approach, particularly in Kenya, as almost all

Figure 6.3.1 High-end dresses from Botswana, Sanitas Tea Gardens
Photo shooting: Gaborone. Image reproduced courtesy of Aobakwe Molosiwa

participants are in the product category of haute couture. This model provides individual and unlimited access to the product to the lessee while they pay a regular fee for the use of a particular item. High-end products (see Figure 6.3.1) used in this way give the fashion house control over the use of the product according to the terms of the lease, but customers also have a sense of individual "ownership" since during the tenure of the lease they are the only ones using the item. An additional benefit is the product take-back option provided for by a lease arrangement. Extended producer responsibility is one option participants were open to (e.g. "... checks that enable sustainability by holding the business owner accountable ..." (BW10). Additional services, such as accessories, can then be offered in this arrangement.

Initial Implementation of S.PSS models

Product-oriented S.PSS models are highly possible with ready-to-wear clothing/apparel (see sample in Figure 21 in plate section), mostly in Botswana, as all participants are in the product category and already provide services attached to the sold product in the form of maintenance, repair, advice, and consultancy. Product-related service such as repair and supply of buttons and zips or accessories can be attached to the sold products to extend their useful life. Advice and consultancy services can be offered in terms of the frequency of washes (wash cycles) and which specific detergents to use. The fashion house can also provide laundry services that use appropriate washing and drying techniques that again extend garments' useful life and make S.PSS formalwear (or "event") products (Figure 6.3.2) suitable for repeated use.

Although the companies acknowledged the benefits of S.PSS in the fashion industry, there is no systematic approach to implementation. Any efforts to do so are random and uncoordinated. The lack of a systematic structure to guide companies in their implementation of S.PSS in fashion design from an African perspective is arguably a contributory factor to the slow uptake of this approach. A more positive perception of it could pique participants' interest and encourage them to move toward sustainability and S.PSS. The prevalence of non-fashion-related qualifications among both Batswana and Kenyan interviewees could also suggest a lack of background knowledge and skills in fashion design and technical dynamics in the industry. This could contribute to a lack of knowledge-informed strategies such as S.PSS, which constantly need reviewing and the application of new knowledge. However, the findings offer valuable information on how design interventions could be developed to assist fashion design companies in Africa to move toward sustainability and S.PSS.

Figure 6.3.2 Evening dresses from Botswana in the context of events, My Star Botswana Grand Finale, Gaborone
Image reproduced courtesy of Aobakwe Molosiwa

CONCLUSION

This study has provided insights into Botswana's and Kenya's fashion industries in terms of what needs to be done in order for S.PSS models to be adopted. Participants' perceptions of sustainability and S.PSS demonstrate a clear lack of knowledge about both concepts. This could be attributed to the fact that some company founders do not possess the relevant qualifications in fashion design. Those who do have such qualifications did not always have corporate mission or vision statements in place that relate to sustainable fashion design. It may well be that courses on sustainable fashion are difficult to access, and thus it would be helpful for higher-education institutions to review their curriculum to offer them. The low level of sustainability knowledge is also displayed by the companies in both countries by their failure to develop green markets. The authors make the following recommendations as a result of the findings and what they could mean:

1. Capacity-building initiatives need to be developed in order to empower participants' efforts to move toward sustainability and to recognize S.PSS as a possible business strategy.

2. The concept of Fairtrade needs to be promoted rigorously to educate both producers and consumers about fairly traded products and services so that they can promote and support the same. This should contribute to the better treatment and dignity of employees in the workplace.

3. Design thinking needs to be promoted in the fashion industry in Botswana and Kenya in order to take advantage of the exploratory, adaptable, and flexible design-led approach to problem solving with tools to investigate user needs. Through design, fashion houses could be able to co-create dematerialized solutions with their customers, thus, promoting a move away from traditional concepts of ownership.

Although this study has provided an overview of sustainability and S.PSS in the two countries included, further work needs to be undertaken through action research to uncover successful S.PSS strategies and possible implementation routes.

REFERENCES

Armstrong, C., and K. Niinimäki (2014), "Empathic fashion product-service systems for sustainable development," *Proceedings of the Global Fashion Conference*, 19–21, November, School of Arts, Ghent, Belgium.

Armstrong, C. M., K. Niinimäki, C. Lang, and S. Kujala, S. (2016), "A Use-orientated Clothing Economy? Preliminary Affirmation for Sustainable Clothing Consumption Alternatives," *Sustainable Development,* 24: 18–31.

Baines, T., and H. W. Lightfoot (2013), "Servitization of the Manufacturing Firm: Exploring the Operations Practices and Technologies That Deliver Advanced Services," *International Journal of Operations & Production Management*, 34(1): 2–35.

Braun, V., and V. Clarke (2006), "Using Thematic Analysis in Psychology," *Qualitative Research in Psychology*, 3(2): 77–101.

Briceno, T., and S. Stagl (2006), "The Role of Social Processes for Sustainable Consumption," *Journal of Cleaner Production,* 14(17): 1541–51.

De Lille, C., E. R. Abbingab, and M. Kleinsmann (2012), "A designerly approach to enable organizations to deliver product-service systems," in *Proceedings of the DMI 2012 International Research Conference: Leading through design*, Boston.

Dissanayake, D. G. K., and P. Sinha, P (2012), "Sustainable Waste Management Strategies in the Fashion Industry Sector," *International Journal of Environmental, Cultural, Economic and Social Sustainability*, 8(1): 77–90.

Dyer, W. G., and A. L. Wilkins (1991), "Better Stories, Not Better Constructs, to Generate Better Theory: A Rejoinder to Eisenhardt," *Academy of Management Review,* 16: 613–19.

Fletcher, K. (2012), "Durability, Fashion, Sustainability: The Processes and Practices of Use," *Fashion Practice,* 4(2): 221–38.

Horn, M. J., and L. M. Gurel (1981), *The Second Skin.* 3rd ed. Boston: Houghton Mifflin Company.

Hutter, L., P. Capozucca, and S. Nayyar (2010), "A roadmap for Sustainable Consumption," *Deloitte Review,* 7: 45–59.

Manzini, C., and C. Vezzoli (2000), "Product-service Systems and Sustainability: Opportunities for Sustainable Solutions." Paper presented in a workshop on product-service systems held by UNEP DTIE, Paris, June.

Manzini, C., and C. Vezzoli (2003), "A Strategic Approach to Develop Sustainable Product Service Systems: Examples Taken from the 'Environmentally Friendly Innovation' Italian Prize," *Journal of Cleaner Production,* 11: 851–57.

Morelli, N. (2003), "Product-service Systems, a Perspective Shift for Designers: A Case Study—the Design of a Telecentre," *Design Studies.* 24(1): 73–99.

Mulgan, G. (2006), "The Process of Social Innovation," *Innovations,* 1(2): 145–62.

Neu, W.A., and S. W. Brown (2005), "Forming Successful Business-to-business Services in goods-dominant firms," *Journal of Service Research,* 8(1): 3–17.

Niinimäki, K. (2012), "Proactive Fashion Design for Sustainable Consumption," *Nordic Textile Journal,* 1: 60–69.

Oliva, R., and R. Kallenberg (2003), "Managing the Transition from Products to Services," *International Journal of Service Industry Management.* 14(2): 160–72.

Phills, J. A., K. Deiglmeier, and D. T. Miller (2008), "Rediscovering Social Innovation," *Stanford Social Innovation Review,* 6(4) 34–43.

Prahalad, C. K., and V. Ramaswamy (2004), "Co-creating value with customers," *Strategy & Leadership,* 32(3): 4–9.

Ramaswamy, V., and F. Gouillart (2010), *The Power of Co-creation.* New York: Free Press.

Ramsamy-Iranah, S., and N. Budhai (2013), "Developing a New Concept of Reversible Textile Furnishing," *International Journal of Home Economics,* 6(2): 286–304.

Silverman, D. (2001), *Interpreting Qualitative data Methods for Analysing Talk, Text and Interaction.* London: SAGE Publications.

Vezzoli, C., and E, Manzini (2008), *Design for Environmental Sustainability.* New York: Springer.

Vezzoli, C., C. Kohtala, and A. Srinivasan (2014). *Product-service System Design for Sustainability.* Sheffield: Greenleaf.

Zwass, V. (2010), "Co-Creation: Toward a Taxonomy and an Integrated Research Perspective," *International Journal of Electronic Commerce,* 15(1): 11–48.

CHAPTER 6.4

A SPOTLIGHT ON: DESIGNING SUSTAINABLE INDIGENOUS FABRIC AND ATTIRE FOR YOUNG WOMEN IN ZIMBABWE'S TERTIARY INSTITUTIONS

Mercy Rugedhla, Solusi University, Zimbabwe

Potlako Peoesele Disele, Richie Moalosi, and Lily Clara Fidzani, University of Botswana, Botswana

INTRODUCTION

Sustainability is an essential component in textile design because it helps to prevent challenges that affect people as well as animals and the environment. It can be improved by the use of certified organic, natural, highly renewable fibers, the use of non-toxic processes and low impact or natural dyes, as well as recycling, and environmentally appropriate packaging, among other approaches (Kadolph 2010; Pasricha 2010). Gwilt (2012) proposes the integration of sustainable design strategies during the fashion design process, as these will improve product value. The concept of sustainability also relates to indigenous knowledge systems. However, little in-depth research has been conducted on the design of sustainable indigenous fabrics within the

context of Zimbabwe. It is against this background that this chapter will discuss sustainability in textiles and the design of a Zimbocentric fabric from the perspective of indigenous knowledge systems.

INDIGENOUS KNOWLEDGE SYSTEMS AND ECO-FRIENDLY DESIGNS

Carvalho and Santos (2016) advocate for eco-friendly products to avoid the use of non-renewable resources and production procedures that put the environment and people at risk. It has been observed that natural dyes are eco-friendly to use due to their higher level of affinity with the environment. The valuable knowledge base of indigenous knowledge (IK) will be explored to identify important sustainability components, e.g. natural dyes that can be used in the design of indigenous fabric that could lead to a more acceptable, appropriate, and culturally sensitive medium for identification for Zimbabwean women in tertiary institutions.

DRESS IN ZIMBABWE

Clothing announces who people are and who they want to be. There is no dress that is specifically Zimbabwean and thus people often wear the African attire (see Figure 22, plate section). In 2005, attempts by the then Minister of Education, Sports, Arts and Culture in Zimbabwe to launch a "national" dress were unsuccessful because many people associated it with politics. In 2012, one designer made another attempt and launched the *Nhowe* dress, which also failed because people felt that it did not portray their identity. Another fabric called *Retso* was promoted too, but it was unacceptable to the majority of Zimbabwean Christian women because it was associated with those practicing traditional African religion.

RESEARCH METHOD

A mixed method approach will be used in order to harness the strengths of the qualitative and quantitative methods. According to Creswell et al. (2004), these methods complement each other since none of them is sufficient by itself to capture the trends and details of the situations in research. The study will be divided into the following three phases: fieldwork; design; and conducting a customer satisfaction survey in order to choose the best Zimbocentric fabric. All qualitative textual and visual material will be analyzed using content analysis, and quantitative data will be interrogated using SPSS to perform univariate analysis that will assess customers' acceptance of the Zimbocentric fabric.

POSSIBLE OUTCOMES OF THE STUDY

The researchers believe that analogies from nature possess a wealth of historical imagery that can be used to inspire design solutions. It is anticipated that local symbols, motifs, and patterns may be transformed as visual clues in creating a well-defined novel cultural fabric. In designing a culturally acceptable fabric and garment, it is important to develop a design framework that defines the key elements of Zimbabwe's culture and outline how they can be made applicable in designing cultural-oriented fabric and attire.

CONCLUSION

This ongoing study posits that IK is vital in the preservation of cultural heritage in that it emphasizes people's lifestyles and cultural values. IK will be used to design sustainable cultural fabric to satisfy a need which was expressed by young women in Zimbabwe's tertiary institutions. The sustainable approach was adopted because it enhances IK by encouraging eco-friendly designs.

REFERENCES

Carvalho, C., and G. Santos. (2016), "Sustainable and
   Biotechnology," *Natural or Bio Dyes Resources in
   Textiles*, 6(1): 1–5.

Creswell, J. W., M. D. Fetters, and N. V. Ivankova (2004),
   "Designing a Mixed Method Study in Primary Care,"
   Annals of Family Medicine, 2(1): 7–12.

Gwilt, A. (2012), "Integrating Sustainable Strategies in
   the Fashion Design and Process: A Conceptual
   Model of the Fashion Designer in Haute Couture,"
   PhD thesis, School of Architecture and Design
   College of College and Social Context, RMIT
   University.

Kadolph, S. J. (2010), *Textiles*. 11th ed. New York:
   Pearson.

Pasricha, A. (2010), "Exploration of the Meaning of
   Sustainability in Textiles and Apparel Discipline and
   Prospects for Curriculum Enhancement." PhD Thesis,
   School of Hospitality and administration
   Management, LOWA State University.

SUSTAINABLE FASHION AND THE UNITED ARAB EMIRATES VISION 2021

Ayesha Siddequa, Founder and Creative Director of Future Fashion, UAE

INTRODUCTION

In a region that makes headlines due to wars and political turmoil, the United Arab Emirates (UAE) is a rare oasis of political and economic stability in the Middle East. This stability, coupled with vision and determination, has enabled the UAE to become an extremely popular international business hub. For Dubai, fashion means business. The retail sector makes up a third of Dubai's economy; consisting of over 40 mega malls, according to the Oxford Business

Figure 6.5.1 View of city

Image reproduced courtesy of Harikrishnan Balakrishnan

Figure 6.5.2 The Three Spheres of Sustainability[1]
Image reproduced courtesy of Charles Moffatt

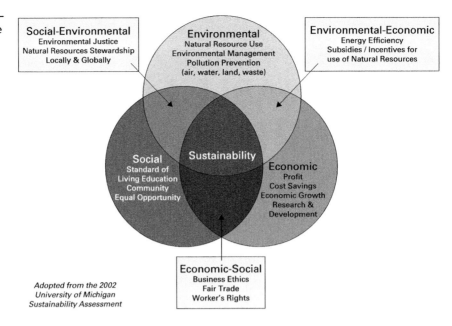

Social-Environmental
Environmental Justice
Natural Resources Stewardship
Locally & Globally

Environmental
Natural Resource Use
Environmental Management
Pollution Prevention
(air, water, land, waste)

Environmental-Economic
Energy Efficiency
Subsidies / Incentives for
use of Natural Resources

Social
Standard of
Living Education
Community
Equal Opportunity

Sustainability

Economic
Profit
Cost Savings
Economic Growth
Research &
Development

Economic-Social
Business Ethics
Fair Trade
Worker's Rights

Adopted from the 2002
University of Michigan
Sustainability Assessment

Group. Shopping is tax-free and the UAE is home to more than forty mega malls. This chapter explores sustainable fashion within the context of UAE Vision 2021.

SUSTAINABLE FASHION

Sustainable fashion is an approach to designing, sourcing, and manufacturing clothing that benefits the community while also minimizing environmental impact. As a phrase, it can be used to describe both fashion businesses that aim to reduce their ecological footprint through environmentally conscious manufacturing process, and those companies that aim to support communities through offering fair wages and working conditions. The key question is: will sustainable fashion ever become anything more than a niche product?

While the choice between sustainably- and unsustainably-produced clothing ought to be simple for consumers, many are put off by the higher price tag. However, as Friederike von Wedel-Parlow so aptly summed it up: "Cheaply produced clothing doesn't compensate for the resulting environmental damage. If we add these costs into the end price, then ecologically produced clothing would be cheaper, because it doesn't lead to damage that will later affect the public." Friederike von Wedel-Parlow, Director of the Esmod Berlin International University of Art for Fashion

The Urgent Need for Change

Global population growth and the related need for further economic development will continue to drive increasing consumption. Each year, for example, the UK consumes and disposes of 1.1 million tonnes of clothes. Some 48 percent of these items are reused and 14 percent recycled, while the remainder winds up in landfill (31 percent) or incinerated (7 percent) (Gould 2013). The growing sales volumes in the fashion industry mean that its already significant environmental impact only escalates as the global population rises to the expected 9 billion by 2050. Innovative and transformative solutions are urgently needed to solve or reduce the industry's significant impacts in areas such as water and energy use, emissions, and toxic chemicals (Mistra Future Fashion 2013).

"Eventually, there aren't going to be resources to sustain fast fashion, so to me it seems to be a very vulnerable business model," says Alex McIntosh, the business and research manager at the London College of Fashion's Centre for Sustainable Fashion (Centre for Sustainable Fashion 2015). Approximately 60 to 75 million people are employed in the textile, clothing, and footwear sector worldwide. Over 80 percent of employees within the fast fashion industry do not even earn a living wage (Clean Clothes 2015). Industry estimates suggest that 20 to 60 percent of garment production is sewn at home by workers employed informally (Siegle 2011). Similar to the growing environmental impact, the impact felt on communities that are supplying our fast fashion needs is already severe. Cheaper retail prices have triggered unbearable working conditions and lower wages at the "bottom of the pyramid." Since the current fast fashion model is simply not sustainable, we will need the involvement of everyone connected within the industry—journalists, brands, consumers, governments, and even the United Nations and the World Bank—to bring about changes so desperately needed in the apparel and the environment and economic development.

The UN's newly adopted Sustainable Development Goals (SDGs), for example, are all about social inclusion, economic prosperity, and environmental sustainability—three pillars that need to be at the epicenter of the apparel industry. According to Jorma Ollila, (World Bank Council for Sustainable Development Chairman): "Business as usual in the face of global climate change and population growth is not an option. We need big changes in industrial systems, business models, economic assumptions, market rules and governance frameworks to tackle the huge challenges facing us all at once. Business needs to be part of the solution."

UAE VISION 2021—TO MAKE UAE ONE OF THE TEN MOST SUSTAINABLE COUNTRIES IN THE WORLD

Over the past century, UAE has experienced a dramatic transformation. In 1900, it was estimated that only 10,000 people lived in the desert-like country. UAE currently has a population of over 9.1 million people, however, and receives between ten and fourteen million visitors per year (Bagherian 2017).

The humble origins of the country hitherto dependent on fishing and pearl diving were altered dramatically after oil was discovered in the 1950s. When Abu Dhabi became the first of the Emirates to start exporting oil in 1962, it saw the first signs of the economic success it enjoys today. All economic sectors, from finance, fashion, tourism, construction, and so on, have reaped the benefits of the oil trade. In 2014, His Highness Sheikh Mohammed bin Rashid Al Maktoum, Vice-President and Prime Minister of the UAE and Ruler of the Emirate of Dubai, launched a seven-year UAE National Agenda leading to the UAE Vision 2021, a year that will coincide with the country's fiftieth National Day. Vision 2021 aim is to make the UAE one of the world's best countries in many sectors, from education to healthcare, economy, standard of living, fair government, and infrastructure. The performance indicators set against the Vision generally compare the UAE against global benchmarks and are actively monitored by the government to ensure targets will be achieved by 2021 (Vision 2021 2014)

Figure 6.5.3
Fishing boats
Image reproduced courtesy of Mohammed Ehtesham

Figure 6.5.4
Metro link
Image reproduced courtesy of David Kagerer

UNDERPINNING THE WIDER UAE 2021 VISION: A SPECIFIC FRAMEWORK

According to Abdullah Al Shaibani, Secretary-General of the Executive Council of Dubai: "Dubai continues to flourish and rise, and launching Dubai Plan 2021 supports Dubai's development, ensuring its sustainability in line with long term well thought out standards that align with leadership's vision and that fulfill the needs of all of Dubai's people." The UAE framework embraces six development themes that define Dubai's Vision for 2021:

1. The People: "City of Happy, Creative & Empowered People."

2. The Society: "An Inclusive & Cohesive Society."
3. The Experience: "The Preferred Place to Live, Work & Visit."
4. The Place: "A Smart & Sustainable City."
5. The Economy: "A Pivotal Hub in the Global Economy."
6. The Government: "A Pioneering and Excellent Government."

WHAT DOES UAE VISION 2021 MEAN FOR THE COUNTRY'S FASHION INDUSTRY?

The seven Emirates are just forty-four years old, but the growth of UAE, its strong heritage, and the richness of its culture are substantial. As part of this, the country enjoys one of the most successful and dynamic fashion industries in the world. Ranked seventh on the 2015 Global Retail Development Index, UAE has the highest market attractiveness/retail development score (97.6 percent) globally. It continues to hold its eleventh position as the world's biggest clothing importer with an import value of $4 billion (Hassan 2016). The UAE manufacturing sector contributes around 15 percent of the UAE's GDP. Efforts are ongoing to boost the contribution of this vital sector (Made in UAE 2017).

WHY EMBRACE THE VISION?

One main reason for businesses to adopt an ethical commercial approach is that consumers are becoming more ethically conscious. They are reading about sustainability and making informed choices that affect their purchases. People are starting to learn about the pollution involved in traditional textile manufacture, and "greener" choices are starting to look more appealing. According to a 2012 report by the Boston Consulting Group, 80 percent of American shoppers said that they were willing to pay higher prices for products made in the United States, and in fact nearly 60 percent of shoppers said they had consciously chosen more expensive US-made products in the previous month (Cline 2013).

In the West, ethical fashion is a mature market; it has already taken off and continues gaining momentum. In the Middle East, the fashion sector's focus remains on brand labels. Fashion is one of the region's main industries, alongside construction, tourism, food, and trade, but the ethical approach has yet to take off. And that needs to change—urgently. Even though gas supplies are currently plentiful, most Middle Eastern fashion empires must remember that they will eventually run out. Just as the gas will not last forever, neither will the brand labels that rely on this precious resource, not unless they start to make some dramatic changes. For example, the traditional dress of women in the Middle East, the abaya, is made principally from synthetic fabric, like polyester. Polyester is made from chemically produced fibers, which are ultimately derived from coal, oil, or natural gas. Polyester factories are responsible for massive amounts of air pollution and water pollution, and may cause human health problems.

It is essential that we start acknowledging our environment and championing change in the region. By taking gas for granted, companies are taking their profit and growth for granted, they are taking their business for granted, and their country's culture for granted. The UAE has always been forward-thinking and at the front of the fashion game, it cannot afford to fall behind as the West has already invested so much in sustainable resources and ethical fashion.

CULTURAL VALUES

The Qur'an states that all business transactions should be done within a clear and transparent ethical framework (2:282); corruption, deception, and bribery are outlawed, and shareholders, suppliers, and competitors must be treated fairly and with respect. As for quality standards, the Qur'an (26:181–83) states that one must "Give just measure and cause no loss (to others by fraud). And weight with scales true and upright. And withhold not things justly due to men, nor do evil in the land of working mischief." The Prophet Muhammad's teachings also encourage fair treatment in the workplace, and discourage discrimination against minorities or other groups (Beekun & Badawi 2005).

....

"What we have done for ourselves alone dies with us; what we have done for others and the world remains and is immortal." Albert Pike

The country's forefathers identified what resources were available to them and utilized them as effectively as possible, using oil to great cultural and financial success. This resourcefulness and determination is very much part of the country's culture, and are qualities that are needed for the UAE to keep evolving in a post-peak-oil era. Depleting oil stocks will be a growing concern, especially for industries highly dependent on energy.

SPREADING AWARENESS

The substantial environmental improvements in areas such as the quality of air, the preservation of water resources, and the contribution of clean energy addressed in the Vision 2021 agenda are hugely important in the fashion industry.

Fashion is the second largest of the key industries that are draining these precious resources globally. The global fashion apparel industry has surpassed the market size of US$1 trillion as of 2013, and now it represents nearly 2 percent of the world's GDP (BusinessVibes 2015). It is our responsibility to look at the changing world, to embrace the need for sustainability, and to celebrate our originality and ingenuity. A shift in mindset is required; the need for sustainability and responsible choices is a necessity, rather than a choice.

It was expected that by 2018 Dubai would have replaced Paris as the third most popular tourist destination in the world. Many developments are geared toward high-end fashion retail, which could be correlated to the rise in luxury tourism in the Emirates (Hassan 2016). Fashion production methods traditionally rely on excessive quantities of water, the use of pollutants, and the depletion of precious fossil-fuel supplies. It has been predicted by the World Resources Institute that between 2007 and 2025, water use will increase by 50 percent in developing countries and 18 percent in developed nations (WWF 2013). The obvious solution to this would be to recycle the water, but pesticides used often make recycling water impossible. Farmers need to be re-educated in alternative farming methods that involve avoiding pesticides and thus facilitate the recycling of water. Levi's proved that this was possible when they made 100,000 pairs of jeans using 100 percent recycled water (Eco Watch 2014). Nike's moonshot ambition is to double its business while halving the company's environmental impact. It has set three strategic aims to guide this work: minimize environmental footprint; transform manufacturing; and unleash human potential (Jones 2016).

WHO IS LEADING THE WAY?

Beyond the multi-national giants, local companies are also acknowledging the importance of environmental issues and taking steps to address them. The Dubai-based Chalhoub Group has been the leading partner for luxury across the Middle East since 1955. As an expert in retail, distribution, and marketing services, the Group has become a major player in the beauty, fashion, and gift sectors regionally. During this time, it has remained committed to responsible business behaviors, considering the impact of their operations on local communities, the people they

work with, and the surrounding environment. As a member of the United Nations Global Compact (UNGC), the Group is fully committed to supporting the SDGs. Its strategy is aligned with the Dubai 2021 plan and the UAE Green Growth strategy, which promotes sustainable development in the Middle East (Chalhoub Group 2016).

At Chalhoub Group, we know that the fashion industry is one of the most polluting industries in the world—with 10 percent of the world's CO_2 emissions and the second largest consumer of water. This is why we have an ambitious sustainability strategy to help us reduce our impact on the planet. We continuously assess the environmental impact of our supply chain, our stores, our warehouses, and our offices, and we have an unequivocal commitment to become a more sustainable business."

Marc Ruiviejo Cirera, Senior Sustainability Executive at Chalhoub Group

Figure 6.5.5 Bedouin woman
Photographer: Zenab S.

In the UAE, there are now many alternative fashion initiatives, including high-end consignment and resale stores, and both online and physical ethical fashion stores that have opened over the last few years, like Future Fashion, RETOLD, Garderobe, So Chic, and more, giving the customers a way into owning a sustainable wardrobe.

Local businesses like D-Grade, the Islamic Fashion and Design Council, Goumbook, Sustainability Advisory, Green Emirates, Sustainability Tribe and many others aim to provide resources of the widest range of information on green and sustainable lifestyles, products, and businesses in the region. According to Maria Sillanpaa, founding director of Sustainability Advisory:

> Fast fashion is a sign of our times. As with fast food a decade or so ago, awareness of its insidious and wide-ranging impacts on the planet and its people is gradually growing amongst consumers and other stakeholders. We have a long way to go, but as with any emerging sustainability issue, it is the pioneers that do the heavy lifting—the awareness raising, the sharing of pivotal practices, and, most importantly, by consuming and producing fashion differently.

Fashion plays a significant economic role in the UAE, especially in Dubai. This makes it especially important that the concrete links between sustainable fashion and the Dubai Vision 2021 are explored, and taken forward as part of the wider economic diversification plans for the country.

UAE's vision for the future shows that it is committed to being a pioneer in the field of sustainability, and it will continue do so for its growing fashion industry. To stay ahead of the game, to remain cutting edge and current, it needs to fully embrace the changes that have been laid out in the National Agenda. The country will support its home-grown fashion designers and encourage the most environmental and ethical production methods. It will do its bit to protect this beautiful world. "The UAE is more than coming into its own, particularly with the internal emphasis on homegrown designers," says Jane Monnington Boddy, director of Colour and Womenswear at trend forecaster WGSN. "For this part of the world [the Middle East], it is absolutely correct to say that it is and will continue to be a fashion hub" (Judge 2017).

Dubai's market for apparel and footwear is estimated to be worth $12.8 billion, registering 5.5 percent annual growth in sales since 2010, according to a report by the Dubai Chamber of Commerce and Industry based on data from Euromonitor International (Emirates 24/7 2014). This pioneering spirit; its ethical intelligence, and sustainable fashion celebrate the true heart of UAE culture. The essence of that culture lies in not only moving with the tide, but having a firm hand on the tiller. Sustainability is the future, and UAE will be among its pioneers.

CONCLUSION

The first step to fixing a problem is to admit there is one, and it is becoming more obvious these days that the contemporary fashion industry is very unsustainable. In order to implement systemic change, there must first be a market for sustainable products, and currently that is quite small (*The Guardian* 2011). Until the cost of sustainable fashion falls, or the prices of fast fashion increase to cover its current environilentnl and social externalities, the proposition looks attractive on paper, but will remain a challenge for the majority of budget-conscious consumers.

Raising awareness as to why clothes are so cheap is key. Making sustainable garments a reality for high street fashion requires action from all key players. There can only be positive changes for businesses if sustainable business practices are implemented: reputational, meeting changing consumer expectations, saving costs, building brand loyalty, and more. According to the WBCD: "The continuing commitment by business to behave ethically and contribute to economic development while improving the quality of life of the workforce and their families as well as of the local community and society at large."

The future of fashion is changing, and its focus on sustainability and preserving the health of the planet as well as looking after our communities, is something that resounds deeply at the heart of the Arab culture. UAE's culture is built from a durable and united social fabric, and it aims to make the future a sustainable one.

NOTE

1. http://fashion.lilithezine.com/Sustainable-Clothing-Fashion.html

REFERENCES

Anon. (2005), "Doing Business with Islam: Can Corporate Social Responsibility be a Bridge Between Civilisations?" *Social Science Research Network.*

Bagherian, B. (2017), *Baharash.* Available online at: http://www.baharash.com/dubai-smart-city/

Beekun, R. I., and J. A. Badawi (2005), "Balancing Ethical Responsibility among Multiple Organizational Stakeholders: The Islamic Perspective," *Journal of Business Ethics.*

Business Vibes (2015), "30 Shocking Figures and Facts in Global Textile and Apparel Industry," *Business 2 Community.* Available online at: http://www.business2community.com/fashion-beauty/30-shocking-figures-facts-global-textile-apparel-industry-01222057#AABuOFHeV9ThMEl6.97

Centre for Sustainable Fashion (2015), "Home page." Available online at: http://sustainable-fashion.com/

Chalhoub Group (2016), "Sustainability Report 2016." Available online at: http://chalhoubgroup.com/uploads/pdf_file/Sustainabiliy-Report-2016.pdf

Child Poverty Action Group (2016), "Child Poverty Facts and Figures." Available online at: http://www.cpag.org.uk/child-poverty-facts-and-figures

Clean Clothes (2015), "Facts on the Global Garment Industry." Available online at: https://cleanclothes.org/resources/publications/factsheets/general-factsheet-garment-industry-february-2015.pdf

Cline, E. (2013), "Can Fashion Clean Up Its Act," *The National.* Available online at: https://www.thenation.com/article/can-fashion-clean-its-act/ (accessed 2017).

Eco Watch (2014), "Levi's Makes 100,000 Pairs of Jeans With 100% Recycled Water." Available online at: https://www.ecowatch.com/levis-makes-100-000-pairs-of-jeans-with-100-recycled-water-1881869424.html

Emirates 24/7 (2014), "Dubai World's Next Fashion Capital: Billions of Dollars in Planned Investments." Available online at: http://www.emirates247.com/news/emirates/dubai-world-s-next-fashion-capital-billions-of-dollars-in-planned-investments-2014-02-14-1.538245

Emirates 24/7 (2016), Available online at: http://www.emirates247.com/news/emirates/dubai-world-s-next-fashion-capital-billions-of-dollars-in-planned-investments-2014-02-14-1.538245

Feeding America (2016), Available online at: http://www.feedingamerica.org/hunger-in-america/impact-of-hunger/hunger-and-poverty/hunger-and-poverty-fact-sheet.html?referrer=https://www.google.co.uk/

Fletcher, K. (2007), Available online at: http://katefletcher.com/slow-fashion-consultancy/

Gould, H. (2013), *The Guardian.* Available online at: https://www.theguardian.com/sustainable-business/sustainable-fashion-blog/alternative-business-models-live-chat (accessed May 5, 2017).

The Guardian (2011), "Sustainability in the Fashion Business," Available online at: Available at: https://www.theguardian.com/sustainable-business/sustainable-ethical-fashion-business

Hassan, W. (2016), "UAE's Apparel Industry and Clothing sector lucrative for investment in 2016." s.l.: Research Konnection.

Index Mundi (2016), "United Arab Emirates Below Poverty Line." Available online at: http://www.indexmundi.com/united_arab_emirates/population_below_poverty_line.html

Jones, H. (2016), "Top Things to Know about Sustainable Innovation at Nike." Available online at: http://news.nike.com/news/sustainable-innovation

Judge, L. (2017), "The Future of Fashion in the UAE." Available online at: http://fridaymagazine.ae/fashion-beauty/women/the-future-of-fashion-in-the-uae-1.1962736

Made in UAE (2017), Available online at: http://www.makeinuae.ae/

Menkes, S. (2011), "In Praise of Slow Fashion at Hermès," *New York Times* (2011). Available online at: http://www.nytimes.com/2011/03/07/fashion/07iht-rhaider07.html

Mistra Future Fashion (2013), "Research for Systemic Change in Fashion." Available online at: http://mistrafuturefashion.com/ (accessed May 15, 2017).

Moffat, C. (2012), "Sustainable Clothing and Sustainable Fashion," *Fashion Lilithezine*. Available online at: http://fashion.lilithezine.com/Sustainable-Clothing-Fashion.html (accessed May 2017).

Shah, A., 2013. "Poverty Facts and Stats," *Global Issues*. Available online at: http://www.globalissues.org/article/26/poverty-facts-and-stats

Siegle, L. (2011), *To Die for: Is Fashion Wearing Out the World?*. London: Fourth Estate.

Vision 2021 (2014), "UAE Vision 2021." Available online at: https://www.vision2021.ae/en

WWF (2013), "The Impact of a Cotton T-Shirt," *WWF*. Available online at: https://www.worldwildlife.org/stories/the-impact-of-a-cotton-t-shirt

CHAPTER 6.6

A SPOTLIGHT ON: SHAHIRA MEHREZ, EGYPT
The Continuation of Culture

Maggie Jonk, Ryerson University, Canada

"This is what you should focus on; this is what matters." Shahira Mehrez, a researcher and collector, is quick to dismiss her own ready-to-wear collection when asked about cultural preservation and sustainability. Instead, she prefers to focus on the work of Chant Avedissian, and clearly outlines the difference between herself—the preserver—and designer Avedissian—the transposers (Mehrez 2017). Avidly preserving Egyptian material culture for over fifty years, Mehrez provides a wealth of knowledge and physical examples of traditional making techniques from within her collection to designers willing to commit to understanding the practices and their origin. However, Mehrez notes that few designers are willing to do this.

Mehrez acknowledges how her research contributes to the sustainable continuation of Egyptian textile and clothing traditions, but she does not consider herself a designer. Through working with traditional Egyptian makers, Mehrez produces a collection of ready-to-wear garments. She argues that hers are reproductions of the past, noting that the role of a designer is to deeply understand their inspiration and to

transpose. In order to meaningfully contribute to the perpetuation of a tradition, she maintains that designers must engage with tradition, "adapting it to a new form that allows it to survive," thus creating an exchange between the old principles, the new, and the contemporary needs of modern society (Mehrez 2017).

An example of this exchange is found in the work of Avedissian, Egyptian artist and designer. With the collection of Mehrez serving as a source of inspiration, Avedissian interpreted specific Egyptian textile traditions through a series of clothing and textiles, namely the Nubian Girgar and Bedouin Flat Weave. Through an understanding of color theories, traditional pattern-cutting techniques, usage of shape and textures, and finishing, Mehrez explains how Avedissian moved the traditional to the contemporary in a sustainable way (see Figures 6.6.1 and 6.6.2).

Emerging United Arab Emirates-based Palestinian designer Faisal El Malak's work exemplifies this practice as well, with his pieces incorporating hand-woven fabrics from around the region. El Malak works with traditionally

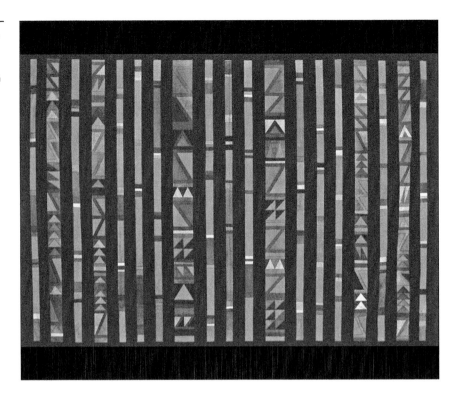

Figure 6.6.1 Variation on the Bedouin Flat Weave by Chant Avedissian for Shahira Mehrez
Image courtesy of Shahira Mehrez

Figure 6.6.2 Bedouin Flat Weave from the collection of Shahira Mehrez. Inspiration for Chant Avedissian
Image courtesy of Shahira Mehrez

patterned fabrics, noting the difficulties he faced when trying have more contemporary patterns woven. Instead, he finds beauty in the tradition, and showcases it through carefully cut contemporary men's and women's wear (see Figures 6.6.3 and 6.6.4). Sourcing these fabrics, he noted, has been challenging. Difficulties include access, political uncertainty in the countries where his makers are based, and working between the local, traditional industry and an international, contemporary industry (El Malak 2017).

Figure 6.6.3 Vest and skirt from Yemini hand-woven textiles by Faissal Al Malak
Image courtesy of Faissal El-Malak

Figure 6.6.4 Short-sleeve top from Yemini hand-woven textiles by Faissal Al Malak
Image courtesy of Faissal El-Malak

Avedissian and El Malak are few among the many who find inspiration in the material culture of the Middle East and North Africa. While often reproduced, Mehrez argues that, unlike Avedission and El Malak, most designers are grafting their rich culture onto the increasingly present western culture, through a lack of understanding and application of cultural practices and traditions. She sites colonialization and "auto-colonialization," as described by Hassan Fathy, as catalysts in the interruption and liquefaction of traditional culture, leaving many without knowledge of the principles found within traditional craft (Mehrez

2017). Through a process of devaluing, forgetting, and then grafting without understanding, regional making practices are not being preserved, but rather superficially produced. Mehrez advocates that contemporary designers within the region need to take an interest in creating a pluralistic design practice, building on their tradition of incorporating the many outside cultural practices that have passed through the region throughout its dynamic history, while maintaining a thorough understanding of their own (Mehrez 2017). Sass Brown, sustainable fashion advocate and scholar, predicts that the new luxury market will be one centered on traditional and artisanal making techniques, arguing that there will be a substantial place for tradition within the contemporary industry (Brown 2015). Designers such as El Malak are now tasked with moving the work of scholars such as Shahira Mehrez into Brown's new luxury market, in a way, which is not trend-based but sustainable in nature. Reflecting on the industry as a whole, Mehrez summarized: "what I want to say is that fashion is the end result of a way of thinking; fashion is not the most important thing, the most important thing is the way we think. Our fashion, our traditional crafts, showed how pluralistic we were because we were accepting from the other. We were taking what they have, we were using it in our clothes, in our furniture, our jewelry, so this is what we want to preserve" (Mehrez 2017). And it is through the preservation of these traditions that regional designers such as El Malak and Avedissian are creating clothing with meaning, consequently changing production techniques, and influencing consumption and post-consumption attitudes.

REFERENCES

El Malak, F. (2017), Conversations with Faissal El Malak, Tashkeel Studio.

Brown, S. (2015), "Can Global Craft & Artisanship be the Future of Luxury Fashion?" Proceedings of the PLATE Conference. Nottingham: Nottingham Trent University.

Mehrez, S. (2017), Conversations with Shahira Mehrez, Dokki Apartment, Cairo.

CONCLUDING REMARKS

Alison Gwilt, Alice Payne, and Evelise Anicet Rüthschilling

Internationally there are large clothing brands, small fashion labels, and artisan makers developing products that are circular, environmentally conscious, and/or ethically made. Some of these are respected global brands, such as H&M, Patagonia, and Nike, while others are making a difference at a local and/or national level. Although these companies do raise awareness to sustainable fashion, there has been difficulty in "seeing" sustainable fashion as a truly international movement. *Global Perspectives on Sustainable Fashion* has tried to present a wide variety of narratives from researchers, designers, makers, and activists in different communities, countries, and continents. They represent the many varied environmental, ethical, social, and economic aspects that have shaped the development of fashion for sustainability in different nations. Although each author has examined aspects of sustainable fashion in their own way, the dimensions of environmental and ethical production come to the fore, and alongside the apparel production critical to the livelihoods of individuals and to the economics of nations. Nevertheless, it is evident to us that many of our regional neighbors are being encouraged or motivated to reduce the impacts associated with fashion production and consumption—and this is a positive dimension that has been, perhaps, less acknowledged in the research community.

There are some significant insights to be gained from this book. It is clear to us that in Latin America (Part 1) there is renewed vigor in capitalizing on local systems, and in revitalizing traditional methods and processes for new opportunities. At the same time there is a "resistance" to feeding social norms focused on growing consumption, which is leading designers, makers, and consumers to embrace slower and local practices. Meanwhile in North America and Europe (Parts 2 and 3) the contributions in these sections clearly reflect a move to "undo" and correct years of environmental and social "damage." Moreover, this is leading to a desire to improve, or reconfigure, or look for entirely new, radical approaches to the fashion system that broadly encompass slow, local, and circular business models. Similar concerns are found throughout Asia and Oceania (Parts 4 and 5), with many practitioners adopting a waste-to-resource philosophy in which they draw on the local materials at hand, whether post-consumer clothing waste or pre-consumer manufacturing waste, to create new garments. From the perspective of workers, texts on major apparel exporting nations in Asia reveal both the benefits and complexities of large-scale manufacturing, and the work of many in addressing these challenges. In Africa and the Middle East (Part 6) we can observe a real growth and motivation in exploring and capitalizing on new business models and opportunities. Moreover, there is a recognition that cultural heritage can play a crucial part in projecting a "homegrown" identity within an independent fashion system, which can serve the needs of local people.

As we further reflect on the contributions presented in this book we have identified across the regions that:

- There are many different regional perspectives on how "sustainability" is defined. Some contributions focus on the importance of cultural sustainability to their region, while others focus on social justice, or on environmental issues. Further, in acknowledging that all perspectives play a part in contributing to a "global picture," we elected at the start of this work to leave the authors to explore the field from their viewpoint, and the contributions speak to sustainability concerns that are universal as well as intensely local.
- Within the contributions we have been exposed to inequalities in the global fashion system, and the impact that changing consumption habits are having, both negatively and positively, on communities elsewhere.
- Essential to many contributions is the importance of activists and campaign groups

in raising awareness. To many of our authors, these have helped shape and drive the pace at which change has been occurring within their domestic market. Moreover, they play an important role in acting as a conduit for change between industry and consumers.

In closing, this book arose from our motivation to share the experiences of others, to learn from and avoid the mistakes of many, and to support and engage others to take action. Therefore we now have to consider the future—and seek out what we think may be the big challenges and opportunities on a domestic and international scale. Many of our contributors have highlighted the connections between nations; whether through fiber production, or through manufacturing, or through wearing and purchasing, the world's clothes are already "global" in origins and in destinations. These interconnections between countries can be viewed simply as evidence of the tangled supply chains of globalized fashion production. But the connections also suggest improved futures for fashion: offering opportunities for transparent production and collaboration, and opportunities to learn from the practices and industries of other regions. Finally, a key aim for us has been to see this book as a celebration of the big and small achievements; of the drive and motivations of dedicated people who want to see a difference, and the hope that step by step these accomplishments may be built upon by others to change the industry.

RESOURCES

This list has been compiled with the help of our contributing authors, who kindly suggested resources that are important to their respective regions.

KEY BOOKS AND REPORTS
Latin America

Anicet, A., P. Bess, and A. C. Broega (2012), "A quantificação da sustentabilidade no design têxtil," in A. M. S. De Carli and B. L. S. Venzon (eds), *Moda: sustentabilidade e emergências,* 135–47. Caxias do Sul, Brazil: EDUCS.

Berlim, L. G. (2012), *Moda e Sustentabilidade, uma reflexão necessária.* São Paulo: Estação das Letras e Cores.

Berlim, L. G. (2016), "Transformações no Campo da Moda: Crítica, Ética e Estética", PhD thesis, Federal Rural University of Rio de Janeiro, UFRRJ, Brazil. Available online at: https://tede.ufrrj.br/jspui/handle/jspui/2139

Bossle, M. B. (2011), "Comércio justo no Brasil e a comercialização de produtos do algodão orgânico," Master's dissertation at Graduate Program in Business Administration, UFRGS, Brazil. Available online at: http://www.lume.ufrgs.br/handle/10183/30370

Ganem, M. (2016), *Design Dialógico: Uma Estratégia Para Gestão Criativa de Tradições.* São Paulo: Estação das Letras e Cores.

Gardetti M. A., and S. S. Muthu (2015), *Handbook of Sustainable Luxury Textiles and Fashion, Vols 1 and 2.* Singapore: Springer.

Lima, B. L., et al. (2017), "Critérios para avaliação da sustentabilidade em marcas de moda," *Design e Tecnologia,* [S.l.], 7(14): 59–68. Available onlinet at: https://www.ufrgs.br/det/index.php/det/article/view/403 and http://dx.doi.org/10.23972/det2017iss14pp59-68

Muthu, S. S., and M. A. Gardetti (2016), *Green Fashion, Vols 1 and 2.* Singapore: Springer.

Muthu, S. S., and M. A. Gardetti (2016), *Sustainable Fibers for the Fashion Industry, Vols 1 and 2.* Singapore: Springer.

Rüthschilling, E. A., and A. Anicet (2018), "Slow Surface Design and Contemporary Technology Applied in Fashion," *Moda Palavra* 11(21). Available online at: http://revistas.udesc.br/index.php/modapalavra/article/view/10698 and http://dx.doi.org/10.5965/1982615x11212018079

Santos, A., F. Ceschin, S. B. Martins, and C. Vezzoli (2016), "A Design Framework for Enabling Sustainability in the Clothing Sector," *Latin American Journal of Management for Sustainable Development,* 3(1): 47–65.

Sarmento, F. (2014), "Design para a sociobiodiversidade: perspectivas para o uso sustentável da borracha na Floresta Nacional do Tapajós," PhD thesis, USP Faculdade de Arquitetura e Urbanismo, São Paulo, Brazil. DOI 10.11606/T.16.2014.tde-28072014-111246_ and http://www.teses.usp.br/teses/disponiveis/16/16134/tde-28072014-111246/pt-br.php

Schulte, N. (2015), *Reflexões sobre moda ética: contribuições do biocentrismo e do veganismo.* Florianópolis: UDESC, Brasil.

Todeschini, B. V., et al. (2017), "Innovative and sustainable business models in fashion industry: entrepreneurial drivers, opportunities and challenges," *Business Horizons,* Elsevier. Available online at: https://doi.org/10.1016/j.bushor.2017.07.003

North America

Brydges. T (2017), "Made in Canada: The Strategies, Spaces and Working Lives of Independent Designers in the Canadian Fashion System," PhD Thesis, Uppsala University, Sweden. Available online at: http://www.diva-portal.org/smash/record.jsf?pid= diva2%3A1113383&dswid=1854

Cline, E. L. (2012), *Overdressed: The Shockingly High Cost of Cheap Fashion.* New York: Portfolio.

Ellen MacArthur Foundation (2017), "A New Textiles Economy: Redesigning Fashion's Future." Available online at: http://www.ellenmacarthurfoundation.org/ publications

Hethorn, J., and C. Ulasewicz (2015), *Sustainable Fashion: What's Next?* New York: Fairchild Books.

Rissanen, T., and H. McQuillan (2015), *Zero Waste Fashion Design.* London: Fairchild Books.

Europe

Black, S. (2013), *The Sustainable Fashion Handbook.* London: Thames & Hudson. Youth Fashion Summit archive: the archives hold valuable teaching material for students. Available online at: http:// youthfashionsummit.com/archive/

Eyskoot, M. (2014), *Talking Dress.* Haarlem: Becht.

Fletcher, K., and I. Klepp, eds (2018), *Opening Up the Wardrobe: A Methods Book.* Oslo: Novus Forlag

Gwilt, A. (2014), *A Practical Guide to Sustainable Fashion.* London: Fairchild Books.

Modint (2017), "Sustainable Material Guide— Netherlands: Engelstalig." Available online at: http:// modint.nl/2017/01/09/modints-sustainable-material- guide-smg/

Niinimäki, K., ed. (2013), *Sustainable Fashion: New Approaches.* Available online at: https://shop.aalto.fi/ media/attachments/1ee80/SustainableFashion.pdf

Asia (Western, Central, South Central, Eastern)

Chattopadhyay, K. D. (1985), *Handicrafts of India.* New Delhi: Indian Council for Cultural Relations.

Ho, P.Y., and T. M. Choi (2012), "A Five-R Analysis for Sustainable Fashion Supply Chain management in Hong Kong: A Case Analysis," *Journal of Fashion Marketing and Management,* 16(2): 161–75.

Jaitl, J. (2012), *Craft Atlas of India.* New Delhi: Niyogi Books.

Ko, E., and Fashion Marketing Research Lab (2015), *Sustainable Fashion Brand Marketing.* Seoul: Gyomoon. Available online at: https://www. researchgate.net/publication/292150455_ Sustainable_Fashion_Brand_Marketing (accessed 18 April 2018).

Lopez-Acevedo, G., and R. Raymond (2016), *Stitches to Riches?: Apparel Employment, Trade, and Economic Development in South Asia.* Washington, DC: World Bank Publications.

Von Busch, O. (2017), *Moda Praksisi [Fashion Condition].* İstanbul: Yeni İnsan Yayınevi Publishers.

Na, Y., and D. K. Na (2015), "Investigating the Sustainability of the Korean Textile and Fashion Industry," *International Journal of Clothing Science and Technology,* 27(1): 23–33.

Oxfam Hong Kong (2009), *Good Fashion: A Guide to Being an Ethical Clothing Company.* Available online at: http://www.oxfam.org.hk/web/files/csr/Good_ Fashion_en.pdf (accessed April 18, 2018).

Kipöz, S., ed. (2015), *Sürdürülebilir Moda (Sustainable Fashion).* İstanbul: Yeni İnsan Pub.

Southeast Asia and Oceania

Cornish, P. (2017), "Dawn of Vietmanese Fashion," *Asia Life Magazine.* Available online at: https://www. asialifemagazine.com/vietnam/dawn-of-vietnamese- fashion/ (accessed viewed April 18, 2018).

Tearfund (2017), *The Ethical Fashion Report.* Available online at: https://www.tearfund.org.nz/ ethicalfashionguide (accessed April 18, 2018).

Diviney, E., and S. Lillywhite (2009), *Travelling Textiles: A Sustainability Roadmap of Natural Fibre Garments.* Fitzroy, Victoria: Brotherhood of St Laurence.

Nimbalker, G., J. Mawson, C. Cremen, H. Wrinkle, and E. Eriksson (2018), *Australian Fashion Report.* Sydney: Baptist World Aid. Available online at: Australia: https://baptistworldaid.org.au/resources/ 2018-ethical-fashion-guide/ (accessed April 18, 2018).

English, B., and L. Pomazan, eds (2010), *Australian Fashion Unstitched: The Last 60 Years.* Port Melbourne, Vic.: Cambridge University Press.

Fair Labour Association (2014), *Promoting Sustainable Compliance in Vietnam*. Available online at: http://www.fairlabor.org/sites/default/files/documents/promoting_sustainable_compliance_in_vietnam_final_2009_to_2014_.pdf (accessed April 18, 2018).

Milburn, J. (2017), *Slow Clothing: Finding Meaning in What We Wear*. Brisbane: First Edition.

Payne, A (2014), "Spinning a Sustainable Yarn: Environmental Sustainability and Brand Story in the Australian Fashion Industry," *International Journal of Fashion Studies* 1(2): 185–208.

Press, C. (2017), *Wardrobe Crisis: How We Went from Sunday Best to Fast Fashion*. Melbourne: Nero.

Scopes (2017), *Special issue, Fashion Today and Tomorrow: Considering an Interconnected Global System of Challenges and Promise*. Available online at: http://www.thescopes.org/art-and-design-15/ (accessed April 18, 2018).

World Bank (2018), *World Bank Report: Vietnam*. Available online at: http://www.worldbank.org/en/country/vietnam (accessed April 18, 2018).

ILO (2017), "Stitching a Future: Stories of Hope and Success in Vietnam's Garment Industry." Available online at: http://www.ilo.org/hanoi/Whatwedo/Publications/WCMS_618334/lang--en/index.htm (accessed 18 April 2018).

Better Factories Cambodia (2018), "International Labour Organization: Resources and Publications." Available online at: https://betterwork.org/where-we-work/cambodia/our-resources-and-publications/ (accessed April 18, 2018).

HRW (2018), "Human Rights Watch Cambodia." Available online at: https://www.hrw.org/cambodia (attached April 18, 2018).

Africa and the Middle East

Child Poverty Action Group (2016), "Child Poverty Facts and Figures." Available online at: http://www.cpag.org.uk/child-poverty-facts-and-figures

Index Mundi (2016), "United Arab Emirates Below Poverty Line." Available online at: http://www.indexmundi.com/united_arab_emirates/population_below_poverty_line.html

Olsson, J., J. Perzon, T. Haglund-Flemström, and S. Sjöberg (2016), *Trend report: Future of sustainable fashion*. Available online at: https://www.accenture.com/t20170410T044051Z__w__/us-en/_acnmedia/Accenture/Conversion-Assets/DotCom/Documents/Global/PDF/Consulting/Accenture-HM-Global-Change-Award-Report.pdf (accessed July 9, 2018).

Forum for the Future (2010), *Fashion futures 2025: Global Scenarios for a Sustainable Fashion Industry*. Available online at: https://www.forumforthefuture.org/sites/default/files/images/Forum/Projects/Fashion-Futures/FashionFutures_2025_FINAL_SML.pdf

SUSTAINABLE FASHION BRANDS, LABELS, AND BUSINESSES

Latin America

NCC Ecobrands do grupo (Natural Cotton Color)
Important sustainable fashion brand in Brazil. Uses genetically colored organic cotton, works with a network of workers including lacemakers, embroiderers, and artisans from throughout Northeastern Brazil, especially Paraíba. Participates in international sustainable fashion fairs, and exports to more than ten countries.

http://www.naturalcottoncolor.com.br/index.php; http://www.nccecobrands.com.br/

Osklen
Brazilian sustainable fashion brand in operation since 1998. Products are available in the United States, Greece, Japan, and Uruguay.

https://www.osklen.com.br/

Ateliê Vivo
A making facility open to the public. People can build their knowledge and skills in manfacturing clothes.

http://www.atelievivo.com.br/

Contextura
Sustainable fashion brand based on artistic and scientific research.

http://www.contextura.art.br

Cosecha Vintage
> Argentinian brand, established in 2009, that reuses materials to construct new garments.
>> http://www.cosechavintage.com.ar
>> https://www.facebook.com/CosechaVintage/

Cúbreme
> Argentina sustainable fashion brand.
>> http://cubreme.com

Flávia Aranha
> Premium fashion brand that represents Brazil at international fairs.
>> http://flaviaaranha.com/

Flávia Amadeu
> Natural latex jewelry from the Amazon.
>> https://www.flaviaamadeu.com/

Insecta Shoes
> Vegan shoe brand.
>> https://www.insectashoes.com/

Márcia Ganem
> Brand that uses the traditional methods of making lace, using recycled raw materials and innovative design.
>> http://marciaganem.com/

Portal Ecoera
> Hub for brands and products with sustainable attributes.
>> http://www.portalecoera.com.br

Therapy Recycle and Exorcise (alternative and disruptive)
> http://therapy-recycle-and-exorcise.tumblr.com

North America

Comrags
> Designed by Gunhouse and Cornish in Toronto. Comrags has been designing and making women's clothing in Canada since 1983.
>> https://www.comrags.com

Eileen Fisher Renew
> Take-back program for Eileen Fisher clothing. Unwanted and/or damaged clothing is resold or remanufactured for resale.
>> https://www.eileenfisher.com/renew

Fabscrap
> Textile reuse and recycling service for the US fashion industry.
>> http://fabscrap.org/

Goodwill Industries
> US-based charities collecting and recycling donated clothing
>> http://www.goodwill.org/

Lucien Matis
> Toronto-based womenswear designer specializing in daywear and embellished eveningwear.
>> https://www.lucianmatis.com/

INLAND
> Online showcase of sustainable Canadian fashion brands.
>> https://www.instagram.com/made_inland/

Mara Hoffman
> New York-based womenswear designer that focuses on sustainable materials, processes, and production in order to improve and extend garment life.
>> https://www.marahoffman.com/

The Renewal Workshop
> US-based clothing company that remanufactures discarded garments and textiles into new clothing products, upcycled materials, or recycled fiber.
>> https://renewalworkshop.com/en/home

Triarchy
> Canadian sustainable denim brand.
>> https://triarchy.com

Europe

Aiayu
> Danish luxury clothing label that promotes artisan methods and traditional skills. Garments are made by local craftspeople in Bolivia, India, and Nepal.
>> https://www.aiayu.com

Carcel
> Working with natural fibers, the Danish company produces small ranges of garments in partnership

with the Cuscos Women's Prison, Peru. The company's next collection will be developed in conjunction with correctional services in Thailand.
https://carcel.co

Filippa K
Established Swedish fashion brand that incorporates a number of sustainable initiatives within its business model and practices. This includes a garment-leasing service, and a take-back garment service that feeds into their own-brand secondhand store.
https://www.filippak.com/en/filippakworld/ourmethod

Freitag
Swiss-based company developing recycled bags and materials.
https://www.freitag.ch/en

Asia (Western, Central, South Central, Eastern)

Argande
Turkish label promoting Anatolian handicrafts.
http://www.argande.com

Bhusattva
Indian sustainable luxury brand.
http://www.bhusattva.com/home.html

Eco Party Mearry
Korean-based upcycling design brand.
http://mearry.beautifulstore.org/

Esquel Group
Global textile and garment manufacturer with a vertically integrated supply chain
http://www.esquel.com/en/index1.html

Fab India
Platform promoting brands featuring Indian crafts.
https://www.fabindia.com

House of Lonali
Sri Lankan independent ethical fashion label using pre-consumer waste.
https://www.lonali.com/

NEEMIC
Beijing-based fashion label using reclaimed materials and GOTS certified fabrics.
http://neemic.asia/

Oh Seven Days
Turkish label using reclaimed materials.
https://ohsevendays.com/

Re:Code
Upcycling brand that provides a value-added life to discarded products.
https://www.kolonmall.com/Content/445

Reflect
Turkish activist fashion.
https://www.reflect.ist/

Restore Jeans
Turkish sustainable denim brand.
https://restorejeans.com

Southeast Asia and Oceania

Children of Promise
New Zealand-based sustainable fashion label.
https://www.copthelabel.com/

Elisa Jane Carmichael
Artist and fashion designer from the Quandamooka people of Moreton Bay, Queensland, Australia.
http://elisajanecarmichael.com.au/

FASHION4FREEDOM
Platform connecting designers and manufacturers in Vietnam to promote ethical and transparent supply chains.
http://www.fashion4freedom.com/

Full Circle Fibres
Australian-grown and manufactured cotton yarns and fabrics.
http://fullcirclefibres.com/

Grace Lillian Lee
Artist and designer collaborating with Australian indigenous communities and art centers to create fashion performances as a

platform for cultural expression and celebration.
http://gracelillianlee.com/

Ipa Nima
Artisanal handbags, ethically made in Vietnam.
http://ipa-nima.com/

Lána
Australian clothes sharing platform.
https://lana.global/

Lanh My Silk
Natural silk fabric manufactured in Vietnam.
https://medium.com/factoryfinder-stories/lanh-my-a-story-5d4d704509d8

Kilomet 109
Vietnam-based label working with artisans to create adaptable clothing.
http://kilomet109.com/

Kowtow
New Zealand designer label working with sustainable materials.
https://nz.kowtowclothing.com/

NICO
Australian eco underwear label.
https://nicounderwear.com/

Pactics
https://pactics.com

Rant clothing
Australian label specializing in local, environmentally conscious production.
https://www.sustainablefashion.com.au/

Seljak Brand
Australian label creating recycled wool blankets.
https://www.seljakbrand.com/

Sinerji
Australian label specializing in organic clothing that utilizes natural dyes.
http://www.sinerji.com.au/

The Social Studio, Melbourne and *The Social Outfit, Sydney*
Social enterprises providing skills training to recent migrants.
http://www.thesocialstudio.org/ | https://thesocialoutfit.org/

Thunderpants
New Zealand fair trade certified underwear label.
https://www.thunderpants.co.nz/

Tonle
Cambodian label working with pre-consumer textile waste.
https://tonle.com

Well Made Clothes
Australian online marketplace promoting ethical fashion and consumer education.
https://wellmadeclothes.com.au/

Africa and the Middle East

BOTOCY Creations
https://www.facebook.com/Botocy

GildedSands
https://gildedsands.blogspot.com/

ORGANIZATIONS AND ADVISORY GROUPS
Latin America

Design & Sustainability Research Center of the UFPR
http://www.sacod.ufpr.br/portal/dedesign/design-e-sustentabilidade/
Center of Studies on Creative Economy, Culture and Innovation
http://www.ufrgs.br/obec/neccult/
Research Group on Sustainability and Innovation, UFRGS
http://www.ufrgs.br/gps
Research Center on Sustainable Fashion, UFRGS
http://www.ufrgs.br/lit/?pg=home&lab=Nms

Centro Textil Sustentable
www.ctextilsustentable.org.ar

Centro de Estudios para el Lujo Sustentable
www.lujosustentable.org

Centro Metropolitano de Diseño
CMD.gov.ar

ESPLAR,Centro de Pesquisa e Assessoria
www.esplar.org.br

EMBRAPA, Brazilian Agricultural Research Corporation
Ministry of Agriculture, Livestock, and Food Supply has developed a natural cotton color and a natural colored seed without chemicals, saving 70 percent of water production.
https://www.embrapa.br/en/international

IBD Certifications
http://ibd.com.br/pt/Default.aspx
http://ibd.com.br/en/IbdOrganico.aspx

Instituto E
The E-Institute is an OSCIP—Civil Society Organization of Public Interest—that believes sharing information is the first step in promoting sustainable human development. The mission of the E-Institute is to transform and position Brazil as "the country of sustainable human development" through networks.
http://institutoe.org.br/

Justa Trama
http://www.justatrama.com.br/home

Organic Cotton from Northeast Brazil
https://vimeo.com/4352540

Inexmoda
Colombian NGO network for the fashion industry
https://inexmoda.org.co/

Fashion Radicals
Online editorial for fashion culture in Colombia.
http://www.fashionradicals.com/

Semana Sostenible
Environmental and sustainability editorial from Colombia.
http://sostenibilidad.semana.com/

Focus Magazine
Colombian fashion editorial.
http://focusmag.co/

Ecofashion Latam
Sustainable fashion network in Colombia
http://ecofashionlatam.com/

North America

Better Buying
Ratings platform designed to assist brands and retailers highlight areas for improved purchasing practices.
http://www.betterbuying.org/Home/purchasing-practices

Cleaner by Design, Natural Resources Defense Council
Aims to reduce the environmental impacts in manufacturing that is created by companies outsourced overseas. The website contains a wide range of reports and factsheets about the impacts of manufacturing.
http://www.nrdc.org/international/cleanbydesign/

Cradle-to-Cradle Products Innovation Institute
The Fashion Positive Innovation Hub
Initiative formed to provide a information platform for designers, brands, and suppliers on the Cradle-to-Cradle certified product standard.
https://www.fashionpositive.org/

Fair Labor Association (FLA)
The FLA is made up of universities, companies, and organizations and aims to protect workers rights around the world. It offers tools and resources to industry, and although based in the Unites States, has other international offices.
http://www.fairlabor.org/

The Fashion Exchange
Established by George Brown College, the Fashion Exchange fosters relationships between fashion

educators, industry partners, community organizations, and fashion graduates to work toward a sustainable fashion industry.
http://www.fashionexchangetoronto.com/

National Resource Defense Council
US-based, non-profit, advocacy group working internationally to protect the environment.
https://www.nrdc.org/

NYC Fair Trade Coalition
Volunteer-run, grassroots organization that educates consumers, and supports and promotes Fairtrade businesses and retailers.
https://www.nycfairtradecoalition.com/

Patagonia Action Works
Established by the US-based Patagonia clothing company, Action Works supports and connects environmental activist groups with the wider community.
https://www.patagonia.com/actionworks/

RE\SET by The Collections
Network platform for emerging designers and labels in Canada.
https://reset.fashion/

Sustainable Apparel Coalition
Consortium of clothing manufacturers and retailers, footwear, and textile industry companies working for sustainable production.
https://apparelcoalition.org/

Europe

The Clean Clothes Campaign (CCC)
Alliance of NGOs and trade unions from fifteen European states, although also works with organizations in the US, Australia, and Canada. Covers a wide range of issues from women's rights to consumer advocacy and poverty reduction.
http://www.cleanclothes.org/

Copenhagen Fashion Summit
Influential sustainability event for the fashion industry.
https://copenhagenfashionsummit.com

Ethical Fashion Forum
Although UK-based, the network is international. The website provides a wide range of resources for designers and producers; members may attend webinars and other events.
http://www.ethicalfashionforum.com/

Fair Wear Foundation (FWF)
Independent no-profit organization based in based in Amsterdam but with international reach. Provides advice and support to industry to improve labor conditions for garment workers. Good, accessible resources are available on the website.
http://www.fairwear.org/home/

Fashion Revolution
UK-based activist NGO formed in response to the Rana Plaza factory collapse disaster in Bangladesh in 2013. The organization works with partners across the world.
https://www.fashionrevolution.org/

Labour Behind The Label
Campaign to improve the conditions for workers in the clothing industry. The site provides access to a wide variety of educational resources. Part of the international Clean Clothes Alliance.
http://www.labourbehindthelabel.org/

Nordic Fashion Association, Nordic Initiative Clean & Ethical (NICE)
Organization established to support industry cooperation across the Nordic region, and at the same time it specifically places an educational focus on sustainable fashion.
http://nordicfashionassociation.com/

Asia (Western, Central, South Central, Eastern)

The Alternative
Sustainable living magazine and online platform based in Bangalore, India.
http://www.thealternative.in/campaign/sustainable-fashion/

Beijing Fashion Collective
Organization for local fashion designers to share resources, skills, and opportunities.
http://www.beijingfashioncollective.com

Clean Clothes Campaign Turkey
Turkish arm of the global campaign to support the empowerment of workers in the textile and garment industries, and improve working conditions.
http://www.temizgiysi.org

Craft Council of India
Founded in 1964 to protect and enhance India's craft heritage.
www.craftscouncilofindia.org

Earthy Zest
Online platform maintaining lists of Indian sustainable fashion brands.
https://www.earthyzest.com/blog/2017/12/25/ultimate-list-indian-ethical-recycling-sustainable-fashion-brands/

Impact Hub Istanbul
Co-working spaces centered around social entrepreneurship.
http://impacthubist.net/

Joint Apparel Association Forum Sri Lanka (Jaafsl)
Sri Lankan industry association promoting ethical production.
http://www.srilankaapparel.com/

Kiple
Korean peer-to-peer collaborative consumption platform that allows users to buy and sell secondhand children's clothing online.
www.kiple.net

Korea Fashion Association
Peak industry body for fashion in Korea.
http://koreafashion.org

Redress
Hong Kong-based NGO that aims to promote sustainability in fashion within Asia. A good range of resources can be found on the website. Pays particular attention to reducing fabric waste, either during manufacture or at garment end-of-life.
http://redress.com.hk/

Redress, Sustainable Fashion Educator Pack
https://www.redressdesignaward.com/educatorpack/

Redress, External Resources
https://www.redressdesignaward.com/learn/additional-resources/

Self Employed Women's Association
South Asian trade union representing the rights of poor self-employed female workers.
http://www.sewa.org

Sharing City Seoul
City-wide strategy for promoting shared use of public and private resources.
http://english.sharehub.kr/

Sol Inspirations
US-based organization promoting eco-fashion.
http://www.sol-inspirations.org/

South Asian Apparel Leadership Forum
Initiative of the Sri Lanka Export Development Board to promote Sri Lankan apparel.
http://www.srilankabusiness.com/apparel/

The Foundation for the Support of Women's Work
Turkish non-profit civil-society organization aiming to improve the quality of life and economic situation of low-income women and strengthen their leadership in local development.
http://www.kedv.org.tr/?lang=en

The Open Closet
An NGO run together with support from Seoul Metropolitan City that permits people to share clothes.
https://theopencloset.net/

The Sharing Economy
Korean sharing platform for clothing.
http://www.theclozet.co.kr/

Upasana–The Conscious Fashion Hub
Indian platform devoted to tackling social issues surrounding waste, pollution and workers' rights.
http://www.upasana.in

Woorigachi
Korean sustainable fashion introduction.
www.woorigachi.com/xe/board_wGuS57/127292

Yeşilist
Turkish online platform promoting sustainability.
https://www.yesilist.com/kategori/hayat/moda/

Yeşil Yama
Turkish online platform promoting green living.
http://yesilyama.com

Southeast Asia and Oceania

Australian Fashion Council
Australia's peak body for the fashion and textiles industries.
https://ausfashioncouncil.com/

Australian Wool Innovation
Non-profit organization that invests in research and development in the support and promotion of Australian wool.
https://www.wool.com/

Buy Nothing New month
Australian organization promoting reuse and buying secondhand.
https://www.buynothingnew.com.au/pledge/

Conscious Consumers
New Zealand-based accreditation system.
https://consciousconsumers.nz/our-accreditation/

Cotton Australia
Peak industry body representing Australian cotton.
http://cottonaustralia.com.au/

Ethical Clothing Australia
Works with the local textile and fashion industry to ensure that Australian workers receive fair wages and decent conditions. Is particularly helpful with meeting Australian compliance laws and regulations.
http://www.ethicalclothingaustralia.org.au/home/home

Good on you
Australian app offering guidance on ethical shopping.
https://goodonyou.eco/

The Formary
New Zealand project transforming waste fibers into luxury fibers.
http://www.theformary.com/

Fair Labor Association
http://www.fairlabor.org/our-work/special-projects/project/promoting-sustainable-corporate-social-responsibility-vietnam

Fashion Revolution Vietnam
Vietnamese arm of Fashion Revolution.
http://fashionrevolution.org/country/vietnam/

Fashion Revolution—Garment Worker Diaries
Fashion Revolution's project with garment workers in Cambodia, Bangladesh, and Vietnam.
https://www.fashionrevolution.org/garment-worker-diaries/

International Fashion Week Vietnam
http://vietnaminternationalfashionweek.com/en

Shop Ethical app
Australian app for ethical shopping.
https://www.ethical.org.au/3.4.2/

Sustainable Business Network
New Zealand network of small businesses, international corporations, non-government organizations, local authorities, health boards, and individuals.
https://sustainable.org.nz/

Space Between
Project by Massey University's School of Design, aimed at developing new ways to design, make and use locally-produced fashion.
https://creative.massey.ac.nz/enterprise/space-between/

The Solidarity Center, Cambodia
Organization working with Cambodian unions and other partners to advance rights of workers.
https://www.solidaritycenter.org/where-we-work/asia/cambodia/

Workers Information Center
Cambodian women garment workers' union.
http://wic.unitedsisterhood.org

Walk Sew Good
Project with two women, Megan O'Malley and Gab Murphy, walking through Southeast Asia in search of positive fashion stories.
https://walksewgood.com

Africa and the Middle East

African Cotton & Textile Industries Federation (ACTIF)
http://www.actifafrica.com/

Design Society Development DESIS Lab
www.designsocietydevelopment.org

Sustainable Cotton Cluster
http://cottonsa.org.za/sustainable-cotton-cluster/contact-the-cluster/

Sustainability Institute—Early Childhood Development
www.sustainabilityinstitute.net

United Nations Development Programme, through the Sustainable Development Goals
http://hdr.undp.org/

INDEX